CHANGE AND CONTINUITY
IN THE 1996 AND 1998 ELECTIONS

Paul R. Abramson
MICHIGAN STATE UNIVERSITY

John H. Aldrich
DUKE UNIVERSITY

David W. Rohde
MICHIGAN STATE UNIVERSITY

Washington, D.C.

Copyright © 1999 Congressional Quarterly Inc.
1414 22nd Street, N.W.
Washington, D.C. 20037

CQ Press on the Web: http://books.cq.com
CQ Press customer service: (800) 638-1710; (202) 822-1475

Printed in the United States of America

Cover design by Rich Pottern Design

Library of Congress Cataloging-in-Publication Data

Abramson, Paul R.
    Change and continuity in the 1996 and 1998 elections / Paul R. Abramson, John H. Aldrich, David W. Rohde.
        p.   cm.
    Includes bibliographical references.
    ISBN 1-56802-474-6
    1. Presidents—United States—Election—1996. 2. United States. Congress—Elections, 1996. 3. United States. Congress—Elections, 1998. 4. Elections—United States. 5. United States—Politics and government—1993–   I. Aldrich, John Herbert, 1937– . II. Rohde, David W. III. Title.
JK526   1996k
324.973'0929—dc21   99-18220
                                                                  CIP

To Joseph A. Schlesinger

Contents

Tables and Figures

Tables

Figures

Preface

A political earthquake on November 8, 1994, brought the Republicans control of the House of Representatives for the first time in forty years and of the Senate for the first time in eight. These developments placed President Bill Clinton on the political defensive. Yet two years later he easily won reelection, the first Democratic president to do so since Franklin D. Roosevelt was reelected (for the third time) in 1944. Despite losing nine seats, the Republicans retained control of the House, and they gained two seats in the Senate. The 1996 contest was the first election since 1928 in which the Republicans had won control of the House in two consecutive elections. Moreover, it was also the first election in U.S. history in which the Democrats won the presidency without gaining control of the House. Indeed, the Democrats won the presidency in nineteen of the forty-two presidential elections held between 1828 and 1992, and in all nineteen of their victories they also won control of the House.

The Republicans retained control of both the House and Senate in the 1998 midterm elections, but they lost five House seats while holding their own in the Senate. The 1998 election was unusual, especially in light of historical patterns, for it was the first midterm election since 1934 in which the party holding the White House gained seats in the House. In fact, the party controlling the presidency lost strength in the House in thirty-eight of the thirty-nine midterm elections held between 1842 and 1994.

In 1988, with George Bush's election, the Republicans had won the presidency for three elections in a row, and many scholars argued that the GOP was becoming the dominant party in presidential elections. What happened to Republican presidential dominance? What are the prospects for the Democrats to build a new presidential majority? And what happened to Democratic congressional dominance? What are the prospects for ending divided government, and which party is likely to end it? Have the major political parties weakened their hold on the U.S. electorate, and, if so, what are the prospects for a new political party?

To answer these questions, one cannot view the 1996 and 1998 elections as isolated events; rather, one needs to study them in their historical context. To do this, we have examined a broad range of evidence, from past election results to public opinion surveys of the electorate conducted since 1944.

We employ many sources, but we rely most heavily on the 1996 survey of the American electorate conducted by the Survey Research Center and the Center for Political Studies (SRC-CPS) of the University of Michigan as part of an on-going project funded by the National Science Foundation. We use every one of the twenty-four election studies conducted by the Michigan SRC-CPS between 1948 and 1996, often referred to as the National Election Studies.

These surveys, which are disseminated by the Inter-university Consortium for Political and Social Research (ICPSR), can be analyzed by scholars through-out the United States. The ICPSR provided these data in April 1997. Unless oth-erwise indicated, all of the tables and figures in Chapters 2, 4–8, and 10 are based on surveys obtained through the ICPSR. The standard disclaimer holds: the con-sortium is not responsible for our analyses or interpretations.

Several institutions aided us financially. John H. Aldrich was a visiting profes-sor in the Department of Government at Harvard University when most of this book was written, and he is grateful for its support. The Department of Political Science at Duke University also provided assistance. Paul R. Abramson and David W. Rohde received support from the Department of Political Science and the Political Institutions and Public Choice Program at Michigan State University. Rohde also received assistance from a Michigan State University fund for Distin-guished University Professors.

Many individuals helped us with this effort. Bryan Marshall at Michigan State University helped us with the data analysis for Chapters 2, 9, 10, and 11, and Jamie Carson at Michigan State University assisted with the analysis for Chapter 11. Mark Berger at Duke University assisted with the data analysis for Chapters 6, 7, and 8. Walter Dean Burnham at the University of Texas at Austin provided us with estimates of turnout among the politically eligible population, and Mar-tin O'Connell of the U.S. Bureau of the Census answered questions about the census survey of U.S. turnout.

Others helped us by commenting on several of these chapters. At Michigan State University, Darren W. Davis, Mark P. Jones, Michael Mintrom, Dennis Patterson, and Joseph A. Schlesinger provided numerous suggestions for Chap-ter 12. Jack Dennis at the University of Wisconsin, Robert E. O'Connor at Pennsyl-vania State University, and an anonymous reviewer provided us with suggestions based upon their reading of *Change and Continuity in the 1992 Elections*.

Once again we are thankful to the staff at CQ Press. Brenda Carter and Gwenda Larsen guided us in preparing our manuscript. Joanne S. Ainsworth and Christopher M. Karlsten copyedited our manuscript, and Talia Greenberg assisted in its production.

Like our earlier books, this book was a collective enterprise, but we divided the labor. Abramson had the primary responsibility for Chapters 3, 4, and 5; Aldrich for Chapters 1, 6, 7, and 8; and Rohde for Chapters 2, 9, 10, and 11. Abramson and Aldrich are primarily responsible for Chapter 12. We must also take some responsibility for the electoral outcome in 1996, since we all voted for Clinton. Yet, although each of us made several trips to the nation's capital during Clinton's first term, none of us slept in the Lincoln bedroom. In fact, none of us even entered the White House during the Clinton presidency.

Paul R. Abramson
John H. Aldrich
David W. Rohde

PART 1

The 1996 Presidential Election

Presidential elections in the United States are partly ritual, a reaffirmation of our democratic values. But they are far more than ritual. The office confers great powers upon the occupant, and those powers have expanded during the course of American history. It is precisely because of these immense powers that presidential elections have at times played a major role in determining public policy.

The 1860 election, which brought Abraham Lincoln and the Republicans to power and ousted a divided Democratic party, focused on whether slavery should be extended into the western territories. Following Lincoln's election, eleven southern states attempted to secede from the Union, the Civil War erupted, and slavery itself was abolished. An antislavery plurality (Lincoln received only 40 percent of the popular vote) set in motion a chain of events that freed some four million African-Americans.

The 1896 election, in which the Republican William McKinley defeated the Democrat and Populist William Jennings Bryan, beat back the challenge of western and agrarian interests to the prevailing financial and industrial power of the East. Although Bryan mounted a strong campaign, winning 47 percent of the vote to McKinley's 51 percent, the election set a clear course for a policy of high tariffs and the continuation of a gold standard for American money.

The twentieth century also witnessed presidential elections that determined the direction of public policy. In 1936 the incumbent Democrat, Franklin D. Roosevelt, won 61 percent of the popular vote and his Republican opponent, Alfred M. Landon, only 37 percent, a margin that allowed the Democrats to continue to consolidate the economic, social, and welfare policies of the New Deal.

Lyndon B. Johnson's 1964 landslide over the Republican Barry M. Goldwater provided the clearest set of policy alternatives of any election of this century. Johnson, who received 61 percent of the popular vote to Goldwater's 38 percent, saw his election as a mandate for his Great Society programs, the most far-reaching social legislation enacted since World War II.

Goldwater offered "a choice, not an echo," advocating far more conservative social and economic policies than Johnson's. Ironically, the election also appeared to offer a choice between escalating American involvement in Vietnam and restraint. But American involvement expanded after the election, and four years later the Democrats lost the presidency.

WHAT DID THE 1996 ELECTION MEAN?

Only the future will determine the ultimate importance of the 1996 election. Some scholars argue that elections have become less important for deciding public policy, and there is doubtless some truth in their argument.[1] But presidential elections often do have important policy consequences. The 1996 election did not offer dramatic choices, mainly because after the Republican victories in the 1994 midterm election, Bill Clinton moved to the political center and did not offer dramatic new initiatives for his second term. If the "era of big government is over," as Clinton proclaimed in his State of the Union message in 1996, so too was the era of big new campaign promises. Clinton's signing of welfare reform legislation, opposed by many liberal Democrats, signaled a move to the political center as did his accepting the goal of balancing the budget by the year 2002. He also advocated some traditional positions on social values, such as the death penalty, school uniforms, and a "V-chip" to allow parents to control television programming.

But despite moving to the political center, he clearly differed from Bob Dole. Dole specifically proposed a program for a 15 percent across-the-board cut in the federal income tax, whereas Clinton wanted any tax cuts to be specifically targeted. Clinton was opposed to major changes in Medicare and Medicaid, was more supportive of environmental protection, and favored gun control. He wanted to reform, but continue, affirmative action. He differed markedly from Dole on abortion rights. His decision to veto a bill that would have made a late-term abortion procedure (often referred to as "partial birth" abortions) illegal led Dole to charge that Clinton favored "abortion on demand." Under the presidencies of Ronald Reagan and George Bush, new Supreme Court appointments had come close to placing the *Roe v. Wade* decision, which prevents the states from outlawing abortion, in jeopardy. As Clinton's two Supreme Court appointments during his first term, Ruth Bader Ginsberg and Stephen Breyer, made clear, Clinton was committed to appointing justices who supported abortion rights. Moreover, voters who were disenchanted with the Republican and Democratic parties had the opportunity to vote for H. Ross Perot, now running as head of the newly formed Reform party.

Clinton won reelection easily, becoming the first Democrat to be reelected to the presidency since Franklin D. Roosevelt was reelected (for the third time) in 1944. But the Republicans held control of both the House and the Senate, the first time they had maintained control in two successive elections since 1928. Between 1828 and 1996, the Democrats had won the presidency twenty times, but 1996 was the only time they had won the White House without also winning control of the U.S. House of Representatives. Because divided government would continue, many expected relatively little change in public policy. The budget agreement passed by Congress and signed by Clinton in the summer of 1997 demonstrated that there could be bipartisan cooperation. But the possibilities for substantial government retrenchment were clearly limited compared with the possibilities for change under a united Republican presidency and Congress. The "Republican revolution," so boldly proclaimed after the 1994 midterm election, had ended, with Republican representatives complaining about the lack of leadership from Newt Gingrich, the newly reelected Speaker of the House.

Skeptics ask, Do elections matter?[2] The answer, clearly, is yes. Presidential elections not only can change the direction of public policy, they can also change the direction of American politics.[3] The 1996 election can only present clues about the future of American electoral politics. During the Republican presidential victories of the 1980s, many political scientists raised the possibility that a partisan realignment had occurred or was about to occur. In 1985 President Reagan himself proclaimed that a Republican realignment was at hand. "The other side would like to believe that our victory last November was due to something other than our philosophy," he asserted. "I just hope they keep believing that. There's a change happening in America. Realignment is real."[4]

In November 1984 Reagan had won 59 percent of the popular vote. Bush's election in 1988 (with 53 percent of the vote) raised the possibility of continued Republican dominance. But in 1992 Bush won only 37 percent of the popular vote, a 22-point decline from Reagan's high-water mark. Not only had the Republican winning streak of three straight victories been broken, but the Republicans suffered one of the greatest popular vote declines since the Civil War. And in 1996 Dole won only 41 percent of the popular vote.

Obviously, the 1992 and 1996 presidential elections call into question any claims about a pro-Republican realignment. But Clinton won only 43 percent of the popular vote in 1992 and only 49 percent in 1996. In 1992 nearly one out of five voters had voted for Perot, and in 1996 one out of ten voters voted for Perot and for other minor-party candidates. The divided partisan outcome also suggests that a substantial number of Clinton voters voted for Republican House and Senate candidates. Many voters appear to have reservations about both of the major political parties. This raises the possibility that past voting patterns are breaking down, something that political scientists have called a dealignment.

What do the terms *realignment* and *dealignment* mean? Political scientists define *realignment* in different ways, but they are all influenced by the seminal writings of V. O. Key, Jr., who began by developing a theory of "critical elections" in which "new and durable electoral groupings are formed."[5] Elections like that of 1860, in which Lincoln's victory brought the Republicans to power; the election of 1896, in which McKinley's victory consolidated Republican dominance; and the 1932 election, which brought the Democrats under Roosevelt to power, are obvious choices for this label.

But Key later argued that realignments take place over a series of elections—a pattern he called "secular realignment." During these periods, "shifts in the partisan balance of power" occur.[6] In this view, the first Republican realignment might be seen as having begun in 1856, when the newly formed Republican party displaced the Whigs as the major competitor to the Democrats, and as having been consolidated by Lincoln's reelection in 1864 and Ulysses S. Grant's election in 1868. The realignment of the late nineteenth century may well have had its beginnings in 1892, when the Democrat Grover Cleveland won the election but the Populist party, headed by James B. Weaver, won 8.5 percent of the popular vote, won four states, and gained electoral votes in two others. The realignment may have been consolidated by McKinley's reelection against Bryan in 1900 and Theodore Roosevelt's victory in 1904. The New Deal realignment, forged by Franklin D. Roosevelt, may be seen as beginning in Herbert C. Hoover's 1928 triumph over Alfred E. Smith (the first Roman Catholic to be nominated by the Democratic party). Although Smith was badly defeated, he carried two New England states, Massachusetts and Rhode Island, which later became the most Democratic states in the nation.[7] As Key points out, the beginnings of a shift toward the Democrats can be seen in Smith's defeat.[8] The term *New Deal* was not coined until 1932. Yet the New Deal coalition was not created by the 1932 election but after that, and it was consolidated in Roosevelt's 1936 landslide over Landon and his 1940 defeat of Wendell Willkie.

Although scholars disagree about how long it takes to create a new partisan alignment, all agree that durability is an essential element of realignment. As James L. Sundquist writes, "Those who analyze alignment and realignment are probing beneath the immediate and transitory ups and downs of daily politics and periodic elections to discover fundamental shifts in the structure of the party system." According to Lawrence G. McMichael and Richard J. Trilling, a realignment is "a significant and durable change in the distribution of party support over relevant groups within the electorate."[9]

Partisan realignments in the United States have had five basic characteristics. First, party realignments have always involved changes in the regional bases of party support. Between 1852 and 1860, the Republicans replaced the Whigs. In all of the presidential elections between 1836 (when the Whigs first opposed the Democrat Martin Van Buren) and 1852, the Whigs drew at least some of their electoral support from the slave states. The last Whig candidate to be elected, Zachary Taylor in 1848, won 72 of his 163 electoral votes from the fifteen slave states.[10] In his 1860 victory, Lincoln did not win a single electoral vote from the slave states, and in twelve of them he did not even compete. But Lincoln won all of the electors in seventeen of the eighteen free states, as well as a majority of the electoral votes in New Jersey. Subsequent realignments do not reveal this degree of regional polarization, but they all display regional shifts in party support.

Second, past party realignments appear to have involved changes in the social group bases of party support. Even during a period when a party becomes dominant, some social groups may be moving to the losing party. During the 1930s, for example, Roosevelt gained the support of industrial workers, but at the same time he lost support among business owners and professionals.

Third, past realignments have been characterized by the mobilization of new groups into the electorate. Between Calvin Coolidge's Republican landslide in 1924 and Roosevelt's third-term victory in 1940, turnout rose from 44 percent to 59 percent, an increase of 15 percentage points. Although some long-term forces were pushing turnout upward, the sharp increase in turnout between 1924 and 1928, and again between 1932 and 1936, resulted at least partly from the mobilization of new social groups into the electorate. Ethnic groups that were predominantly Catholic were mobilized to support Smith in 1928, and industrial workers were mobilized to support Roosevelt in 1936.

Fourth, past realignments have occurred when new issues have divided the electorate. The most obvious example is the emergence of the Republican party, which reformulated the controversy over slavery to form a winning coalition. By opposing the extension of slavery into the territories, Republicans divided the Democratic party. No issue since slavery has divided America as deeply, but subsequent realignments have always been based on the division of the electorate over issues.

Lastly, most political scientists argue that partisan realignments occur when voters change not just their voting patterns but the way they think about the political parties. For example, in 1932 many voters who thought of themselves as Republicans voted against Hoover. Many of these voters returned to the Republican side in subsequent elections, but others began to think of themselves as Democrats. Likewise, in 1936 some voters who thought of themselves as Democrats may have voted against Roosevelt's policies. Some of these Democrats returned to the Democratic fold during subsequent elections, but others began to think of themselves as Republicans.

During the three Republican victories of the 1980s, some of these changes occurred. As we will see, there were shifts in the regional bases of party support and there were changes in the distribution of party loyalties among the electorate. There were further shifts among some social groups (especially southern whites) away from the Democratic party, and some argued that the Republicans were establishing a winning position on issues that gained votes in presidential elections. Despite these changes, however, the Republicans never emerged as the majority party among the electorate, although they came close to parity with the Democrats in the mid-1980s. Moreover, even though the Republicans gained control of the U.S. Senate between 1981 and 1987, they never came close to winning a majority in the U.S. House of Representatives. Clearly, if there was a realignment, it was incomplete, leading some scholars, such as Michael Nelson, to speculate about the possibilities of a "split-level realignment," a pattern in which the Republicans became the dominant party in presidential elections while the Democratic dominance of the House of Representatives remained intact.[11] And Byron E. Shafer argued that a "new electoral order" had been achieved. The 1988 election, Shafer argued, had institutionalized a new division in American politics. Beginning in 1968, with the controversy over the Vietnam War, a new system began. "What was to emerge, instead of realignment," he wrote, "was a different *type* of electoral order: one in which there was a new Republican majority to lay claim to the presidency, an old Democratic majority to keep the House, and a wavering Democratic majority to strive to hold on to the Senate."[12]

But this electoral order was disrupted by Clinton's election in 1992 and appears to have ended with the Republican capture of the House in 1994. Indeed, Clinton's victory called into serious question the thesis that a pro-Republican realignment had occurred, while the Republican control of the U.S. House of Representatives in 1994 and 1996 calls into question any thesis that a pro-Democratic majority had been restored. And the large vote for Perot in 1992, as well as the large vote for Perot and other minor-party candidates in 1996, raises the prospect of the breakdown of the traditional party system. Thus, the term *dealignment,* introduced by Ronald Inglehart and Avram Hochstein in 1972, may provide a better description of current political realities. A dealignment is a condition in which old voting patterns break down without being replaced by newer ones. Most scholars who use this term stress the weakening of party loyalties as a key component. As Russell J. Dalton, Paul Allen Beck, and Scott C. Flanagan point out, dealignment was originally viewed as a preliminary stage leading to a new partisan realignment. But, they argue, dealignment "may be a regular feature of electoral politics."[13]

As Dalton and Martin P. Wattenberg have written, "Whereas realignment involves people changing from one party to another, dealignment involves people gradually moving away from all parties." "Many scholars," Dalton and Wattenberg write, "express concern about political dealignment trends because they fear the loss of the stabilizing, conservative equilibrium that party attachments provide to electoral systems."[14] Wattenberg argues that American presidential elections have become increasingly centered upon political candidates. The large Perot vote in 1992, Dalton and Wattenberg argue, may well have come mainly from voters who have few feelings—either positive or negative—about the political parties.

The concept of dealignment is by no means restricted to U.S. politics. Bo Särlvik and Ivor Crewe have analyzed British politics in the 1970s as the "decade of dealignment."[15] And Harold Clarke and his colleagues argue that Canadian politics may have reached the stage of "permanent dealignment." "A dealigned system," they write, "is one in which volatility is paramount, where there are frequent changes in electoral outcomes as well as lots of individual flexibility."[16]

Scholars disagree about the meaning of the 1996 election and have used both *realignment* and *dealignment* to describe it. Everett Carll Ladd sees the election as a continuation of a realignment that began in the late 1960s. Writing after the 1996 election, he argues that "the partisan realignment that ushered in our contemporary era is now fully mature." But this is a new type of realignment, Ladd argues, that has not led to domination by either party, since it is primarily a "philosophical realignment."[17] Walter Dean Burnham argues that a new realignment had occurred in the 1960s but that it was disrupted by the victory of the Republicans in the 1994 congressional elections. That Republican victory, he argues, created "an abrupt break with a previous political equilibrium governing congressional elections" and was one of the largest breaks with past voting patterns in U.S. history. Because the Republicans retained control of Congress in 1996, he states, "the 1996 election is thus to be regarded as a confirming event following a historically rare level of upheaval." Burnham goes on to say, "This is not a partisan realignment old-style, since Dole was not elected president. It is, however, its functional equivalent given the current organization of the electoral market."[18]

Nelson, who had earlier argued that a "split-level realignment" had occurred, now maintains that "the most recent realignment took place more than sixty years ago, and many scholars wonder whether another ever will occur." Instead, he writes, "Dealignment, the word usually used to describe the contemporary era, creates a fertile field in which third parties may flourish."[19] And James W. Ceaser and Andrew E. Busch argue that there is now a very large segment of "dealigned voters." "Trends favoring dealignment could be seen in the growing importance of the floating and nonattached voter, the growing space for third-party candidates, and the positive embrace of divided party control."[20]

Raising questions about prospects for alignment and dealignment leads to three basic questions that we will ask throughout our book. First, what happened to Republican presidential dominance? Did it end mainly because the electorate judged Bush a failure, or did the Republican coalition contain conflicting components that contributed to his defeat? Did Dole's failure to recapture the presidency for the GOP result mainly from a poor campaign, or did it also demonstrate that the Republicans may face fundamental problems rebuilding a winning presidential coalition?

Second, what are the prospects for the Democrats to build a new presidential majority? Were Clinton's victories something genuinely new, or did his winning coalitions resemble those of past Democratic winners? Did Clinton win reelection in 1996 based on his policy positions on newly emerging issues, or did he win mainly because voters were relatively satisfied with the economy and with the job he was doing as president?

Last, what ended Democratic congressional dominance? With the 1992 election, the Democrats had won the U.S. House in twenty consecutive elections, by far the longest period of one-party dominance in U.S. history.[21] The capture of the House by the Republicans in the 1994 midterm election was largely unexpected, and they managed to hold it by only a narrow margin in 1996. Even so, we can ask if the Republicans are in a position to establish long-term dominance in future legislative elections. What are the prospects for ending divided government between the Democratic and the Republican parties, and which party is likely to end it?

SURVEY RESEARCH SAMPLING

Our book relies heavily on surveys of the American electorate. It draws on telephone polls held during the election years, an exit poll conducted outside voting stations by the Voter News Service, and on interviews conducted inside the respondents' households by the National Opinion Research Center and by the U.S. Bureau of the Census. But we rely for the most part on nationwide interviews conducted mainly in the respondents' households during the two months before and the two months after the 1996 election by the Survey Research Center and the Center for Political Studies (SRC-CPS) of the University of Michigan. The SRC has been conducting surveys of the American electorate in every presidential election since 1948, and of every midterm election since 1954; these surveys are generally known as the National Election Studies (NES). Since 1952 the NES surveys have measured party identification and feelings of political efficacy. The CPS, founded in 1970, has developed valuable questions for measuring issue preferences. The NES data are the best and most comprehensive source of information about the political attitudes and partisan loyalties of the American electorate.

Readers may question our reliance on the NES survey of 1,714 Americans, when there are some 189 million Americans of voting age.[22] Would we obtain similar results if all adults had been surveyed?[23] The NES surveys use a procedure called multistage probability sampling to select the particular individuals to be interviewed. These procedures ensure that the final sample is likely to represent the entire U.S. adult citizen population (except for Americans living in institutions, on military bases, or abroad).[24]

Given the probability procedures used to conduct the NES surveys, we are able to assess the likelihood that the results represent the entire U.S. resident citizen population. The 1996 survey sampled about only one American adult in 100,000, but, provided that the sample is drawn properly, the representativeness of a sample depends far more on the size of the sample than on the size of the population being studied. For most purposes, samples of 1,500 are adequate to study the electorate. With samples of this size, we can be fairly confident (confident to a level of .95) that the results we obtain fall within 3 percentage points of the results we would get if the entire adult population had been surveyed.[25] For example, when we find that 40 percent of the sample in the 1996 NES survey thought that the nation's economy had gotten better in the past year, we can be fairly confident that between 37 (40 − 3) and 43 (40 + 3) percent of the entire electorate thought that the economy was improving. The actual result could be less than 37 percent or more than 43 percent. But a confidence level of .95 means that the odds are 19 to 1 that the proportion in the entire electorate falls within this range.

The range of confidence becomes wider when we look at subsamples of the electorate. When we examine groups of 500 respondents, the range of confidence grows to ±6 percentage points. Because the likelihood of error grows as our subsamples become smaller, we often supplement our analysis with the reports of other surveys.

Somewhat more complicated procedures are necessary to determine whether the difference between two groups is likely to reflect the relationship that would be found if the entire population were sampled. The probability that such differences reflect real differences in the total population is largely a function of the size of the groups being compared.[26] Generally speaking, when we compare the results based on the entire 1996 sample with an earlier NES survey, a difference of 4 percentage points is sufficient to be reasonably confident that the difference is real. For example, back in 1988, when Bush was elected, only 19 percent thought that the nation's economy had gotten better in the last year. In 1996, as we saw, 40 percent thought the economy was improving. Because this difference is greater than 4 points, we can be reasonably confident that the electorate was more likely to think the national economy was improving in 1996 than they were to think it was improving back in 1988.

When we compare subgroups of the electorate sampled in 1996 (or subgroups sampled in 1996 with subgroups sampled in earlier surveys), a larger percentage point difference is necessary for us to be reasonably confident that differences do not result from chance. For example, when we compare men with women a difference of about 6 points is necessary. When we compare blacks with whites, a difference of about 9 points is necessary, since only about 200 blacks are sampled in most NES surveys.

These numbers provide only a quick ballpark estimate of the chances that the reported results are likely to represent the entire population. Better estimates can be obtained by using formulas presented in many statistics textbooks. To make such calculations, or even a ballpark estimate of the chance of error, the reader must know the size of the groups being compared. For this reason, we always report in our tables and figures either the number of cases on which our results are based or the information necessary to approximate the number of cases.[27]

THE 1996 CONTEST

Part 1 of our book follows the chronology of the campaign itself. We begin with the struggle to gain the Republican party presidential nomination. Even though Clinton looked highly vulnerable, he faced no opposition for the Democratic party nomination. But eleven major Republicans sought their party's nomination, although only eight were still actively campaigning when the election year began.

Chapter 1 examines the Republican nomination process, although we also discuss Clinton's activities during the nomination phase. We begin by examining who chose to run for the Republican presidential nomination, with the goal of understanding the regularities that govern presidential nominations. We examine the rules that structure the nomination contest, showing how the electorate has a far larger role in choosing presidential candidates than they did before the reforms introduced after the 1968 election. These new rules, we argue, make it very likely that the nominee will be chosen before the presidential nominating convention is held. We explain why Dole won his party's nomination, and why he won so quickly. But we also show how Dole's early victory limited his ability to campaign effectively after he had locked up his party nomination. We examine his decision to resign from the Senate and his surprising choice of Jack Kemp as his running mate. We also analyze the party conventions, showing how Dole controlled the Republican National Convention and projected a far less strident image than the Republicans did at the 1992 convention.

Having gained their party's nomination, Clinton and Dole faced the task of winning the 270 electoral votes needed to win the general election. In Chapter 2 we look at the strategies of both candidates. As we shall see, although historical patterns seemed to favor the Republicans, the circumstances in 1996 favored Clinton. We examine the strategy for reelection that Clinton developed after the devastating Democratic losses in the 1994 midterm elections and show how he also developed a coherent electoral vote strategy. Dole appeared largely unprepared for the postconvention campaign and vacillated between an electoral vote strategy that wrote off California as unwinnable and one that made California a key part of a winning coalition. We look briefly at the Perot campaign, explaining why Perot never played an important role in the 1996 contest. As in all presidential elections since 1976, there were presidential debates. We show why Dole made no gains in his two debates against Clinton and why Kemp failed to make gains for his ticket in his debate against Al Gore. We examine Clinton's final efforts to protect his lead, and Dole's final ninety-six-hour campaign marathon. Finally, we discuss whether the campaign affected the results, making use of the 1996 NES survey to gain insights into that question.

Chapter 3 presents and interprets the election results. We discuss the election rules and see how the electoral college transformed Clinton's 49 percent of the popular vote into 70 percent of the electoral vote. We examine the overall pattern of results, showing how a pattern of Republican presidential dominance ended. Because states are the building blocks on which electoral vote majorities are based, the results are discussed state by state. We pay particular attention to electoral change in the South, because in the past half-century the South has been transformed from the most solidly Democratic region into one of the strongest regions for the Republicans in presidential elections. Finally, we examine the electoral vote balance. We argue that neither party is in a dominant position and that each has a mixture of problems and opportunities.

Chapter 1

The Nomination Struggle

January and February 1996 were difficult for Senator and presidential candidate Bob Dole (R-Kan.). The two positions he held were pulling him in sometimes quite opposite directions. As the majority leader in the Senate, he was involved, among many other things, in difficult negotiations, being torn between supporting the position of the conservative members of his own party (led in the negotiations by Speaker of the House Newt Gingrich of Georgia) and supporting the position of the opposite party (led in negotiations by President Bill Clinton). An impasse in negotiations over the budget process had already resulted in two partial shutdowns of the federal government, and the public believed that the Republicans, especially the Speaker, were to blame. Yet, Dole's famous abilities as senator to find common ground were severely tested by virtue of his campaign. To win his party's presidential nomination that year, he needed the support of members of the large and active conservative wing of his party, and because they had never felt he was "one of them," he had to win them over to his side. To align with the president in negotiations was to risk his ability to convince conservatives that he was at least acceptable to them. To side with the Speaker, however, was to side with those who were losing the public relations campaign and to position himself poorly for defeating the president in November. Moreover, while Dole was the acknowledged front-runner for the nomination, he faced stiff challenges both within the ranks of his party's elected leadership and from a new source, a rich outsider to politics, Steve Forbes, Jr. Dole stood by the conservatives, leaving it to Gingrich to give in to the president. Dole did so presumably in part on the grounds that he could not possibly defeat Clinton in the fall if he were not nominated by his party in the first place. Even so, Dole won by only a small margin in the first major contest of the year, the Iowa caucuses, and he actually lost the first primary of the year, in New Hampshire, to the outspoken conservative commentator and former speechwriter Patrick Buchanan.

Although in January and February it appeared that it would be a long campaign before the winner of the Republican nomination would emerge, in fact

Dole was able to withstand this crisis and defeat his rivals easily and early. Of course, Dole's path to the nomination was necessarily more difficult than Clinton's, because Clinton had worked hard to ensure that no major candidate would contest his nomination. In fact, the Democratic nomination in 1996 was the first effectively uncontested Democratic campaign since President Lyndon B. Johnson was nominated for a full term in 1964 (having assumed the presidency from the vice presidency in 1963 because of the assassination of John F. Kennedy). Thus, the 1996 nomination was also the first uncontested Democratic campaign since the reforms that created the current nomination system were initiated. Moreover, although Dole's campaign faced a crisis point in January and February, that he effectively won nomination in March meant that the two nomination campaigns of 1996 were resolved sooner than in any other year since the new nomination system was created in time for the 1972 elections.

While the campaigns may have had unique features, we shall see that they shared a great deal in common with prior campaigns under this nomination system. In this chapter we examine some of these regularities, and seek to understand some of the newer features, revealed in the 1996 nomination contests. We turn next to an examination of the first step of the nomination process, the decision of politicians to become—or not to become—presidential candidates. Then we examine some of the rules of the nomination system they face. Finally, we consider how the candidates ran and why Dole and Clinton succeeded in their quests.

WHO RAN

Eleven major Republicans sought their party's nomination, but only eight were still actively campaigning for the nomination by January 1, 1996. As we noted above, only Clinton sought his party's nomination. Just those facts alone reveal several important regularities in the new nomination system. First, when the incumbent seeks renomination, only a very few candidates will contest him, and perhaps no one will at all. In 1972, although the incumbent president Richard M. Nixon did face two potentially credible challengers to his renomination, they were sufficiently ineffective that he was essentially uncontested, just as Ronald Reagan was actually uncontested for renomination in 1984. The other incumbents, Gerald R. Ford in 1976, Jimmy Carter (the only Democratic incumbent besides Clinton in this era) in 1980, and George Bush in 1988, each faced one, or at most two, credible challengers. Bush was expected to have little difficulty in defeating his challenger, Buchanan, but had some problems at the outset, in part because he did not anticipate any struggle. Still, as we described in our earlier volume, he in fact defeated Buchanan rather easily.[1] Ford and Carter, however, had great difficulty in defeating their opponents (Reagan and Sen. Edward R. "Ted" Kennedy [D-Mass.], respectively). The latter two contests, although demonstrating that incumbents are not assured victory simply because they hold the office, nonetheless confirm the power of presidential incumbency, because both were victorious even though facing the strongest imaginable challengers and even though both were relatively weak incumbents. Clinton, not in as weak a position as either of them (but not in as strong a position as Nixon or Reagan), carefully planned to ensure that potential challengers, such as the Reverend Jesse Jackson Jr. and Robert Casey, the former governor of Pennsylvania, were dissuaded from trying.

A second regularity is the large number of candidates—eight—who ran for the Republican nomination in 1996. This size field is quite typical for parties that do not have an incumbent president seeking the nomination. There have been six such campaigns since 1980, and the number of major candidates that are in the race as the year begins varies remarkably little: seven Republicans in 1980, six in 1988, and eight in 1996; eight Democrats in each of the years 1984, 1988, and 1992. The eight Republican candidates in 1996 were Lamar Alexander (Tenn.), who most recently had been secretary of education in the Bush administration and had been governor directly before then; Buchanan, a former speechwriter in the Nixon administration and more recently a media commentator; Dole; Forbes; Sen. Phil Gramm (Texas); Alan Keyes, a former government official; Sen. Richard G. Lugar (Ind.); and Morry Taylor, a businessman. The three Republicans who had formally begun presidential campaigns in 1995 but withdrew before the year had ended were Rep. Robert K. Dornan (Calif.);[2] Sen. Arlen Specter (Penn.); and Gov. Pete Wilson (Calif.). This typical and relatively large list of candidates indicates the attraction of the office to ambitious politicians and those who aspire to be politicians.

This list of Republicans reveals further regularities typical of nominations in the last quarter century. A third is that, although one might expect current officeholders to dominate the list of candidates, a significant fraction of them do not hold office during the campaign. In 1996 only the three senators (and Clinton) were actually in office when running, and one of these, Dole, felt it wise to resign from office for the general election campaign. The substantial proportion of out-of-office candidates illustrates the extremely large amount of time, energy, and effort required to run for a presidential nomination. In addition, it exemplifies the (apparently increasing) attraction voters have to the "nonpolitician," the candidate who can claim to have played little or no role in politics, especially in Washington politics. The modest, if surprising, showing of Buchanan in 1992, who took great pains to be seen as an outsider, was trumped by the nearly 20 percent of the vote that the businessman H. Ross Perot won in that general election. Perhaps it is therefore no surprise that two businessmen, Forbes and Taylor, made concerted bids for the 1996 nomination. But Keyes, whose bid was focused on strongly conservative ideological appeals, especially on abortion, was reminiscent of other, earlier contenders who focused their campaigns more on a strong issue appeal than on an expectation of victory, such as Jackson in 1984 and 1988 and the Republican Rev. Pat Robertson in 1988.

A fourth regularity is that, of those candidates who were politicians, most held or had recently held high political office. Including Clinton, a president, three senators, and a cabinet officer (who had just retired from a governorship) ran in 1996, and, in addition, a representative, a senator, and a governor ran in 1995. This regularity follows from "ambition theory," developed originally by Joseph A. Schlesinger to explain how personal ambition and the pattern and prestige of office tend to emerge from political offices that provide the strongest electoral bases.[3] This base for the presidency includes the offices of vice president, senator, governor, and, of course, the presidency itself.

Except for the apparently increasing attractiveness of the nonpolitician, most candidates in 1996, as in all earlier campaigns under the new nominating system, have emerged from such a strong electoral base. Table 1-1 reports such data for 1996 and for all campaigns from 1972 through 1996 together. Seventy-two percent of all candidates emerge from the four offices that provide a strong electoral base. In addition, Gramm was the only Republican up for reelection to his currently held office, and Gramm was the beneficiary of the so-called Johnson law in Texas, whereby candidates can be elected to more than one office at a time, choosing which they prefer after the election. The law, passed to permit Johnson to run for both vice president and senator in 1960, meant that Gramm, like the other Republican senators, could retain his current office even if he lost the presidential race (although, as we noted, Dole chose to forfeit his current office to enhance his chances of winning the presidency).

A final regularity is that a relatively large list of potentially strong, attractive candidates did *not* run. This list included the immediate past vice president, Dan Quayle; Jack Kemp, who would become the Republican nominee for vice president; the former secretary of state James Baker III; the former cabinet member William Bennett, then a currently best-selling author; and several prominent governors, especially Tommy Thompson of Wisconsin and Christine Todd Whitman of New Jersey. Each of these potential candidates had been the object of considerable speculation and media scrutiny in 1995, as had the (at best vague) possibility of a Gingrich candidacy. The most intensely followed decision, however, was that of the former chairman of the Joint Chiefs of Staff during the Persian Gulf War, Gen. Colin Powell. His book-signing tour in late 1995 created a near "feeding frenzy" among the media, as the nation awaited not only his decision about the campaign but also his conclusion about his partisan preferences (which turned out to be Republican). General Powell, like the rest of the potential contenders in 1995 and so many others in preceding elections, decided either that the office itself was not particularly attractive to him or that the rigors of running were too great or both (or, as then-senator Walter F. Mondale, Jr., of Minnesota put it when he dropped out of the 1976 Democratic presidential nomination campaign in 1974, he lacked the "fire in the belly" for the job and its required campaign).

Still, eight is a substantial number of contenders. Evidently they concluded that the rigors of running were worth the prize that would come from winning. How they ran for office depended on two major factors: who else was running

TABLE 1-1   Current or Most Recent Office Held by Declared Candidates
for President: Two Major Parties, 1972–1996

Office held[a]	Percentage of all candidates holding that office	Number 1972–1996	Number 1996
President	8%	6	1
Vice president	3	2	0
U.S. senator	39	31	3
U.S. representative	11	9	0
Governor	22	17	0
U.S. cabinet	4	3	1
Other	5	4	1
None	9	7	3
Total	101%	79	9

[a]Office held at time of candidacy or office held most recently prior to candidacy.

Sources: The list of candidates between 1976 and 1992 is found in *Congressional Quarterly's Guide to U.S. Elections*, 3d ed. (Washington, D.C.: Congressional Quarterly, 1994), 562, while those in 1972 may be found in ibid., 522–525. The 1996 candidates are listed earlier in this chapter.

and the rules (both formal and informal) of the nomination campaign. All knew, as 1996 opened, that a large and reasonably diverse set of opponents faced them. Their next question, then, was how to win in the remarkably complex "game" of nomination campaigns that emerged in 1972—and has been revised for every election since then.

THE RULES OF THE NOMINATION SYSTEM

The method used for nominating presidential candidates by the two major parties is unique and amazingly complicated. To add to the complication, the various formal rules, laws, and procedures for the nomination are changed sometimes in large ways and invariably in numerous small ways every four years. And above and beyond the formal rules are informal standards and expectations, often set by the media or the candidates themselves, that help shape each campaign. As variable as the rules are, however, the basic shape of the current nomination system was set in a series of reforms in the late 1960s and early 1970s. This nomination system of 1972 (as we call it, because it was effectively in place in time for the 1972 campaigns) has one pair of overriding characteristics that define it as its own system. Beginning in 1972, for the first time, the major-party presidential nominees were selected in public and by the public. As a result, all serious candidates have sought the nomination by seeking the support of the public, campaigning to them through the various media of communications.

The complexity of the nomination contests is a consequence of four major factors. One of these, federalism, or the state as unit of selection for national nominees, is virtually as old as the Republic. Two factors, the rules concerning the selection (and perhaps instruction) of delegates to the convention and the rules concerning financing the campaign, are the (often-revised) products of the reform period. The final one, the reaction of candidates to these rules and to their opponents, is the invariable consequence of keen competition for a highly valued goal.

Federalism, or State-Based Delegate Selection

National conventions were first held to select presidential nominees for the 1832 presidential election, and it has been true for every nomination from then to today that it is the vote of delegates attending the national nominating conventions that selects the nominees.[4] Delegates have always been allocated at the state level and, whatever particulars may apply, each state selects its parties' delegates through procedures adopted by its state party organizations or by state law (which determines primary elections, their dates, rules, and procedures) or by both. Votes at the convention are cast by state delegation, and in general, the state (including the District of Columbia, and various territories) is the basic unit of the nomination. Thus, there are really fifty-one separate delegate selection contests in each party (plus several for the territories and the like that have voting powers). There is no national primary, nor is there serious contemplation of one.

The fact that there are more than fifty separate contests in each campaign creates numerous layers of complexity, two of which are especially consequential. First, each state is free to select any method of choosing delegates consistent with the general rules of the national party. Many states choose to select delegates via a primary election, which is a state-run election like any other, except that each of the two major parties holds its own primary for the selection of delegates for its convention (as well as, often, for the selection of its candidates for various other electoral offices). Indeed, the Democratic party requires that its party's primaries be open only to those who register as Democrats.[5] Other states use a combination of caucuses and conventions. Caucuses are simply local-level meetings of party members. Those in attendance choose some from their midst to attend higher-level conventions, perhaps at the county level, then the congressional, state, and eventually national conventions. Those attending the caucuses typically report their preferences for the presidential nomination (Democrats must do so), perhaps endorse possible platform proposals, and conduct additional party business in addition to selecting delegates to attend succeeding conventions.

The second major consequence of this federalism is that the states are free (within bounds) to choose when to hold their primaries or caucuses.[6] As a result, they are spread out over time. New Hampshire has held the first primary in the nation since it began to hold primaries in 1920; its law requires that it be held before any other primary, and since 1976 it has held its primary in February. A more recent tradition, which began in 1976, is that Iowa holds the first caucus, in advance of the New Hampshire primary (a "tradition" challenged by other states). The primary season in 1996 ended, as usual, in early June. In prior years, the primary season ended with something of a flourish because June primaries included the largest single prize, California. Even though California moved the date of its primary to earlier in the year in 1996, delegate selection still spread over essentially the same time as in previous years. The result is a months-long process that features dramatic ebbs and flows of candidates' fortunes. The lengthy and dynamic nature of these more than fifty events preceded the reforms that created the nomination system of 1972, but those reforms have greatly accentuated the importance of length and enhanced its dynamism.[7]

The Nomination System of 1972: Delegate Selection

Through 1968 presidential nominations were won by appeal to the party leadership. To be sure, public support and even primary election victories could be important in a candidate's campaign, but their importance would lie in the credibility they would give his (or, very rarely, her) candidacy to party leaders. But the 1968 Democratic nomination, as so much that year, was an especially tumultuous one, with the result that the Democratic party began a series of reforms that created one of the two major components of the new nomination system of 1972, that concerning delegate selection. Although the Republican party was much less aggressive in reforming its delegate selection procedures, they also did so, if to a lesser degree. Moreover, the most consequential results of these reforms for our purposes, the proliferation of presidential primaries and media treatment of some caucuses (notably Iowa's) as essentially primary-like, spilled over to the Republican side in full measure.

In 1968 Sens. Eugene J. McCarthy (Minn.) and Robert F. Kennedy (N.Y.) ran highly visible, public, primary-oriented campaigns. Before the second primary, in Wisconsin, President Johnson surprisingly announced that he would not seek renomination. Vice President Hubert H. Humphrey took his place in representing the establishment of the Democratic party. Humphrey, however, waged no *public* campaign, winning nomination without entering a single primary.[8] The controversial nomination split an already deeply divided party. Whether Humphrey would have won had Kennedy not been assassinated the night he defeated McCarthy in the California primary, effectively eliminating McCarthy as a serious contender, is unknowable. It was clear to Democrats, however, that the nomination process should be opened to more diverse candidacies and that public participation should be more open and more efficacious, perhaps even determinative.

The most obvious consequences of these reforms were the increasing decisiveness of the public in each state's delegate selection proceedings (even binding delegates to vote in support of the candidate for whom they were chosen) and the proliferation of presidential primaries.[9] Caucuses and conventions were made more timely and were better publicized; in short, they were made more primary-like. The media have treated Iowa's caucuses as critical events, and their coverage of them is similar to their coverage of primaries—how many "votes" were "cast" for each candidate, for example. At the state level, many concluded that primary elections were the easiest way of conforming with the new Democratic rules in 1972. Thus, the number of states holding Democratic primaries increased from seventeen in 1968 to twenty-three in 1972 to thirty in 1976, with the number of Republican primaries essentially the same. In 1988, for example, thirty-five states held Republican primaries (thirty-three held Democratic ones), which selected three of every four delegates to the Republican convention that year. In 1996, forty-two Republican primaries were held, or 80 percent of all delegate-selecting units (the states, the District of Columbia, and Puerto Rico). Caucuses are more common in smaller states, and fully 87 percent of Republican delegates were chosen in primaries in 1996. Thus, it is fair to say that for the Republicans the new system has become one based all but exclusively on primaries.[10]

Although the requirements had been changed by one or both national parties (usually the Democrats) every four years since 1972, delegate selection rules at the national level were not changed for 1996. That does not mean that delegate selection procedures were the same in 1996 as in 1992. State legislatures, state parties, or both may change their requirements every four years as well, and many do.

States in fact altered delegate selection procedures in one very consequential way. More states would select more delegates earlier than ever before. Most significantly, for example, California changed its primary date from its traditional first Tuesday in June to March 26. This "front loading," as it is called, has been happening fairly consistently since 1972. In that year a majority of Republican delegates to be chosen by primary were not selected until the ninth week after the first primary, New Hampshire's, and the three-quarter mark was not hit until the very last day of the primary season, some fourteen weeks after the New Hampshire primary (the primary season was two weeks shorter in 1972 than in 1996). In 1988 the 50 percent mark was hit in the fifth week, and the 75 percent mark in the twelfth week of the season. In 1996 the 50 percent mark was hit three weeks after New Hampshire's primary, and the threequarter mark was hit three weeks later (or only a month and a half after the New Hampshire primary), according to the calculations of William G. Mayer.[11]

The rationale for front loading is clear enough. California's (actual or near) end-of-season primary was least consequential in the 1964 Republican and the 1972 Democratic nomination contests. Once candidates, media, and other actors realized, and reacted to, the implications of the reformed nomination system, the action shifted to the earliest events of the season. Most important, the nomination was effectively won well before the last primary. In 1988 several southern states (and others) aligned their primaries to be held on the same early March date to maximize their regional influence over the nomination campaigns. More and more state parties and legislatures realized that front loading brought more attention in the media, more expenditures of time and money by the candidates, and more influence to their states.

If the rationale for front loading was clear by 1996, the consequences were not. Some argued that long-shot candidates could propel to the front of the pack by gathering momentum in Iowa and New Hampshire and, before the well-known candidates could react, lock up the nomination early. This rationale seemed to reflect the dynamics of the 1984 Democratic presidential nomination, with Mondale reeling from Sen. Gary Hart's (Colo.) strong showing in Iowa and victory in New Hampshire. Mondale slowly regained his lead in March, however, and went on to victory. Hart's victories in and immediately after the New Hampshire primary, by this argument, indicated that little-known long shots could win the nomination based on these early showings, especially if, because of front loading, most delegates were selected before a candidate like Mondale could recover.

The alternative argument was that increasing front loading helps those who begin the campaign with several advantages associated with being a front-runner, such as name recognition, support from state and local party or related organizations, and, most of all, money. Indeed, as the primary season has become more front loaded, the well-known, established, and financed candidates have increasingly come to dominate the primaries. Sen. George McGovern (S.D.) and Carter won the Democratic nominations in 1972 and 1976 even though they began as little-known and ill-financed contenders. Bush, successful in the 1980 Iowa Republican caucuses, climbed from, in his words, "an asterisk in the polls" (where the asterisk is commonly used to indicate less than 1 percent support) to become Ronald Reagan's major contender and eventual vice-presidential choice. And as we noted, Hart nearly defeated former vice president Mondale in 1984. In 1988 the two strongest candidates at the start of the Republican race, Bush and Dole, contested most vigorously, with Bush winning. Gov. Michael Dukakis of Massachusetts was the most well financed and best-organized Democrat and won nomination surprisingly easily. Clinton's victory in 1992, then, appeared the culmination of the trend toward the strongest and most well financed candidate's seemingly insuperable advantages. For his part, he was able to withstand scandal and defeat in the early going and essentially cruise to victory. One important reason was illustrated by Sen. Paul Tsongas (Mass.). He defeated the field in New Hampshire and, as usual, the victory and its consequent media attention opened doors to fund-raising possibilities unavailable to him even days earlier. Yet he faced the dilemma that taking the time to raise the funds and use them to increase the chances of winning votes would let too many primaries pass without his competition. Conversely, if he campaigned in those primaries, he would not have the opportunity to raise and direct the funds he needed to be an effective competitor. Front loading had, simply, squeezed too much into too short a time frame after the New Hampshire primary for him to be able to capitalize on early victories as, say, Carter had in 1976 in winning nomination and election.

The Nomination System of 1972: Campaign Finance

The second part of the reforms of the presidential nomination process began with the Federal Election Campaign Act of 1971, but it was the amendments of 1974 and 1976 that fully altered the nature of campaign financing. The Watergate scandal exposed substantial abuses in both raising and spending money in the 1972 presidential election (facts that were revealed in part as a result of the implementation of the 1971 act). The resulting reforms limited contributions by individuals and groups, virtually ending the influence of individual "fat cats" and requiring presidential candidates to raise money in a broadly based campaign. Small donations for the nomination could be matched by the federal government, and any candidate who accepted matching funds would be bound by limits on what he or she could spend (a provision that limited Dole's campaign efforts in the spring after he won the primaries but before the nominating conventions).

These provisions and others, such as the creation of the Federal Election Commission to monitor campaign financing, altered the way nomination campaigns were funded. Still, just as candidates learned over time how to compete most effectively within the new delegate selection process, so too did candidates learn how to campaign in light of the financial regulations. Perhaps most important, presidential candidates learned that, while it is not as true for them as their congressional peers that "early money is like yeast," it *is* true, or so they believed in 1996, that lots and lots of early money is necessary to compete effectively.[12] Gramm proved to be a remarkable raiser of early money. On February 23, 1995, he raised more than $4 million at one dinner. In words that did not necessarily help his public image, he declared at that dinner that "I have the most reliable friend you can have in American politics, and that is ready money."[13] He eventually proposed a standard of raising between $20 million and $26 million before the primary season as a measure of serious viability.

Clearly, Dole and Forbes mounted strong campaigns after the New Hampshire primary and had lots of money, and both Dole and Buchanan (who also competed effectively) had strong organizations in numerous locales to help their campaigns. Indeed, front loading has made strong, early fund-raising and organizational building critical tasks. Equally clearly, little-known outsiders like Carter in 1976 or Tsongas in 1992 are quite unlikely to be able to raise much capital (financially and/or organizationally) before the primary season. But we said above that lots of early money may be *necessary* to compete effectively. Necessity is not sufficiency. Gramm raised the necessary resources. Money was not, by itself, sufficient, however, as he received too little public support, and he withdrew from competition two days after finishing fifth in the Iowa caucuses.

WHY DOLE WON

The story of the 1996 campaign, like all earlier campaigns in this new nomination system, was at base the story of what actions the public took in reaction to

the candidates. While that story ordinarily begins in Iowa, its status as first caucus in the nation was challenged by Louisiana's party-run, primary-like caucus
(Alaska, Guam, and Hawaii began their caucuses before Iowa, as well). A pact
among Republican candidates (urged by Iowans) to ignore Louisiana was broken by Buchanan and Gramm. Gramm's defeat there weakened public perceptions of his candidacy, and his well-financed campaign ended with his fifth-place
showing in Iowa. Dole carried Iowa, but by a very small margin over Buchanan,
with Alexander coming in third. This was considered something of a defeat for
Dole by the media, because Iowa is near his home state and because he had
handily defeated the incumbent vice president, Bush, there four years earlier.
Still, it was better than the actual (if narrow) defeat he suffered in New Hampshire by Buchanan, with Alexander again coming in third. Forbes then polled
close victories in Delaware and Arizona (offset by Dole victories in the Dakotas)
in the week following the New Hampshire primary. But the next Saturday Dole
won the South Carolina primary, and then two weeks after the New Hampshire
primary, he won all eight primaries, and, indeed, every primary thereafter. What
looked to be a competitive contest in February reverted to a lopsided Dole victory march, and he was assured of a majority of the convention delegates by the
end of March 26, the day of the California, Nevada, and Washington primaries.
The results of the Republican caucuses and primaries are reported in Tables 1-2
and 1-3, respectively.

The main question in regard to this campaign, we believe, is why did Dole win
so quickly?[14] We believe the answer is that front loading the primary season led
to an even more highly front-loaded campaign—and that process gives the advantage to the initial front-runner. The advantage is sufficiently strong that a
clear front-runner can withstand substantial setbacks without losing control of
the nomination.

Dole was the clear front-runner as the primary season began. This was his
fourth national campaign, and among his opponents only Buchanan had experienced even one. Dole began the year as the overwhelming first choice among
Republicans in the electorate for the nomination. In Gallup polls in 1995 and
early 1996, he consistently was the first choice of 45 to 50 percent of the Republicans; Gramm took second place, with 10 to 13 percent support. To be sure,
when Powell was included in the poll, Dole and Powell received about one-third
support each (whereas including Gingrich barely changed Dole's—or Gramm's—
support), but then, Powell was never an actual candidate. Dole would have had
an advantage over Powell in having raised, rather than having to raise, the multiple millions of dollars needed, and Dole had the advantage over all other Republicans in having the support of a large number of elected Republicans,
including governors of key states. These endorsements meant that in addition to
his own extensive organizational efforts, aid became available from many state
and local party organizations. In short, Dole was known by the public and liked
at least sufficiently that many were willing to support him, and he was well financed and well organized. No one else could come close to matching those

TABLE 1-2 Republican Caucus Results, 1996

	Total vote	Alexander	Buchanan	Dole	Forbes	Keyes	Others/ uncommitted
Alaska (Jan. 27–29)	9,172	0.6%	**32.6%**	17.1%	30.7%	9.8%	9.2%
Louisiana (Feb. 6)	22,846	—	**44.4**	—	—	4.0	51.6
Iowa (Feb. 12)	96,451	17.6	23.3	**26.3**	10.2	7.4	15.1
Wyoming (March 2)	915	7.2	19.8	**40.4**	17.6	6.7	8.3
Minnesota (March 5)	28,256	4.6	33.1	**41.2**	10.3	9.5	1.4
Washington (March 5)	26,158	2.1[a]	28.1	**36.4**	21.8	7.9	3.8
Missouri (March 9)	10,000[c]	—	**36.5**	28.5	0.9[b]	9.2	25.0

Note: In most cases, results are based on straw votes of caucus participants at first-round caucus events. However, in Louisiana, where Patrick J. Buchanan and Sen. Phil Gramm of Texas were the main competitors, voters balloted directly for national convention delegates, while in Missouri the results reflected the preferences of delegates selected to the next stage of the caucus process. Percentages do not always add to 100 percent because of rounding. The winner's percentage is indicated in boldface.

[a] Alexander withdrew from the race March 6.
[b] Forbes withdrew from the race March 14.
[c] Turnout estimate.
— Indicates that candidate was not listed on the caucus ballot or his votes were not tabulated separately.

Source: Congressional Quarterly Weekly Report, August 3, 1996, 62.

TABLE 1-3 Republican Primary Results, 1996

	Total vote	Alexander	Buchanan	Dole	Forbes	Keyes	Others/uncommitted
New Hampshire (Feb. 20)	208,993	22.6%	27.2%	26.2%	12.2%	2.7%	9.1%
Delaware (Feb. 24)	32,773	13.3	18.7	27.2	32.7	5.3	2.8
Arizona (Feb. 27)	347,482	7.1	27.6	29.6	33.4	0.8	1.5
North Dakota (Feb. 27)	63,734	6.3	18.3	42.1	19.5	3.2	10.6
South Dakota (Feb. 27)	69,170	8.7	28.6	44.7	12.8	3.4	1.8
South Carolina (March 2)	276,741	10.4	29.2	45.1	12.7	2.1	0.6
Puerto Rico (March 3)	238,748	0.5	0.4	97.9	0.5	0.0	0.7
Colorado (March 5)	247,752	9.8	21.5	43.6	20.8	3.7	0.6
Connecticut (March 5)	130,418	5.4	15.1	54.4	20.1	1.7	3.3
Georgia (March 5)	559,067	13.6	29.1	40.6	12.7	3.1	0.9
Maine (March 5)	67,280	6.6	24.5	46.3	14.8	1.8	5.9
Maryland (March 5)	254,246	5.5	21.1	53.3	12.7	5.4	2.0
Massachusetts (March 5)	284,833	7.5	25.2	47.7	13.9	1.8	3.8
Rhode Island (March 5)	15,009	19.0	2.6*	64.4	0.9*	0.2*	12.9
Vermont (March 5)	58,113	10.6[a]	16.7	40.3	15.6	—	16.8
Florida (March 12)	898,070	1.6	18.1	56.9	20.2	1.9	1.3
Louisiana (March 12)	77,789	2.1	33.1	47.8	13.2	3.2	0.6
Mississippi (March 12)	151,925	1.8	25.9	60.3	8.0	1.9	2.1
Oklahoma (March 12)	264,542	1.3	21.5	59.3	14.1	2.4	1.4
Oregon (March 12)	407,514	7.0	21.3	50.8	13.3	3.5	4.1
Tennessee (March 12)	289,043	11.3	25.2	51.2	7.7	2.7	1.9
Texas (March 12)	1,019,803	1.8	21.4	55.6	12.8[b]	4.1	4.2
Illinois (March 19)	818,364	1.5	22.7	65.1	4.9	3.7	2.1
Michigan (March 19)	524,161	1.5	33.9	50.6	5.1	3.1	5.9
Ohio (March 19)	955,017	2.0	21.5	66.4	6.0	2.9	1.1

(Table continues)

TABLE 1-3 (continued)

	Total vote	Alexander	Buchanan	Dole	Forbes	Keyes	Others/ uncommitted
Wisconsin (March 19)	576,575	1.9	33.8	**52.3**	5.6	3.1	3.3
California (March 26)	2,452,312	1.8	18.4	**66.1**	7.5	3.8	2.5
Nevada (March 26)	140,637	2.3	15.2	**51.9**	19.2	1.4	10.0
Washington (March 26)	120,684	1.3	20.9	**63.1**	8.6	4.6	1.4
Pennsylvania (April 23)	684,204	—	18.0	**63.6**	8.0	5.8	4.5
District of Columbia (May 7)	2,941	—	9.5	**75.5**	—	—	15.0
Indiana (May 7)	498,444	—	19.4	**70.6**	9.9	—	—
North Carolina (May 7)	283,213	2.7	13.0	**71.5**	4.1	4.1	4.5
Nebraska (May 14)	170,591	2.6	10.4	**75.7**	6.2	3.0	2.1
West Virginia (May 14)	125,413	2.9	16.3	**68.8**	4.9	3.8	3.3
Arkansas (May 21)	42,648	—	23.5	**76.5**	—	—	—
Idaho (May 28)	118,715	—	22.3	**62.3**	—	5.0	10.4
Kentucky (May 28)	103,206	3.2	8.1	**73.8**	3.3	3.7	7.8
Alabama (June 4)	143,295	—	15.7	**74.9**	—	3.6	5.8
Montana (June 4)	114,463	—	24.4	**61.3**	7.2	—	7.1
New Jersey (June 4)	209,998	—	11.0	**82.3**	—	6.7	—
New Mexico (June 4)	67,122	3.9	8.2	**75.4**	5.7	3.2	3.7

Note: Results are based on official returns for the primaries held through April, except for Ohio, and on nearly complete but unofficial returns for the primaries held in May and June, except for Idaho and Nebraska, where official returns were available. Percentages may not add to 100 because of rounding. The New York primary March 7 (not included) was for election of delegates only. The winner's percentage is indicated in boldface.

[a] Alexander withdrew from the race March 6.

[b] Forbes withdrew from the race March 14.

*Votes won by Buchanan, Forbes, and Keyes in Rhode Island were write-ins.

— Candidates or uncommitted line not listed on ballot.

Source: Congressional Quarterly Weekly Report, August 3, 1996, 63.

advantages, and they define the very idea of what it means to be the front-runner. Moreover, each of those resources proved useful at one point or another: experience and popular support at each step; money to counter the advertising blitz that cost Forbes more than $20 million by the end of February 1996; and organizational and elected leadership support in such states as South Carolina that helped counter Forbes's money and Buchanan's support from conservative groups. Thus, the ingredients that went into making Dole the initial front-runner were the ingredients that enabled him to withstand challenges and survive in a highly truncated primary season.

THE CONVENTIONS

The sudden Dole victory left both parties with nearly four months until their national conventions. The 1992 nominations were not effectively decided until late spring (itself an unusually early time), and the remaining vacuum in time was quickly filled by Perot's rise as an independent candidate, to the point that he led in the national polls in early June. In 1996 Clinton, like Bush four years earlier, could simply be president and, as such, attract media attention. But Clinton was proving to be a remarkable fund-raiser and, unlike his predecessor, had no primary opposition and therefore had the full allotment of nomination funding available. He chose to spend significant sums in the primary season (which, after all, continued into June) and later. Dole, however quickly he might have vanquished his competition, was running close to the spending limits, which restricted his ability to contest Clinton's advertising, done in the primary season but oriented toward the general election.

On May 15, in part in an effort to combat Clinton's lead in the polls and campaigning that was at least reinforcing that lead, Dole announced that he was resigning from the Senate as of June 11. His retirement was a touching and positively assessed event. Nonetheless, perhaps because he lacked the resources (and by then opportunities) to capitalize on it effectively, his poll numbers did not increase noticeably.

Dole had one final—and major—decision in preparation for the convention and transition to the general election campaign, selection of his vice-presidential running mate. Technically, the presidential nominee-to-be would be simply announcing his preference, "hoping" that some delegate would nominate that candidate and that the convention would approve it. In reality, of course, the nominee gets his wishes, even in the rare case (Bush's selection of Quayle in 1988, perhaps) when the name engenders controversy. When Dole chose Jack Kemp as his running mate, he was widely praised, particularly for selecting an experienced (but younger) candidate long noted for his deep beliefs in conservative economic principles and commitment to social policies that, while conservative, were also designed to include minorities and the disadvantaged.

The 1992 Republican convention was widely criticized for its strident conservative speeches. Bush was perceived as having lost control of his party's convention, and many thought that at least symptomatic if not causative of his losing campaign thereafter. Dole wanted, of course, to avoid a comparable situation. The most explosive issue facing Republicans since at least the 1980 campaign was abortion. Their strong opposition to abortion was criticized by some as closing the "big tent" of the party to moderates on the issue, let alone pro-choice advocates. Pro-choice forces sought to moderate the strict pro-life planks, and Dole sought a compromise in the platform. Debate raged in public, with the final compromise reflecting more the pro-life than the Dole compromise position. Still, the main event, Dole's nominating convention, held in San Diego, proved to be well run, free of major controversy, and a generally positive send-off for the Doles. The "talk show" style speech given by Elizabeth Dole, currently the head of the American Red Cross and a two-time former cabinet member, probably attracted the most positive reviews.

The Democratic convention returned to Chicago for the first time since its debacle in and outside the convention hall in 1968. But although a Richard Daley was mayor of the city in both cases (father and son, respectively), times had changed. Clinton's renomination attracted little controversy. The platform reflected Clinton's moderate and not particularly ambitious goals for the second term (or at least his not particularly ambitious campaign themes). His acceptance speech, like Dole's, was sound, not especially inspiring, and achieved its primary aim of holding his front-running position firm as the general election campaign formally began.

Chapter 2

The General Election Campaign

Once they have been nominated, candidates choose their general election campaign strategies based on their perceptions of what the electorate wants, the relative strengths and weaknesses of their opponents and themselves, and their chances of winning. A candidate who is convinced that he or she has a dependable lead may choose strategies very different from those used by a candidate who believes he is seriously behind. A candidate who believes that an opponent has significant weaknesses is more likely to run an aggressive, attacking campaign than one who does not perceive such weaknesses.

After the conventions, Bill Clinton had a solid lead in the trial heats in national polls. Many observers, however, believed that the race would eventually tighten up—perhaps because of Clinton's "ethical problems" or Bob Dole's promise of a tax cut or other reasons—and that Dole really could win. They believed that the campaign could really make a difference. Part 2 of this book examines in detail the impact of particular factors (including issues and evaluations of Clinton's job performance) on the voters' decisions. This chapter provides an overview of the campaign—an account of its course and a description of the context within which strategic decisions were made.

THE STRATEGIC CONTEXT AND CANDIDATES' CHOICES

One aspect of the strategic context that candidates must consider is the track record of the parties in recent presidential elections. In presidential races the past is certainly not entirely prologue, but it is relevant. From this perspective, the picture was not particularly encouraging for the Democrats, whereas it offered hope to the GOP. From 1952 through 1992 there had been eleven presidential elections, and the Republicans had won seven of them. Similarly, the GOP had won three of the last five races, and two of their three victories were electoral college landslides.

The nature of the American system for electing presidents requires that we examine the state-by-state pattern of results. U.S. voters do not directly vote for president or vice president. Rather, they vote for a slate of electors pledged to support a presidential and a vice-presidential candidate. Moreover, in every state except Maine and Nebraska the entire slate of electors that receives the most popular votes is selected. In no state is a majority of the vote required. Since the 1972 election, Maine has used a system in which the plurality-vote winner for the whole state wins two electoral votes. In addition, the plurality-vote winner in each of Maine's two House districts receives that district's single electoral vote. Beginning in 1992 Nebraska allocated its five electoral votes in a similar manner: the statewide plurality-vote winner gained two votes, and each of the state's three congressional districts awarded one vote on a plurality basis.

If larger states used the district plan employed by Maine and Nebraska, the dynamics of the campaign would be different. For example, candidates might target specific congressional districts and would probably campaign in all large states, regardless of how well they were doing in the statewide polls. But given the winner-take-all rules employed in forty-eight states and the District of Columbia, candidates cannot safely ignore the pattern of past state results. And a state-by-state analysis of the five presidential elections from 1976 through 1992 suggests that the Democrats did not face an easy task in the effort to win the 270 electoral votes required for victory.

As Figure 2-1 reveals, twelve states voted Republican in all five of these elections. Only one state (Minnesota) and the District of Columbia were equally loyal to the Democrats. (See Chapter 3 for a discussion of long-term voting patterns.) These perfectly loyal states provided a prospective balance of 73 electoral votes for the Republicans to only 13 for the Democrats. More problematic for the Democratic candidates were the next groups of states. Eighteen states had voted Republican in every election but one, with a total of 243 electoral votes. Balancing these were only three small states (Hawaii, Rhode Island, and West Virginia) with 13 electoral votes that had supported the Democrats in four of the five contests. Thus, if each state's political leanings were categorized on the basis of the last five elections, one might expect that 316 electoral votes were likely to go to the GOP (46 more than needed for victory), whereas only 26 were as likely to go to the Democrats.

If this previous pattern were to govern the 1996 election completely, then prospects would have been dark for the Democratic ticket. But, of course, things were not that simple, and many factors made Democratic chances considerably better than they had been in the past. The most important of these was that Clinton was the incumbent and Dole was the challenger. This meant that Clinton had the advantages of the office at his disposal: he could command media attention at will and he could consider the political effects of the governmental decisions he made. Incumbency also meant something else: Clinton had won the previous election. That is, in his 1992 contest with George Bush he had assembled a winning electoral college coalition. If he could just persuade the people who had voted for him before to choose him again he would go a long way toward

FIGURE 2-1   States That Voted Republican at Least Four out of Five Times,
1976–1992

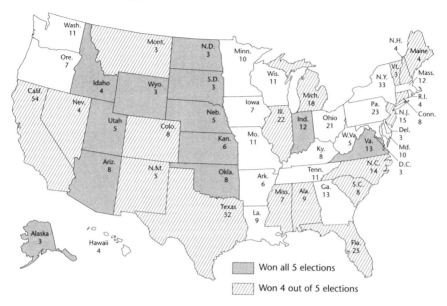

Note: Each state's electoral vote equals the total number of its representatives and senators in Congress. The electoral votes are the number allocated to each state for the 1992, 1996, and 2000 elections.

Source: Election results based on *Presidential Elections 1789–1992* (Washington, D.C.: Congressional Quarterly, 1995), 70–74.

winning. Dole, in contrast, faced the far more daunting task of getting millions of 1992 voters to change their minds. This was not impossible; after all, both Jimmy Carter and Bush had been recently defeated as incumbents. It was just that getting people to change their minds about an incumbent candidate is generally more difficult than getting them to persist.

Far more important than the simple fact of incumbency, however, was the public's evaluation of Clinton's performance and of the state of the nation. When Carter and Bush had faced the voters in their reelection campaigns, their approval ratings in polls were decidedly negative. Clinton was in much better shape. During the fight with the Republican Congress in late 1995 and early 1996—and in the wake of two shutdowns of the federal government—his approval rating had moved into the positive range, and it had stayed above 50 percent almost without exception since February.[1] More specific evaluations also augured well for the president's prospects. For example, the state of the economy was relatively good—and, politically more important, it was regarded as good by the electorate. At the end of August, 37 percent of the respondents in a national poll said that the state of the economy was good or excellent, and 52 percent said that the economy was getting better. This was in contrast to 10 percent and 29 percent, respectively, that had held the same opinions in a survey approximately four years earlier, leading into the 1992 election.[2] Moreover, Clinton was starting to get personal credit for the performance of the economy. This had not been the case during most of his presidency, when his approval rating on handling the economy had generally been in the 30 to 40 percent range. At the beginning of September, however, a CBS News/*New York Times* poll showed that Clinton's economic approval rating had reached 55 percent.[3] By the election, according to the National Election Studies (NES) survey, his economic approval rating had climbed to 66 percent. Even on foreign policy, far from Clinton's strong suit in the eyes of the electorate during his first term, Clinton was seen to be doing well. During a confrontation with Iraq, Clinton ordered a missile strike against that nation. Survey respondents registered 69 percent approval for the missile attack and 63 percent support for the president's handling of the situation with Iraq.[4] Overall, 64 percent of survey respondents labeled Clinton's first term a success (up from 44 percent who had the same opinion in December of 1994).[5]

The Clinton campaign had (as it did in 1992) a firm strategic plan with a strong geographic focus.[6] In the wake of the devastating Democratic losses in the 1994 elections, and in conflict with the GOP Congress in 1995-1996, Clinton arrived at a synthesis between the pressures from competing groups of advisers. One group, mostly holdovers from 1992, urged tending to the party's liberal base and defending its established programs, whereas the other, newer group (chief among them campaign adviser Dick Morris) pressed Clinton to move to the center. Clinton did both, proposing, for example, his own version of a balanced budget (which angered many liberal Democrats) while opposing the GOP Congress's priorities by vetoing its budget bills. The latter events precipitated the government shutdowns, which in turn led to the rise in Clinton's approval ratings above the 50 percent mark.[7] Perhaps the best illustration of this mixed strategy was the president's 1996 State of the Union address in which he declared, "The era of big government is over. But we cannot go back to the time when our citizens were left to fend for themselves."[8] The speech also included a range of new small proposals (in both scope and cost) but no major initiatives.

The geographic strategy was largely an updating of the successful approach of four years earlier. Clinton's strategists planned heavy purchases of media time beginning in April of 1996, targeted on twenty-three states that they believed would determine the outcome of the election.[9] The states totaled 310 electoral votes, and Clinton had carried all but two of them (Florida and North Carolina) in his initial campaign. This plan left two other groups of states with lower priority for campaigning. One group (sixteen states, with 129 electoral votes) was deemed to be too favorable to Dole; the president had lost all of them in 1992. The second set (eleven states plus the District of Columbia, with 99 electoral votes) had all gone to Clinton four years before and were thought to be relatively safe. This media-intensive strategy was made feasible by the president's substantial financial advantage we mentioned in the preceding chapter. Because of his contested nomination, Dole spent heavily, and by the end of March he had only about $2 million left until general election funds became available at the end of

August. Clinton, having no contest, had about $21 million remaining for that period.[10]

In contrast to the incumbent's situation, the Dole campaign was largely unprepared for the postconvention campaign. Dole essentially acted as his own campaign manager, resisting the efforts of professionals to shape his strategy and message. Mostly, choices were put off: "Mr. Dole was always arguing that important campaign decisions could be delayed."[11] Almost by default, Dole's proposal for a 15 percent across-the-board tax cut became the initial campaign theme. It quickly became apparent, however, that the proposal was not making headway with the voters. By the beginning of September, a *New York Times* poll showed that 64 percent of respondents said that Dole would not be able to cut taxes that much if he were elected, and that was up from 51 percent who had thought that in the previous poll.[12]

Regarding geographic strategy, the campaign was also indecisive. Some people in Dole's inner circle argued that the campaign had to focus or risk losing everywhere. But focus on what? Two proposed courses were offered, one concentrating on a western strategy that would try to win California, the other targeting states in the East. "Typically, Scott Reed [Dole's campaign manager] hesitated. Instead, he ordered up a third map—a play-everywhere scenario."[13]

Of course this was a difficult choice because it really revolved around a strategic issue that had often faced Democratic presidential candidates in previous elections: how do you persuade a large number of voters to change their minds when you are far behind in the polls? Waiting for the voters to move of their own volition, or for the incumbent to make a serious mistake, did not seem promising, and the positive theme of a tax cut wasn't working. That left "going negative," but that strategy also did not look too promising. First of all, the GOP had been attacking Clinton's administration for bad policies and ethical lapses for four years, and Clinton was ahead anyway. One poll at the beginning of September showed that 56 percent thought that Dole had the higher moral character, as opposed to 33 percent for Clinton. Despite that, however, approval of the job that Clinton was doing as president had peaked at 60 percent.[14] Making things even more difficult, the same survey indicated that 29 percent of respondents believed that the Dole campaign had already been too personally negative, whereas only 5 percent thought that of the Clinton campaign.[15] Yet there was little choice. Dole "would have to go negative, he knew, not because he wanted to but because there was no place else to go."[16]

FROM LABOR DAY TO THE DEBATES

The Republicans: Searching for a Strategy

Lacking tangible gains in the polls from his tax proposal, Dole tried various appeals and tactics during the month of September. It was striking that at the beginning of the month the candidate of the party that had controlled the White House for twenty of the previous twenty-eight years invoked the image of a Democratic president, comparing himself to Harry S. Truman and vowing to emulate Truman's come-from-behind victory in 1948.[17] In an address to the American Legion, he contrasted his values with Clinton's, attacking the president's opposition to a constitutional amendment to ban flag burning. He also contended that the rise in drug use during the previous four years had been encouraged by the standards set by the White House.[18] He attacked the Clinton-sponsored Family and Medical Leave Act as an interference by government in the affairs of businesses.

Most of all, Dole tried the time-tested charge that Clinton was a liberal, although this line of assault was rendered less effective by the equally frequent GOP attack that the president was a "waffler," not firmly committed to any position or principle. The Republican candidate also tried to use his ties in the Senate to deny legislative successes to Clinton. He wrote to his successor as majority leader, Sen. Trent Lott of Mississippi, criticizing the proposed treaty banning chemical weapons, and the GOP majority put off consideration of the treaty until 1997. Dole also called for a provision in the immigration bill under consideration to permit the states to deny public education to children who were illegal immigrants.[19]

With regard to geographic strategy, the campaign continued to demonstrate the same uncertainty of focus noted above. In the middle of September, Dole campaigned in Connecticut despite trailing Clinton by nearly two to one in polls, talking about tax cuts and the president's character. At the same time, the Republican campaign committed large amounts of media money to California even though surveys indicated that Clinton had about a 20-point lead.[20] In contrast, the Republicans spent no media money for two weeks at the beginning of the month in the more closely contested midwestern states of Illinois, Missouri, and Wisconsin. Continuing to reflect the campaign's view that the race could be won in the late weeks, one Dole official indicated that "the vast majority of the money is budgeted for October."[21]

By late September, however, Dole strategists had reportedly developed a firmer geographic focus. First they counted on a group of sixteen "core states" (with 135 electoral votes) that had been dependably Republican in the past. Next there was a "must-win" category of seven states (with 77 votes) where Clinton was ahead, but most of which had been with the GOP in a majority of the last five elections. A daunting aspect of this plan was that even if Dole could win all states in both of these categories, he would still be 58 electoral votes short of the 270 he needed. That left him pinning his hopes on a final group of six states (66 votes), in all of which Clinton had double-digit leads, to put him over the top. The character of the campaign was also becoming more determined; an adviser indicated that about two-thirds of the remainder of the advertisements would be negative.[22]

The Democrats: Playing from Strength

During September the president pursued his campaign, deftly playing both offense and defense. His national lead gave his organization the luxury of focusing substantial time and money on the South, normally the core of Republican strength. Early in the month, for example, Clinton spent two full days in Florida— a prize with twenty-five electoral votes that he lost narrowly in 1992. He particularly emphasized his conflicts with the GOP Congress over Medicare, an important issue in a state with a large percentage of retirees. And unlike four years earlier, when the Clinton campaign organization in Florida had a budget of $50,000 and no real office, by the time of his visit the Democratic National Committee had already spent $3.2 million on TV ads and the organization had opened fourteen regional offices.[23] By concentrating resources on southern states, the Democrats forced the GOP to allocate time and money there that they would rather channel elsewhere. It also complicated the GOP's message: to attract southern votes the Republicans often needed to emphasize issues and positions that might not be as appealing to voters in pivotal large northern states.[24]

Emphasizing his mixed strategy, Clinton claimed credit for having signed the compromise welfare-reform bill in August (an action not popular with many liberals) while strongly defending his Family Leave Act. On the latter issue, after Dole publicly emphasized his opposition to the law, the Clinton campaign quickly produced a television ad that featured a couple describing the time they had spent with their daughter before she died. A narrator indicated the president's support and Dole's opposition, and the ad closed with the mother saying: "President Clinton understands the struggles that families go through."[25] Perhaps the high point of the success of the mixed strategy was when, in mid-September, the Fraternal Order of Police (the nation's largest police organization) endorsed the president for reelection. In 1992 the group had endorsed President Bush.

Another aspect of the president's strategy was the continuous effort to link Dole to the unpopular Republican Speaker of the House, Newt Gingrich. Indeed, Democratic television ads almost invariably linked the two names together, to the point that many analysts observed that "Dole-Gingrich" became a single word. The president also persisted with a campaign theme that was, ironically, supplied by Dole in his nomination acceptance speech. That speech had included the line: "Age has its advantage. Let me be a bridge to an America that only the unknowing call myth." In his own acceptance speech, Clinton indicated that while Dole wanted to offer a bridge to the past, he wanted to be a bridge to the future, "to the 21st century, wide enough and strong enough to take us to America's best days."[26] The continuous use of this image was seen as a way to remind the electorate of Dole's age in contrast with Clinton's relative youth without seeming negative. Unfortunately for Dole, he often helped to reinforce the image, as when he referred to the "Brooklyn Dodgers" rather than the "Los Angeles Dodgers" on a campaign trip to California.

Perot: A Shadow of the Past

One of the most remarkable aspects of the 1992 presidential race was the showing by Ross Perot. He won nearly a fifth of the popular vote as an independent, although no electoral votes, spending $65 million of his own money in the process. In fact, he believed that he should have won, taking great stock in exit poll data that indicated that 40 percent of respondents said they would have voted for him if they believed he "had a chance to win" (31 percent said they would have voted for Clinton, and 27 percent for Bush.)[27] He blamed the media (for not taking him seriously) and the Republicans (for urging voters not to waste their votes in support of him) for his failure.

In the wake of that election, Perot's activities largely revolved around efforts to turn the movement he headed into an established third party. He asserted that the new Reform party was not his to control, and he actually urged David Boren, a former Democratic senator from Oklahoma, to seek the party's presidential nomination. Boren refused, but one fairly prominent politician did become actively interested—Richard Lamm, the former Democratic governor of Colorado. Lamm, like Perot, had long been concerned about the budget deficit and political reform issues, and he actively courted delegates to the Reform party's convention in August. Perot, however, still was the bankroller for the party and kept control of its apparatus. For example, Lamm complained that he was even unable to get a list of the party's members. In due course, Ross Perot became the first presidential nominee of the Reform party. Needing a running mate, he was unsuccessful in persuading professional politicians to join him on the ticket and eventually settled on Pat Choate, a Washington policy analyst.

Perhaps the biggest surprise of the Perot campaign occurred shortly after he won the nomination, when he announced that he would accept federal campaign funds. Based on his previous showing, this amounted to about $29 million, less than half of what he had spent of his own money in 1992. This decision produced some negative reactions among his followers and also considerably limited the resources available to his campaign because by accepting federal funding he had to accept federal campaign spending limits. Perot launched his 1996 campaign with a thirty-minute "infomercial," as he had in 1992, but this time only about one-third as many viewers tuned in.[28] Then, in the middle of September, he was struck another blow when the Commission on Presidential Debates ruled that he should be excluded from the presidential debates in 1996 on the grounds that he had no realistic chance of winning in November.[29] This calculation was based, in part, on Perot's single-digit showings in all major polls. He sought a court injunction to stop the debates, but without success. Clearly, Perot was not going to play as prominent a role in the 1996 election as he had in 1992.

THE DEBATES: A DEMOCRATIC "HAT TRICK"

The campaign organizations of the two major-party candidates agreed to three debates, two presidential and one vice-presidential, to be held sometime between

October 6 and October 16. Neither candidate's preparations for the first debate went very well. In Dole's case, he faced even more pointedly the strategic choices that had confronted him throughout the campaign: what issues to raise in order to change the voters' minds, and whether to go negative against the president. He practiced for two days, consistently exceeding time limits for questions and refusing to watch tapes of his performance. Clinton practiced with the former Senate majority leader George Mitchell of Maine, who played Dole's part. Mitchell took a hard-hitting approach, targeting the ethics issue. Clinton was unable to keep his cool, frequently getting angry, and admitting afterward that Mitchell "beat me like a drum."[30]

In the actual debate, however, Dole did not pursue Mitchell's aggressive course. His strategy was to try to allay his image of being dour and mean-spirited by frequently using humor to make his points, and most observers agreed that he was successful. That choice, however, made it difficult to attack Clinton effectively. He did urge the president to "stop scaring the seniors" on the Medicare issue, but he largely avoided direct criticisms of Clinton, saying, "I don't like to get into personal matters." Clinton, in turn, painted a picture of a nation at peace, with a strong economy. He also attacked Dole's 15 percent tax cut, calling it a "$550 billion tax scheme that will blow a hole in the deficit."[31] The "overnight" polls all showed essentially the same results: about half the respondents thought that Clinton had won the debate, compared with about 30 percent for Dole. More important for Dole, there was virtually no change in support for the candidates among those who watched.

Three nights later, the vice-presidential debate was held. It was, if anything, even less conflictual than the Dole-Clinton contest. Jack Kemp emphasized at the outset that he and Dole did not see the Democratic candidates "as our enemy. We see them as our opponents." Al Gore, in turn, indicated that he and his running mate had "enormous respect" for their GOP challengers. The vice president frequently challenged the budget implications of Dole's tax plan, and Kemp expressed negative views on the administration's foreign policy, but there was little in the way of fireworks. Postdebate surveys gave the victory to Gore, and some Republicans were very critical of Kemp for being unwilling to go on the attack.

The second presidential debate offered Dole what many thought was his last real chance to move the electorate. In the days leading up to that meeting, the question of how negative to get continued to face the GOP candidate. Campaigning after the first debate, Dole charged that Clinton's "word is no good," and his organization released a new commercial that charged that the country suffered from a "moral crisis" and that "the problem is in the White House." The next day he indicated that he might have some "surprises" for Clinton in the next debate.[32] Dole's advisers, however, remained divided on tactics for the debate. Several senior advisers argued that it would be politically ruinous for their candidate to come across as too negative. One said: "It's a very, very risky proposition. . . . There's a tremendous downside, tremendous backlash potential."[33]

Dole even asked a crowd at a New Jersey campaign stop, "Should I get tougher on Clinton?" (They approved.) But the day before the debate he sounded as if he had made up his mind, sharply attacking Clinton's competence and ethics, saying, "No administration has shown more arrogance, but few have displayed more ethical failures."[34]

Whatever Dole's plans were in advance, however, circumstances kept him from making a heavy negative assault. Unlike the first debate, which had the candidates remain behind podiums answering questions from a moderator, the second used the "town meeting" format at which Clinton excelled in 1992. The audience consisted of 113 uncommitted voters from the San Diego area, who asked questions when called on by the moderator. The candidates were permitted to come out from behind the podiums when answering, and Clinton frequently did so, seeking to dominate the space. Dole began aggressively, demanding that the president pledge that he would not pardon any of his former associates who were convicted as a result of the Whitewater investigation, but none of the questions that followed related to this topic, making it difficult for Dole to follow up, although he tried to go on the attack where feasible. Indeed, most of the questions were regarded as "softballs" by observers, and both candidates emphasized familiar themes.

This was not a recipe for changing a lot of minds in the electorate. Polls again showed that viewers regarded Clinton as the winner of the debate by about two to one and that few changed their minds about which candidate they preferred. It appeared, moreover, that even Dole's limited attacks had backfired. In CBS News/*New York Times* polls before and after the debates, respondents were asked whether each candidate was spending more time explaining what he would do as president or attacking his opponent. The proportion that thought that Dole was spending more time attacking increased thirteen points (from 50 to 63 percent), whereas the proportion that said that Clinton was doing more explaining rose five points (from 68 to 73 percent).[35] With less than three weeks to election day, GOP prospects were not encouraging.

FINAL EFFORTS

In the home stretch, the Clinton campaign generally persisted in its previous patterns. A substantial amount of the president's campaign time continued to be allocated to the South and other usually Republican territory. For example, the day after the second presidential debate, Clinton visited Orange County, California, a conservative stronghold. His campaign also released a new TV ad featuring James Brady, the former press secretary to President Ronald Reagan who had been seriously injured during the 1981 assassination attempt on the president. Brady contended that President Clinton "had the integrity to do what was right" by fighting for gun control.[36] Later in the month he even campaigned in Alabama, the first time he had set foot in the state during his presidency.

During the last few weeks, Clinton also campaigned in eastern states in an effort to influence the congressional races and enhance the probability of the Democrats' winning back House and Senate majorities. This was done carefully, because his campaign believed that direct partisan appeals would not work; there was some evidence that moderate voters were comfortable with divided party control. Instead the Democrats sought to encourage high levels of turnout, with the president telling people "It's your responsibility" to vote, and warning that "It's not over yet." He also devoted increasing amounts of time to raising campaign funds for Democratic congressional candidates.[37] In addition, Clinton sought to maximize the benefits of the gender gap by emphasizing issues that surveys indicated were important to women, like the Family and Medical Leave Act and funds for breast cancer research.

From the beginning of October, the Republican campaign was debating how to allocate its resources in the closing weeks—specifically, whether to make an all-out effort in California. The state had fifty-four electoral votes, one-fifth of the total needed to win the election. It had been regarded by analysts as a Clinton stronghold, with polls giving the president about a 20-point lead. Some advisers, however, thought it offered the campaign its best chance, and that the GOP effort could profit from the campaign in support of the anti-affirmative action initiative that was also on the California ballot. By the middle of the month, a consensus was reached that the California strategy was the way to go, partly because of the results from a recent Field poll (a respected independent survey of California) that showed Clinton's lead at 10 points. The Dole people would spend $4 million in California in the last two weeks, money drawn from allocations planned for Ohio, New Jersey, and other states in the East and Midwest.

More generally, Dole accelerated his attacks on Clinton. He particularly emphasized the questions that had recently been raised about possibly illegal donations to the Democratic party by foreign sources. "Come clean, Mr. President!" he demanded, and said: "Every day we have a new scandal involving the foreign corruption of America. This must stop and must stop today. Our elections are not for sale to some foreign influence or some foreign interest."[38] Dole, however, grew increasingly frustrated because his attacks did not seem to be having much effect on the voters' intentions. In a visit to Florida late in October, he said: "I wonder sometimes what people are thinking about—if people are thinking at all. . . . Wake up, America!" He also blamed the "liberal media" for not reporting the failings of the Clinton administration because they wanted him to be re-elected.[39]

This frustration also led to one of the more bizarre episodes of the campaign. Dole's campaign manager, Scott Reed, was dispatched late in October to visit Ross Perot and ask him to drop out of the race and endorse the Republican candidate. Much to Reed's chagrin, the supposedly secret meeting was leaked to the press even before he and Perot met in Dallas, and reactions almost universally were that the gambit indicated that the Dole campaign was in desperate shape. Perot, in contrast, enjoyed the new spotlight the incident cast on his own lagging campaign, characterizing the GOP proposal as "weird and totally incon-sequential." One of Perot's advisers said the Republicans were "so desperate they'll go to the one person they locked out of the debates."[40] In the closing days of the campaign, Perot vigorously attacked Clinton's character. At his final public speech, he compared President and Mrs. Clinton to Bonnie and Clyde and contended that a president "should live in the center of the field of ethical behavior and hold himself to a much higher standard than is it legal or illegal." He then went on to host a one-hour infomercial on all three networks on election night.[41]

President Clinton ended what he called "my last campaign" with a series of stops, some in states that were perceived to have the potential to go either way in the presidential race, and others in states that had close Senate races. On the Sunday before election day, he campaigned in Florida, urging Americans to re-ject the "politics of division and gridlock," and to say "no to racial and religious hatred." The next day, Clinton began early with a stop in New Hampshire, then visited four states in the Midwest, finally ending the campaign at home in Arkansas.[42]

Bob Dole offered the most dramatic end to the 1996 presidential race. He committed himself to a ninety-six-hour nonstop campaign swing before the November 5 voting. This tour crisscrossed the country, with many stops each day. On Sunday, November 3, for example, he visited seven cities, five of them in California. At one event, he urged his supporters, "Don't watch the scoreboard. . . . Don't pay any attention to the polls. You are the polls." On the final day, Dole campaigned mostly in the Southwest, speaking only briefly at each stop and some-times turning to his wife for help as his voice began to fail him. Speaking to reporters about the four-day nonstop effort, he said: "I couldn't think of any-thing else. . . . It's my last option." As a symbolic note, the Republicans scheduled the last stop for Independence, Missouri—Truman's home—early Tuesday morn-ing.[43] Dole ended the campaign as he began, tying his appeal to the memory of the Democratic president who had succeeded to the office at the death of Franklin D. Roosevelt, while Bill Clinton sought to become the first Democratic president since Roosevelt to be reelected.

DID THE CAMPAIGN MATTER?

It is appropriate to ask whether the general election campaign made any differ-ence, and the answer depends on the yardstick used to measure the campaign's effects. Did it determine the winner? Did it affect the choices of a substantial number of voters? Did it put issues and candidates' positions clearly before the voters? Were the issues that were addressed different from those that would have been considered otherwise? Did it produce events that will have a lasting impact on American politics? We cannot provide firm answers to all of these questions, but we can shed light on some of them.

In regard to events, there did not seem to be anything particularly novel about the campaign. Presidential debates were held again (albeit without Perot this time), and one used the town meeting format that voters seem to like and the media do not. These features may well persist. The potentially most important innovation of the campaign was the rise of the Reform party. Whether it survives to become a lasting third party is very much in doubt. Furthermore, it does not appear that the issues agenda of the campaign was markedly affected by it, unlike in 1992, when Perot succeeded in raising the matter of balancing the budget to prominence in the public's mind. That issue, and others from four years earlier, remained, but only the specifics of the complaints about Clinton's character appeared to be new.

Regarding the outcome, there is no evidence that the general election campaign made a difference. Clinton led in the polls all year and throughout the two-month campaign, and he won a comfortable victory (albeit a somewhat narrower one than had been expected), which largely mirrored his 1992 win. There is, however, reason to believe that the campaign did have some influence on voters' choices. Research on the 1996 campaign by Thomas M. Holbrook, building on his work on earlier campaigns, indicates that "some aspects of the campaign did influence levels of candidate support during the campaign period."[44] More specifically, certain events (like Dole's policy proposals and the revelations about foreign donations to the Democrats near the end of the campaign) did have some positive effect on Dole's and, to a lesser degree, Perot's support. They did not, however, have any systematic effect on Clinton's support, which was instead more strongly related to national conditions like presidential approval and economic evaluations. In particular, Holbrook's analysis indicated that the impact of campaign events was less in 1996 than in earlier elections.

Another perspective on this question is offered by data from the 1996 NES survey. Table 2-1 shows the percentage of respondents that reported voting for each of the top three candidates, controlling for their party identification and when they claimed to have made the vote choice.[45] Overall, about 28 percent of the sample indicated that they knew all along how they were going to vote (up about 10 points from 1992). Not surprisingly, it was in this group that Clinton's support was strongest. About 47 percent, however, said they decided after the conventions, and 29 percent claimed their decision was made during the last two weeks before the vote. In this last group, the president's support was lower than in other categories. One should also note that within each party identification category, defection from party identification tended to be more likely among respondents who decided late than those who decided earlier. Of particular interest is the pattern of the Perot vote. The totals show that his support was substantially higher among those who decided after the conventions than earlier. Very few of the respondents claimed to have known they would support Perot all along, or even before the fall, despite his earlier campaign and activities during the intervening years.

Thus there is evidence that the choices of some voters were affected by the campaign. In general, however, the summary judgment would have to be that

TABLE 2-1   Vote for President, by Time of Vote Decision and Party
Identification, 1996 (in percentages)

Party identification	Vote	When voter decided			
		Knew all along	Through conventions	After conventions through debates	Last two weeks or later
Strong Democrat	Clinton	96	100	96	88
	Dole	1	0	1	4
	Perot	3	0	3	8
	(N)	(100)	(63)	(33)	(48)
Weak Democrat	Clinton	92	98	82	65
	Dole	4	2	12	22
	Perot	5	0	6	13
	(N)	(59)	(41)	(37)	(59)
Independent, leans Democrat	Clinton	82	87	77	64
	Dole	2	8	12	7
	Perot	16	5	11	29
	(N)	(25)	(35)	(28)	(41)
Independent, no partisan leanings	Clinton	44	75	39	30
	Dole	31	25	44	43
	Perot	25	0	17	27
	(N)	(8)	(4)	(16)	(24)
Independent, leans Republican	Clinton	28	27	24	23
	Dole	61	70	68	62
	Perot	12	3	8	15
	(N)	(21)	(33)	(25)	(42)
Weak Republican	Clinton	10	16	22	24
	Dole	90	79	60	60
	Perot	0	5	18	16
	(N)	(39)	(46)	(26)	(68)
Strong Republican	Clinton	0	0	14	16
	Dole	100	100	86	75
	Perot	0	0	0	8
	(N)	(69)	(73)	(20)	(30)
Total	Clinton	58	52	56	47
	Dole	38	46	35	38
	Perot	4	2	9	16
	(N)	(321)	(295)	(185)	(314)

Note: Numbers in parentheses are the total cases on which percentages are based. The numbers are weighted.

the campaign mattered relatively little, and we probably should not have expected it to. As we discuss in detail in Chapter 7, elections involving incumbents tend to be referenda on presidential performance. During the second half of the twentieth century, when we have dependable measurements of the public's evaluation of the president's performance, there have been nine elections in which an incumbent president could face the electorate. (In two elections, 1960 and 1988, the incumbent was constitutionally ineligible to run again.) In five of those elections, including 1996, the president had approval ratings above 50 percent during the spring before the vote—that is, before the general election campaign, and even well before the selection of the opposing nominee by his party's convention. In all five instances, the incumbent won comfortably. In four cases, however, the incumbent's approval was below 50 percent. In all of those instances, he either withdrew from the race or lost.[46]

Furthermore, not only was Clinton evaluated on his and the economy's performance (and little on his personal character), but also Dole was so well known to the electorate because of his career that there was relatively less for them to learn about the challenger than usual. The public's evaluation of a president's performance is shaped by years of experience with his actions and their public consequences. It would be unlikely, indeed, that those evaluations could be significantly changed by nine weeks or so of rhetoric, which is, after all, what a campaign is.

Chapter 3

The Election Results

Despite his ninety-six-hour campaign marathon, Bob Dole did little to reduce Bill Clinton's margins in the preelection polls. Although most polls predicted a somewhat larger Clinton victory than actually materialized, there was little suspense while the results were reported on election night, November 5. Because the television networks were relying partly on exit polls to project state-by-state victories, and because all of the networks relied on polls conducted by the same polling organization (Voter News Service), the networks called a Clinton electoral college victory within a minute of the polls closing in nine states at 9:00 p.m. Eastern Standard Time. At the time Clinton's victory in the polls was projected, the polls were still open in Idaho, Iowa, Montana, Nevada, and Utah (where they were scheduled to close at 10:00 p.m. EST); California, Hawaii, Oregon, and Washington (where they closed at 11:00 p.m. EST); and Alaska (where they closed at midnight EST).

In the final tally, Clinton had carried thirty-one states and the District of Columbia, and Dole had carried nineteen. H. Ross Perot, running as the Reform party candidate, finished third in every state and in the District of Columbia. Clinton won 47.4 million votes, Dole won 39.2 million, and Perot tallied 8.1 million. In addition, Ralph Nader, the Green party candidate, who was on the ballot in twenty-one states, won nearly 700,000 votes, and Harry Browne, the Libertarian candidate, who was on the ballot in all fifty states, won nearly half a million. Clinton won 49.2 percent of the popular vote, failing to attain his goal of winning a popular vote majority. Dole won 40.7 percent of the popular vote, while Perot won 8.4 percent, with 1.7 percent going to other candidates. Clinton's 8.5 percent margin over Dole was somewhat larger than his 5.6 percent margin over George Bush in 1992. Clinton also won a slightly larger share of the major-party vote, gaining 54.7 percent in 1996 compared with 53.5 percent in 1992. In 1980 Ronald Reagan had won by 9.7 percentage points over Jimmy Carter, and in 1984 he had defeated Walter F. Mondale by a massive 18.2 points. In 1988 Bush had prevailed over Michael S. Dukakis by 7.7 points. Still, Clinton won both his victories by a far more comfortable margin than Jimmy Carter had in 1976, since Carter won by a mere 2.1 percentage points over Jerry Ford. Table 3-1 presents the official election results, by state, for the 1996 election.[1]

Clinton's electoral vote tally was also impressive. As Figure 3-1 reveals, Clinton won 379 electoral votes to 159 for Dole, and Perot won none. This is very close to the 1992 outcome, in which Clinton won 370 electoral votes to Bush's 168 (with Perot winning none). In fact, the state-by-state outcome is very similar. In 1996 Clinton won two states that Bush carried in 1992 (Arizona and Florida). He carried twenty-nine of the thirty-two states that he won in 1992 (all but Colorado, Georgia, and Montana) and the District of Columbia. Clinton's two victories fell short of the three previous Republican victories. In 1980 Reagan captured forty-four states and 489 electoral votes, and in 1984 he carried forty-nine states and 525 electoral votes. In 1988 Bush carried forty states and 426 electoral votes. But, once again, Clinton's margin of victory was far more comfortable than Carter's. Carter had carried only twenty-four states and the District of Columbia for a total of 297 electoral votes. Far more important, unlike Carter, Clinton was reelected, becoming the first Democratic president to win reelection since Franklin D. Roosevelt in 1944.

THE PEROT VOTE AND THE ELECTION RULES

Perot fared far worse in the popular vote than he had in 1992, when he won almost twenty million votes, nearly a fifth of the total vote cast. But even in 1992 he won no electoral votes. Although Clinton failed to gain a majority of the popular vote, it seems likely that he would have won in a direct popular vote contest. But he was clearly the beneficiary of the U.S. electoral system. As we saw in Chapter 2, U.S. voters do not vote directly for president or vice president. Rather, they vote for a slate of electors pledged to support presidential and vice-presidential candidates. Moreover, in every state except Maine and Nebraska, the slate that receives the most popular votes wins all of the state's electoral votes. In no state is a majority of the vote required. In fact, Clinton (or, to be precise, the slate of electors pledged to Clinton) won a majority of the vote in eighteen states (and the District of Columbia), yielding 230 electoral votes. Dole, in contrast, won a majority of the votes in only six states, yielding only 32 electoral votes.

The plurality-vote winner-take-all system has an important consequence. It tends to transform a nationwide plurality of the popular vote into an absolute majority of the electoral votes. And it takes an absolute majority of the electoral votes for the electoral college to produce a winner. If there is no majority winner in the electoral college, the U.S. House of Representatives, voting by state delegations, chooses among the three candidates with the largest number of electoral votes. But the House has not chosen a president since 1825, mainly because the plurality-vote system is very likely to produce a winner in the electoral college. The majority-vote winner is usually the presidential candidate with the most

TABLE 3-1   Official Presidential Election Results, by States, 1996

(Based on reports from the secretaries of state for the 50 states and the District of Columbia)

State	Total vote	Bill Clinton (Democrat) Votes	%	Bob Dole (Republican) Votes	%	Ross Perot (Reform Party) Votes	%	Other Votes	%	Plurality (D/R)	
Alabama	1,534,349	662,165	43.2	769,044	50.1	92,149	6.0	10,991	0.7	106,879	R
Alaska	241,620	80,380	33.3	122,746	50.8	26,333	10.9	12,161	5.0	42,366	R
Arizona	1,404,405	653,288	46.5	622,073	44.3	112,072	8.0	16,972	1.2	31,215	D
Arkansas	884,262	475,171	53.7	325,416	36.8	69,884	7.9	13,791	1.6	149,755	D
California	10,019,484	5,119,835	51.1	3,828,380	38.2	697,847	7.0	373,422	3.7	1,291,455	D
Colorado	1,510,704	671,152	44.4	691,848	45.8	99,629	6.6	48,075	3.2	20,696	R
Connecticut	1,392,614	735,740	52.8	483,109	34.7	139,523	10.0	34,242	2.5	252,631	D
Delaware	271,084	140,355	51.8	99,062	36.5	28,719	10.6	2,948	1.1	41,293	D
District of Columbia	185,726	158,220	85.2	17,339	9.3	3,611	1.9	6,556	3.5	140,881	D
Florida	5,303,794	2,546,870	48.0	2,244,536	42.3	483,870	9.1	28,518	0.5	302,334	D
Georgia	2,299,071	1,053,849	45.8	1,080,843	47.0	146,337	6.4	18,042	0.8	26,994	R
Hawaii	360,120	205,012	56.9	113,943	31.6	27,358	7.6	13,807	3.8	91,069	D
Idaho	491,719	165,443	33.6	256,595	52.2	62,518	12.7	7,163	1.5	91,152	R
Illinois	4,311,39_	2,341,744	54.3	1,587,021	36.8	346,408	8.0	36,218	0.0	754,723	D
Indiana	2,135,842	887,424	41.5	1,006,693	47.1	224,299	10.5	17,426	0.8	119,269	R
Iowa	1,234,075	620,258	50.3	492,644	39.9	105,159	8.5	16,014	1.3	127,614	D
Kansas	1,074,300	387,659	36.1	583,245	54.3	92,639	8.6	10,757	1.9	195,586	R
Kentucky	1,388,703	636,614	45.8	623,283	44.9	120,396	8.7	8,415	0.6	13,331	D
Louisiana	1,783,959	927,837	52.0	712,586	39.9	123,293	6.9	20,243	1.1	215,251	D
Maine	605,897	312,788	51.6	186,378	30.8	85,970	14.2	20,761	3.4	126,410	D
Maryland	1,780,870	966,207	54.3	681,530	38.3	115,812	6.5	17,321	1.9	284,677	D
Massachusetts	2,556,785	1,571,763	61.5	718,107	28.1	227,217	8.9	39,698	1.6	853,656	D
Michigan	3,848,844	1,989,653	51.7	1,481,212	38.5	336,670	8.7	41,309	1.1	508,441	D
Minnesota	2,192,640	1,120,438	51.1	766,476	35.0	257,704	11.8	48,022	2.2	353,962	D

State	Total Vote									Plurality	
Mississippi	893,857	394,022	44.1	439,838	49.2	52,222	5.8	7,775	0.9	45,816	R
Missouri	2,158,065	1,025,935	47.5	890,016	41.2	217,188	10.1	24,926	1.2	135,919	D
Montana	407,261	167,922	41.2	179,652	44.1	55,229	13.6	4,458	1.1	11,730	R
Nebraska	677,415	236,761	35.0	363,467	53.7	71,278	10.5	5,909	0.9	126,706	R
Nevada	464,279	203,974	43.9	199,244	42.9	43,986	9.5	17,075	3.7	4,730	D
New Hampshire	499,175	246,214	49.3	196,532	39.4	48,390	9.7	8,039	1.6	49,682	D
New Jersey	3,075,807	1,652,329	53.7	1,103,078	35.9	262,134	8.5	58,266	1.9	549,251	D
New Mexico	556,074	273,495	49.2	232,751	41.9	32,257	5.8	17,571	3.2	40,744	D
New York	6,316,129	3,756,177	59.5	1,933,492	30.6	503,458	8.0	123,002	1.9	1,822,685	D
North Carolina	2,515,807	1,107,849	44.0	1,225,938	48.7	168,059	6.7	13,961	0.6	118,089	R
North Dakota	266,411	106,905	40.1	125,050	46.9	32,515	12.2	1,941	0.7	18,145	R
Ohio	4,534,434	2,148,222	47.4	1,859,883	41.0	483,207	10.7	43,122	1.0	288,339	D
Oklahoma	1,206,713	488,105	40.4	582,315	48.3	130,788	10.8	5,505	0.5	94,210	R
Oregon	1,377,760	649,641	47.2	538,152	39.1	121,221	8.8	68,746	5.0	111,489	D
Pennsylvania	4,506,118	2,215,819	49.2	1,801,169	40.0	430,984	9.6	58,146	1.3	414,650	D
Rhode Island	390,284	233,050	59.7	104,683	26.8	43,723	11.2	8,828	2.3	128,367	D
South Carolina	1,151,689	506,283	44.0	573,458	49.8	64,386	5.6	7,562	0.7	67,175	R
South Dakota	323,826	139,333	43.0	150,543	46.5	31,250	9.7	2,700	0.8	11,210	R
Tennessee	1,894,105	909,146	48.0	863,530	45.6	105,918	5.6	15,511	0.8	45,616	D
Texas	5,611,644	2,459,683	43.8	2,736,167	48.8	378,537	6.7	37,257	0.7	276,484	R
Utah	665,629	221,633	33.3	361,911	54.4	66,461	10.0	15,624	2.3	140,278	R
Vermont	258,449	137,894	53.4	80,352	31.1	31,024	12.0	9,179	3.6	57,542	D
Virginia	2,416,642	1,091,060	45.1	1,138,350	47.1	159,861	6.6	27,371	1.1	47,290	R
Washington	2,253,837	1,123,323	49.8	840,712	37.3	201,003	8.9	88,799	3.9	282,611	D
West Virginia	636,459	327,812	51.5	233,946	36.8	71,639	11.3	3,062	0.5	93,866	D
Wisconsin	2,196,169	1,071,971	48.8	845,029	38.5	227,339	10.4	51,830	2.4	226,942	D
Wyoming	211,571	77,934	36.8	105,388	49.8	25,928	12.3	2,321	1.1	27,454	R
Total	96,277,872	47,402,357	49.2	39,198,755	40.7	8,085,402	8.4	1,591,358	1.7	8,203,602	D

Source: America Votes 22: A Handbook of Contemporary American Election Statistics, ed. Richard M. Scammon, Alice V. McGillivray, and Rhodes Cook (Washington, D.C.: Congressional Quarterly, 1998), 9.

FIGURE 3-1   Electoral Votes by States, 1996

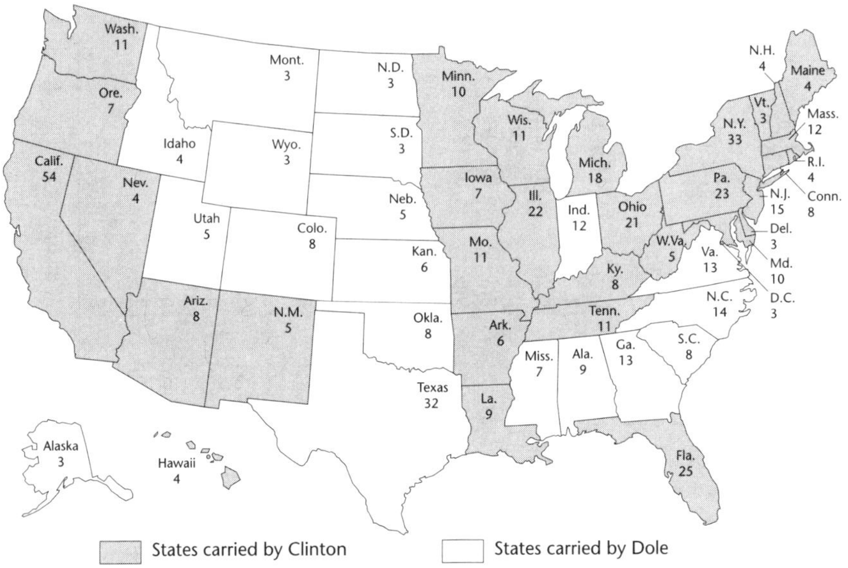

Note: Clinton won 379 electoral votes; Dole won 159 electoral votes.

Source: America Votes 22: A Handbook of Contemporary American Election Statistics, ed. Richard M. Scammon, Alice V. McGillivray, and Rhodes Cook (Washington, D.C.: Congressional Quarterly, 1998), 9.

popular votes. Indeed, in forty of the forty-two elections held from 1832 through 1996, the candidate with the most popular votes has received an absolute majority of the electoral votes (the two exceptions were in 1876 and 1888).[2] During this period there have been fourteen elections in which a candidate won a plurality (but not a majority) of the popular vote and won a majority of the electoral vote.[3]

The system takes a heavy toll on third-party or independent candidates. A successful third-party or independent candidate usually receives a far smaller share of the electoral vote than of the popular vote.[4] We can review the fate of the four most successful independent or third-party candidacies (in popular votes) since World War II: those of George C. Wallace (who won 13.5 percent of the popular vote in 1968); John B. Anderson (who won 6.6 percent in 1980); and Perot in 1992 and 1996. In 1980 and 1992 Anderson and Perot, respectively, had some modest regional bases of support. Both fared better in New England than elsewhere, and both fared worst in the South.[5] In addition, in 1992 Perot did well in the mountain states, and he even finished second in two states—Maine, where he came in ahead of Bush, and Utah, where he came in ahead of Clinton.[6] In 1996 Perot fared somewhat better in New England, but regional differences were very small. In the fifty states, Perot's overall level of support ranged from a low of 5.6 percent in Tennessee to a high of 14.2 percent in Maine. Wallace, in contrast, clearly had a regional basis of support. Even though he won a smaller share of the popular vote than Perot won in 1992, he came in first in five states (winning a majority of the popular vote in Alabama and Mississippi) and gained forty-six electoral votes (including one faithless elector from North Carolina). But even Wallace won only 8.5 percent of the electoral vote, less than his popular vote share.[7]

The U.S. plurality-vote system can be seen as a confirmation of Duverger's law, a proposition advanced by Maurice Duverger in the early 1950s. According to Duverger, "the simple-majority single-ballot system favors the two-party system." In other words, a plurality-vote win system in which there are no runoff elections tends to favor the dominance of two political parties. Indeed, Duverger argued, "the American procedure corresponds to the usual machinery of the simple-majority single-ballot system. The absence of a second ballot and of further polls, particularly in the presidential elections, constitutes in fact one of the historical reasons for the emergence and the maintenance of the two-party system."[8]

According to Duverger, the principle applies for two reasons. First, the plurality-vote system has a "mechanical" effect. Third-place parties may earn a large number of votes but fail to gain a plurality of the vote in many electoral units. Second, the plurality-vote system has a "psychological" effect. Some voters who prefer a party or candidate whom they think cannot win will cast a vote for their first choice among the major-party candidates. This behavior is often called sophisticated or strategic voting. William H. Riker defines strategic voting as "voting contrary to one's immediate tastes in order to obtain an advantage in the long run."[9] As we shall see in Chapter 6, it seems highly likely that at least some voters who preferred Perot decided instead to vote for Clinton or Dole.

Of course, we cannot know what the results would have been if an alternative system had been used, because some voters might have voted differently if the election rules had been different. But as Gerald M. Pomper pointed out after the 1992 election, the electoral college does have one virtue: it produces a clear winner who is recognized as the legitimately elected president despite his minority count in the popular vote. "The existing system, while hard to justify in democratic philosophy, [gives] the nation a clear, immediate, and legitimate verdict."[10] If the president were elected by a direct popular vote, a runoff election might be necessary. For example, in the French Fifth Republic, the president is directly elected by the popular vote, and an absolute majority is required to win. All six presidential elections held under these rules (1965, 1969, 1974, 1981, 1988, and 1995) have required a runoff.[11] Moreover, in 1996 (as well as in 1968, 1980, and 1992) the U.S. system probably produced a Condorcet winner, that is, a candidate who would have won in a head-to-head contest against any opponent. As we shall show in Chapter 6, it seems highly likely that Clinton would have won in a two-person contest against either Dole or Perot.[12]

THE PATTERN OF RESULTS

Two basic facts emerge from the 1996 presidential election results. First, despite his minority-vote status, Clinton's victory substantially reduces the Republican pattern of dominance in postwar presidential elections. With Clinton's victory, the Republicans have won only a bare majority (seven) of the thirteen elections held since World War II. Moreover, the Democrats and the Republicans have now split the last six presidential elections, although the Republican victories were won by substantially larger margins. In fact, the Republicans have won a majority of the popular vote six times since World War II (1952, 1956, 1972, 1980, 1984, and 1988), whereas the Democrats have won a popular-vote majority only twice (1964 and 1976). Moreover, the average (mean) level of Republican presidential support has been 49.1 percent, whereas the average Democratic vote has been 45.9 percent.

This slight Republican advantage goes hand in hand with a pattern of considerable electoral volatility during the postwar years. Between 1952 and 1984, neither party was able to win three elections in a row, although Bush's 1988 victory broke this pattern. The high level of change since World War II sets the postwar era in sharp contrast with most of American electoral history. Table 3-2 shows the presidential election results since 1832, the first election in which parties used national nomination conventions to select their candidates. From 1832 though 1948 we find four periods in which a single party won a series of three or more elections. The Republicans won six elections in a row from 1860 through 1880, although in 1876 Rutherford B. Hayes beat Samuel J. Tilden by a single electoral vote, and Tilden won a majority of the popular vote. The Republicans also won four elections from 1896 through 1908, as well as three between 1920 and 1928. The Democrats won five straight elections between 1932 and 1948.

After 1948 a period of volatility began. But although no party was able to manage three straight wins, until 1980 the winning party was able to pull off a second presidential victory. The Republicans won in 1952 and 1956, the Democrats in 1960 and 1964, and the Republicans in 1968 and 1972. In all three cases the second win was bigger than the first, and in both 1964 and 1972 the second win was by a substantially greater margin. The Democrats won the White House in 1976, but they failed to hold it in 1980. The 1980 and 1984 Republican victories followed the earlier pattern, a win followed by a bigger win. Moreover, Reagan was elected by a substantially greater margin than he won by in 1980. But in 1988, with Bush's election, this pattern of volatility was broken. With Clinton's victory in 1992, volatility returned. Clinton won in 1996 by only a slightly larger margin than in 1992.

The 1976 and 1980 elections are the only successive elections in the twentieth century in which incumbent presidents lost. There were similar periods in the nineteenth century, however. Four elections were lost by the incumbent party from 1840 through 1852, a period of alternation between the Democrats and the Whigs, and again from 1884 and 1896, a period of alternation between the Republicans and the Democrats. Both of these periods preceded major realign-

TABLE 3-2   Presidental Election Results, 1832–1996

Election	Winning candidate	Party of winning candidate	Success of incumbent political party
1832	Andrew Jackson	Democrat	Won
1836	Martin Van Buren	Democrat	Won
1840	William H. Harrison	Whig	Lost
1844	James K. Polk	Democrat	Lost
1848	Zachary Taylor	Whig	Lost
1852	Franklin Pierce	Democrat	Lost
1856	James Buchanan	Democrat	Won
1860	Abraham Lincoln	Republican	Lost
1864	Abraham Lincoln	Republican	Won
1868	Ulysses S. Grant	Republican	Won
1872	Ulysses S. Grant	Republican	Won
1876	Rutherford B. Hayes	Republican	Won
1880	James A. Garfield	Republican	Won
1884	Grover Cleveland	Democrat	Lost
1888	Benjamin Harrison	Republican	Lost
1892	Grover Cleveland	Democrat	Lost
1896	William McKinley	Republican	Lost
1900	William McKinley	Republican	Won
1904	Theodore Roosevelt	Republican	Won
1908	William H. Taft	Republican	Won
1912	Woodrow Wilson	Democrat	Lost
1916	Woodrow Wilson	Democrat	Won
1920	Warren G. Harding	Republican	Lost
1924	Calvin Coolidge	Republican	Won
1928	Herbert C. Hoover	Republican	Won
1932	Franklin D. Roosevelt	Democrat	Lost
1936	Franklin D. Roosevelt	Democrat	Won
1940	Franklin D. Roosevelt	Democrat	Won
1944	Franklin D. Roosevelt	Democrat	Won
1948	Harry S. Truman	Democrat	Won
1952	Dwight D. Eisenhower	Republican	Lost
1956	Dwight D. Eisenhower	Republican	Won
1960	John F. Kennedy	Democrat	Lost
1964	Lyndon B. Johnson	Democrat	Won
1968	Richard M. Nixon	Republican	Lost
1972	Richard M. Nixon	Republican	Won
1976	Jimmy Carter	Democrat	Lost
1980	Ronald Reagan	Republican	Lost
1984	Ronald Reagan	Republican	Won
1988	George Bush	Republican	Won
1992	Bill Clinton	Democrat	Lost
1996	Bill Clinton	Democrat	Won

Sources: *Presidential Elections 1789–1992* (Washington, D.C.: Congressional Quarterly, 1995), 34–74; *America Votes 22: A Handbook of Contemporary American Election Statistics,* ed. Richard M. Scammon, Alice V. McGillivray, and Rhodes Cook (Washington, D.C.: Congressional Quarterly, 1998), 9.

ments of the parties. After the Whig party's loss in 1852, the Republican party replaced it. Although many Whigs, including Lincoln, became Republicans, the Republican party was not just the Whig party renamed. The Republicans had transformed the American political agenda by capitalizing on opposition to slavery in the territories.[13] Their political base was different from that of the Whigs, because the Republicans had no southern support. But they created a base in the Midwest, something the Whigs never established.

The 1896 contest, the last in a series of four incumbent losses, is usually viewed as a critical election because it solidified Republican dominance. Although the Republicans had won all but two of the elections after the Civil War, many of their victories were by narrow margins. In 1896 the Republicans emerged as the clearly dominant party, gaining a solid hold in Connecticut, New Jersey, New York, and Indiana, states they had frequently lost between 1876 and 1892. After William McKinley's defeat of William Jennings Bryan in 1896, the Republicans established a firmer base in the Midwest, New England, and the mid-Atlantic states. They lost the presidency only in 1912, when the GOP was split, and in 1916, when Woodrow Wilson ran for reelection.

The Great Depression ended Republican dominance. The emergence of the Democrats as the majority party was not preceded by a series of incumbent losses. The Democratic coalition, forged in the mid-1930s, relied heavily on the emerging working class and at least partly on the mobilization of new groups into the electorate.

As the emergence of the New Deal coalition demonstrates, a period of electoral volatility is not a necessary condition for a partisan realignment. Nor, perhaps, is volatility a sufficient condition. In 1985 Reagan himself proclaimed that a Republican realignment had occurred. Political scientists were skeptical about this claim, mainly because the Democrats continued to dominate in the U.S. House of Representatives. With Bush's victory in 1988, however, some argued that a "split-level" realignment had occurred.[14] But although Bush's election suggested that a period of Republican dominance had arrived, Clinton's 1992 victory called such a thesis into question, and his 1996 reelection casts further doubt on the idea that a realignment had occurred. Still, the capture of the House of Representatives by the Republicans in 1994, along with their continued control in 1996, calls into question any notion that Democratic dominance has been reestablished.

STATE-BY-STATE RESULTS

Politicians, journalists, and political scientists are fascinated by how presidential candidates fare in each state because states deliver the electoral votes necessary to win the presidency. The presidential contest can be viewed as fifty-one separate elections, one for each state and the District of Columbia.

As we saw in Chapter 2, the candidate with the most votes in each state, with the exception of Maine and Nebraska, wins all of the state's electoral votes. Regardless of how a state decides to allocate its electors, the number of electors for each state is the sum of its senators (two) plus the number of representatives in the House. In 1996 the number of electors ranged from a low of three in Alaska, Delaware, Montana, North Dakota, South Dakota, Vermont, Wyoming, and the District of Columbia to a high of fifty-four in California. There are 538 electors and an absolute majority is required for a candidate to be elected by the electoral college. In 1996, the ten largest states, which have between fourteen and fifty-four electors, had 54 percent of the total population, but they chose only 48 percent of the electors. The twenty-two smallest states and the District of Columbia, each of which has between three and seven electors, are overrepresented in the electoral college. They make up 13 percent of the population, but they choose 19 percent of the electors.

In the actual election contest, however, candidates focus on the larger states, unless polls indicate that they are unwinnable. Despite being underrepresented on a per capita basis, California still provides one-fifth of the electors necessary to win the presidency. Even so, in 1992 Bush quit campaigning in California in early September because the polls showed that Clinton had a commanding lead. In contrast, even though most polls showed that Clinton had a commanding lead in 1996, Dole focused on California during the final weeks of his campaign, although this strategy may have been chosen mainly to help the Republicans retain control of the U.S. House of Representatives.

States are the building blocks of winning presidential coalitions, but state-by-state results can be overemphasized and can even be misleading. First, as we saw, in forty of the forty-two elections between 1832 and 1996, the candidate with the largest popular vote has also gained a majority of the electoral vote. Thus, candidates can win by gaining a broad base of support throughout the nation, even though they must also consider the likelihood of winning specific states. Moreover, given the nature of national television coverage, candidates must run national campaigns. They can make special appeals to states and regions, but these appeals may be broadcast through the national media.

Second, comparing state-by-state results can be misleading because these comparisons may conceal change. To illustrate this point we can compare the results of the two closest postwar elections—John F. Kennedy's victory over Richard M. Nixon in 1960 and Carter's over Ford in 1976. There are many parallels between these two Democratic victories. In 1960 and 1976 the Republicans did very well in the West, and both Kennedy and Carter needed southern support to win.[15] Kennedy carried six of the eleven states of the old Confederacy (Arkansas, Georgia, Louisiana, North Carolina, South Carolina, and Texas) and gained 5 of Alabama's 11 electoral votes, for a total of 81 electoral votes. Carter carried ten of these states (all but Virginia) for a total of 118 electoral votes.

The demographic basis of Carter's support was quite different from Kennedy's, however. In 1960 only 29 percent of the African-American adults in the South were registered to vote, compared with 61 percent of the white adults. According to our analysis of survey data from the National Election Studies (NES), only one voter out of fifteen who supported Kennedy in the South was an African-American. After the Voting Rights Act of 1965, however, black registration increased. In 1976, 63 percent of the African-Americans in the South were registered to vote, compared with 68 percent of the whites.[16] We estimate that about one out of three southerners who voted for Carter was black. A comparison of state-by-state results conceals this massive change in the social composition of the Democratic presidential coalition.

Third, state-by-state comparisons do not tell us why a presidential candidate received support. Of course, such comparisons can lead to interesting speculation, especially when dominant political issues are related to regional differences. But it is also necessary to turn to surveys, as we do in Part 2, to understand the dynamics of electoral change.

With these qualifications in mind, we can turn to the state-by-state results. In our earlier books we presented maps displaying Reagan's margin of victory over Carter in 1980, Reagan's margin over Mondale in 1984, Bush's margin over Dukakis in 1988, and Clinton's margin over Bush in 1992.[17] In Figure 3-2 we present a map that shows Clinton's state-by-state margin over Dole. These maps clearly reveal differences among these three Republican victories, and also show patterns of continuity that are found in the two Democratic victories.

In 1980 Reagan did far better in the West than in other regions. We consider eighteen states as western from the standpoint of presidential elections, and Reagan won thirteen of them by a margin of 20 percentage points or more. Outside the West, he won only a single state (New Hampshire) by a 20-point margin. Although he carried ten southern states, he carried many of them by relatively narrow margins.

In 1984 the West no longer appeared distinctive. Reagan won by a larger overall margin than in 1980, and he had an impressive margin in many more states. Although Reagan still had a massive margin in the West, he now carried seventeen states outside the West by a margin of 20 points or more. His biggest gains were in the South. In 1980 he carried none of the eleven southern states by a 20-point margin. In 1984 he carried ten of them by a margin of at least 20 points, and he carried Tennessee by 16 points. Although southern blacks voted overwhelmingly for Mondale, his losses in the South were still massive. Whereas in 1980 Carter had won more than one-third of the southern white vote, only about one white southerner in four supported Mondale.

The 1988 results show a clear improvement for the Democrats. Dukakis won two New England states (including his home state of Massachusetts), gaining nearly half (49.9 percent) of the vote in this region. He carried three midwestern states (Iowa, Minnesota, and Wisconsin). Dukakis fared slightly worse than Carter in the border states, where he won only West Virginia. Like Mondale, Dukakis lost all eleven southern states.

Bush's overall margin of victory was much smaller than Reagan's margin over Mondale in 1984, and it was somewhat smaller than Reagan's margin over Carter.

FIGURE 3-2   Clinton's Margin of Victory over Dole, 1996

More than 20%   Between 10% and 15%   Less than 5%

Between 15% and 20%   Between 5% and 10%   Dole win

Source: America Votes 22: A Handbook of Contemporary American Election Statistics, ed. Richard M. Scammon, Alice V. McGillivray, and Rhodes Cook (Washington, D.C.: Congressional Quarterly, 1998), 9.

Moreover, Bush's regional strength differed from Reagan's. Bush's best region was the South, and he was far less dominant in the West than Reagan. Bush won five southern states by a margin of 20 points and three others by 15 to 20 points. He won the three remaining states by a margin of 10 to 15 points. Bush thus won every southern state by more than his national margin (7.7 points) and carried the South as a whole by 17.5 points over Dukakis.

In the eighteen states we view as western, Bush actually lost three states and won by less than 10 percentage points in five others, including California, which he carried by less than 5 points. If we restrict our attention to the eight mountain states, we find that Bush carried five by a margin greater than 20 points, but he carried the remaining three by less than 10 points. The combined result for these states shows Bush with a 16.8 margin over Dukakis, slightly smaller than his margin in the South. Bush's overall margin in all eighteen western states was only 7.5 points, slightly less than his national margin.

In 1992, as in 1988, the South was the best region for the Republicans. Clinton lost seven of the eleven southern states, and he won three others by less than 5 points, winning by a wider margin only in his native Arkansas. For all eleven states, Bush won 42.6 percent of the popular vote, compared with 41.2 percent for Clinton, and the South was the only region where Bush won a majority of the electoral votes, carrying 108 of the South's 147 electors. Among the eighteen states we classify as western, Clinton and Bush each won nine. Clinton even won four of the eight mountain states, although three of his wins were by less than 5 percentage points. But the mountain states were Perot's best region, and he won 25.2 percent of the vote there. Bush won 38.1 percent of the vote in these states, with Clinton winning 36.3 percent. But by winning by nearly 1.5 million votes over Bush in California, Clinton fared better in the eighteen western states than Bush. He carried 41.2 percent of all the western votes, compared with 35.6 percent for Bush. His margin over Bush in the West was the same as his national margin.

In 1996 Dole slipped slightly in the South compared with Bush, but he still won seven southern states, carrying 96 of its 147 electoral votes. But Clinton actually won slightly more popular votes in the region than Dole, carrying 46.2 percent of the vote to Dole's 46.1 percent. Dole did better than Clinton in the mountain states. Although Perot won 12 percent or more of the vote in Idaho, Montana, and Wyoming, his overall share of the vote in the mountain states fell to 8.7 percent, and Dole appears to have been the beneficiary. Dole carried five of these eight states, winning 23 of their 40 electoral votes. He also won a plurality of the popular vote, winning 46.4 percent to Clinton's 42.6 percent. But Clinton won California by 1.3 million votes. In the eighteen western states, Clinton won 46.7 percent of the popular vote and Dole carried 42.1 percent.

As Figure 3-2 reveals, Clinton's greatest margin of victory was in New England and the mid-Atlantic states. He carried every midwestern state except Indiana, and he carried Illinois and Minnesota by more than 15 percentage points. He won California and Washington by more than 10 percentage points and carried traditionally Democratic Hawaii by more than 20 points. Clinton won by a narrow margin in Arizona, but that ended an eleven-election winning streak for the Republicans. Arizona was the only state to have voted consistently for the same party since Eisenhower's 1952 victory.

These regional differences led some scholars to speculate that a "new sectionalism" was developing. As Bill Schneider notes, Clinton did well in three areas of the country: the Northeast (in which Schneider includes Maine, Vermont, New Hampshire, Massachusetts, Rhode Island, Connecticut, New York, New Jersey, Pennsylvania, Delaware, Maryland, and West Virginia); the Midwest (Ohio, Michigan, Illinois, Wisconsin, Minnesota, and Iowa); and the West (Washington, Oregon, California, and Hawaii). According to Schneider, "Those are the states where Yankee liberalism and progressivism have deep historic roots. Let's call that section of the country the Progressive Belt."[18]

In our view it seems too early to proclaim a new sectionalism, especially when twelve of these twenty-two states voted for Bush in 1988. Instead, we would reach two basic conclusions from these state-by-state results. First, it seems clear that the South has been transformed into a Republican region. Second, with only a slight increase in regional distinctiveness in 1996, these results point to a marked decline in regional differences that has characterized postwar American politics.

As we can see, the Republicans do not have complete dominance in the South, but in both of the last elections they won a majority of southern electoral votes, and in both of these elections over half of their electoral votes came from the South. Despite fielding a ticket with two southerners, the Democrats would have won both the 1992 and 1996 elections without carrying a single southern state. Lyndon B. Johnson was the only other Democratic winner since World War II who would have won without southern electoral votes, but Johnson, unlike Clinton, won an electoral vote landslide. Harry S. Truman in 1948, Kennedy in 1960, and Carter in 1976 all needed southern electoral votes to win.

Indeed, it is instructive to compare Clinton's victories in 1992 and 1996 with Jimmy Carter's victory in 1976. Although Carter actually won many southern states by narrow margins, his electoral vote victory depended very heavily on southern electoral votes. Of the 297 electoral votes he won, 118 came from southern states. Of the 370 electoral votes that Clinton won in 1992, only 39 came from the South; of the 379 votes he won in 1996, only 51 did.

Clearly, the South has been transformed from the most Democratic region of the country to one of the most Republican. As we shall see in Chapter 9, a similar if less dramatic shift has occurred in congressional elections. In congressional elections, regional differences between the parties, pronounced in the 1950s, were negligible by the 1990s. Perhaps the most striking feature of the last four presidential elections has been the absence of regional differences, which can be shown through statistical analysis.

Joseph A. Schlesinger has analyzed state-by-state variation in presidential elections from 1832 through 1988, and we have updated his analysis through 1996. His measure is the standard deviation in the states in the percentage voting Democratic. State-by-state variation in 1996 was 6.70 points. This is somewhat larger than state-by-state variation in 1984 (5.84 points), 1988 (5.60 points), or 1992 (5.96 points), but somewhat below state-by-state variation in 1980 (7.95 points). But what is most striking in Schlesinger's analysis is the relatively low level of state-by-state variation in all thirteen postwar elections. According to his analysis, all fifteen of the presidential elections from 1888 through 1944 displayed more state-by-state variation than any of the thirteen postwar elections. To a large extent, the decline in state-by-state variation results from the transformation of the South.[19]

ELECTORAL CHANGE IN THE POSTWAR SOUTH

The transformation of the South was a complex process, but the major reason for the change was simple. As V. O. Key, Jr., brilliantly demonstrated in *Southern Politics in State and Nation* (1949), the major factor in southern politics is race: "In its grand outlines the politics of the South revolves around the position of the Negro. . . . Whatever phase of the southern political process one seeks to understand the trail of inquiry leads back to the Negro."[20] And it is the changed position of the national Democratic party toward African-Americans that has smashed Democratic dominance in the South.[21]

Between the end of Reconstruction and the end of World War II, the South was a Democratic stronghold. In fifteen of the seventeen elections from 1880 through 1944, all eleven southern states voted Democratic. In his 1920 victory over James M. Cox, the Republican Warren G. Harding narrowly carried Tennessee, but the ten remaining southern states voted Democratic. The only major southern defections occurred in 1928, when the Democrats ran Alfred E. Smith, a Roman Catholic. The Republican candidate, Herbert C. Hoover, won five southern states. Even so, six of the most solid southern states—Alabama, Arkansas, Georgia, Louisiana, Mississippi, and South Carolina—voted for Smith, even though all but Louisiana were overwhelmingly Protestant.[22] After southern blacks lost the right to vote in the South, the Republicans ceded these states to the Democrats. Although the Republicans, as the party of Lincoln, had black support in the North, they did not attempt to enforce the Fifteenth Amendment, which bans restrictions on voting on grounds of "race, color, or previous condition of servitude."

In 1932 a majority of African-Americans remained loyal to Hoover, although by 1936 Franklin D. Roosevelt won the support of northern blacks. Roosevelt made no effort to win the support of southern blacks, most of whom were effectively disfranchised. Even as late as 1940 about 70 percent of the nation's blacks lived in the states of the old Confederacy. Roosevelt carried all eleven of these states in each of his four elections. His 1944 victory, however, was the last contest in which the Democratic candidate carried all eleven southern states.

World War II led to a massive migration of African-Americans from the South, and by 1948 Truman, through his support for the Fair Employment Practices Commission, made explicit appeals to blacks. In July 1948 Truman issued an executive order ending segregation in the armed services.[23] These policies led to defections by the "Dixiecrats" and cost Truman four southern states (Alabama, Louisiana, Mississippi, and South Carolina). But Truman still won all seven of the remaining southern states. Adlai E. Stevenson de-emphasized appeals to blacks, although Dwight D. Eisenhower made inroads.

In 1952 Eisenhower captured Florida, Tennessee, Texas, and Virginia, and in 1956 he won Louisiana as well. In 1960 Kennedy also played down appeals to African-Americans, and southern support was vital to his win over Nixon. By choosing a Texan, Lyndon B. Johnson, as his running mate, Kennedy may have helped himself in the South. Clearly, Johnson's presence on the ticket helped Kennedy win in Texas, which he carried by only 2 percentage points over Nixon.[24]

But if Johnson as running mate aided the Democrats in the South, Johnson as president played a different role. His support for the Civil Rights Act of 1964, as well as his explicit appeal to African-Americans, helped end Democratic dominance in the South. Goldwater, the Republican candidate, had voted against the Civil Rights Act, creating a sharp difference between the presidential candidates.

By 1968 Humphrey, who had long been a champion of black causes, carried only one southern state, Texas, which he won with only 41 percent of the vote. (He was probably aided by Wallace's candidacy, since Wallace gained 19 percent of the Texas vote.) Wallace's third-party candidacy carried Alabama, Arkansas, Georgia, Louisiana, and Mississippi, while Nixon carried the remaining five southern states. Nixon carried every southern state in 1972, and his margin of victory was somewhat greater in the South than outside the South. Although Carter won ten of the eleven southern states (all but Virginia), he carried a minority of the vote among white southerners.

In 1980 Reagan carried every southern state except Georgia, Carter's home state. In his 1984 reelection he carried every southern state, and his margin of victory was greater in the South than outside the South. In 1988 Bush carried all eleven southern states, and the South was his strongest region. As we saw, Clinton made some inroads in the South in 1992 and somewhat greater inroads in 1996. All the same, the South was the only predominantly Republican region in the 1992 election, and in 1996 Dole won a majority of the electoral votes only in the South and the mountain states. The transformation of the South is clearly the most dramatic regional change in postwar American politics.

THE ELECTORAL VOTE BALANCE

The Republicans dominated presidential elections from 1972 through 1988. After his relatively narrow win over Hubert H. Humphrey in 1968, Nixon swept forty-nine states in his defeat of George S. McGovern four years later. Although Carter won a narrow victory in 1976, the Republicans swept most states during the Reagan and Bush elections, winning forty-nine states in Reagan's 1984 triumph over Mondale.

As a result of these victories the Republicans repeatedly carried many states over the course of these five elections.[25] Some scholars went so far as to argue that the Republicans held an electoral vote lock. According to Marjorie Randon Hershey, the Republicans won so many states during recent elections that they had a "clear and continuing advantage in recent presidential elections."[26] This advantage, Hershey argued, came mainly from Republican strength in a large number of small states, which, as we have seen, are overrepresented in the electoral college. But Michael Nelson argued that the Republicans did not have an electoral college advantage, and James C. Garand and T. Wayne Parent maintained that the electoral college was biased toward the Democrats.[27]

We can test for the presence of a possible pro-Republican bias in the electoral college in 1996 by asking what the results would have been if Dole and Clinton had received the same percentage of the popular vote. As Clinton won by 8.5 percentage points, we will add 4.25 percentage points to Dole's vote in every state and subtract 4.25 percent from Clinton's. This hypothetical shift moves Arizona, Florida, Kentucky, Missouri, Nevada, New Mexico, Ohio, Oregon, and

FIGURE 3-3   Results of the 1988, 1992, and 1996 Elections

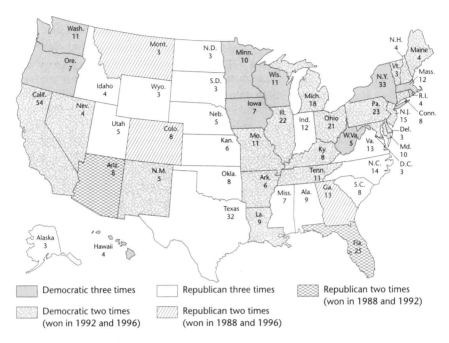

Source: Presidential Elections 1789–1992 (Washington, D.C.: Congressional Quarterly, 1995), 73–74; *America Votes 22: A Handbook of Contemporary American Election Statistics,* ed. Richard M. Scammon, Alice V. McGillivray, and Rhodes Cook (Washington, D.C.: Congressional Quarterly, 1998), 9.

Tennessee from the Clinton column to the Dole column. This would boost Dole to 259 votes and Clinton would retain his electoral vote majority. In 1992, however, there may have been a slight bias in favor of the Republicans.[28]

If partisan biases exist in the electoral college they are very small. Of course, even a small bias can lead to the electoral college's electing a plurality-vote loser, just as it did in 1876 and 1888.[29] The probability that a "wrong winner" will be elected is smaller than it was before World War II, since in the earlier elections the Democrats often won southern states by large popular-vote majorities

Today's elections are more national in scope, and the electoral college provides no significant barrier to either party. Indeed, the last three elections show a fairly even balance. Figure 3-3 illustrates the combined results of the 1988, 1992, and 1996 elections. We show the states that the Democrats won in all three elections and the states that the Democrats won in two of the last three contests. The latter are all states that the Democrats lost in 1988 but won in 1992 and 1996, because in both of his victories, Clinton won every state that Dukakis carried. We show the five states that the Republicans have won in two of the last three elections. Here two patterns are possible. The Republicans won two of these states in 1988 and 1992 and three of them in 1988 and 1996. We also show those states that the Republicans won in all three elections.

The ten states, and the District of Columbia, that the Democrats have won in all three of the last elections yield 107 electoral votes. The nineteen states that the Democrats lost in 1988 but carried in 1992 and 1996 bring 239 electoral votes. The two states the Republicans won in 1988 and 1992 are worth 33 electoral votes, and the three states they won in 1988 and 1996 are worth 24 votes. The Republicans won sixteen states in all three elections, and they yield 135 electoral votes.

This mixture shows problems and opportunities for both parties. The Republicans have strong prospects in the South, but they may have overinvested in that region. For example, the conservative appeals that helped Bush and Dole in the South may have cost them votes in California. The Democrats have demonstrated that they can win the presidency without the South, but many of their victories in the Midwest have been in states that Clinton won by relatively narrow margins. The potential for the Republicans gaining a "lock" on the presidency has disappeared, but the Democrats have no solid hold on an electoral college majority.

To assess the future prospects for the major political parties, as well as the prospects for new political parties, we must go beyond analyzing official election statistics. To determine the way social coalitions have been transformed, and the issue preferences of the electorate, we must use surveys to study the attitudes and behavior of individuals. Likewise, we must analyze surveys to study the extent to which the 1996 election resulted from a response to improved economic conditions and the extent to which it was an endorsement of Clinton's policies. And we must study surveys to examine the way in which the basic party loyalties of the American electorate have changed during the postwar years. Part 2 of our study uses survey data to examine prospects for change and continuity in American electoral politics.

PART 2

Voting Behavior in the 1996 Presidential Election

The collective decision reached on November 5, 1996, was the product of 189 million individual decisions. Two choices faced American citizens eighteen years of age and older: whether to vote and, if they decided to vote, how to cast their ballots. How voters make up their minds is one of the most thoroughly studied subjects in political science—and one of the most controversial.[1]

Voting decisions can be studied from at least three theoretical perspectives.[2] First, voters may be viewed primarily as members of social groups. Voters belong to primary groups of family members and peers; secondary groups, such as private clubs, trade unions, and voluntary associations; and broader reference groups, such as social classes and ethnic groups. Understanding the political behavior of these groups is the key to understanding voters, according to the pioneers of this approach, Paul F.. Lazarsfeld, Bernard R. Berelson, and their colleagues. Using their simple "index of political predisposition," they classified voters according to their religion (Catholic or Protestant), socioeconomic level, and residence (rural or urban) to predict how they would vote in the 1940 presidential election. Lazarsfeld and his colleagues maintained that "a person thinks, politically, as he is, socially. Social characteristics determine political preference."[3] This perspective is still popular, although more so among sociologists than political scientists. The writings of Robert R. Alford, Richard F. Hamilton, and Seymour Martin Lipset provide excellent examples of this sociological approach.[4]

A second approach emphasizes psychological variables. To explain voting choices in the 1952 and 1956 presidential elections, Angus Campbell, Philip E. Converse, Warren E. Miller, and Donald E. Stokes, scholars at the University of Michigan's Survey Research Center (SRC), developed a model of political behavior based on social-psychological variables, and their model was presented in their classic book, *The American Voter*.[5] They focused on attitudes likely to have the greatest effect just before the moment of decision, particularly attitudes toward the candidates, parties, and issues. Party identification emerged as the major social-psychological variable that influences voting decisions. The Michigan approach is the most prevalent among political scientists, although many de-emphasize its psychological underpinnings. The work of Philip E. Converse provides outstanding examples of this research tradition.[6] The recent book by Warren E. Miller and J. Merrill Shanks, *The New American Voter*, provides an excellent example of this approach and is especially useful for understanding the long-term forces that have transformed the American electorate.[7]

A third approach draws heavily on the work of economists. According to this perspective, citizens weigh the cost of voting against the expected benefits of voting when deciding whether to go to the polls. And when deciding whom to choose on election day, voters calculate which candidate favors policies closest to their policy preferences. Citizens are thus viewed as rational actors who attempt to maximize their expected utility. Anthony Downs and William H. Riker helped to found the rational choice approach.[8] The writings of Riker, Peter C. Ordeshook, John A. Ferejohn, and Morris P. Fiorina provide excellent examples of this point of view.[9]

How, then, do voters decide? In our view none of these perspectives provides a complete answer. Although individuals belong to groups, they are not always influenced by their group memberships. Moreover, classifying voters by social groups does not explain why they are influenced by social forces. Placing too much emphasis on psychological factors, however, can lead us away from the political forces that shape voting behavior. The assumptions of economic rationality may lead to clearly testable propositions; still, the data used to test them are often weak, and the propositions that can be tested are often of limited importance.[10]

Although taken separately none of these approaches adequately explains voting behavior, taken together they are largely complementary. Therefore, we have chosen an eclectic approach that draws on insights from each viewpoint. Where appropriate, we employ sociological variables, but we also use social-psychological variables, such as party identification and feelings of political efficacy. The rational choice approach guides our study of the way issues influence voting behavior.

Part 2 begins with an examination of the most important decision of all: whether to vote. One of the most profound changes in postwar American politics has been the decline of electoral participation. Although turnout grew fairly consistently between 1920 and 1960, it fell in 1964 and in each of the next four elections. Turnout rose slightly in 1984, but in 1988 it dropped to a postwar low. Turnout rose some 5 percentage points in 1992, but in 1996 it fell 6 percentage points, yielding the lowest turnout since 1924. In the 1960 contest between John F. Kennedy and Richard M. Nixon, 63 percent of the adult population voted; in 1996, only 49 percent voted. Turnout is somewhat higher in the United States than in Switzerland, but it is about 20 points lower than turnout in Canada. And turnout is much higher in all the remaining industrialized democracies. But although turnout was very low in 1996, it was not equally low among all social groups, and we examine group differences in detail. Drawing mainly on a social-psychological perspective, Chapter 4 studies changes in attitudes that have contributed to the decline in electoral participation. We attempt to explain why turnout was especially low in 1996 and try to determine whether low turnout affected electoral outcomes. Finally, we attempt to determine whether low turnout threatens democracy itself.

In Chapter 5 we examine how social forces influence the vote. The National Election Studies (NES) surveys enable us to analyze the vote for Clinton, Dole, and Perot by race, gender, region, age, occupation, union membership, and religion. The impact of these social forces has changed considerably during the past half-century. Support for the Democratic party among the traditional members of the New Deal coalition of white southerners, union members, the working class, and Catholics has eroded. Despite two Clinton victories, it seems unlikely that the old New Deal coalition can be restored.

Chapter 6 examines attitudes toward both the candidates and the issues. Because Clinton won in a three-person contest, it is possible that the outcome would have been different if Perot had not been a candidate. However, as we shall show, it seems quite likely that Clinton would have won in a head-to-head contest against *either* Dole or Perot. Turning to issues, we begin by examining the concerns of the electorate and by doing so demonstrate how decreased concern with economic issues increased Clinton's chances. We attempt to assess the extent to which voters based their votes on issue preferences. We pay special attention to the abortion controversy, not because it was the major issue for most voters, but because the NES survey data on this issue reveal that voters do not decide on the basis of issues unless they know where the candidates stand on those issues. And we pay special attention to the issue preferences of Perot voters.

We then turn to how presidential performance influences voting decisions. Recent research suggests that many voters decide how to vote on the basis of "retrospective" evaluations of the incumbents. In other words, what incumbents have done in office—not what candidates promise to do if elected—affects how voters decide. In Chapter 7 we assess the role of retrospective evaluations in the last seven presidential elections. Voters' evaluations of Gerald R. Ford's performance in 1976 played a major role in the election of Jimmy Carter, whereas four years later the voters' evaluations of Carter played a major role in the election of Ronald Reagan. To a very large extent, Bush's defeat in 1992 resulted from negative evaluations of his performance as president. As we shall see, to a very large extent Clinton's reelection in 1996 resulted from positive evaluations of his performance. Last, we pay special attention to the retrospective evaluations of Perot voters.

How closely do voters identify with a political party? And how does this identification shape issue preferences and the evaluations of the incumbent and the incumbent party? Chapter 8 explores the impact of party loyalties on voting choices during the postwar era. Beginning in 1984 there was a shift in party loyalties toward the Republican party, but that shift ended and was possibly reversed in 1992. We shall find that although the balance between the parties did not change between 1992 and 1996, there was a small increase in the party loyalties of the electorate. In 1996 party loyalties appear to have played a major role in shaping issue preferences, retrospective evaluations, and voting choices. Still, one out of ten voters voted for neither of the major parties, most of them voting for Perot. We pay special attention to the party identification of Perot voters, for the eight million Perot voters could still play a crucial role in future elections, especially given the very close partisan balance between the two major parties.

Chapter 4

Who Voted?

Before discovering how people voted in the 1996 presidential election, we must answer an even more basic question: Who voted? Only 49 percent of the adult population voted for president, a 6 percent decline from the 1992 election and the lowest turnout since 1924. Turnout is lower in the United States than in any other industrialized democracy except Switzerland.[1] Even though Bill Clinton won by 8 million votes over Bob Dole, the 85 million Americans who did not vote could easily have elected Dole, or they could have chosen H. Ross Perot. In principle, nonvoters could have elected any alternative candidate, since many more Americans chose not to vote than voted for Clinton. Yet, it is unlikely that increased turnout would have affected the outcome of the presidential election, although it might have affected the congressional elections. Before we study turnout in the 1996 elections, however, we must place the election in a broader historical context.[2]

Historical records can be used to determine how many people voted in presidential elections, and we can derive meaningful estimates of turnout for elections as early as 1828. Turnout is calculated by dividing the total number of votes cast for president by the voting-age population.[3] But should the turnout denominator (that is, the voting-age population) include all persons old enough to vote, or should it include only those eligible to vote? The answer to this question greatly affects our estimate of turnout in all presidential elections through 1916, because few women were legally eligible to vote until 1920.

Although women gained the right to vote in the Wyoming Territory as early as 1869, even by 1916 only eleven of the forty-eight states had fully enfranchised women, and these were mainly western states with small populations.[4] The Nineteenth Amendment, which granted women voting rights in all states, was ratified only a few months before the 1920 election. Because women were already voting in some states, it is difficult to estimate turnout before 1920. Clearly, women should be included in the turnout denominator in those states where they had the right to vote. Including them in those states where they could not vote leads to very low estimates of turnout.

Table 4-1 presents two sets of turnout estimates between 1828 and 1916. The first column, compiled by Charles E. Johnson, Jr., calculates turnout by dividing the number of votes cast for president by the voting-age population. The second, based on Walter Dean Burnham's calculations, measures turnout by dividing the total presidential vote by the total number of Americans eligible to vote. Burnham excludes southern blacks before the Civil War, and from 1870 on he excludes aliens where they could not vote. But the major difference between Burnham's calculations and Johnson's is that Burnham excludes women from his turnout denominator in those states where they could not vote.

Most political scientists would consider Burnham's calculations to be more meaningful than Johnson's. For example, most political scientists argue that turnout was higher in the nineteenth century than it is today. But even if we reject this interpretation, both sets of estimates reveal the same pattern of change. There is clearly a large jump in turnout after 1836, for both the Democrats and the Whigs began to employ popular appeals to mobilize the electorate. Turnout jumped markedly in the 1840 election, the "Log Cabin and Hard Cider" campaign in which the Whig candidate, William Henry Harrison, the hero of Tippecanoe, defeated the incumbent Democrat, Martin Van Buren. Turnout waned after 1840, but it rose rapidly after the Republican party, founded in 1854, polarized the nation by taking a clear stand against the extension of slavery into the territories. In Abraham Lincoln's election in 1860, four out of five white men went to the polls.

Turnout waxed and waned after the Civil War, peaking in the 1876 contest between Rutherford B. Hayes, the Republican winner, and Samuel J. Tilden, the Democratic candidate. As the price of Hayes's contested victory, the Republicans agreed to end Reconstruction in the South. Having lost the protection of federal troops, many African-Americans were prevented from voting. Although some southern blacks could still vote in 1880, overall turnout among blacks dropped sharply, which in turn reduced southern turnout. Turnout began to fall nationwide by 1892, but it rose in the 1896 contest between William Jennings Bryan (Democrat and Populist) and William McKinley, the Republican winner. Turnout dropped in the 1900 rerun between the same two men.

By the late nineteenth century, African-Americans were denied the franchise throughout the South, and poor whites often found it difficult to vote as well.[5] Throughout the country registration requirements, which were in part designed to reduce fraud, were introduced. Because individuals were responsible for getting their names on the registration rolls before the election, the procedure created an obstacle that reduced electoral participation.[6]

Introducing the secret ballot also reduced turnout. Before this innovation,

TABLE 4-1   Turnout in Presidential Elections, 1828–1916

Election year	Winning candidate	Party of winning candidate	Percentage of voting-age population who voted	Percentage eligible to vote who voted
1828	Andrew Jackson	Democrat	22.2	57.3
1832	Andrew Jackson	Democrat	20.6	56.7
1836	Martin Van Buren	Democrat	22.4	56.5
1840	William H. Harrison	Whig	31.9	80.3
1844	James K. Polk	Democrat	30.6	79.0
1848	Zachary Taylor	Whig	28.6	72.8
1852	Franklin Pierce	Democrat	27.3	69.5
1856	James Buchanan	Democrat	30.6	79.4
1860	Abraham Lincoln	Republican	31.5	81.8
1864[a]	Abraham Lincoln	Republican	24.4	76.3
1868	Ulysses S. Grant	Republican	31.7	80.9
1872	Ulysses S. Grant	Republican	32.0	72.1
1876	Rutherford B. Hayes	Republican	37.1	82.6
1880	James A. Garfield	Republican	36.2	80.6
1884	Grover Cleveland	Democrat	35.6	78.3
1888	Benjamin Harrison	Republican	36.3	80.5
1892	Grover Cleveland	Democrat	34.9	78.3
1896	William McKinley	Republican	36.8	79.7
1900	William McKinley	Republican	34.0	73.7
1904	Theodore Roosevelt	Republican	29.7	65.5
1908	William H. Taft	Republican	29.8	65.7
1912	Woodrow Wilson	Democrat	27.9	59.0
1916	Woodrow Wilson	Democrat	32.1	61.8

[a]The estimate for the voting-age population is based on the entire U.S. adult population. The estimate for the eligible population excludes the eleven Confederate states that did not take part in the election.

Sources: The estimates of turnout among the voting-age population are based on Charles E. Johnson, Jr., *Nonvoting Americans,* ser. P-23, no. 102 (U.S. Department of Commerce, Bureau of the Census, Washington, D.C.: U.S. Government Printing Office, 1980), 2. The estimates of turnout among the population eligible to vote are based on calculations by Walter Dean Burnham. Burnham's earlier estimates were published in U.S. Department of Commerce, Bureau of the Census, *Historical Statistics of the United States: Colonial Times to 1970,* ser. Y-27-28 (Washington, D.C.: U.S. Government Printing Office, 1975), 1071–1072. The results in the table, however, are based on Burnham, "The Turnout Problem," in *Elections American Style,* ed. A. James Reichley (Washington, D.C.: Brookings Institution, 1987), 113–114.

most voting in U.S. elections was public. Ballots were printed by the political parties; each party produced its own. Ballots differed in size and color, and any observer could see how each person voted. In 1856 Australia adopted a law calling for a secret ballot to be printed and administered by the government. The

"Australian ballot" was first used statewide in Massachusetts in 1888. By the 1896 election, nine out of ten states had followed Massachusetts's lead.[7] Although the secret ballot was introduced to reduce coercion and fraud, it also reduced turnout. When voting was public, men could sell their votes, but candidates were less willing to pay for a vote if they could not see it delivered. Ballot stuffing was also more difficult when the state printed and distributed the ballots.

As Table 4-1 shows, turnout trailed off rapidly in the early twentieth century. By the time of the three-way contest among Woodrow Wilson (Democrat), William Howard Taft (Republican), and Theodore Roosevelt (Progressive) in 1912, fewer than three out of five eligible Americans went to the polls. In 1916 turnout rose slightly, but just over three-fifths of the eligible Americans voted, and only one-third of the total adult population went to the polls.

TURNOUT FROM 1920 THROUGH 1996

It is easier to calculate turnout after 1920, and we have provided estimates based on U.S. Bureau of the Census statistics. Although there are alternative ways to measure the turnout denominator, they lead to relatively small differences in the overall estimate of turnout.[8]

In Table 4-2 we show the percentage of the voting-age population that voted for the Democratic, Republican, and minor-party and independent candidates in the twenty elections held from 1920 through 1996. The table also shows the percentage that did not vote, as well as the overall size of the voting-age population. In Figure 4-1, we show the percentage of the voting-age population that voted in each of these twenty elections.

As Table 4-2 reveals, Clinton received the vote of only about 24 percent of the voting-age population in both 1992 and 1996. Seventeen of the eighteen previous winners from 1920 through 1988 exceeded this total. Calvin Coolidge, the sole exception, won with a similar share in 1924. In fact, *losing* presidential candidates in eight elections (Wendell Willkie in 1940, Thomas E. Dewey in 1944, Adlai E. Stevenson in 1952 and 1956, Richard M. Nixon in 1960, Barry M. Goldwater in 1964, Hubert H. Humphrey in 1968, and Gerald Ford in 1976) equaled or exceeded Clinton's share.

Clinton's low share of the vote in 1996 results from two factors. First, he received only 49 percent of the total vote. Second, turnout was very low in 1996. But Dole did decidedly worse than Clinton. He received the votes of only 20 percent of the voting-age population. The only major-party candidates to win a smaller share were James M. Cox in 1920 and John W. Davis in 1924. Dole gained a slightly smaller share than Herbert C. Hoover in 1932, Alfred M. Landon in 1936, George S. McGovern in 1972, and George Bush in 1992.

As Figure 4-1 makes clear, turnout increased in seven of the ten elections from 1920 through 1960. Two of the exceptions—1944 and 1948—result from the social dislocations during and shortly after World War II. Specific political events

TABLE 4-2   Percentage of Adults Who Voted for Each Major Presidential Candidate, 1920–1996

Election year	Democratic candidate		Republican candidate		Other candidates	Did not vote	Total	Voting-age population
1920	14.8	James M. Cox	26.2	*Warren G. Harding*	2.4	56.6	100	61,639,000
1924	12.7	John W. Davis	23.7	*Calvin Coolidge*	7.5	56.1	100	66,229,000
1928	21.1	Alfred E. Smith	30.1	*Herbert C. Hoover*	.6	48.2	100	71,100,000
1932	30.1	*Franklin D. Roosevelt*	20.8	Herbert C. Hoover	1.5	47.5	100	75,768,000
1936	34.6	*Franklin D. Roosevelt*	20.8	Alfred M. Landon	1.5	43.1	100	80,174,000
1940	32.2	*Franklin D. Roosevelt*	26.4	Wendell Willkie	.3	41.1	100	84,728,000
1944	29.9	*Franklin D. Roosevelt*	25.7	Thomas E. Dewey	.4	44.0	100	85,654,000
1948	25.3	*Harry S. Truman*	23.0	Thomas E. Dewey	2.7	48.9	100	95,573,000
1952	27.3	Adlai E. Stevenson	34.0	*Dwight D. Eisenhower*	.3	38.4	100	99,929,000
1956	24.9	Adlai E. Stevenson	34.1	*Dwight D. Eisenhower*	.4	40.7	100	104,515,000
1960	31.2	*John F. Kennedy*	31.1	Richard M. Nixon	.5	37.2	100	109,672,000
1964	37.8	*Lyndon B. Johnson*	23.8	Barry M. Goldwater	.3	38.1	100	114,090,000
1968	26.0	Hubert H. Humphrey	26.4	*Richard M. Nixon*	8.4	39.1	100	120,285,000
1972	20.7	George S. McGovern	33.5	*Richard M. Nixon*	1.0	44.8	100	140,777,000
1976	26.8	*Jimmy Carter*	25.7	Gerald R. Ford	1.0	46.5	100	152,308,000
1980	21.6	Jimmy Carter	26.8	*Ronald Reagan*	4.3	47.2	100	163,945,000
1984	21.6	Walter F. Mondale	31.3	*Ronald Reagan*	.4	46.7	100	173,995,000
1988	23.0	Michael S. Dukakis	26.9	*George Bush*	.5	49.7	100	181,956,000
1992	23.7	*Bill Clinton*	20.6	George Bush	10.8	44.9	100	189,524,000
1996	24.1	*Bill Clinton*	19.9	Bob Dole	4.9	51.0	100	196,509,000

Note: The names of winning candidates are italicized.

Sources: Results for 1920 through 1932 are based on U.S. Department of Commerce, Bureau of the Census, *Statistical Abstract of the United States, 1972* (Washington, D.C.: U.S. Government Printing Office, 1972) 358, 373; results for 1936 through 1992 are based on *Statistical Abstract of the United States, 1996* (Washington, D.C.: U.S. Government Printing Office, 1996), 269, 287. For 1996 the voting-age population is based on U.S. Department of Commerce, Bureau of the Census, *Projection of the Voting-Age Population for States for the November 1996 Election, October 4, 1996* (available on the U.S. Census Bureau Web site [http://www.census.gov/population/www/socdemo/voting/tabcon.html]). For 1996 the number of votes cast for each candidate and the total number of votes cast for president are based on *America Votes 22: A Handbook of Contemporary American Election Statistics,* ed. Richard M. Scammon, Alice V. McGillivray, and Rhodes Cook (Washington, D.C.: Congressional Quarterly, 1998), 9.

FIGURE 4-1   Percentage of Voting-Age Population That Voted for President, 1920–1996

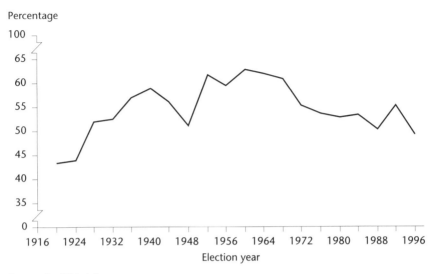

Sources: See Table 4-2.

explain why more people voted in certain elections. The jump in turnout from 1924 to 1928 resulted from the candidacy of Alfred E. Smith, the first Roman Catholic to receive a major-party nomination, and the increase from 1932 to 1936 resulted from Franklin D. Roosevelt's efforts to mobilize the lower social strata, particularly the industrialized working class. The extremely close contest between Nixon and the second Catholic candidate, John F. Kennedy, partly accounts for the high turnout in 1960. Turnout rose to 62.8 percent of the voting-age population and to 65.4 percent of the politically eligible population.[9] This was far below the percentage of the eligible Americans that voted between 1840 and 1900, although it was the highest percentage of the voting-age population that had ever voted in a presidential election (see Table 4-1). Nonetheless, U.S. turnout in 1960 was still far below the average level of turnout attained in most Western democracies.

Although short-term changes were driving turnout upward in specific elections, long-term changes were also driving turnout upward. The changing social characteristics of the electorate contributed to increasing turnout. For example, women who came of age to vote before the Nineteenth Amendment often failed to exercise their right to vote, but women who came of age after 1920 had higher turnout and gradually replaced the older women.[10] Because all states restricted voting to citizens, many immigrants failed to enter the electorate. But after 1921, as a result of restrictive immigration laws, the percentage of the population that was foreign born declined. Moreover, levels of education have been rising throughout the twentieth century, a change that boosts turnout. Americans who have attained higher levels of education are much more likely to vote than those who have lower educational levels.

As Figure 4-1 shows, the trend toward increasing turnout was reversed after 1960. By 1960, generational replacement among the female electorate had largely run its course. In the 1960s and 1970s, immigration laws were reformed, again increasing the noncitizen population. Educational levels, however, continued to rise, a change that might have been expected to increase turnout. After the passage of the Voting Rights Act of 1965, turnout rose dramatically among African-Americans in the South, and their return to the voting booth spurred voting among southern whites. Less restrictive registration laws during the last three decades made it easier to vote. The National Voter Registration Act, better known as the "motor-voter" law, which went into effect in January 1995, may have added nine million additional registrants to the voter rolls.[11]

Despite these changes, overall turnout declined after 1960. Except for a small increase in participation from 1980 to 1984, turnout declined continuously from 1960 through 1988, and in 1988 only 50.3 percent of the voting-age population voted. Turnout rose 5 percentage points in 1992, which may have partly resulted from Perot's candidacy.[12] In 1996 relatively few attempts were made to mobilize voters until late in the campaign. In the last ten days of the campaign, both the Democrats and the Republicans worried about the effect of low turnout. Given Clinton's large and consistent lead in the preelection polls, the Democrats worried about complacency. The Republicans feared that their supporters might be too discouraged to vote. In addition to efforts by the political parties, the American Federation of Labor and Congress of Industrial Organizations (AFL-CIO) distributed literature to union members urging them to vote, and the Christian Coalition distributed 45 million voter guides in some 120,000 churches.[13] These efforts were aimed mainly at attempting to win control of the U.S. House of Representatives, because few partisans thought that turnout would affect the presidential election results. Despite these last-minute efforts, as well as the increased registration resulting from the motor-voter law, turnout fell 6 percentage points. We examine both the long-term and short-term forces that contributed to the decline in turnout later in this chapter.

TURNOUT AMONG SOCIAL GROUPS

Although turnout was low in 1996, it was not equally low among all social groups. To compare turnout among social groups, we rely on the National Election Studies (NES) survey conducted by the Survey Research Center and the Center for Political Studies of the University of Michigan, although we supplement these results with the Current Population Survey conducted by the U.S. Bureau of the Census.[14] The 1996 NES survey is based exclusively on whether or not respondents said that they voted, and reported turnout is substantially higher than actual turnout. In 1996 actual turnout among the politically eligible population was about 51 percent. But among 1,521 respondents who were interviewed after the 1996 presidential election, 76.3 percent said that they voted.[15] All previous NES surveys also overestimate turnout, although the discrepancy between reported turnout and actual turnout is greater in 1996 than in any previous NES study.

There are three basic reasons that the NES studies exaggerate turnout. First, even though they are asked a question that supplies reasons for not voting, some nonvoters falsely claim that they voted.[16] Vote validation studies, in which the NES has directly checked voting and registration records, suggest that about 15 percent of the respondents who claim to have voted have not actually voted, whereas only a handful of actual voters say that they did not vote.[17] Second, the NES surveys do not perfectly represent the voting-age population. Lower socioeconomic groups, which have very low turnout, are underrepresented. Third, during presidential years the same respondents are interviewed before and after the election. Being interviewed before an election provides a stimulus to vote and thus increases turnout among the NES sample.[18]

Race, Gender, and Age

Table 4-3 compares reported turnout among basic social groups using the NES surveys. Our analysis begins by comparing whites and African-Americans. As the table shows, whites were 8 percentage points more likely to report voting than blacks. According to the Current Population Survey, 56.0 percent of the whites said that they voted, whereas 50.6 percent of the blacks reported voting.[19] As we mentioned in note 17, all eight vote validation studies show that blacks are more likely than whites to claim falsely to have voted, so it seems likely that these differences are greater than these surveys suggest.[20] Of course, racial differences in turnout are far smaller than they were before the Voting Rights Act of 1965. The first Current Population Survey of U.S. voter turnout, conducted in 1964, found that whites were 12.5 percentage points more likely to vote than nonwhites. Racial differences in turnout may have been lowest in 1984, when Jesse Jackson's first presidential candidacy mobilized blacks to vote.[21] Given the relatively small number of blacks sampled in the NES survey, we cannot make many comparisons among blacks. Southern blacks were less likely to vote than blacks outside the South.[22] Young blacks were very unlikely to report voting, as were blacks who had not graduated from high school. However, the NES survey showed that black women and black men were equally likely to vote. In fact, most surveys show that black women are more likely to vote than black men.

As Table 4-3 shows, among whites, those who identified as Hispanic were less likely to vote than non-Hispanics, mainly because turnout was very low among Mexican-Americans.[23] The NES survey includes only citizens, and, as Census Bureau surveys of turnout show, differences in turnout between Hispanics and non-Hispanics are substantially greater when comparisons are made among the

TABLE 4-3   Percentage of Electorate Who Reported Voting for President, by Social Group, 1996

Social group	Voted	Did not vote	Total	(N)[a]
Total electorate	76	24	100	(1,521)
Electorate, by race				
African-American	69	31	100	(161)
White	77	23	100	(1,308)
Whites, by Hispanic identification				
Identify as Hispanic	67	33	100	(107)
Do not identify as Hispanic	78	22	100	(1,197)
Whites, by gender				
Females	76	24	100	(673)
Males	79	21	100	(635)
Whites, by region				
New England and Mid-Atlantic	82	18	100	(252)
North Central	76	24	100	(344)
South	74	26	100	(348)
Border	74	26	100	(70)
Mountain and Pacific	80	20	100	(293)
Whites, by birth cohort				
Before 1924	85	15	100	(125)
1924–1939	84	16	100	(240)
1940–1954	82	18	100	(340)
1955–1962	77	23	100	(282)
1963–1970	70	30	100	(219)
1971–1978	52	48	100	(100)
Whites, by social class				
Working class	70	30	100	(463)
Middle class	83	17	100	(675)
Farmers	84	16	100	(32)
Whites, by occupation of head of household				
Unskilled manual	64	36	100	(109)
Skilled, semiskilled manual	72	28	100	(354)
Clerical, sales, other white collar	75	25	100	(175)

(Table continues)

TABLE 4-3 (continued)

Social group	Voted	Did not vote	Total	(N)[a]
Whites, by occupation of head of household (continued)				
Managerial	81	19	100	(268)
Professional and semiprofessional	92	8	100	(232)
Whites, by level of education				
Eight grades or less	55	45	100	(42)
Some high school	54	46	100	(100)
High school graduate	70	30	100	(391)
Some college	81	19	100	(356)
College graduate	89	11	100	(268)
Advanced degree	89	11	100	(149)
Whites, by annual family income				
Less than $10,000	58	42	100	(97)
$10,000 to $14,999	57	43	100	(81)
$15,000 to $19,999	69	31	100	(84)
$20,000 to $24,999	68	32	100	(85)
$25,000 to $29,999	76	24	100	(98)
$30,000 to $34,999	73	27	100	(103)
$35,000 to $39,999	73	27	100	(84)
$40,000 to $49,999	81	19	100	(140)
$50,000 to $59,999	90	10	100	(124)
$60,000 to $74,999	88	12	100	(144)
$75,000 to $89,999	89	11	100	(74)
$90,000 and over	89	11	100	(126)
Whites, by union membership[b]				
Member	83	17	100	(242)
Nonmember	76	24	100	(1,061)
Whites, by religion				
Jewish	97	3	100	(29)
Catholic	80	20	100	(390)
Protestant	79	21	100	(693)
None, no preference	68	37	100	(172)
White Protestants, by whether born again				
Not born again	78	22	100	(342)
Born again	80	20	100	(344)

Social group	Voted	Did not vote	Total	(N)[a]
White Protestants, by religious commitment				
Medium or low	77	23	100	(307)
High	81	19	100	(217)
Very high	90	10	100	(105)
White Protestants, by religious tradition				
Mainline	84	16	100	(294)
Evangelical	74	26	100	(296)
Whites, by social class and religion				
Working-class Catholics	75	25	100	(128)
Middle-class Catholics	84	16	100	(220)
Working-class Protestants	72	28	100	(257)
Middle-class Protestants	86	14	100	(331)

[a]The numbers are weighted.
[b]Whether respondent or family member in union.

total adult population. According to the 1996 Current Population Survey, only 26.7 percent of all Hispanics voted.

Table 4-3 shows that white men were slightly more likely to vote than white women, although among the total adult population gender differences are even smaller. Surveys consistently show that men outvoted women in all presidential elections through 1976. The 1980 presidential election seems to mark a historic change, for the participation advantage of men was eliminated. In recent Census Bureau surveys women have been slightly more likely to vote than men. In 1996, according to the Current Population Survey, 55.5 percent of the women voted, while 52.8 percent of the men did.

Of course, we do not need surveys to study turnout in the various regions of the country. Because the Census Bureau estimates the total voting-age population for each state, we can measure turnout merely by dividing the total number of votes cast for president within each state by its voting-age population. In 1996 turnout varied greatly from state to state, from a low of 39.3 percent in Nevada to a high of 64.5 percent in Maine. Official statistics show that turnout was lowest in the South, where only 45.6 percent of the voting-age population voted; outside the South, 50.4 percent voted.

Official election statistics do not present results according to race, so we need surveys to study relative turnout among whites and blacks within each region.

As Table 4-3 shows, white turnout in the South was lower than it was outside the South. Seventy-four percent of the whites in the South said they voted; outside the South, 79 percent voted. The relatively low level of turnout in the South results partly from low educational levels within that region.[24] But regional differences have declined dramatically during the past three decades. According to the 1964 Census Bureau survey, southern whites were 15 percentage points less likely to vote than whites outside the South, and nonwhite southerners were 28 points less likely to vote than nonwhites outside the South.

As did previous surveys, the 1996 NES survey finds that turnout is very low among young Americans. Among whites born after 1970 (those too young to have voted in 1988), only 52 percent claim to have voted. Unlike previous surveys, the 1996 NES survey shows no decline in voting among older Americans. In fact, there is little evidence that older Americans disengage from politics. Even in previous surveys, which found somewhat lower levels of turnout among older Americans, the lower turnout among the elderly resulted from their relatively low levels of formal education.[25] The 1996 Current Population Survey also reveals a strong relationship between age and voting. Among respondents between the ages of eighteen and twenty, only 31.2 percent voted; among those between twenty-one and twenty-four years old, 33.4 percent voted; and among those between the ages of twenty-five and forty-four, 49.2 percent voted. Among persons between the ages of forty-five and sixty-four, 64.4 percent voted, and among those sixty-five years and over, 67.0 percent reported voting.

Young Americans have relatively high levels of formal education, and one might therefore expect them to have high levels of turnout. Low participation among the young, however, appears to be a life-cycle phenomenon. As young Americans age, marry, have children, and develop community ties, their turnout tends to increase.

Social Class, Income, and Union Membership

As Table 4-3 shows, there were clear social-class differences in voting in 1996. Middle-class whites (nonmanually employed workers and their dependents) were 13 percentage points more likely to report voting than working-class whites (manually employed workers and their dependents).[26] Farmers registered above-average levels of turnout, although the number of farmers sampled is too small to lead to reliable conclusions. Although the distinction between the middle class and working class is crude, it appears to capture a meaningful division, for in most elections when we further divide respondents according to occupation we find that clerical, sales, and other white-collar workers (the lowest level of the middle class) are clearly more likely to vote than skilled and semiskilled manual workers.

Annual family income was also related to turnout, with reported turnout very low among whites with annual incomes below $15,000 a year.[27] Reported turnout was very high among whites with annual family incomes of $50,000 and above. Americans with high family incomes tend to have higher levels of formal education, and both education and income contribute to turnout; however, education has a greater effect on turnout than income does.[28]

Surveys over the years have found a weak and inconsistent relationship between union membership and turnout. Although being in a household with a union member may create organizational ties that stimulate turnout, members of union households tend to have somewhat lower levels of formal education than nonmembers. Nevertheless, as Table 4-3 reveals, in 1996 whites in union households were somewhat more likely to report voting than whites in households with no union members.

Religion

In most postwar elections, higher percentages of white Catholics than of white Protestants have voted, but these differences have eroded. As Table 4-3 reveals, in 1996 white Catholics and white Protestants were equally likely to vote. Jews have much higher levels of formal education than gentiles and have always had higher turnout. They registered very high reported turnout in 1996, but the number of Jews sampled is too small to reach reliable conclusions. Whites with no religious preferences had lower than average turnout.

In recent elections, fundamentalist Protestant leaders have launched get-out-the-vote efforts to mobilize their followers, and we examined turnout among white Protestants in some detail. We found only limited evidence that these mobilization efforts were successful. We began by exploring differences among white Protestants with differing religious views. As we show in Table 4-3, reported turnout was similar among white Protestants who said they had been "born again" and those who did not have this religious experience.[29] However, we should remember that born-again Christians are more likely to live in the South, and that the South is a region of low turnout. Among white Protestants in the South, 60 percent said that they were born again; outside the South, only 44 percent said they had had this experience. Outside of the South, white Protestants who were born again and those who were not born again were equally likely to vote. Among white southern Protestants, those who were born again were 9 percentage points more likely to say they voted than those who had not been born again.

David C. Leege and Lyman A. Kellstedt argue that religious commitment is an important dimension of political behavior. We classified white Protestants according to their level of commitment. To receive a score of "very high" on this measure respondents had to report praying several times a day, to attend church at least once a week, to say that religion provided "a great deal" of guidance in their lives, and to believe that the Bible was literally true or "the word of God."[30] White Protestants with very high levels of religious commitment were more likely to vote than those with lower levels of religious commitment. White Protestants in the South had somewhat higher levels of religious commitment than those outside the South. Religious commitment was more strongly related to reported turnout outside of the South; white Protestants outside the South with very high commitment were 14 percentage points more likely to vote than those with lower levels. As we shall see in Chapters 5 and 10, religious commitment was strongly related to the way white Protestants voted.

Beginning in 1990 the NES surveys have included detailed questions that allow us to distinguish among Protestant denominations and thus allow us to conduct analyses of religious differences that could not be conducted with earlier NES surveys. We can now divide white Protestants into four basic groups: Evangelicals, mainline Protestants, those with ambiguous affiliations, and nontraditional Protestants. Most white Protestants can be classified into the first two categories, which, according to Kenneth D. Wald, make up almost half the total adult population.[31] According to R. Stephen Warner, "The root of the [mainline] liberal position is the interpretation of Christ as a moral teacher who told his disciples that they could best honor him by helping those in need." In contrast, Warner writes, "the evangelical position sees Jesus (as they prefer to call him) as one who offers salvation to anyone who confesses his name." Liberal, or mainline, Protestants stress the importance of sharing their abundance with the needy, while Evangelicals stress the importance of sharing their creed. Evangelicals, Warner argues, see the Bible as a source of revelation about Jesus, "treasure it and credit even its implausible stories. . . . Liberals argue that these stories are timebound, and they seek the deeper truths that are obscured by myth and use the Bible alongside other texts as a source of wisdom."[32]

As Table 4-3 reveals, white mainline Protestants were 10 percentage points more likely to report voting than white Evangelicals.[33] White southerners are more likely to be Evangelicals than whites outside the South. Among white southern Protestants who can be classified as belonging to these two religious traditions, 59 percent were Evangelicals; outside the South, only 45 percent were. Evangelicals also tend to have lower levels of formal education. Among white Protestants who had graduated from college, only 32 percent were Evangelicals; among those who had never attended college, 62 percent were. However, the tendency of more mainline Protestants than Evangelicals to vote was found in both the South and outside the South, and at all levels of formal education except for respondents with advanced degrees.

In Table 4-3 we also take a closer look at differences between white Protestants and white Catholics by showing the combined effect of social class and religion. We still find no differences between Protestants and Catholics, although within each religious group middle-class whites are more likely to vote than working-class whites.

Education

We found a strong relationship between formal education and turnout. As Raymond E. Wolfinger and Steven J. Rosenstone demonstrate, formal education is the most important variable in explaining differences in turnout in the United States.[34] Better-educated Americans have skills that reduce the information costs of voting and can acquire information about how to vote more easily than less-educated Americans; they are also more likely to develop attitudes that contribute to political participation, especially that citizens have a duty to vote and that they can influence the political process.

As Table 4-3 shows, among whites who did not graduate from high school, just over half claimed to have voted; among whites who graduated from college and those who have advanced degrees, nearly nine out of ten said that they voted. Even though surveys may somewhat exaggerate the relationship between education and turnout, the tendency of better-educated Americans to be more likely to vote than less-well-educated Americans is one of the most consistently documented relationships in voting research.[35] The 1996 Census Bureau survey also found a very strong relationship between education and turnout. Among respondents with less than a high school education, only 29.9 percent voted; among those with some high school, 33.8 percent voted; and among high school graduates, 49.1 percent did. Among those with some college-level education, 60.5 percent voted, and among college graduates, turnout was 72.6 percent.

WHY HAS TURNOUT DECLINED?

Clearly, turnout within educational groups must have been declining so fast that the effect of rising educational levels was canceled out. This suggests that the decline of turnout since 1960 results from the offsetting of some forces that stimulated turnout by others that depressed it. Analysts have studied the decline of turnout extensively. Some have focused on social factors, such as changing educational levels and the changing age distribution among the electorate. Some scholars have studied political attitudes, such as changes in partisan loyalties, as a major source of turnout change. Others have analyzed institutional changes, such as the easing of registration requirements. And, finally, some scholars have pointed to the behavior of political leaders, arguing that they are making less of an effort to mobilize the electorate. Some changes, such as the rise in educational levels and the easing of registration requirements, should have increased turnout in national elections. Because turnout rates declined in spite of these forces, Richard A. Brody views the decline of turnout as a major puzzle for students of American politics.[36]

We began to explore this puzzle by examining the relationship between educational levels and reported turnout among whites in all presidential elections between 1952 and 1996. We divided whites into five educational levels: college graduate, some college, high school graduate, some high school, and eight grades or less. African-Americans have substantially lower levels of formal education than whites, and southern blacks have been enfranchised only since 1965. Therefore, including blacks in our analysis would substantially obscure the relationships we are studying.

The NES surveys show only a slight drop in turnout among whites with a college education, and they were nearly as likely to vote in 1996 as they were in 1960. But turnout dropped within all four of the other educational categories, and it dropped markedly among all three groups that had not attended college. Several studies of earlier Census Bureau surveys also suggest that turnout declined most among Americans who were relatively disadvantaged.[37] Ruy A. Teixeira's analysis of census surveys shows a 10-point decline in turnout among college graduates from 1964 to 1988, although the drop was greater among the lower educational categories; as in our analysis of NES data, he found that the decline in turnout was greatest among those who had not attended college.[38] And Jan E. Leighley and Jonathan Nagler's analysis of census surveys shows a similar pattern. In addition, studies by Teixeira and by Leighley and Nagler show that turnout declines were greater among manually employed workers. But Leighley and Nagler argue that the study of turnout inequalities should focus on differences in income, since government policies affect Americans differentially according to their income levels. Their analyses suggest that the decline in turnout was consistent across all income categories.[39]

But it is the rise in educational levels among the electorate that creates the greatest problem in accounting for the decline of turnout. Although the increase in education among the electorate did not prevent the decline in turnout, it played a major role in slowing down the decline. From 1960 through 1996, the level of education among the white electorate increased substantially, an increase that resulted almost entirely from generational replacement.[40] According to the NES surveys, the percentage of the white electorate that had not graduated from high school fell from 47 percent in 1960 to 13 percent in 1996. During this same period, the percentage who had graduated from college rose from 11 percent to 29 percent. Between 1960 and 1996 reported turnout among the white electorate fell 6 percentage points. An estimate based on an algebraic standardization procedure suggests that if the educational level of the electorate had not increased, turnout would have declined 17 percentage points.[41] Although this procedure provides only a preliminary estimate of the impact of rising educational levels on the decline of turnout, our analysis suggests that the overall decline of turnout would have been nearly three times as great if educational levels had not risen.

Other social changes also tended to push turnout upward. In a comprehensive attempt to explain the decline of turnout between 1960 and 1988, Teixeira studied changes in turnout using the NES surveys. He found that increases in income and the growth of white-collar employment tended to retard the decline of turnout. But the increase in educational levels, according to Teixeira's estimates, is by far the most important of these changes, and its influence is three times as great as the impact of occupational and income changes combined.[42]

Steven J. Rosenstone and John Mark Hansen have also used the NES surveys to provide a comprehensive explanation of the decline of turnout during these years. Their analysis also demonstrates that the increase in formal education was the most important factor preventing an even greater decline in voter participation. They also estimate the effect of easing voter registration requirements. They find that reported turnout declined 11 percentage points in the 1960s through the 1980s, but they estimate that turnout would have declined 16 points if it had not been for the combined impact of rising educational levels and liberalized election laws.[43]

Although some social forces slowed down the decline in electoral participation, other forces contributed to the decline. After 1960 the electorate became younger, as the baby boom generation (generally defined as persons born between 1946 and 1964) came of age. As we have seen, young Americans have relatively low levels of turnout, although as the baby boomers age (by 1996 they were between the ages of thirty-two and fifty), one might expect turnout to rise. The proportion of Americans who were married declined, and because married people are more likely to vote than unmarried people, this social change reduced turnout. And church attendance declined, reducing the ties of Americans to their communities. Teixeira identifies these three changes as major shifts that contributed to the decline of turnout and argues that the decline in church attendance was the most important of these changes.[44] Rosenstone and Hansen also examined changes that tended to reduce turnout, and their analysis suggests that a younger electorate was the most important social change reducing electoral participation.[45] Warren E. Miller argues that the decline of turnout results mainly from the entry of a post-New Deal generation (defined as Americans first eligible to vote in 1968) into the electorate.[46] This change, Miller argues, results not merely from the youth of these Americans, but from generational differences that contribute to lower levels of electoral participation. During the late 1960s and early 1970s a series of events—the Vietnam War, Watergate, and the failed presidencies of Ford and Carter—Miller argues, created a generation that withdrew from political participation. We agree that generational replacement contributed to the decline of turnout, but analyses by Teixeira and by Rosenstone and Hansen suggest that Miller may have overestimated its impact.[47]

Most analysts of turnout agree that attitudinal change contributed to the decline of electoral participation. Our own analysis has focused on the effect of attitudinal change, and we have examined the erosion of party loyalties and the decline of what George I. Balch and others have called feelings of external political efficacy, or the belief that the political authorities respond to attempts to influence them.[48] These are the same two basic attitudes studied by Teixeira in his first major analysis of the decline of turnout, and they are among the political attitudes studied by Rosenstone and Hansen.[49] We found these attitudinal changes to be important factors in the decline of turnout from 1960 through 1980, as did Teixeira.[50] We have also estimated the impact of these attitudinal changes on turnout in the 1984, 1988, and 1992 elections.[51] Although the effect of the decline in partisan loyalties and the erosion of political efficacy on the overall decline of turnout has varied from election to election, these variables have always played a major role in accounting for the decline of electoral participation among the white electorate. And they play a major role in accounting for the decline of turnout among whites between 1960 and 1996.

The measure of party identification we use is based on questions designed to gauge psychological attachment to a partisan reference group.[52] In Chapter 8 we discuss how party identification contributes to the way people vote. But party loyalties also contribute to *whether* people vote. Strong feelings of party identification contribute to psychological involvement in politics, as Angus Campbell and his colleagues argue.[53] Party loyalties also reduce the time and effort needed to decide how to vote and thus reduce the costs of voting.[54] In every presidential election from 1952 through 1996, strong partisans have been more likely to vote than any other category of partisan strength. In every election since 1960, independents with no partisan leanings have been the least likely to vote.

Between 1952 and 1964, the percentage of whites who were strong party identifiers never fell below 35 percent. The percentage of strong identifiers fell from 36 percent in 1964 to 27 percent in 1966, and it continued to fall through 1978, when only 21 percent of whites strongly identified with either party. Since then party identification has rebounded somewhat, but in 1996 only 30 percent of the whites were strong party identifiers. The percentage of whites who were independents with no partisan leanings averaged about 8 percent between 1952 and 1964. This percentage increased to about 14 percent of the white electorate between 1974 and 1980. Since then, however, this percentage has declined, and in 1996 the percentage fell to only 8 percent. For a detailed discussion of party identification from 1952 through 1996 and tables showing the distribution of party identification during these years, see Chapter 8.

Feelings of political effectiveness also contribute to electoral participation. Citizens may expect to gain benefits from voting if they believe that the government is responsive to their demands. Conversely, those who believe that political leaders will not or cannot respond to popular demands may see little reason for voting. In every presidential election between 1952 and 1992, Americans with high feelings of political effectiveness were the most likely to report voting, and those with low feelings of political effectiveness were the least likely to vote.

From 1960 to 1980 feelings of political effectiveness declined markedly. Scores on our measure are based on the responses to the following two statements: "I don't think public officials care much what people like me think" and "People like me do not have any say about what the government does."[55] In 1956 and 1960, 64 percent of the white electorate felt they were highly efficacious. The decline in feelings of political effectiveness began in 1964, and by 1980 only 39 percent scored high. Feelings of political effectiveness rose somewhat in 1984, fell in 1988, and rose slightly by 1992, at which time 40 percent scored high. But feelings of political efficacy fell sharply in 1996, and only 28 percent of the whites surveyed scored high on our measure. The percentage scoring low on this measure was only 15 percent in 1956 and 1960, but the percentage rose in 1964 and by 1980, 30 percent scored low. The percentage scoring low fell in 1984, but it rose in 1988, falling again in 1992. In 1992, 34 percent of the whites surveyed

TABLE 4-4   Percentage of Whites Who Reported Voting for President,
by Strength of Party Identification and Sense of External Political
Efficacy, 1996

Scores on external political efficacy index	Strength of party identification							
	Strong partisan		Weak partisan		Independent who leans toward a party		Independent with no partisan leaning	
	%	(N)	%	(N)	%	(N)	%	(N)
High	94	(141)	78	(134)	76	(79)	56	(18)
Medium	96	(105)	82	(111)	86	(70)	48	(23)
Low	84	(160)	66	(232)	66	(158)	51	(61)

Note: The numbers in parentheses are the totals on which percentages are based. The numbers are weighted using the time-series weight.

scored low on this measure. In 1996, with feelings of political efficacy falling, 47 percent of the whites surveyed scored low.

Although feelings of partisan loyalty and feelings of political effectiveness are both related to turnout, in most NES surveys they are weakly related to each other. In 1996 the relationship between party identification and feelings of political efficacy was stronger in the NES survey than in most earlier surveys, with strong partisans having the highest feelings of political effectiveness and independents with no partisan leanings the lowest. Table 4-4 shows the combined effect of these political attitudes on the turnout of whites in 1996.

In 1996, unlike previous surveys, turnout was equally high among whites with both high and medium levels of feelings of political efficacy, but, as in all previous surveys, it was lowest among whites with feelings of low effectiveness. Reading down each column shows that in three of the four partisan strength categories, whites with feelings of low political effectiveness are the least likely to report voting. Reading across each row, we find that strong party identifiers are always the most likely to vote, regardless of their level of feelings of political efficacy. Independents with no partisan leanings are always the least likely to vote, regardless of their feelings of political effectiveness. As in most previous surveys, there are no consistent differences in reported turnout between weak partisans and independents who leaned toward a party.[56] These attitudinal variables have a strong cumulative impact. Among whites with strong party loyalties and high feelings of political effectiveness, more than nine out of ten say that they voted; among independents with no partisan leanings and low feelings of political effectiveness, only half say that they voted.

The decline in party loyalties and the erosion of feelings of political efficacy clearly contribute to the decline of turnout. A preliminary assessment of the effect of these factors can be derived through a simple algebraic standardization procedure.[57] According to our calculations, the combined impact of these attitudinal changes accounts for 64 percent of the decline of turnout, with the decline of feelings of political effectiveness being more than five times as important as the weakening of partisan loyalties.

Our estimates clearly demonstrate that these attitudinal changes are important, but they are not final estimates of the impact of these changes. We do not claim to have solved the puzzle of political participation, and we believe that comprehensive tests, such as those conducted by Teixeira and by Rosenstone and Hansen are needed to study the 1992 and 1996 NES results. As Teixeira demonstrates, a comprehensive estimate of the impact of attitudinal changes must calculate the contribution of the change in attitudes to the decline that would have occurred if there had been no social forces retarding the decline of turnout. In Teixeira's analysis, for example, the decline in party loyalties and the erosion of feelings of political efficacy accounted for 62 percent of the decline of turnout from 1960 through 1980. But these attitudinal changes accounted for only 38 percent of the larger decline that would have occurred if changes in educational levels, income, and occupational patterns had not slowed the decline of turnout.

We analyzed the combined effect of rising educational levels, the erosion of feelings of political efficacy, and the decline of party loyalties on reported turnout among whites between 1960 and 1996. Our estimates suggest that attitude change accounted for 37 percent of the decline in turnout that would have occurred if rising educational levels had not slowed the decline of turnout.[58]

A comprehensive analysis of the impact of attitudinal factors would take into account other attitudes that might have eroded turnout. As has been well documented, there has been a substantial decline in political trust during the past three decades.[59] In 1964, when political trust among whites was highest, 77 percent of the whites said the government in Washington could be trusted to do what is right just about always or most of the time, and 74 percent of the blacks endorsed this view.[60] Political trust reached a very low level in 1980, when only 25 percent of the whites and 26 percent of the blacks trusted the government. In 1992, 29 percent of the whites and 26 percent of the blacks trusted the government. Feelings of political trust were still very low in 1996, but they were higher than in the 1992 election, especially among blacks. Among both whites and blacks, 32 percent trusted the government in Washington to do what is right just about always or most of the time. Back in 1964, 63 percent of the whites and 69 percent of the blacks said the government was run for the benefit of all.[61] By 1980, only 19 percent of the whites and 34 percent of the blacks held this view. In 1992, 20 percent of the whites and 19 percent of the blacks trusted the government on this question. In 1996, with a slight rebound in trust, 26 percent of the whites and 32 percent of the blacks said the government was run for the benefit of all. But in 1996, as in most previous elections, there was little difference in turnout between whites who tended to trust the government and those who were politically cynical. Whites who trusted the government just about always or most of the time were no more likely to vote than those who said the government could be trusted only some of the time or never. However, among whites who said the government was run for the benefit of all ($N = 336$), 83 percent said that they voted; among those who said it was run for a few big interests ($N = 923$), only 73 percent said that they voted.

Scholars will also need to investigate short-term forces that may have contributed to low turnout in 1996. Rosenstone and Hansen's analysis points to one possibility. They focus on the declining role of political parties in mobilizing the electorate, which they view as the primary cause of turnout decline.[62] The key variable in their measure of party mobilization is whether respondents report being contacted by a political party.[63] Rosenstone and Hansen present a fascinating analysis that focuses on the effect of elite behavior on the participation of the electorate. But there are problems with their interpretation. The percentage of Americans who say that they were contacted by a political party actually increased after the 1960 presidential election. In 1960, 22 percent of the electorate said they were contacted by a political party; in 1980, 32 percent said they were contacted. Yet turnout declined substantially. In 1992 only 20 percent claimed to have been contacted by a political party, but turnout was higher than in 1980. In 1996, 29 percent of the respondents said that they were contacted by a political party, and those who were contacted were substantially more likely to vote than those who were not. Among whites who said they were contacted by a political party ($N = 399$), 90 percent said that they voted; among whites who said they were not contacted ($N = 912$), only 70 percent said that they voted. But even though there was a substantial relationship between party contacts and voting, and even though party contacts increased, overall turnout fell some 6 percentage points.[64]

In most elections, Americans who think the election will be close are more likely to vote than those who think that the winner will win by quite a bit.[65] Even though these differences are not large, the percentage of those viewing the election as close has varied greatly from contest to contest.[66] Orley Ashenfelter and Stanley Kelley, Jr., report that the single most important factor accounting for the decline of turnout between 1960 and 1972 was "the dramatic shift in voter expectations about the closeness of the race in these two elections."[67] The percentage who thought the presidential election would be close fell dramatically between 1992 and 1996. In 1992, 85 percent of the whites interviewed thought the election would be close; in 1996 only 52 percent did. But this change cannot account for the decline of turnout, since in 1996, respondents who thought the election would be close were no more likely to vote than those who thought that the winner would win by quite a bit.

Finally, we may examine the possibility that the weakness of Perot's 1996 candidacy contributed to the decline of turnout. If this were a cause of the declining turnout between 1992 and 1996, we would expect relatively high abstention rates among respondents who voted for Perot in the 1992 election. But reported turnout in 1996 was relatively high among supporters of all three candidates in the

1992 election. Among whites interviewed in 1996 who said that they had voted for Bush four years earlier ($N = 287$), 92 percent said that they voted; among those who voted for Clinton in 1992 ($N = 415$), 89 percent said that they voted; and among those who voted for Perot in 1992 ($N = 182$), 85 percent said that they voted.

DOES LOW TURNOUT MATTER?

For the last decade Democratic party leaders have debated the importance of increasing turnout. Some argue that low turnout was a major reason for the Democratic presidential election losses. The Democrats could win, they argue, if the party could mobilize disadvantaged Americans. In 1984 the Democrats and their supporters launched major get-out-the-vote efforts, but turnout increased less than 1 percentage point, and in 1988 turnout reached a postwar low. Other Democrats argue that the main problem the party faced was defections by its traditional supporters. Of course, attempting to increase turnout and attempting to win back defectors are not mutually exclusive strategies, but they can lead to contradictory tactics. For example, mobilizing African-Americans may not be cost-free if doing so leads to defections among white Democrats.

In fact, as James DeNardo has pointed out, from 1932 through 1976 there was only a very weak relationship between turnout and the percentage of the vote won by Democratic presidential candidates.[68] In our analyses of the 1980, 1984, and 1988 presidential elections, we argued that under most reasonable scenarios increased turnout would not have led to Democratic victories.[69] In 1992 increased turnout went along with a Democratic victory, although not an increased Democratic share of the vote. Our analyses suggest that Clinton did benefit somewhat from increased turnout but that he gained more by converting voters who had supported Bush four years earlier.[70]

Despite a decline of 6 percentage points in turnout in 1996, Clinton was easily reelected. Even so, there is some evidence that low turnout among Democrats cost Clinton votes. The U.S. House race, however, was much closer. Nationwide, the Republicans won 48.9 percent of the popular vote for the U.S House of Representatives, while the Democrats won 48.5 percent. Low turnout could have thwarted the Democratic attempt to regain the House, although the evidence is by no means conclusive.

We begin this discussion by examining turnout among party identifiers. In 1980, 1984, and 1988 strong Republicans were more likely to vote than strong Democrats, and weak Republicans were more likely to vote than weak Democrats.[71] In 1992, however, partisan differences were small, because the increase in turnout between 1988 and 1992 was somewhat greater among Democrats than among Republicans.

In Table 4-5 we show the percentage of the electorate who reported voting, according to their party identifications, their policy preferences, and their evalu-

TABLE 4-5 Percentage of Electorate Who Reported Voting for President, by Party Identification, Issue Preferences, and Retrospective Evaluations, 1996

Attitude	Voted	Did not vote	Total	(N)[a]
Electorate, by party identification				
Strong Democrat	89	11	100	(201)
Weak Democrat	72	28	100	(260)
Independent, leans Democratic	69	31	100	(164)
Independent, no partisan leaning	52	48	100	(100)
Independent, leans Republican	77	23	100	(150)
Weak Republican	79	21	100	(225)
Strong Republican	96	4	100	(198)
Electorate, by scores on the balance of issues measure[b]				
Strongly Democratic	84	16	100	(76)
Moderately Democratic	73	28	100	(99)
Slightly Democratic	64	36	100	(170)
Neutral	73	27	100	(434)
Slightly Republican	70	30	100	(266)
Moderately Republican	82	18	100	(235)
Strongly Republican	90	10	100	(241)
Electorate, by summary measure retrospective evaluations[c]				
Strongly Democratic	76	24	100	(21)
Moderately Democratic	80	20	100	(119)
Leans Democratic	74	26	100	(212)
Neutral	75	25	100	(155)
Leans Republican	75	25	100	(67)
Moderately Republican	79	21	100	(97)
Strongly Republican	86	14	100	(87)

[a]Numbers are weighted.
[b]Chapter 6 describes how the "balance of issues" measure was constructed.
[c]Chapter 7 describes how the "summary measure of retrospective evaluations" was constructed.

ations of Clinton and the Democratic party performance. Turning first to party identification, we find that strong Republicans were more likely to vote than strong Democrats, weak Republicans were more likely to vote than weak Democrats, and independents who leaned toward the Republican party were more likely to vote than independents who felt closer to the Democratic party. If Democrats within each of these categories had voted at the same level as Republicans and had supported Clinton at the same level as Democrats within these categories who did vote, Clinton's overall share of the popular vote would have increased 1.6 percentage points. More important, if Democrats within each partisan category had voted at the same level as Republicans and had supported Democratic congressional candidates at the same level as strong Democrats, weak Democrats, and independents who leaned Democratic who did vote, the overall share of the Democratic House vote would have increased 1.4 percentage points. Whether this increased turnout among Democrats would have actually changed control of the House depends on how these votes were distributed across closely contested congressional districts. Indeed, the Republicans won eleven House districts by 2 percentage points or less, and a 1-point Democratic gain, coupled with a 1-point GOP loss, would have changed the outcome in these districts.

In Chapter 6 we shall examine the issue preferences of the electorate. Our measure of issue preferences is based on each voter's view on nine issues—reducing or increasing government services, decreasing or increasing defense spending, private versus government health insurance, government job guarantees, government aid for blacks, the proper approach to reducing crime, two questions about government protection of the environment, and a question about the role of women in society. In 1980 there was no systematic relationship between issue preferences and turnout, although in 1984, 1988, and 1992, respondents with pro-Republican views were somewhat more likely to vote than those with pro-Democratic views. In 1984 and 1988 these biases cost the Democratic presidential candidate about 2 percentage points. In 1992 they cost Clinton less than 1 percentage point. As Table 4-5 shows, in 1996, respondents with strongly pro-Republican views on the issues were 6 points more likely to report voting than those with strongly pro-Democratic views, those with moderately pro-Republican views were 9 points more likely to vote than those with moderately pro-Democratic views, and those with slightly pro-Republican views were 6 points more likely to vote than those with slightly pro-Democratic views. Assuming that respondents with pro-Democratic views were as likely to vote as those with pro-Republican views, and assuming that they were as likely to support Clinton as respondents with these views who did vote, Clinton would have gained about 0.8 of a percentage point. According to our estimates, an increase in turnout among pro-Democratic respondents would have added only half a percentage point to the Democratic share of the House vote.

In Chapter 7 we shall study the retrospective evaluations of the electorate. Our measure of retrospective evaluations has three components: (1) an evaluation of Clinton's performance as president; (2) an assessment of how good a job the government was doing solving the most important problem facing the country; and (3) a judgment about which party would do a better job solving that problem.[72] In 1980, respondents who expressed negative views of Carter and the Democrats were more likely to vote than those with positive views; given that negative views prevailed, these biases hurt Carter. In both 1984 and 1988, respondents with positive views of the Republicans were more likely to vote than those with negative views, although in 1992 these pro-Republican biases were eliminated. In 1996, respondents with strongly pro-Republican views were 10 points more likely to vote than those with strongly pro-Democratic views, but there were no differences in turnout between respondents with moderately pro-Republican views and those with moderately pro-Democratic views, or between respondents who leaned toward the Republicans and those who leaned toward the Democrats. Given that few respondents were strongly pro-Democratic, these biases had little effect. Had turnout differences been eliminated, Clinton would have gained about 0.7 of a percentage point, and the total Democratic share of the House vote would have increased about 1 percentage point.

Clearly, increased turnout would not have affected the presidential election outcome, and unless the Democratic gains in the U.S. House vote were registered in closely contested House races, this increased turnout would not have allowed the Democrats to recapture control of the House. Given that increased turnout may not have affected the outcome, some might argue that low turnout does not matter. Some scholars have argued that in many elections (although not in the last four presidential elections), the policy preferences of voters and nonvoters have been similar to the preferences of Americans who did not go to the polls. Turnout has been low in postwar elections, but in many of them the voters reflected the sentiments of the electorate as a whole.[73]

Despite this evidence, we cannot accept the conclusion that low turnout is unimportant. We are especially concerned that turnout is low among disadvantaged Americans. Some believe that turnout is low among the disadvantaged because political leaders structure policy alternatives in a way that provides disadvantaged Americans with relatively little choice. Frances Fox Piven and Richard A. Cloward, for example, acknowledge that the policy preferences of voters and nonvoters are similar, but they argue that this similarity results from the way that elites have structured policy choices. "Political attitudes would invariably change over time," they maintain, "if the allegiance of voters at the bottom became the object of partisan competition, for then politicians would be prodded to identify and articulate the grievances and aspirations of lower income voters in order to win their political support, thus helping them give form and voice to a distinctive political class."[74]

We cannot accept this argument either, mainly because it is highly speculative, and there is little empirical evidence to support it. The difficulty in supporting this view may partly result from the nature of survey research, because questions about policy preferences are usually framed along the lines of controversy as defined by the mainstream political leaders. Occasionally, however, surveys pose radical policy alternatives, and they often ask open-ended questions that allow respondents to state their policy preferences. We find little concrete evidence that low turnout leads current political leaders to ignore the policy preferences of the American electorate.

Nevertheless, low turnout among Americans can scarcely be healthy for a democracy. Even if low turnout seldom affects electoral outcomes, it may undermine the legitimacy of elected political leaders. The large bloc of nonparticipants in the electorate may be potentially dangerous, because this means that many Americans have weak ties to the established parties and leaders. The prospects of electoral instability, and perhaps political instability, thus increase.[75]

Does low turnout imply that a partisan realignment has occurred or is likely to occur? Low turnout in the 1980 election led some scholars to question whether Reagan's victory presaged a pro-Republican realignment. As Gerald M. Pomper argued at the time, "Elections that involve upheavals in party coalitions have certain hallmarks, such as popular enthusiasm."[76] Indeed, past realignments have been characterized by increases in turnout. As Table 4-1 shows, turnout rose markedly from 1852 to 1860, a period when the Republican party formed, replaced the Whigs, and gained control of the presidency. Turnout also rose in the Bryan-McKinley contest of 1896, which is generally considered a realigning election. As both Table 4-2 and Figure 4-1 show, turnout rose markedly after 1924, increasing in 1928 and again in 1936, a period when the Democrats emerged as the majority party.

Of course, there is no necessary reason that a future party realignment, should one occur, must bear all the hallmarks of previous realignments. But it would be difficult to consider any alignment as stable when nearly half of the politically eligible population does not vote.

Chapter 5

Social Forces and the Vote

Ninety-six million Americans voted for president in 1996. Voting is an individual act, but group memberships influence voting choices because people who share social characteristics may share political interests. Group similarities in voting behavior also may reflect past political conditions. The partisan loyalties of African-Americans, for example, were first shaped by the Civil War; black loyalty to the Republican party, the party of Lincoln, lasted through the 1932 presidential election, but by 1936 most blacks outside the South had shifted to the Democrats. The steady Democratic voting of southern whites, a product of these same historical conditions, lasted even longer, perhaps through 1960.

It is easy to see why group-based loyalties persist over time. Studies of pre-adult learning suggest that partisan loyalties are often transmitted from generation to generation. And because religion, ethnicity, and, to a lesser extent, social class are also transmitted from generation to generation, social divisions have considerable staying power. Moreover, the interaction of social group members with each other may reinforce similarities in political attitudes and behaviors.

Politicians often think in group terms. They recognize that to win they may need to mobilize the social groups that have supported them in the past and that it is helpful to cut into their opponents' established bases of support. The Democrats think more in group terms than the Republicans do because since the 1930s the Democratic party has been a coalition of minorities. To win, the party has needed to earn high levels of support from the social groups that have traditionally made up its broad-based coalition.

The 1992 contest was unusual, however. Bill Clinton earned high levels of support from only two of the groups comprising the New Deal coalition, African-Americans and Jews. Most of the other groups that made up the New Deal coalition gave less than half of their vote to Clinton. But in the three-way contest of 1992, it took only 43 percent of the vote to win. The 1996 election was much more of a two-candidate fight, and Clinton won with 49 percent of the popular vote. Clinton gained ground among the vast majority of groups we analyze, and he made especially large gains among union members (a traditional component of the New Deal coalition) and among Hispanics. Even so, there is also considerable evidence that the New Deal coalition has weakened. In many respects, Democratic presidential losses during the past three decades may be attributed to the party's failure to hold the basic loyalties of the social groups that made up the coalition forged by Franklin D. Roosevelt in the 1930s. In winning in 1992 and 1996, Clinton only partly revitalized that coalition.

This chapter analyzes the voting patterns of social groups in the 1996 presidential election. To put the 1996 election in perspective, we examine the voting choices of key social groups during the entire postwar period. By studying the social bases of party support since 1944, we discover the long-term trends that weakened the New Deal coalition and thus are better able to understand the distinctive character of Clinton's victory.

HOW SOCIAL GROUPS VOTED IN 1996

Our basic results on how social groups voted for president in the 1996 election are presented in Table 5-1.[1] Excluding respondents for whom the direction of the vote was not ascertained, the 1996 National Election Studies (NES) survey shows that 51.9 percent voted for Clinton, 39.1 percent for Dole, and 7.4 percent for Perot. The NES survey shows Clinton as doing 2.7 points better than he actually did, whereas Dole and Perot fared 1.6 points and 1.0 points worse, respectively. The NES survey shows Clinton winning 57.0 percent of the major-party vote; as we saw in Chapter 3, he actually won only 54.7 percent. This bias is not severe, and it is somewhat less than the pro-Clinton bias in the 1992 NES survey. Nonetheless, readers should bear in mind that the results in our tables somewhat overestimate Clinton's vote.

Despite its tendency to exaggerate Clinton's vote, the 1996 NES survey, which is based on the responses of 1,137 voters, is the single best source of survey data, especially when we study change over time. However, once we examine subsets of the electorate, the number of persons sampled in some social groups becomes rather small. Therefore, we often supplement these results by referring to the exit poll of 16,627 voters conducted by the Voter News Service (VNS) for the television networks.[2]

Race, Gender, and Age

Political differences between African-Americans and whites are far sharper than any other social cleavage.[3] According to the NES survey, 97 percent of the black voters supported Clinton; only 48 percent of the white voters did. The VNS exit poll reports that 84 percent of the black voters supported Clinton, whereas only 43 percent of the white voters did. Even though blacks make up only one-ninth of the electorate, and even though they have relatively low turnout, about one-

TABLE 5-1   How Social Groups Voted for President, 1996 (in percentages)

Social group	Clinton	Dole	Perot	Total	(N)
Total electorate	53	40	8	100	(1,120)
Electorate, by race					
African-American	97	1	2	100	(105)
White	48	44	7	99	(981)
Whites, by Hispanic identification					
Identify as Hispanic	79	19	3	101	(70)
Do not identify as Hispanic	46	46	9	101	(909)
Whites, by gender					
Females	54	38	8	100	(495)
Males	42	49	9	100	(486)
Whites, by region					
New England and					
Mid-Atlantic	54	36	10	100	(201)
North Central	44	47	9	100	(256)
South	43	49	9	101	(253)
Border	48	46	6	100	(50)
Mountain and Pacific	53	40	7	100	(220)
Whites, by birth cohort					
Before 1924	52	44	5	101	(103)
1924–1939	51	45	4	101	(192)
1940–1954	52	38	10	100	(274)
1955–1962	39	54	9	100	(215)
1963–1970	52	37	12	101	(145)
1971–1978	47	43	10	101	(49)
Whites, by social class					
Working class	49	39	11	99	(313)
Middle class	46	47	7	100	(546)
Farmers	57	38	4	99	(26)
Whites, by occupation of head of household					
Unskilled manual	54	38	7	99	(68)
Skilled, semiskilled manual	48	39	12	99	(244)
Clerical, sales, other white collar	49	46	6	101	(125)
Managerial	45	46	9	100	(212)
Professional and semiprofessional	46	48	6	99	(209)

(Table continues)

TABLE 5-1 (continued)

Social group	Clinton	Dole	Perot	Total	(N)
Whites, by level of education					
Eight grades or less	83	13	4	100	(23)
Some high school	71	26	4	101	(51)
High school graduate	48	42	10	100	(267)
Some college	46	43	11	100	(274)
College graduate	43	51	6	100	(232)
Advanced degree	47	49	4	100	(130)
Whites, by annual family income					
Less than $10,000	69	22	10	101	(51)
$10,000 to $14,999	54	34	11	99	(44)
$15,000 to $19,999	66	24	11	101	(55)
$20,000 to $24,999	61	29	11	101	(56)
$25,000 to $29,999	42	51	7	100	(73)
$30,000 to $34,999	53	42	5	100	(74)
$35,000 to $39,999	40	55	5	100	(60)
$40,000 to $49,999	50	47	3	100	(106)
$50,000 to $59,999	47	47	6	100	(109)
$60,000 to $74,999	36	50	14	100	(121)
$75,000 to $89,999	42	52	6	100	(66)
$90,000 and over	41	53	5	99	(111)
Whites, by union membership[a]					
Member	64	26	9	100	(193)
Nonmember	44	48	8	100	(785)
Whites, by religion					
Jewish	86	7	7	100	(29)
Catholic	54	39	8	101	(303)
Protestant	40	52	8	100	(531)
None, no preference	56	30	14	100	(103)
White Protestants, by whether born again					
Not born again	50	42	7	99	(259)
Born again	31	61	8	100	(269)
White Protestants, by religious commitment					
Medium or low	52	44	5	101	(228)
High	32	57	11	100	(170)
Very high	24	72	3	99	(91)

Social group	Clinton	Dole	Perot	Total	(N)
White Protestants, by religious tradition					
Mainline	45	49	6	99	(240)
Evangelical	38	52	10	100	(212)
Whites, by social class and religion					
Working-class Catholics	65	27	8	100	(94)
Middle-class Catholics	49	44	6	99	(178)
Working-class Protestants	42	48	10	100	(177)
Middle-class Protestants	36	56	7	100	(276)

Note: Numbers are weighted. The twenty-three voters for whom direction of vote was not ascertained and the seventeen voters who voted for other candidates have been excluded from these analyses.

ªWhether respondent or family member in union.

sixth of Clinton's total vote came from black voters.[4] Put differently, this suggests that of the 47 million votes that Clinton received, about 8 million came from blacks. Few blacks voted for Perot. According to the NES survey, only about one black in fifty voted for Perot; according to the VNS poll, about one black in twenty-five did.

Because race is such a profound social division, we examine whites and blacks separately.[5] Among African-Americans, as among whites, women were more likely to vote Democratic than men. According to the VNS exit poll, 89 percent of the black women voted for Clinton, whereas only 78 percent of the black men did. Unlike the pattern among whites, however, southern blacks were more likely to vote for Clinton than blacks outside the South. Age differences in blacks' voting preferences were negligible.

Among whites, the small number of voters who identified as Hispanic were much more likely to vote for Clinton than were non-Hispanics.[6] Compared with the 1992 NES survey, Clinton gained 17 points among white Hispanics. Hispanic voters may have been reacting to Republican-sponsored plans to deny welfare services to legal immigrants, attacks on affirmative action, and efforts to establish English as the official language of the United States.[7] According to James W. Ceaser and Andrew E. Busch, Hispanics "may have associated Pat Buchanan's extreme anti-immigration rhetoric with Republicans as a whole."[8] The VNS exit poll reports that among all Hispanics, 72 percent voted for Clinton, 21 percent for Dole, and 6 percent for Perot. Compared with a similar exit poll conducted in 1992, Clinton registered an 11-point gain among Hispanics. He even made substantial gains among Cuban-Americans in South Florida, normally a strongly

Republican bloc. Gains among Hispanic voters may have helped Clinton carry Florida, California, and Arizona.

Gender differences in voting behavior have been pronounced in some European countries, but historically they have been weak in the United States.[9] In the 1980, 1984, and 1988 elections women were less likely to vote Republican for president than were men. Such differences led to a discussion of the "gender gap," and some feminists hoped that women would play a major role in defeating the Republicans. But, as we pointed out earlier, there is no necessary reason that a gender gap will help the Democrats.[10] For example, in 1988 George Bush and Michael S. Dukakis each won half of the women's vote, but Bush won a clear majority among men. Bush benefited from the gender gap in the 1988 election.

In 1992 and again in 1996 Clinton clearly benefited from the gender gap. According to the 1996 NES survey, 54 percent of the white women voted for Clinton, while only 42 percent of the white men did. According to the VNS poll, among all women, 54 percent voted for Clinton, 38 percent for Dole, and 7 percent for Perot; among men, 43 percent voted for Clinton, 44 percent for Dole, and 10 percent for Perot. Among white women, 48 percent voted for Clinton, 43 percent for Dole, and 8 percent for Perot; among white men, Clinton won only 38 percent of the vote, Dole won 49 percent, and Perot gained 11 percent.

As in previous elections, the gender gap was greater among voters of higher socioeconomic status. According to the NES surveys, white women were 11 percentage points more likely to vote for Clinton than white men were. Among whites with annual family incomes above $90,000, women were 18 points more likely to vote for Clinton than were men. Among whites with advanced degrees, women were 30 points more likely to vote for Clinton than men were. Among white women who held advanced degrees ($N = 58$), 64 percent voted for Clinton; among white men with advanced degrees ($N = 72$), only 33 percent voted for Clinton.

As in our analyses of the 1984, 1988, and 1992 NES surveys, we found clear differences between women who were married and those who were single.[11] Single women, in particular, often believed that they had been harmed by the policies of Ronald Reagan and Bush, and the Republican emphasis on "family values" may have cost them votes among women. According to the 1996 NES survey, among all women who had never been married ($N = 66$), 77 percent voted for Clinton; among married women ($N = 373$), 56 percent did. Even though the marriage gap partly results from the relatively large percentage of black women who have never been married, these differences were almost as sharp among white voters. Among white women who had never been married ($N = 48$), 71 percent voted for Clinton; among married white women ($N = 328$), 52 percent did. There was also a marriage gap among men, but it was not as pronounced as among women. Among all men who had never been married ($N = 78$), 54 percent voted for Clinton, while among married men ($N = 393$), 41 percent did. These differences persisted when we examined the relationships among whites. Among white men who had never been married ($N = 71$), 51 percent voted for Clinton; among married white men ($N = 363$), 38 percent did.

The VNS exit poll also reveals that unmarried voters were more likely to support Clinton than those who were married. Among unmarried women, the VNS poll found that 62 percent voted for Clinton, while among married women, 48 percent did. As with the NES survey, the gap was not as large among men. Among unmarried men, according to the VNS poll, 48 percent voted for Clinton, while among married men, only 40 percent did.

Our analysis in Chapter 3 shows that overall regional differences were relatively small. There were, however, clearer regional differences among whites. As Table 5-1 reveals, among whites in the South, Dole won 49 percent of the vote, Clinton won 43 percent, and Perot won 9 percent. The South was the only region where Dole clearly won more white votes than Clinton, although according to the NES survey he narrowly edged out Clinton in the North Central states. The VNS exit poll shows that the South was the only region where Dole clearly won a majority of the white major-party vote. According to this poll, Dole won 56 percent of the white vote in the South, Clinton won 36 percent, and Perot won 8 percent. In the Midwest, Clinton won 45 percent of the white vote, Dole won 43 percent and Perot gained 10 percent, while in the West, Clinton won 43 percent of the white vote, Dole won 44 percent, and Perot won 9 percent. Clinton clearly did best among whites in the East, where he won 51 percent of the white vote, compared with only 37 percent for Dole, and 10 percent for Perot.

In recent years, young Americans have been more likely to identify with the Republican party than older Americans, and in the 1980, 1984, 1988, and 1992 elections the Democrats fared somewhat better among whites who reached voting age before or during World War II (those born before 1924).[12] Clinton did do somewhat better among older voters than younger votes, but age-group differences were relatively small. Dole did best among whites born between 1955 and 1962, who entered the electorate in the 1970s and early 1980s and who may have been influenced by the pro-Republican tide during the early Reagan years. The VNS poll also shows that Dole won the largest share of the major-party vote among whites between the ages of thirty and forty-four (born between 1952 and 1966). Both the NES survey and the VNS exit poll show Perot doing somewhat better among younger voters. To some extent Perot's success among younger voters results from their weaker levels of party identification.

Social Class, Income, Education, and Union Membership

Traditionally, the Democratic party has done well among the relatively disadvantaged. It has done better among the working class, the poor, and voters with low levels of formal education. Moreover, since the 1930s most union leaders have supported the Democratic party, and union members have traditionally been a mainstay of the Democratic presidential coalition. These bases of support persisted in 1996, and Clinton did especially well among union members. Still, differences between working-class and middle-class Americans remained relatively small.

As we shall see, the weak relationship between social class and voting behavior is part of a long-term trend that has eroded class voting. Clinton was a moderate and he reemphasized his moderate image after the Republicans gained control of the 104th Congress. His support for the North American Free Trade Agreement cost him support among union leaders, and his support for welfare reform also cost him support. But in their efforts to end the Republican majority in Congress, unions also mobilized support for Clinton. The Republican appeals to traditional values, however, may have attracted working-class support.

Clinton won a majority of the major-party vote among working-class whites, and an absolute majority among whites who were unskilled manual workers. Clinton clearly fared better among the poor than the affluent. He gained a majority of the vote among whites with annual family incomes below $25,000, whereas Dole gained half the vote among whites with annual family incomes above $60,000. The VNS uses somewhat different categories and does not present its results by race, but the poll shows a similar pattern. Clinton gained a majority of the vote among voters with family incomes below $30,000 and Dole did best among voters with family incomes above $75,000. Both the NES survey and the VNS exit poll show that Perot did somewhat better among voters with relatively low incomes.

Clinton did very well among whites who had not graduated from high school, whereas Dole did best among college graduates. Among whites with advanced degrees, Clinton picked up some support and won nearly half of the major-party vote. The VNS poll does not present the results for whites, but it shows a similar pattern. Clinton did best among voters who had not graduated from high school, winning 59 percent of the vote to Dole's 28 percent. But Clinton's support dropped and Dole's support rose as educational levels increased. Among college graduates without advanced degrees, Dole won out over Clinton 46 percent to 44 percent. But among voters with advanced degrees, Clinton's support rose and Dole's support fell. Clinton won 52 percent of the vote among these highly educated voters, whereas Dole won 40 percent. Both the NES survey and the VNS poll show that Perot did relatively poorly among voters who had graduated from college (including those with advanced degrees).

Some scholars of American politics, such as Walter Dean Burnham and Everett Carll Ladd, argue that the Democrats now tend to fare better among upper and lower socioeconomic groups.[13] This pattern for level of education seems to support their thesis. The Democrats may be appealing to disadvantaged Americans because of their economic policies, and better-educated Americans—and especially better-educated women—may reject the interpretation of traditional values emphasized by the Republicans in recent elections.

Clinton clearly did better among union households, and the NES survey suggests that he gained 16 percentage points among white union households between 1992 and 1996. The VNS exit poll also shows Clinton doing well among union households, and he won 59 percent of their vote compared with 30 percent for Dole and 9 percent for Perot. According to our calculations, the exit poll suggests that Clinton won only 46 percent of the vote among nonunion house-holds, Dole won 44 percent, and Perot won 8 percent. The VNS survey, however, does not show major gains in union support for Clinton between 1992 and 1996, for compared with the exit poll conducted in 1992 it shows only a 4-point gain for Clinton among union households.

Religion

Religious differences, which partly reflect ethnic differences between Catholics and Protestants, have also played an important role in American politics.[14] Roman Catholics have tended to support the Democratic party, and white Protestants, especially outside the South, have tended to favor the Republicans. In all of Roosevelt's elections, and in every election through 1968, Jews strongly supported the Democratic party. Even though Jewish support for the Democrats fell after that, an absolute majority of Jews voted Democratic in every subsequent presidential election except 1980.

As Table 5-1 reveals, Clinton won a majority of the vote among white Catholics, while gaining only two out of five votes among white Protestants. According to the VNS poll, 36 percent of the white Protestants voted for Clinton, 53 percent for Dole, and 10 percent for Perot. Among white Catholics, 48 percent voted for Clinton, 41 percent for Dole, and 10 percent for Perot.[15]

The Republican appeals to traditional values may have had special appeal to religious whites. As we saw in Chapter 1, Dole managed to minimize the role of the religious right at the Republican National Convention. However, he won few concessions for moderate Republicans on the party platform. When Clinton vetoed a bill that would ban a late-term abortion procedure, Dole accused him of supporting "abortion on demand." Jack Kemp, Dole's surprising choice as a running mate, was a pro-life Republican, although he was better known for his economic policies. As Table 5-1 shows, Dole fared better among white Protestants who were "born again"; Dole won three-fifths of the vote among those who were born again, but only two-fifths of the vote among those who had not had this religious experience. As we saw in Chapter 4, white born-again Protestants are more likely to live in the South. Our analysis of the NES survey reveals that differences among Protestants are relatively small in the South. Among southern white Protestants who said they were born-again Christians ($N = 111$), only 33 percent voted for Clinton; among those who said they were not ($N = 64$), 41 percent did. Outside the South, however, differences were substantial. Among white Protestants who identified as born again ($N = 159$), 30 percent voted for Clinton; among those who were not born again ($N = 195$), 53 percent did.

As we noted in Chapter 4, David C. Leege and Lyman A. Kellstedt argue that religious commitment has an important effect on political behavior.[16] Table 5-1 reveals that white Protestants with very high levels of religious commitment were much more likely to vote for Dole than those with high, medium, or low levels of commitment. Among those with medium or low levels, Clinton gained a majority of the vote. As we noted, religious commitment is higher in the South. Religious commitment was related to the vote among white Protestants both in the South and outside the South, although the relationship was stronger outside the South. In the South, among white Protestants who pray several times a day, who attend church at least once a week, who say that religion provides "a great deal" of guidance in their lives, and who believe that the Bible is without error or the "word of God" ($N = 36$), only 30 percent voted for Clinton, whereas Dole gained 52 percent; among white Protestants outside the South with this degree of religious commitment ($N = 56$), only 20 percent voted for Clinton and 77 percent voted for Dole. In both regions, but especially outside the South, there was a substantial drop in support for Dole among white Protestants with lower levels of religious commitment.

Dole also did somewhat better among white Evangelicals than he did among white mainline Protestants. Outside the South, differences are greater. Among white Evangelicals outside the South ($N = 122$), Clinton won 38 percent of the vote and Dole won 53 percent; among white mainline Protestants outside the South ($N = 165$), Clinton gained 48 percent of the vote and Dole won 45 percent.

Many Jews had been clearly opposed to Bush's policies toward Israel, while they were more supportive of Clinton's. Moreover, many Jews may have been alienated from the Republican party because of its emphasis on conservative social values. As Table 5-1 reveals, Clinton received very strong support among Jewish voters. But because the NES survey sampled only 29 Jewish voters, we must supplement this estimate with the VNS survey, which sampled about 500 Jews. According to this survey, 78 percent of the Jews voted for Clinton, 16 percent for Dole, and 3 percent for Perot.

Although Jews remain politically distinctive, the differences between Catholics and Protestants were relatively small. However, when religion and social class are combined, our ability to predict how people will vote is improved. Because working-class voters are more likely to vote Democratic than middle-class voters, and because Catholics are more likely to vote Democratic than Protestants, the tendency to vote Democratic is highest among those who are both working class and Catholic. As Table 5-1 shows, among these voters Clinton won nearly two-thirds of the vote, whereas four years earlier he won less than half of their vote. Among middle-class Protestants, Clinton won only 36 percent of the vote, only a 5-point gain from his 1992 showing.

HOW SOCIAL GROUPS VOTED DURING THE POSTWAR YEARS

How does the 1996 election compare with other presidential elections? Were the relationships in 1996 atypical, or did they result from a long-term trend that has eroded the effect of social forces? To answer these questions we examine the voting behavior of social groups that have been an important part of the Democratic coalition during the postwar years. Our analysis begins with the 1944 presidential election contest between Roosevelt and Thomas E. Dewey and uses a simple measure of social cleavage to assess the effect of social forces over time.

In his lucid discussion of the logic of party coalitions, Robert Axelrod analyzes six basic groups that make up the Democratic presidential coalition: the poor, southerners, blacks (and other nonwhites), union members (and members of their families), Catholics and other non-Protestants, such as Jews, and residents of the twelve largest metropolitan areas.[17] John R. Petrocik's more comprehensive study identifies fifteen coalition groups and classifies seven of them as predominantly Democratic: blacks, lower-status native southerners, middle- and upper-status southerners, Jews, Polish and Irish Catholics, union members, and lower-status border state whites.[18] A more recent study by Harold W. Stanley, William T. Bianco, and Richard G. Niemi analyzes seven pro-Democratic groups: blacks, Catholics, Jews, females, native white southerners, members of union households, and the working class.[19] Our analysis focuses on race, region, union membership, social class, and religion.[20]

The contribution that a social group can make to a party's total vote depends on three factors: the relative size of the group in the total electorate; its level of turnout compared with that of the electorate; and its relative loyalty to a party.[21]

The larger a social group, the greater its contribution can be. African-Americans make up about 12 percent of the electorate, and the white working class makes up 35 percent. Thus, the potential contribution of blacks to a political party is smaller than the potential contribution of the white working class. The electoral power of blacks is diminished further by their relatively low turnout. However, because African-Americans vote overwhelmingly Democratic, their contribution to a party can be greater than their size would indicate. And the relative size of their contribution grows as whites desert the Democratic party.

Race

Let us begin by examining racial differences, which we can trace back to 1944, using the National Opinion Research Center (NORC) study for that year.[22] Figure 5-1 shows the percentage of white and black major-party voters who voted Democratic for president from 1944 through 1996. Although most African-Americans voted Democratic from 1944 through 1960, a substantial minority voted Republican. The political mobilization of blacks spurred by the civil rights movement and the Republican candidacy of Barry M. Goldwater in 1964 ended this Republican voting, and the residual Republican loyalties of older blacks were discarded between 1962 and 1964.[23]

While the Democrats made substantial gains among African-Americans, they lost ground among whites. From 1944 through 1964, the Democrats gained an absolute majority of the white vote in only two elections (1944 and 1964). Since then, they have never won an absolute majority of the white vote. However, in a two-candidate contest the Democrats can win with just under half the white

FIGURE 5-1   Percentage of Major-Party Voters Who Voted Democratic for
President, by Race, 1944–1996

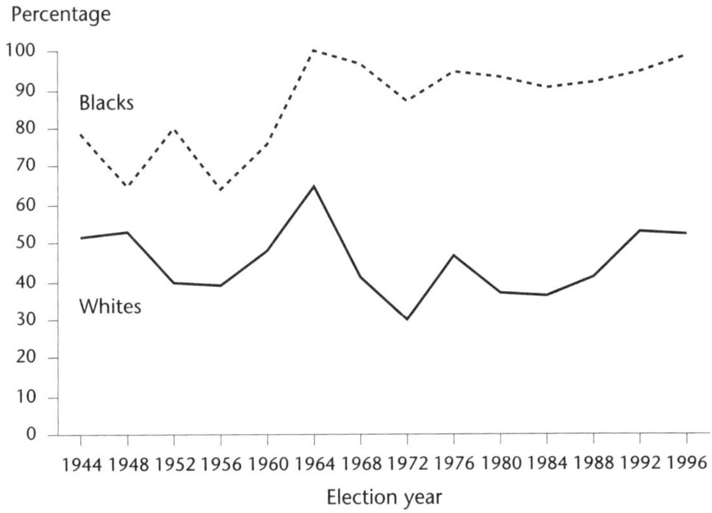

Percentage

Number of:														
Blacks	(52)	(17)	(51)	(50)	(75)[a]	(94)	(87)	(138)	(133)[a]	(105)	(129)	(122)	(188)[a]	(102)[a]
Whites	(1,564)	(364)	(1,127)	(1,213)	(1,340)[a]	(1,014)	(816)	(1,430)	(1,459)[a]	(765)	(1,220)	(1,041)	(1,134)[a]	(900)[a]

[a]These numbers are weighted.

vote, as the 1960 and 1976 elections demonstrate. In the three-way contest of
1992, Clinton was able to win with only about two-fifths of the white vote.

The gap between the two trend lines in Figure 5-1 illustrates the overall difference in the Democratic vote between whites and blacks. Table 5-2 shows overall
levels of "racial voting" in all fourteen elections; the table also presents four other
measures of social cleavage.

From 1944 through 1964 racial voting ranged from a low of 12 percent to a
high of 40 percent. Although African-American support for the Democrats
jumped in 1964, racial voting was held to 36 percentage points because a substantial majority of whites voted Democratic. But racial voting jumped to 56
percent in 1968 (to 61 percent if those who voted for George C. Wallace are
included with Nixon voters), and it did not return to the pre-1968 levels until
the three-candidate contest of 1992. Because very few blacks voted for John B.
Anderson in 1980, or for Perot in either 1992 or 1996, the racial voting score in
these elections is higher if supporters of these candidates are grouped with the
Republicans. In 1980 racial voting rose from 56 to 59 points, in 1992 it jumped
from 41 to 50 points, and in 1996 it rose from 47 points to 50 points.

Not only did African-American loyalty to the Democratic party increase
sharply after 1960, but black turnout rose dramatically from 1960 to 1968 because southern blacks (about half the black population during this period) were

TABLE 5-2 Relationship of Social Characteristics to Presidential Voting, 1944–1996

	Election year													
	1944	1948	1952	1956	1960	1964	1968	1972	1976	1980	1984	1988	1992	1996
Racial voting[a]	27	12	40	25	23	36	56	57	48	56	54	51	41	47
Regional voting[b]														
Among whites	—	—	12	17	6	-11	-4	-13	1	1	-9	-5	-10	-8
Among entire electorate (NES surveys)	—	—	9	15	4	-5	6	-3	7	3	3	2	0	0
Among entire electorate (official election results)	23	14	8	8	3	-13	-3	-11	5	2	-5	-7	-6	-7
Union voting[c]														
Among whites	20	37	18	15	21	23	13	11	18	15	20	16	12	23
Among entire electorate	20	37	20	17	19	22	13	10	17	16	19	15	11	23
Class voting[d]														
Among whites	19	44	20	8	12	19	10	2	17	9	8	5	4	6
Among entire electorate	20	44	22	11	13	20	15	4	21	15	12	8	8	9
Religious voting[e]														
Among whites	25	21	18	10	48	21	30	13	15	10	16	18	20	14
Among entire electorate	24	19	15	10	46	16	21	8	11	3	9	11	10	7

Note: All calculations are based on major-party voters.

[a] Percentage of blacks who voted Democratic minus percentage of whites who voted Democratic.
[b] Percentage of southerners who voted Democratic minus percentage of voters outside the South who voted Democratic.
[c] Percentage of members of union households who voted Democratic minus percentage of members of households with no union members who voted Democratic.
[d] Percentage of working class that voted Democratic minus percentage of middle class that voted Democratic.
[e] Percentage of Catholics who voted Democratic minus percentage of Protestants who voted Democratic.

enfranchised. Moreover, the relative size of the black population increased somewhat during the postwar years. Between 1960, when postwar turnout was at its highest, and 1996, when turnout reached its postwar low, turnout among whites dropped about 15 percentage points. But although black turnout also fell in 1996, it was still well above its levels before the Voting Rights Act of 1965.

From 1948 through 1960, African-Americans never accounted for more than one Democratic vote out of twelve. In 1964, however, Lyndon B. Johnson received about one out of seven of his votes from blacks, and blacks contributed a fifth of the Democratic totals in 1968 and 1972. In the 1976 election, which saw Democratic gains among whites, the black total fell to just over one in seven. In 1980 Jimmy Carter received about one in four of his votes from blacks, and in the next three elections about one Democratic vote in five came from blacks. In 1996, as we saw, about one-sixth of Clinton's total vote came from black voters.

Region

The desertion of the Democratic party by white southerners is among the most dramatic changes in postwar American politics. As we saw in Chapter 3, regional differences can be analyzed using official election statistics. But official election statistics are of limited usefulness in examining race-related differences in regional voting because election returns are not tabulated by race. Survey data allow us to document the dramatic shift in voting behavior of white southerners.

As the data in Figure 5-2 reveal, white southerners were somewhat more Democratic than whites outside the South in the 1952 and 1956 contests between Dwight D. Eisenhower and Adlai E. Stevenson, as they were in the 1960 contest between John F. Kennedy and Richard M. Nixon.[24] But in the next three elections, regional differences were reversed, with white southerners voting more Republican than whites outside the South. In 1976 and 1980, when the Democrats fielded Jimmy Carter of Georgia as their standard-bearer, white southerners and whites outside the South voted very much alike. In 1984 and 1988 white southerners were less likely to vote Democratic than whites in any other region. In 1992 and 1996 the Democratic presidential and vice-presidential candidates, Clinton and Al Gore, were both from the South. Even so, Bush in 1992 and Dole in 1996 did better among white southerners than among whites in any other region.

Regional differences in voting among whites from 1952 through 1996 are presented in Table 5-2. The negative signs for 1964, 1968, 1972, 1984, 1988, 1992, and 1996 reveal that the Democratic candidate fared better among white major-party voters outside the South than he did in the South. As we saw in Chapter 3, Wallace did better in the South than in any other region, whereas Anderson and Perot (in both 1992 and 1996) fared worse in the South than in any other region. If Wallace voters are included with Nixon voters, regional differences among whites increase markedly, moving from −4 to −12. Including Anderson voters with Reagan voters increases the Democratic advantage in the South from 1 to 3

FIGURE 5-2   Percentage of White Major-Party Voters Who Voted Democratic for
President, by Region, 1952–1996

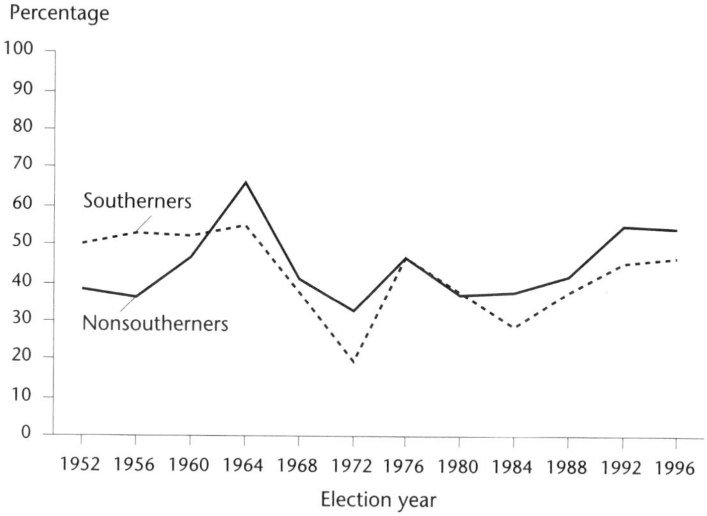

Percentage

Number of:												
Southerners	(152)	(211)	(279)[a]	(163)	(124)	(267)	(266)[a]	(203)	(221)	(198)	(238)[a]	(231)[a]
Nonsoutherners	(975)	(1,002)	(1,061)[a]	(851)	(692)	(1,163)	(1,193)[a]	(562)	(999)	(843)	(897)[a]	(669)[a]

[a]These numbers are weighted.

points, while including Perot voters with Bush voters substantially reduces the Republican advantage among whites, so that regional voting moves from –10 to –5. Including Perot voters with Dole voters, however, has little effect on regional voting among whites (it moves from –8 to –7).

Table 5-2 also presents regional voting for the entire electorate. Here, however, we include two sets of estimates: (1) NES results from 1952 through 1996 and (2) results based on official election statistics. Both sets of figures show that regional differences in voting have declined, but the NES survey somewhat overestimated the Democratic advantage in the South in 1956 and somewhat underestimated the Republican advantage in 1964 and 1972. In 1968, 1984, and 1988, the NES surveys registered a slight Democratic advantage in the South, while the official election statistics show that the Democrats actually fared better outside the South. In both 1992 and 1996 the NES results show the Republicans and Democrats faring equally in both regions, whereas the official election statistics demonstrate that the Republicans actually fared better in the South.

The mobilization of southern blacks and the defection of southern whites from the Democratic party dramatically transformed the demographic composition of the Democratic coalition in the South. Democratic presidential candidates from 1952 through 1960 never received more than one out of fifteen votes in the South from black voters. In 1964 nearly three out of ten of Johnson's southern vote came from blacks, and in 1968 Hubert H. Humphrey received nearly as many votes from southern blacks as from southern whites. In 1972, according to these data, George S. McGovern received more votes from southern blacks than from southern whites.

African-American votes were crucial to Carter's success in the South in 1976. He received about one out of three of his southern votes from blacks in 1976 and again in 1980. In 1984 Walter F. Mondale received about four in ten of his southern votes from blacks, and in 1988 about one in three of the votes Michael S. Dukakis received in the South came from blacks. About a third of Clinton's southern vote in 1992 came from black voters and in 1996 about three in ten of his southern votes came from blacks.[25]

Union Membership

Figure 5-3 shows the percentage of white union members and nonmembers who voted Democratic for president from 1944 through 1996. In all six elections from 1944 through 1964, a majority of the white union members (and their families) voted Democratic. In 1968 Humphrey received a slight majority of the major-party vote cast by white union members, although his total would be cut to 43 percent if Wallace voters were included. The Democrats won 61 percent of the white union vote in 1976, when Carter narrowly defeated Ford. In 1988 Dukakis appears to have won a slight majority of the white union vote, although he fell well short of Carter's 1976 tally. In 1992 Clinton won nearly half the white union vote, although he won about three-fifths of the major-party vote. In 1996, according to the NES survey, Clinton made major gains among union voters, winning 69 percent of the white union vote and 71 percent of the white major-party vote. Conversely, the Republicans have won a majority of the white union vote in only one of these fourteen elections, Nixon's 1972 landslide over McGovern.

Differences between union members and nonmembers are presented in Table 5-2. Because Wallace did better among union members than nonmembers, including Wallace voters with Nixon voters in 1968 reduces union voting from 13 to 10 percentage points. Including Anderson voters with Reagan voters in 1980 has little effect on union voting (it falls from 15 points to 14 points). However, in 1992 Perot did somewhat better among union members than nonmembers, and including Perot voters with Bush voters reduces union voting from 12 points to 8 points. In 1996 Perot may have done slightly better among union members than nonmembers (a relationship confirmed by both the NES and the VNS polls), and when Perot voters are combined with Dole voters, union voting falls from 23 to 20 points. We have also reported the results for the entire electorate, but because blacks are as likely to live in union households as whites, including blacks has little effect on our results.

The percentage of the total electorate composed of white union members and their families declined during the postwar years. Members of white union households made up 25 percent of the electorate in 1952; by 1996 they made up only 16 percent. Turnout among white union households has declined at about the same rate as turnout among nonunion whites. In addition, in many elections

FIGURE 5-3　Percentage of White Major-Party Voters Who Voted Democratic for President, by Union Membership, 1944–1996

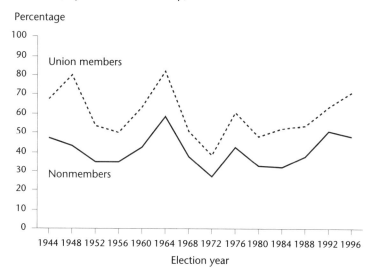

Percentage

Number of:														
Union members[a]	(332)	(94)	(305)	(334)	(342)[c]	(259)	(197)	(366)	(347)[c]	(193)	(278)	(209)	(207)[c]	(175)[c]
Nonmembers[b]	(1,215)	(266)	(815)	(877)	(979)[c]	(755)	(617)	(1,049)	(1,099)[c]	(569)	(941)	(828)	(925)[c]	(723)[c]

[a]Union members or in household with union member.
[b]Not a union member and not in household with union member.
[c]These numbers are weighted.

since 1964 the Democratic share of the union vote has been relatively low. All of these factors, as well as the increased turnout of blacks, have reduced the total contribution of white union members to the Democratic presidential coalition. Through 1960 a third of the total Democratic vote came from white trade union members and members of their families. Between 1964 and 1984 only about one Democratic vote in four came from white union members. In the last three presidential elections only about one in five Democratic presidential votes came from white union members.

Social Class

The broad cleavage in political behavior between manually employed workers (and their dependents) and nonmanually employed workers (and their dependents) is especially valuable for studying comparative voting behavior.[26] In every presidential election since 1936, the working class has voted more Democratic than the middle class. But, as Figure 5-4 shows, the percentage of working-class whites who voted Democratic has varied considerably from election to election. It fell to its lowest level in 1972. Carter regained a majority of the working-class vote in 1976, but he lost it four years later. The Democrats failed to win a major-

FIGURE 5-4   Percentage of White Major-Party Voters Who Voted Democratic for President, by Social Class, 1944–1996

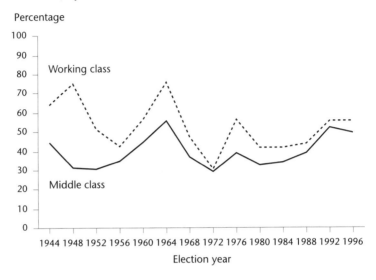

Number of:														
Working-class voters	(597)	(134)	(462)	(531)	(579)[a]	(425)	(295)	(587)	(560)[a]	(301)	(473)	(350)	(393)[a]	(279)[a]
Middle-class voters	(677)	(137)	(437)	(475)	(561)[a]	(454)	(385)	(675)	(716)[a]	(376)	(634)	(589)	(569)[a]	(507)[a]

[a]These numbers are weighted.

ity of the white working-class vote in 1984 and 1988. In 1992 Clinton won only about two-fifths of the white working-class vote, although he did win a clear majority of the major-party vote among working-class whites. In 1996 he won half of the white working-class vote and a clear majority of the major-party vote among working-class whites.

Although levels of class voting have varied since 1944, they are following a downward trend, as Table 5-2 reveals.[27] Class voting is even lower for 1968, falling to 6 points if Wallace voters are included with Nixon voters, because 15 percent of the white working-class voters supported Wallace, while only 10 percent of the white middle-class voters did. Anderson, in contrast, received little support from the working class in 1980, and including Anderson voters with Reagan voters raises class voting to 11 points. In both 1992 and 1996, Perot appears to have done somewhat better among working-class whites than among middle-class whites. Including Perot voters with Bush voters all but eliminates class voting, and working-class whites become only 1 percentage point more likely to vote Democratic than middle-class whites. Including Perot voters with Dole voters reduces class voting among whites to only 4 points.

Class voting trends are affected substantially if African-Americans are included in the analysis. Blacks are disproportionately working class and, as we have seen, they vote overwhelmingly Democratic. In all of the last six elections, including blacks increases class voting somewhat, and the overall trend toward declining class voting is dampened if we study the entire electorate. However, black workers voted Democratic because they were black, not because they were working class. Most middle-class blacks also voted Democratic. In 1996, for example, among the thirty-nine black middle-class voters in the NES survey, 95 percent voted Democratic; among the forty-eight black working-class voters, 96 percent did. It seems reasonable, therefore, to focus on changing levels of class voting among the white electorate.

During the postwar years the proportion of the electorate made up of working-class whites has remained relatively constant, while that of middle-class whites has grown. The percentage of whites in the agricultural sector has declined dramatically. Turnout fell among both social classes after 1960, but it fell more among the working class. As we saw in Chapter 4, only 70 percent of the white working class claimed to have voted in 1996, while 83 percent of the white middle class did. Declining turnout and defections from the Democrats by working-class whites, along with increased turnout by blacks, have reduced the total contribution of working-class whites to the Democratic presidential coalition.

In 1948 and 1952 about half of the total Democratic presidential vote came from working-class whites, and from 1956 through 1964 more than four out of ten Democratic votes came from this social group. In 1968 the total white working-class contribution fell to just over a third and then to under a third in 1972. In 1976, with the rise of class voting, the white working class provided nearly two-fifths of Carter's total vote, but in 1980 just over a third of Carter's total vote came from working-class whites. In 1984 over a third of Mondale's total support came from working-class whites. In 1988 just over a fourth of Dukakis's total support came from the white working class. In both 1992 and 1996 three out of ten of Clinton's total votes came from working-class whites. The middle-class contribution to the Democratic presidential coalition amounted to fewer than three votes in ten in 1948 and 1952, and just under one-third in 1956, stabilizing at just over one-third in the next five elections. In 1980 a third of Carter's total vote came from middle-class whites. In 1984 Mondale received just under two out of five votes from middle-class whites, and in 1988 Dukakis gained just over two out of five. In 1992 more than two out of five votes for Clinton came from middle-class whites and in 1996 nearly half of his votes came from this group. In each of the last four presidential elections, the Democrats have received a larger share of their total vote from middle-class whites than from the white working class. The growing middle-class contribution to the Democratic presidential coalition results from two factors: first, the middle class is growing; and, second, class differences are eroding. The decline in class differences in voting behavior may be part of a widespread phenomenon that is occurring in most advanced industrial societies.[28]

Religion

Voting differences among the major religious groups have also declined during the postwar years. Even so, as Figure 5-5 reveals, in every election since 1944, Jews have been more likely to vote Democratic than Catholics, and Catholics have been more likely to vote Democratic than Protestants.

FIGURE 5-5 Percentage of White Major-Party Voters Who Voted Democratic for President, by Religion, 1944–1996

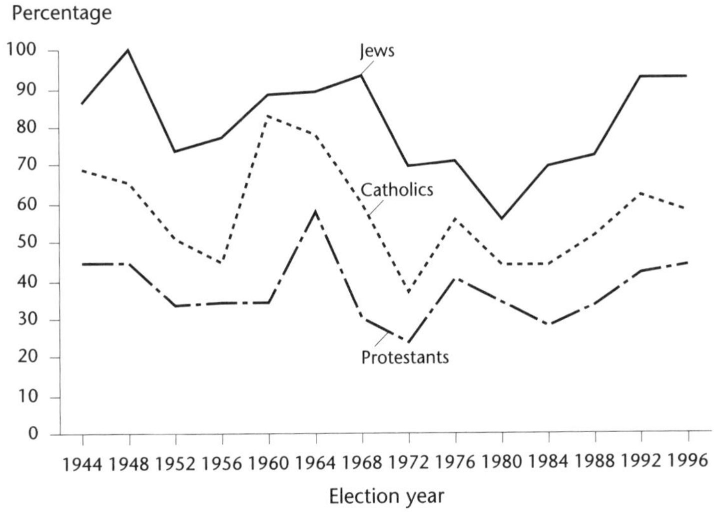

Number of:	1944	1948	1952	1956	1960	1964	1968	1972	1976	1980	1984	1988	1992	1996
Jews	(74)	(19)	(46)	(53)	(53)[a]	(36)	(29)	(36)	(41)[a]	(25)	(36)	(22)	(33)[a]	(25)[a]
Catholics	(311)	(101)	(284)	(288)	(309)[a]	(267)	(206)	(384)	(378)[a]	(188)	(360)	(287)	(301)[a]	(279)[a]
Protestants	(1,183)	(222)	(770)	(841)	(957)[a]	(674)	(533)	(938)	(959)[a]	(490)	(709)	(641)	(642)[a]	(490)[a]

[a]These numbers are weighted.

A large majority of Jews voted Democratic in every election from 1944 through 1968, and, although the Jewish vote for the Democrats dropped in Nixon's 1972 landslide, even McGovern won a majority of the Jewish vote. In 1980 many Jews (like many gentiles) were dissatisfied with Carter's performance as president, and some resented the pressure that he had exerted on Israel to accept the Camp David peace accord, which returned the Sinai Peninsula—captured by Israel in 1967—to Egypt. A substantial minority of Jews voted for Anderson, but Carter still outpolled Reagan among Jewish voters. Both Mondale in 1984 and Dukakis (whose wife, Kitty, is Jewish) in 1988 won a clear majority of the Jewish vote. And the Jewish vote for the Democrats surged in 1992, with Clinton winning about nine out of ten of the major-party votes. In 1996, as we saw, Clinton again won overwhelming Jewish support.

A majority of white Catholics voted Democratic in six of the seven elections from 1944 through 1968. The percentage of Catholics voting Democratic peaked in 1960, when the Democrats fielded a Roman Catholic candidate, and it was still very high in Johnson's landslide victory four years later. Since then, Democratic voting among Catholics has declined precipitously. In 1968 a majority of white Catholics voted Democratic, although Humphrey's total among white Catholics would be reduced from 60 to 55 percent if Wallace voters were included.

In 1992 Clinton won a majority of the major-party vote among white Catholics (see Figure 5-5), and in 1996 he won just over half of the total white Catholic vote, and a clear majority of the major-party vote.

Our simple measure of religious voting shows considerable change from election to election, although there was a clear downward trend through 1980 (see Table 5-2). Even though white Protestants were more likely to vote for Wallace in 1968 than white Catholics were, including Wallace voters in our totals has little effect on relative levels of religious voting (the measure falls from 30 to 29 points). Including Anderson voters has no effect on religious differences. In 1992, however, Perot did somewhat better among white Catholics than among white Protestants, and if Perot voters are included with Republican voters, religious voting falls from 20 to 14 points. Both the NES survey and the VNS exit poll reveal that Perot did equally well among white Protestants and white Catholics in 1996, and including Perot voters with Dole voters has little effect on religious voting (it falls from 14 to 13 points).

Including African-Americans in our calculations substantially reduces religious voting. Blacks are much more likely to be Protestant than Catholic, and including blacks adds a substantial number of Protestant Democrats. The effect of including blacks is greater from 1968 on because black turnout has been higher. In 1996 religious voting is reduced from 14 to 7 points if blacks are included.

The Jewish contribution to the Democratic coalition has declined, partly because Jews did not vote overwhelmingly Democratic from 1972 through 1988, and partly because the proportion of Jews in the electorate declined. From 1972 through 1988, Jews made up only about a twentieth of the Democratic presidential coalition. Despite the upsurge in Jewish Democratic voting in 1992, the NES survey shows that Clinton received only 4 percent of his total vote from Jews, although the major exit poll conducted by Voter Research and Surveys in 1992 suggests that 7 percent of his total vote came from Jews. The 1996 NES survey again shows that 4 percent of Clinton's total vote came from Jews, and the VNS survey suggests that 5 percent did. But although Jews make up only 2.3 percent of the population, over three-fourths of the nation's Jews live in seven large states (New York, California, Florida, New Jersey, Pennsylvania, Illinois, and Massachusetts), which combine for 184 electoral votes.[29]

White Catholics make up just over a fifth of the electorate, and this proportion has remained relatively constant during the postwar years. However, since 1960, turnout has declined more among white Catholics than among white Protestants. As Figure 5-5 shows, the proportion of Catholics voting Democratic has declined, although the Democratic share of the major-party vote increased after 1984. Even so, between 1980 and 1992 the Democrats failed to win an absolute majority of the white Catholic vote, and they won a bare majority in 1996. In addition, increased turnout among blacks has tended to lower the overall contribution of white Catholics to the Democratic coalition.

According to our estimates based on the NES surveys, Harry S. Truman received about a third of his total vote from white Catholics. Stevenson won three-tenths of his vote from white Catholics in 1952 but received only a fourth of his votes from Catholics in 1956. In 1960 Kennedy received 37 percent of his vote from white Roman Catholics, but the Catholic contribution fell to just below three out of ten votes when Johnson defeated Goldwater in 1964. In 1968 three-tenths of Humphrey's total vote came from white Roman Catholics, but only a fourth of McGovern's vote came from white Catholics. Just over a fourth of Carter's vote came from white Catholics in his 1976 victory, but in his loss to Reagan just over a fifth came from this source. Mondale received just under three out of ten votes from white Catholics, and in 1988 Dukakis received a fourth of his vote from this group. According to our estimates based on the NES survey, just under a fourth of Clinton's total vote came from white Catholics in 1992. Our analysis of the 1996 NES survey suggests that just over a fourth (27 percent) of Clinton's total vote came from white Catholics, and our estimates based on the VNS exit poll also reveal that over a fourth of his total vote (28 percent) came from white Roman Catholics.

As the data in Figure 5-6 reveal, the effects of social class and religion are cumulative. In every election from 1944 through 1996, working-class Catholics have been more likely to vote Democratic than any other class-religion combination. In all fourteen elections, white middle-class Protestants have been the least likely to vote Democratic. They are more constant over time than any other group we have

FIGURE 5-6   Percentage of White Major-Party Voters Who Voted Democratic for President, by Social Class and Religion, 1944–1996

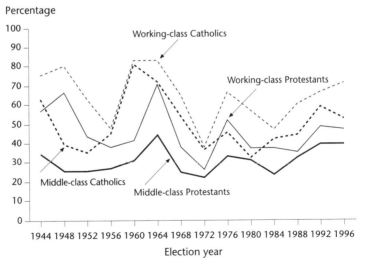

Number of:													
Working-class Catholics	(152)	(61)	(158)	(168)	(179)[a]	(126)	(83)	(176)	(163)[a]	(76)	(156)	(100)	(100)[a]	(86)[a]
Middle-class Catholics	(130)	(28)	(94)	(96)	(109)[a]	(121)	(96)	(176)	(179)[a]	(96)	(177)	(164)	(166)[a]	(167)[a]
Working-class Protestants	(405)	(59)	(279)	(329)	(374)[a]	(280)	(198)	(383)	(367)[a]	(197)	(286)	(218)	(234)[a]	(159)[a]
Middle-class Protestants	(479)	(91)	(302)	(336)	(405)[a]	(287)	(254)	(430)	(457)[a]	(226)	(359)	(349)	(303)[a]	(256)[a]

[a]These numbers are weighted.

studied. An absolute majority voted Republican in every election from 1944 through 1988, and Bush won nearly half of their vote in the three-way contest of 1992. In 1996 Dole captured an absolute majority of the vote among white middle-class Protestants and won three-fifths of the major-party vote.

The relative importance of social class and religion can be assessed by comparing the voting behavior of middle-class Catholics with that of working-class Protestants. Religion was more important than social class in predicting voting choices in 1944, 1956, 1960 (by a considerable margin), 1968, 1972, 1984, 1988, 1992, and 1996. Social class was more important than religion in 1948 (by a great margin), 1952, 1976, and 1980. And class and religion were equally important in 1964. However, beginning in 1968 all of these trend lines began to converge, suggesting that traditional sources of social cleavage are declining in importance.

WHY THE NEW DEAL COALITION BROKE DOWN

Except for race, which increased in importance after 1960, all of the social factors we have examined have declined in importance during the postwar years, although there was some resurgence in the importance of union membership in 1996. The decline in regional differences directly parallels the increase in racial differences. As the national Democratic party strengthened its appeals to African-Americans during the 1960s, party leaders endorsed policies opposed by southern whites, and many of those voters deserted the Democratic party. The migration of northern whites to the South may have also reduced regional differences somewhat.

The Democratic party's appeals to blacks may also have weakened its hold on white groups that traditionally supported it. Robert Huckfeldt and Carol Weitzel Kohfeld clearly demonstrate that Democratic appeals to blacks weakened the party's support among working-class whites.[30] But the erosion of Democratic support among union members, the working class, and Catholics results from other factors as well. During the postwar years, these groups have changed. Although union members do not hold high-paying professional and managerial jobs, they have gained substantial economic advantages. Differences in income between the working class and the middle class have diminished. And Catholics, who often came from more recent immigrant groups than Protestants, have become increasingly middle class as the proportion of second- and third-generation Catholic Americans has become larger, a trend only partly offset by the growing number of white Catholic Hispanics. During the 1950s and 1960s white Catholics were more likely to be working class than were white Protestants. This is no longer true. In 1976, 1980, and 1984 they were just as likely as white Protestants to be middle class, and in the last three elections they were somewhat more likely to be middle class than white Protestants were.

Not only have these groups changed economically and socially, but the historical conditions that led union members, the working class, and Catholics to become Democrats have receded further into the past. While the transmission of partisan loyalties from generation to generation gives historically based coalitions some staying power, the ability of the family to transmit party loyalties has decreased as party identification has weakened.[31] Moreover, with the passage of time, the proportion of the electorate that directly experienced the Roosevelt years has progressively declined. By 1996 only one voter in nine had entered the electorate before or during World War II. New policy issues, often unrelated to the traditional political conflicts of the New Deal, have tended to erode party loyalties among traditional Democratic groups. Edward G. Carmines and James A. Stimson provide strong evidence that race-related issues have been crucial in weakening the New Deal coalition.[32]

Despite the breakdown of the New Deal coalition, the Democrats managed to win the presidency in 1992, and again in 1996. In his 1992 victory, Clinton boosted the Democratic share of the major-party vote among union members, the white working class, Roman Catholics, and even white southerners. Clinton focused on his appeal to middle America, and in both 1992 and 1996 he paid as low a price as possible to gain the black vote. Clinton's victory in 1992 was the first Democratic victory in which blacks made up more than 15 percent of the Democratic coalition. In 1996 he once again won with over 15 percent of his vote coming from blacks. But in 1992, and to a lesser extent in 1996, the white vote was split among three candidates. Our calculations suggest that it would be difficult for the Democrats to win a two-candidate contest in which blacks made up one-fifth or more of their total coalition.

Clinton's victory in 1992 seemed to provide an opportunity to forge a new Democratic coalition, which might have been partly based on some of the components of the old New Deal coalition. But after the Democratic losses of the U.S. House and Senate in the 1994 midterm election, Clinton developed more of a reactive strategy that focused mainly on moving toward the political center. In some respects, he partly revitalized the New Deal coalition, primarily because of the effort of union leaders to end the Republican control of Congress. As a lame-duck president, Clinton's ability to forge a new coalition may be limited. Perhaps, as James Ceaser and Andrew Busch have argued, new coalitions will be formed based on common issue positions rather than the type of demographic groups that both politicians and political scientists employ.[33] Turning to the issue preferences of the electorate provides an opportunity to assess how a Democratic coalition can be forged, and may also suggest strategies that the Republicans can employ to capture the presidency.

Chapter 6

Candidates, Issues, and the Vote

In Chapter 5 we discussed the relationship between various social forces and the vote. The impact of such forces on the vote is indirect. Even though the Democratic New Deal coalition was constructed from members of different groups, people who were members of these groups did not vote for Democrats simply because they were African-Americans, white southerners, union members, Roman Catholics, or Jews. Rather, they usually voted Democratic because that party offered symbolic and substantive policies that appealed to the concerns of members of these groups, because the party nominated candidates who were attractive to members of these groups, and because the party's platforms and candidates were consistent enough that many voters developed long-term partisan loyalties. The long-term decline in class voting, for example, is evidence of the decreasing importance members of the working and middle classes assign to the differences between the parties on concerns that divide blue-collar and white-collar workers. And as we also saw, the changes in such voting patterns from election to election reflect differences in the attractiveness of the candidates and policies the two parties offer and the changing circumstances that have made the parties' appeals more or less important in any given election campaign. That race is the sharpest political division in American politics today does not mean that blacks vote Democratic simply because they are black; as Supreme Court Justice Clarence Thomas and Rep. J. C. Watts (R-Okla.) exemplify, African-Americans may also be conservative ideologically and may identify with and vote for Republicans.

In this and the next two chapters, we examine some of the concerns that underlie voters' choices, connecting the indirect relationship between group membership and the vote. Even though, as we shall see, scholars and politicians disagree among themselves about what factors voters employ, and how they employ them, there is general consensus on several points. First, voters' attitudes or preferences determine their choices. There may be disagreement over exactly which attitudes shape behavior, but most agree that voters deliberately choose to support the candidate they believe will make the best president. There is also general agreement that the most important attitudes in shaping the vote are attitudes toward the candidates, the issues, and the parties.[1]

In this chapter, we first look briefly at the relationship between a measure of candidate evaluations and the vote. In this brief analysis we ignore two of the major components underlying these evaluations: voters' perceptions of the candidates' personal qualities and voters' perceptions of the candidates' professional qualifications and competence to serve as president.[2] As we shall see, there is a very powerful relationship between these summary evaluations of candidates and the vote. It might seem obvious that voters support the candidate they like best, but the presence of a third candidate illustrates the complicated nature of voters' decision making. It appears that in 1992 and 1996 some people may not have voted for the candidate they rated most highly, instead supporting one whom they thought had a better chance of winning, thus seeking to block the election of the candidate they liked least. Voters who do not vote for their first preference for these reasons are called sophisticated or strategic voters.[3]

In a three-way race, it is also possible for the candidate who wins with a plurality of the vote to have been opposed by the majority of the electorate who had divided their vote between the other two contenders. We can use our measures of attitudes toward the candidates to investigate whether this appeared to happen in 1996; we find that Bill Clinton would apparently have been the preferred candidate of a majority if he had run against either Bob Dole or H. Ross Perot alone.

The simple measure of attitudes toward the candidates is, we believe, the most direct influence on the vote itself; helping to shape those attitudes are attitudes toward the issues and the parties. Thus, the first part of our investigation concerns the role of issues. After analyzing what problems most concerned the voters in 1996, we discuss the two basic forms of issue voting, which are referred to as voting based on "prospective" and "retrospective" issues. In this chapter, we investigate the impact of prospective issues. We consider one of the controversies about issue voting: how much information the public has about issues and candidates' positions on them. Our analyses indicate the significance of prospective issues in 1996, and we can make some comparisons of their impact as shown in earlier election surveys. Chapter 7 examines retrospective issues and the vote, and Chapter 8 examines partisan identification and assesses the significance of parties and issues, together, on voting in 1996 and in earlier elections.

ATTITUDES TOWARD THE CANDIDATES

Overall Ratings of the Candidates

Voters faced three major choices in the 1996 election, which makes that election comparable to three other recent elections for which there are National Election

FIGURE 6-1   The "Feeling Thermometer" Shown to Respondents When They Are
Asked to Rate Individuals and Groups

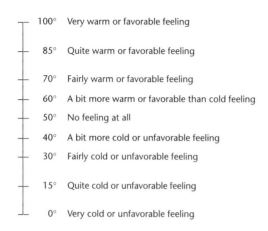

100°   Very warm or favorable feeling

85°   Quite warm or favorable feeling

70°   Fairly warm or favorable feeling

60°   A bit more warm or favorable than cold feeling

50°   No feeling at all

40°   A bit more cold or unfavorable feeling

30°   Fairly cold or unfavorable feeling

15°   Quite cold or unfavorable feeling

0°   Very cold or unfavorable feeling

Source: 1996 National Election Studies, Pre-Election Survey, Respondent Booklet.

Study (NES) surveys, 1968, 1980, and 1992.[4] It seems reasonable to assume that voters support the candidate whom they believe would make the best president. This close relationship can be illustrated by analysis of a measure in the NES surveys called the feeling thermometer. We have reproduced in Figure 6-1 the drawing shown to each respondent. This measure produces a scale that runs from 0 through 100 degrees, with zero indicating very "cold" or negative feelings, 50 indicating neutral feelings, and 100 indicating the "warmest" or most positive evaluation.

In the past, voters knew less about the third candidate than about the nominees of the two major parties. Therefore, fewer respondents ranked third candidates on the thermometer scales, and more of those rated them at the exact neutral point. For example, in the preelection measurement in 1980, 14 percent did not rate John B. Anderson, about three times as many as did not rate Jimmy Carter or Ronald Reagan; in the postelection survey 9 percent failed to rate Anderson, but only 2 percent or fewer failed to rate Carter or Reagan. Many respondents rated Anderson at exactly the neutral point, twice as many as rated Reagan at 50 degrees and more than twice as many as rated Carter at 50 degrees. This lack of voter knowledge was less true of Perot in 1992 and 1996, presumably because of the extremely expensive media advertising campaign he ran in 1992 and the heavier than usual media coverage of him. Still, in 1992, 7 percent did not rate Perot on the preelection feeling thermometer, whereas only 2 percent did not rate Clinton and 1 percent did not rate George Bush. In 1996 only 3 percent did not rate Perot on the preelection feeling thermometer, compared with under 2 percent who failed to rate Dole and less than 1 percent who failed to rate the now-incumbent Clinton. Still, in 1996, respondents appeared to have weak, ambivalent, or indifferent feelings about Perot. In 1992, 24 percent rated Perot at exactly 50 degrees (compared with 15 percent rating Clinton and 14 percent rating Bush at 50 degrees). In 1996 a full 30 percent rated Perot at exactly 50 degrees (the comparable Dole and Clinton figures are 17 and only 7 percent, respectively).

Were Voters "Sophisticated"?

The comparative ranking of the candidates on these scales is usually a very accurate reflection of the vote. Table 6-1 reports the candidate ranked highest by voters in the 1996 postelection survey and the candidate they supported. Included as well are comparable figures from the 1968, 1980, and 1992 NES surveys. In all four cases, those who rated a major-party nominee highest overwhelmingly voted for that candidate. The lowest proportion was the 93 percent who rated Bush highest and voted for him in 1992. In all cases, however, the third candidate fared more poorly. Of those who rated Perot highest in 1996, only 61 percent actually voted for him, a proportion quite comparable to that achieved by Anderson in 1980. These results strongly suggest that at least some voters who preferred Perot strategically voted for Clinton or, more frequently, for Dole.

The most obvious problem facing an independent or third-party candidate is how to attract more of a following, but there is a second obstacle: people find it hard to justify voting for their preferred candidate if they believe he or she has very little chance to win. Many people are unwilling to "waste" their vote. Perot was aware of this fact in 1992 and tried to counter it with the slogan, "Don't waste your vote on politics as usual." The logic against "wasting" votes is a problem faced by third parties in many elections. There is strong evidence that some voters in Canada and Britain, for example, choose not to vote for the party they prefer.[5] Moreover, some voters in U.S. presidential nomination contests also vote for candidates who are not their first choice.[6]

In July 1992 Perot justified his temporary withdrawal from the contest partly on the grounds that he could not win. Perot had just taken the (plurality) lead in the polls, but he argued that his candidacy might lead to a deadlock in which no candidate won a majority of the electoral vote. The U.S. House of Representatives would then need to elect the president, and the House had not chosen a president since it picked John Quincy Adams in 1825 (under the cloud of an alleged "corrupt bargain"). Having the House choose the president, Perot argued, would be "disruptive." In 1996 he never achieved the popular following he had in 1992, and many Americans believed he had no chance of winning.

Independent or third-party presidential candidates such as Perot do not bear the imprimatur of one of the two major parties and the web of support that the label entails. Without a major-party nomination, candidates find it difficult even to recruit a credible running mate. In 1968 Wallace picked a running mate, Gen. Curtis LeMay, whose lack of political experience led him to make statements in

TABLE 6-1   Candidate Thermometer Rankings and the Vote, 1968, 1980, 1992, and 1996 (in percentages)

First place in thermometer rating

A. Voted for in 1968	Nixon	Humphrey	Wallace	Total	(N)
Nixon	96	2	2	100	(418)
Humphrey	2	97	1	100	(353)
Wallace	15	1	84	100	(107)
N-H tie	39	60	2	100	(67)
W-N tie	[4]	—	[5]	—	(9)
W-H tie	—	[3]	—	—	(3)
3-way tie	[3]	[4]	[2]	—	(9)

B. Voted for in 1980	Reagan	Carter	Anderson	Total	(N)
Reagan	97	2	1	100	(409)
Carter	3	97	—	100	(253)
Anderson	18	25	57	100	(111)
R-C tie	40	60	—	100	(40)
A-R tie	88	3	9	100	(34)
A-C tie	7	67	26	100	(27)
3-way tie	24	64	12	100	(25)

C. Voted for in 1992	Bush	Clinton	Perot	Total	(N)[a]
Bush	93	2	6	101	(485)
Clinton	2	95	3	100	(685)
Perot	10	13	77	100	(258)
B-C tie	49	42	8	99	(72)
P-B tie	45	2	52	99	(48)
P-C tie	5	57	38	100	(76)
3-way tie	20	44	37	101	(27)

D. Voted for in 1996	Dole	Clinton	Perot	Total	(N)[a]
Dole	97	3	0	100	(342)
Clinton	3	95	2	100	(533)
Perot	33	6	61	100	(84)
D-C tie	45	49	5	99	(73)
P-D tie	88	9	3	100	(34)
P-C tie	—	48	52	100	(23)
3-way tie	35	29	35	99	(17)

[a]Numbers are weighted.

support of the possible use of nuclear weapons in Vietnam. James Stockdale, who had been a prisoner of war in North Vietnam, was Perot's running mate in 1992, and his lack of political experience also was a liability.[7] Perot's choice in 1996, Pat Choate, was not a liability, but he was perhaps the least well known of these third-party vice-presidential nominees. Wallace in 1968 and Anderson in 1980 faced great financial difficulties. Perot had no financial problems, which may partly account for his relatively high name recognition and popular-vote success in 1992. This made his decision, based on his 1992 showing, to accept the relatively meager federal funding(which barred him from spending his own money), in 1996 so difficult to understand.

Perot in 1992 was a very successful candidate, at least in regard to the popular vote. In a three-candidate race, a candidate opposed by a majority may, by virtue of the rules governing presidential elections, nonetheless win. William H. Riker argues that Woodrow Wilson, the Democratic standard-bearer in 1912, was such a candidate. A majority may have preferred William Howard Taft, the Republican incumbent, to Wilson, and a majority may have preferred Theodore Roosevelt, a former Republican president running under the Progressive or "Bull Moose" party label, to Wilson. With the vote for the other two candidates split, Wilson won with a plurality vote (approximately the same as Bill Clinton's in 1992), which became an electoral college majority by virtue of the states' winner-take-all rule.[8]

As there were no studies of the attitudes of American voters in 1912, we will never know whether Riker's conjectures about that election are correct. By using the feeling thermometers employed in the 1996 NES survey, however, we can at least indirectly determine how Clinton would have done in a two-candidate race against Dole or Perot. Because these thermometer scores are so strongly related to the vote, they can be used to run three mock elections—one pairing Clinton against Dole, another pairing Clinton against Perot, and a third pairing Dole against Perot. Our results, using both the preelection and postelection measurements of the candidate thermometer ratings, are presented in Table 6-2.

In both polls, Clinton was preferred to Dole by a comfortable majority, while only one in three rated Dole over Clinton. When we paired Clinton against Perot, two in three voters ranked Clinton higher than Perot in the preelection and postelection interviews. Table 6-2 also suggests that Dole would have defeated Perot handily. Our main conclusion, therefore, is that Clinton would have been the winner, perhaps an easy winner, in a head-to-head contest against either candidate. The electoral college did not yield a pernicious result. Most social choice theorists would agree with the Marquis de Condorcet that if there is an outcome that would be preferred by a majority over any other alternative, that outcome should be selected. In this sense, Clinton was a Condorcet winner.[9] Although Clinton won just over two out of five votes in 1992, it appears that he was the Condorcet winner in that election. Likewise, Nixon was very likely the Condorcet winner in 1968, and Reagan was the Condorcet winner in 1980.[10]

TABLE 6-2   Comparative Thermometer Ratings of the Candidates, 1996
(Head-to-Head Comparisons, in percentages)

	Clinton versus Dole		Clinton versus Perot		Dole versus Perot	
A. Preelection Survey, Candidate Rated First						
	Clinton	57	Clinton	67	Dole	60
	Tie	9	Tie	9	Tie	14
	Dole	34	Perot	25	Perot	26
	Total %	100	Total %	101	Total %	100
	(N)[a]	(1,680)	(N)[a]	(1,659)	(N)[a]	(1,646)
B. Postelection Survey, Candidate Rated First						
	Clinton	56	Clinton	65	Dole	57
	Tie	11	Tie	9	Tie	17
	Dole	33	Perot	26	Perot	26
	Total %	100	Total %	100	Total %	101
	(N)[a]	(1,504)	(N)[a]	(1,489)	(N)[a]	(1,486)

[a]Numbers are weighted.

RETROSPECTIVE AND PROSPECTIVE EVALUATIONS

Behind these overall evaluations of the candidates are the public's attitudes toward the issues and toward parties (as well as more specific evaluations of the candidates). We begin by considering the role of issues in elections. Concerns about public policy enter into the voting decision in two very different ways. In an election in which an incumbent is running, two questions become important: How has the incumbent president done on policy? And how likely is it that his opponent (or opponents) would do any better? Voting based on this form of policy appraisal is called retrospective voting and is analyzed in Chapter 7.

The second form of policy-based voting involves an examination of the policy platforms advanced by the candidates and an assessment of which candidate's policy promises are most similar to what the voter believes the government should be doing. Policy voting, therefore, involves comparing sets of promises and voting for the set that is most like the voter's own preferences. Voting based on these kinds of decisions may be referred to as prospective voting, for it involves examining the promises of the candidates about future actions. In this chapter, we examine prospective evaluations of the two major-party candidates and how these evaluations relate to voter choice.

The last five elections show some remarkable similarities in prospective evaluations and voting. Perhaps the most important similarity is the perception of where the Democratic and Republican candidates stood on issues. In these five elections, the public saw clear differences between the major-party nominees. In all cases, the public saw the Republican candidates as conservative on most issues, and most citizens scored them as more conservative than the voters rated themselves as being. And in all five elections the public saw the Democratic candidates as being liberal on most issues, and most citizens viewed them as more liberal than the voters rated themselves as being. As a result, many voters perceived a clear choice based on their understanding of the candidates' policy positions. The candidates presented, in the 1964 campaign slogan of Republican nominee Barry M. Goldwater, "a choice, not an echo." The *average* citizen, however, faced a difficult choice. For many, the Democratic nominees were considered to be as far to the left as the Republicans were to the right. On balance, the net effect of prospective issues was to give neither party a clear advantage.

There were also important differences among these elections. One of the most important of these was the mixture of issues that concerned the public. Each election presented its own mixture of policy concerns. Moreover, the general strategies of the candidates on issues differed in each election.[11] In 1980 Jimmy Carter's incumbency was marked by a general perception that he was unable to solve pressing concerns. Reagan attacked that weakness both directly (for example, by the question he posed to the public during his debate with Carter, "Are you better off today than you were four years ago?") and indirectly. The indirect attack was oriented more to the future. Reagan set forth a clear set of proposals designed to convince the public that he would be more likely to solve the nation's problems because he had his own proposals to end soaring inflation, to strengthen the United States militarily, and to regain respect and influence for the United States abroad.

In 1984 Reagan was perceived to be a far more successful president than Carter had been. He chose to run a campaign focused primarily on the theme of how much better things were by 1984 (as illustrated by his advertising slogan, "It's morning in America"). Mondale attacked that claim by arguing that Reagan's policies were unfair and by pointing to the rapidly growing budget deficit. Reagan's counter to Walter F. Mondale's pledge to increase taxes to reduce the deficit was that he, Reagan, would not raise taxes, and that Mondale would do so only to spend them on increased government programs (or, in his words, that Mondale was another "tax and spend, tax and spend" Democrat).

The 1988 campaign was more similar to the 1984 than to the 1980 campaign. Bush continued to run on the successes of the Reagan-Bush administration and promised no new taxes ("Read my lips," he said. "No new taxes!"). Michael S. Dukakis initially attempted to portray the election as one about "competence" rather than "ideology," arguing that he had demonstrated his competence as governor of Massachusetts. By competent management, he would be able to solve the budget and trade deficit problems, for example. Bush, by implication, was less competent. Bush countered that it really was an election about ideology, and that Dukakis was just another *liberal* Democrat from Massachusetts.

The 1992 election presented yet another type of campaign. Bush initially hoped to be able to run as the president who presided over the "new world order," the post-Soviet world, and he used the success of the Gulf war to augment his claim that he was a successful world leader. Clinton attacked the Bush administration on domestic issues, however, barely discussing foreign affairs at all. He sought to keep the electorate focused on the current economic woes, seeking to get the nation moving again. He also argued for substantial reforms of the health care system, and he raised a number of other issues that he expected to appeal to Democrats and to serve as the basis for action, should he become the first Democrat in the White House in twelve years. At the same time, he sought to portray himself not as another "tax and spend" liberal Democrat, but as a moderate, "New Democrat."

In 1996, as we discuss in Chapter 2, Clinton ran a campaign typical of a popular incumbent, focusing on what led people to approve of his handling of the presidency and avoiding speaking of too many specific new programs. Although he had a catchy slogan (handed to him by Dole), "building a bridge to the twenty-first century," his policy proposals were a fairly lengthy series of relatively inexpensive programs that were small in scope. Dole, having difficulty deciding whether to emphasize Clinton's personal failings in the first term or to call for different programs for the future, nonetheless put a significant tax cut proposal at the center of his candidacy.

Each of these general overviews of campaign strategies illustrates prospective and retrospective strategies. All incumbent-party nominees were held accountable for the failings of the current administration by their challengers, and in 1984, 1988, and 1996, the incumbent emphasized his and his party's successes. These were clearly retrospective strategies. But prospective promises also figured prominently in each contest. The challengers in all cases relied heavily on promises of what they would do in office, and all incumbent party candidates attacked those promises. If voters respond to the campaigns of the candidates, we might expect, therefore, to find that both retrospective and prospective policy concerns figure prominently in their decisions.[12]

THE CONCERNS OF THE ELECTORATE

The first question to ask about prospective voting is what kinds of concerns moved the public. The NES surveys ask, "What do you personally feel are the most important problems the government in Washington should try to take care of?" In Table 6-3 we have listed the percentage of responses to what respondents claimed was the single most important problem in broad categories of concerns over the seven most recent elections.[13]

In 1996 the public was far more concerned about domestic issues than about foreign or defense policies. The low levels of concern about the latter might be due to the end of the Cold War, but not only was concern over these questions

TABLE 6-3 Most Important Problem as Seen by the Electorate, 1972–1996 (in percentages)

Problem	1972	1976	1980	1984	1988	1992	1996
Economics	*27*	*76*	*56*	*49*	*45*	*64*	*29*
Unemployment/recession	9	33	10	16	5	23	7
Inflation/prices	14	27	33	5	2	—[a]	—[a]
Deficit/government spending	1	9	3	19	32	16	13
Social issues	*34*	*14*	*7*	*13*	*38*	*28*	*56*
Social welfare	7	4	3	9	11	17	33
Public order	20	8	1	4	19	10	23
Foreign and defense	*31*	*4*	*32*	*34*	*10*	*3*	*5*
Foreign	4	3	9	17	6	2	3
Defense	1	1	8	17	3	1	2
Functioning of government (competence, corruption, trust, power, etc.)	*4*	*4*	*2*	*2*	*1*	*2*	*5*
All others	*4*	*3*	*3*	*3*	*6*	*2*	*4*
Total	*100*	*101*	*100*	*101*	*100*	*100*	*100*
(N)	(842)	(2,337)	(1,352)	(1,780)	(1,657)	(2,003)	(794)
"Missing"	(63)	(203)	(56)	(163)	(118)	(54)	(27)
Percent Missing	7	7	4	7	7	2	4

Notes: Foreign in 1972 includes 25 percent who cited Vietnam. Foreign in 1980 includes 15 percent who cited Iran. Questions asked of randomly selected half sample in 1972 and 1996. Weighted *N* in 1976, 1992, and 1996. All of the subcategories are not included. The total percentages for the subcategories, therefore, will not equal the percentages for the main categories. In 1984 total *N* is 1,543 because 46 respondents were not asked this question, being given a shortened postelection questionnaire. In 1992 the total *N* is 2,487, because 431 respondents either had no postelection interview or were given a shortened form via telephone.

[a] Less than 1 percent of responses.

low in the last three elections, it also was low in 1976, well before the Cold War ended.

The great majority of responses, therefore, concerned domestic issues. In the last seven elections, two major categories of domestic issues dominated. From 1976 through 1992, in good times and bad, by far the more commonly cited was a concern about the economy. In 1972 and 1996 the most frequently cited problems were in the social issues category; an absolute majority in both years cited some social welfare (welfare reform, the environment, health care, and the like) or public order (crime, terrorism, drugs, and related issues) problem. Indeed, social issues have been prominent concerns in each of the last three elections. Together, the economy and social issues accounted for nearly nine in ten responses to this question. Very few cited problems in the "functioning of government" category, such as "gridlock," term limits or other reforms, or government corruption.

While the economy and social issues have been by far the dominant concerns of the public, the particular concerns of the public vary from election to election. In the economy, for example, inflation was a common concern throughout the 1970s, but by 1984, it all but dropped from sight, becoming a literal asterisk in the polls in the last two elections. Unemployment has varied as a concern in rough accord with the actual level of unemployment in the nation. Not surprisingly, concern about the federal budget deficit has also tracked closely the rate of growth (or, in 1996, decline) in the actual deficit. Similarly, in the social issues category, the particular concerns have varied from year to year, most easily understood as following the headlines in the news media and the issues the candidates chose to emphasize in the campaigns. Thus, in 1992, not only was Perot's (and Clinton's) focus on the deficit reflected as a concern of the public, but so too was Clinton's emphasis on the "health care crisis." By 1996 those concerns had waned somewhat, but crime and terrorism, education, and welfare policy had replaced them.

The concerns of the electorate are the backdrop of the campaign. For example, the decline in concern about the economy was good news for the incumbent. Still, three in ten respondents were concerned about the economy, especially the budget deficit. Even for them, however, such concerns did not translate immediately into support for Dole's economic programs (after all, a tax cut might not be the best way to reduce the deficit), or even into opposition to Clinton, and the same holds for those concerned about social issues. A vote, after all, is a choice among alternatives. To investigate these questions, we must look at the voters' issue preferences and their perceptions of where candidates stood on the issues.

ISSUE POSITIONS AND PERCEPTIONS

Since 1972, the NES surveys have included a number of issue scales designed to measure the preferences of the electorate and voters' perceptions of the positions the candidates took on the issues.[14] The questions are therefore especially appropriate for examining prospective issue evaluations. We hasten to add, however, that voters' perceptions of where the incumbent party's nominee stands may well be based in part on what the president has done in office, as well as on the campaign promises he made as the party's nominee. The policy promises of the opposition party's candidate may also be judged partly by what his party did when it last held the White House. Clinton attempted to paint Dole as another "hard-right conservative" and tie him to Speaker Newt Gingrich. Some respondents may have agreed and seen Dole as taking positions similar to those of the Republicans in the 104th Congress, even when Dole did not endorse those policies. Nevertheless, the issue scales generally focus on prospective evaluations and are very different from those used to make the retrospective judgments examined in Chapter 7.

The issue scales will be used to examine several questions: What alternatives did the voters believe the candidates were offering? To what extent did the voters have issue preferences of their own and relatively clear perceptions of candidates' positions? Finally, how strongly were voters' preferences and perceptions related to their choice of candidates?

Figure 6-2 presents the text of one of the 7-point issue scale questions, along with an example of an illustration presented to respondents as they considered their responses. Figure 6-3 shows the nine issue scales used in the 1996 NES survey. The figure presents the average (median) position of the respondents (labeled "self," or "S") and the average (median) perception of the positions of Clinton ("C") and Dole ("D").[15] Several of the scales were created for the 1996 survey, but others have been used for many elections. Issue questions asked in 1996 probe the respondents' own preferences and perceptions of the major-party nominees on whether government spending should be reduced or should be

FIGURE 6-2   Example of a 7-Point Issue Scale: Jobs and Standard of Living
            Guarantees

Question asked by interviewers:

"Some people feel the government in Washington should see to it that every person has a job and a good standard of living. (Suppose these people are at one end of a scale, at point 1.) Others think the government should just let each person get ahead on their own. (Suppose these people are at the other end, at point 7. And, of course, some other people have opinions somewhere in between at points 2, 3, 4, 5, or 6.)

"Where would you place yourself on this scale, or haven't you thought much about this?

"Where would you place Bill Clinton on this scale?

"[Where would you place] Bob Dole?"

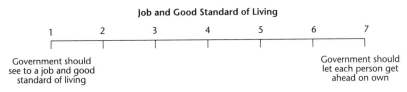

Job and Good Standard of Living

1   2   3   4   5   6   7

Government should   Government should
see to a job and good   let each person get
standard of living   ahead on own

Source: 1996 National Election Studies, Pre-Election Survey, Respondent Booklet.

FIGURE 6-3 Median Self-Placement of the Electorate and the Electorate's
Placement of Candidates on Issue Scales, 1996

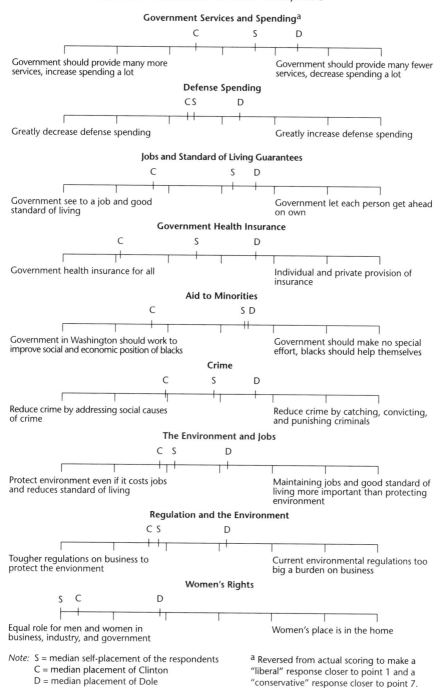

Note: S = median self-placement of the respondents
       C = median placement of Clinton
       D = median placement of Dole

[a] Reversed from actual scoring to make a
"liberal" response closer to point 1 and a
"conservative" response closer to point 7.

increased to provide for greater social services; whether defense spending should be increased or decreased; whether government should guarantee a good living standard; whether health insurance should be the responsibility of the government or the individual; whether the government should provide aid to blacks or they should get ahead on their own; whether crime should be combated by attacking its social causes or by arresting and punishing offenders; whether environmental protections should or should not come at the expense of jobs; whether government regulations to protect the environment should be increased or decreased; and whether women should play a role equal to that of men or should stay at home.[16]

These issues were selected because they were controversial and generally measured long-standing partisan divisions. As a result, the average citizen appears to be reasonably moderate on these issues—in each case but one coming between the positions corresponding to the average placements of the two candidates. On many issues, the typical citizen is very near the center of the scale, especially on the defense spending, jobs and standard of living, health insurance, aid to minorities, and crime scales. On the issues that have been asked about in the past (all but crime), these average citizen stances are quite similar from one election to the next (although self-placement on the jobs scale was rather more conservative in Reagan's initial victory in 1980). The average citizen on the government spending and services scale has typically been just to the left of the middle, so the 1996 average represents a noticeable step to the right. In those years in which the same women's rights scale was used (all but 1984), citizens placed themselves about as far to the "equal role" end as possible, just as in 1996. The two environmental scales (like the crime scale) were new to 1996. The placement of the average citizen is a full point to the environmental side of the middle, suggesting that the reaction against House initiatives in the 104th Congress designed to cut support for the environment reflected beliefs held by the public.

The public has seen the Democratic candidate as more liberal and the Republican candidate as more conservative than the position of the average member of the public on nearly every issue scale asked since 1972 (the women's rights scale being the only exception from 1980 on). This was true in 1996 as well. The result, of course, is that the typical citizen sees a great deal of difference between the two candidates' stances. On average, the candidates are placed 1.7 points apart, which is really quite a substantial spread on 7-point scales. It is, however, very similar to the differences found in preceding election surveys. The candidates were seen as most similar on defense spending (a difference of just under 1 point) and, as befits the controversy surrounding Clinton's health care proposals in his first term, the differences were seen as greatest on that issue (more that 2.5 points).

Although voters saw stark differences between the candidates, the typical voter faced a difficult choice. On average, Clinton was seen about as far to the left of the typical respondent as Dole was to the right. Indeed, taking all nine scales into account, Clinton was on average 0.9 points to the left and Dole was 1.1 units to the right of the ordinary citizen. Thus, on average, Clinton would have a slight advantage over Dole. If the women's rights scale is excluded, however, Clinton remains an average of 0.9 units to the left, but Dole is an average of 0.8 units to the right of the typical citizen. Thus we might imagine that the sharp differences would mean that many voters would have a clear choice based on these issues but that the choices would tend to cancel out, not clearly favoring one candidate or the other. Of course, these data concern average beliefs and perceptions. To consider actual behavior, we must look beyond these averages.

ISSUE VOTING CRITERIA

The Problem

Since voting is an individual action, we must look at the preferences of individuals to see whether prospective issues influenced their vote. In fact, the question of prospective voting is controversial. The authors of the classic study of the American electorate, *The American Voter,* point out that the public is often ill-informed about public policy and may not be able to vote on the basis of issues.[17] They asked what information voters would need before an issue could influence the decision of how to vote, and they specified three conditions. First, the voters must hold an opinion on the issue; second, they must perceive what the government is doing on the issue; and third, they must see a difference between the policies of the two major parties. According to their analysis, only about one-quarter to one-third of the electorate in 1956 could meet these three conditions.

Although it is impossible to replicate their analysis, we can adapt their procedures to the 1996 electorate. In some ways, more recent NES data focus more directly on the actual choice citizens must make, a choice among the candidates. The first criterion is whether the respondent claims to have an opinion on the issue. This is measured by whether respondents placed themselves on the issue scale. Second, the respondents should have some perception of the positions taken by the candidates on an issue. This was measured by whether they could place both major-party candidates on that issue.[18] Although some voters might perceive the position of one candidate and vote on that basis, prospective voting involves a comparison among alternatives, so the expressed ability to perceive the stands of the contenders seems a minimal requirement of prospective issue voting. Third, the voter must see a difference between the positions of the candidates. Failing to see a difference means that the voter perceived no choice on the issue. A voter might be able to satisfy these criteria but misperceive the offerings of the candidates. This leads to a fourth condition that we are able to measure more systematically than was possible in 1956. Does the respondent accurately perceive the relative positions of the two major-party candidates—that is, see Dole as more "conservative" than Clinton? This criterion does not demand that the voter have an accurate perception of what the candidate proposes, but it does expect the voter to see that Clinton, for instance, favored more spending on social services like education and health care than Dole did.

The Data

In Table 6-4 we report the percentages of the sample that met the four criteria on the nine issue scales used in 1996. We also show the average proportion that met these criteria for all scales and compare those averages with comparable averages for all issue scales used in the six preceding elections.[19] As can be seen in column I of Table 6-4, most people felt capable of placing themselves on the issue scales, and this capability was common to all election years.

Fewer people could place both the candidates and themselves on an issue scale than could place just themselves, as can be seen in column II of Table 6-4. Nonetheless, four in five respondents met these two criteria in 1996. Notice that there was relatively little variation across issues: 73 to 88 percent met these criteria on each issue scale. The relatively consistent ability to satisfy the criteria is similar to that obtained in 1984 and thereafter, but different from findings in earlier elections. In 1980, for instance, there were three issue scales on which fewer than half placed themselves and both candidates. The average of 80 percent of respondents who met these two conditions in 1996 marks an all-time high and greatly exceeds the averages in several other election years, especially 1976.

As can be seen in column III of Table 6-4, about two-thirds of the sample met the first two criteria and also saw a difference between the positions of Clinton and Dole. The 1996 result is most similar to those in 1992 and 1984, while the results in the other four elections were substantially lower on average (again, 1976 was especially low). What are we to conclude about these differences in the ability of the electorate to satisfy the criteria and thus to be able to vote on the basis of issues? It seems highly unlikely that the ability of the public to comprehend the electoral process varies so greatly from election to election. Note that there is very little difference among elections in self-placement on issue scales. Rather, the differences are due to perceptions of the candidates' positions. The differences between the election of 1976 and especially the elections of 1984, 1992, and 1996 first appear in the ability to place both candidates on the scales. Perhaps 1976 had relatively low scores because Ford had not run for president before and had been the incumbent for only two years, while Carter was a relatively unknown challenger. And perhaps other elections had higher scores because the incumbent party's candidate had served four or more years in the presidency or the vice presidency. The differences become especially pronounced, however, in the electorate's ability to characterize the candidates' positions. In 1984 the candidates adopted particularly distinctive positions on issues, and this relative clarity was picked up by the electorate. The same seems to be true in 1992 and again in 1996. In 1972, 1980, and 1988, the candidates were only slightly less distinct, and the electorate saw the differences between the candidates only

TABLE 6-4 Four Criteria for Issue Voting, 1996, and Comparisons with 1972–1992 Presidential Elections (in percentages)

Issue scale	Percentage of sample who			
	I Placed self on scale	II Placed both candidates on scale[a]	III Saw differences between Clinton and Dole	IV Saw Clinton more "liberal" than Dole
Government spending/services	86	80	72	62
Defense spending	87	77	67	47
Jobs and standard of living	91	83	70	62
Government health insurance	90	79	70	62
Aid to minorities	92	80	65	59
Crime	96	85	65	55
Jobs and the environment	86	76	59	48
Regulation and the environment	81	73	55	48
Women's Rights	96	88	58	52
Average[b]				
1996 (9)	89	80	65	55
1992 (3)	85	71	66	52
1988 (7)	86	66	52	43
1984 (7)	84	73	62	53
1980 (9)	82	61	51	43
1976 (9)	84	58	39	26
1972 (8)	90	65	49	41

Note: Columns II, III, and IV compare the Democratic and Republican nominees.

[a]Until 1996, respondents who could not place themselves on a scale were not asked to place the candidates on that issue scale. Although they were asked to do so in 1996, we have excluded them from further calculations to maintain comparability with prior surveys.

[b]Number in parentheses is the number of issue scales included in the average for each election year survey.

slightly less clearly. In 1976, by contrast, Ford and Carter were generally described as moderates, albeit moderately conservative and moderately liberal, respectively. The electorate reacted to the relative lack of differences.

In sum, we support Morris P. Fiorina's argument that failure to satisfy the criteria for issue voting does not mean that the electorate has ill-formed preferences and perceptions.[20] Rather, the electorate's ability to perceive differences between the candidates varies because political conditions differ from election to election, and these differences result mainly from differences in the strategies candidates follow. Thus, the "quality" of the responses to these issue questions is based in part on how clearly the candidates articulate their issue positions and on how distinctly the alternative policy platforms are presented to the public.

The data in column IV reflect the ability of the electorate to discern distinctions between the candidates' policy offerings. Averaging these issues together, we see that in 1996, more than half of the respondents satisfied all four issue-voting conditions, the final one being that they saw Clinton as more liberal than Dole. The 1996 data look much like those of 1984 and 1992 in this regard. Once again, the 1976 election stands out in very sharp contrast; barely more than one in four voters could assess the relative positions of the two candidates, while four in ten satisfied all conditions, on average, in the remaining three elections.

The data in Table 6-4 suggest that the potential for prospective issue voting was relatively high in 1996. Therefore, we might expect these issues to be closely related to voter choice. We shall examine voter choice on these issues by trying to find the answers to two questions. First, how often did people vote for the closer candidate on each issue? Second, how strongly related to the vote is the set of all issues taken together?

APPARENT ISSUE VOTING IN 1996

Issue Criteria and Voting on Each Issue

The first question is to what extent did people who were closer to a candidate on a given issue actually vote for that candidate? That is, how strong is apparent issue voting?[21] In Table 6-5 we report the proportion of major-party voters who voted for Clinton by where they placed themselves on the issue scales. We divided the seven points into the set of positions that were closer to where the average citizen placed Clinton and Dole (see Figure 6-3).[22]

As can be seen in Table 6-5, there is a strong relationship between the voters' issue positions and the candidate they supported on eight of the nine issues—all but the women's rights scale. Those who adopted positions at the "liberal" end of each scale were very likely to vote for Clinton. If we define *liberal* as adopting position 1 or 2, then the lowest proportion of support Clinton received was more than seven in ten on these eight scales. Clinton rarely received half the vote from those at the conservative end of the scales, while those with moderate views on

TABLE 6-5 Percentage of Major-Party Voters Who Voted for Clinton, by Seven-Point Issue Scales, 1996

Issue scale	1	Closer to median perception of Clinton			Closer to median perception of Dole			(N)
		2	3	4	5	6	7	
Government spending/services[a]	94	83	78	66	36	17	17	
(N)[b]	(41)	(72)	(157)	(278)	(176)	(135)	(67)	(928)
Defense spending	86	81	69	52	39	34	63	
(N)	(34)	(95)	(166)	(292)	(219)	(97)	(33)	(936)
Jobs and standard of living	93	80	84	70	53	35	23	
(N)	(55)	(59)	(97)	(206)	(192)	(226)	(126)	(963)
Government health insurance	87	85	78	67	46	23	28	
(N)	(99)	(97)	(113)	(192)	(172)	(156)	(112)	(941)
Aid to minorities	91	97	84	64	51	39	41	
(N)	(39)	(36)	(89)	(205)	(202)	(229)	(165)	(964)

(Table continues)

TABLE 6-5 (continued)

Issue scale	1	2	3	4	5	6	7	(N)
		Closer to median perception of Clinton			Closer to median perception of Dole			
Crime	74	82	68	59	49	39	50	
(N)	(114)	(77)	(89)	(237)	(129)	(167)	(185)	(998)
Jobs and the environment	75	71	61	48	27	45	51	
(N)	(95)	(169)	(183)	(253)	(133)	(68)	(29)	(931)
Regulation and the environment	82	72	66	50	36	19	17	
(N)	(109)	(156)	(181)	(204)	(124)	(66)	(47)	(886)
Women's rights	69	48	41	46	38	26	55	
(N)	(491)	(193)	(95)	(116)	(44)	(36)	(27)	(1,002)

[a] Reversed from actual scoring to make a "liberal" response closer to 1 and a "conservative" response closer to 7.

[b] Numbers in parentheses are the totals on which percentages are based. Numbers are weighted.

each issue fell in between these two extremes of support. The pattern of support we would expect from voting on the basis of these issues is particularly clear on those issues that have long defined the traditional cleavages between the two parties (the top five scales on the table). The results on these and, indeed, nearly all of the issue scales, then, show a substantial relationship between the public's opinions and their perceptions of candidates on prospective issues.

The information on issues can be summarized, as it is in Table 6-6, to illustrate what happened when voters met the various conditions for issue voting. In the

TABLE 6-6   Apparent Issue Voting, 1996, and Comparisons with 1972–1992 (in percentages)

Issue scale	Placed self on issue scale	Met all four issue voting criteria	Placed self but failed to meet all three other criteria
Government spending/services	74	82	47
Defense spending	61	75	41
Jobs and standard of living	60	68	39
Government health insurance	65	72	44
Aid to minorities	57	68	33
Crime	57	71	33
Jobs and the environment	62	76	42
Regulation and the environment	67	78	47
Women's rights	62	76	44
Averages[a]			
1996 (9)	63	74	41
1992 (3)	62	70	48
1988 (7)	62	71	45
1984 (7)	65	73	46
1980 (9)	63	71	48
1976 (9)	57	70	50
1972 (8)	66	76	55

Note: An "apparent issue vote" is a vote for the candidate closer to one's position on an issue scale. The closer candidate is determined by comparing self-placement to the median placements of the two candidates on the scale as a whole. Respondents who did not place themselves or who were equidistant from the two candidates are excluded from the calculations.

[a]Number in parentheses is the number of issue scales included in the average for each election year survey.

first column of Table 6-6, we report the percentage of major-party voters who placed themselves closer to the average perception of Clinton or Dole and who voted for the closer candidate. To be more specific, the denominator is the total number of major-party voters who placed themselves closer to the electorate's perception of Clinton or Dole. The numerator is the total number of major-party voters who were both closer to Clinton and voted for him plus the total number of major-party voters who were both closer to Dole and voted for him.

If voting were unrelated to issue positions, we would expect 50 percent to vote for the closer candidate on average. In 1996, 63 percent voted for the closer candidate. This is a higher percentage on average than in 1976, but it is about the same as in other elections.

These figures do not tell the whole story, however, for those who placed themselves on an issue but failed to meet some other criterion were unlikely to have cast a vote based on that issue. In the second column of Table 6-6, we report the percentage of those who voted for the closer candidate on each issue and met all four conditions on that issue. The third column reports the percentage that voted for the closer candidate and failed to meet all three of the remaining conditions.

Those who met all four conditions were much more likely to vote for the closer candidate on any issue. Indeed, there is relatively little difference, on average, across all seven elections. In each case, at least seven of ten such voters supported the closer candidate. For those who failed to meet the last three of the conditions on issue voting, in contrast, voting was essentially random with respect to the issues.

The strong similarity of all seven election averages in the second column suggests that issue voting seems more prevalent in some elections than others because elections differ in regard to the number of people who clearly perceive differences between the candidates. In all elections, at least seven in ten voters who satisfied all four conditions voted consistently with their issue preferences. As we saw earlier, the degree to which such perceptions vary from election to election depends more on the strategies of the candidates than on the qualities of the voters. Therefore, the relatively low percentage of apparent issue voting in 1976, for instance, results from the perception of small differences between the two rather moderate candidates. The large magnitude of apparent issue voting in 1996 results from the remarkable clarity with which most people saw the positions of Clinton and Dole.

The Balance of Issues Measure

Prospective issue voting means that voters compare the full set of policy proposals made by the candidates. As we have noted, nearly every issue is strongly related to the vote so we might expect the set of all issues to be even more strongly so. To examine this relationship, we constructed an overall assessment of the issue scales, what we call the balance of issues measure. We did so by giving individuals a score of +1 if their positions on an issue scale were closer to the average perception of Dole, a –1 if their positions were closer to the average perception of Clinton, and a score of 0 if they had no preference on an issue. These scores for all nine issue scales were added up together, creating a measure that ranged from –9 to +9. For instance, respondents who were closer to the average perception of Clinton's positions on all nine scales received a score of –9. A negative score indicated that the respondent was, on balance, closer to the public's perception of Clinton, while a positive score indicated the respondent was, overall, closer to the public's perception of Dole.[23] We collapsed this 19-point measure into categories, running from strongly Democratic through neutral to strongly Republican.[24]

The results are reported in Table 6-7. As can be seen in row A, only one in twenty respondents was strongly Democratic; three times as many were strongly Republican. Essentially the same was true of the two moderate scores. The Republicans also held an advantage in the comparison of the two slightly partisan-leaning categories. Nearly three in ten, however, were neutral.

This balance of issues measure was, indeed, strongly related to the vote, as the findings for the individual issues would suggest (see Table 6-7, row B). Clinton won the vast majority of the vote from those in the strongly and moderately Democratic categories, and seven of eight from the slightly Democratic category. He even won more than seven in ten votes from those in the neutral category, and a majority from those in the slightly Republican category. His support dropped off dramatically from that point. Indeed, decline in Democratic voting across the net balance of issues categories in 1996 is as strong as it was in 1972 and nearly as strong as in 1984, the two strongest cases in the past seven elections.[25]

The Abortion Issue

We give special attention to the public policy controversy about abortion, for two reasons. First, abortion is an especially divisive issue. The Republican national platform has taken a strong "pro-life" stand since 1980, and the Democratic party has become increasingly "pro-choice." Indeed, abortion is one of the most contentious issues in government at all levels, between the two parties and among members of the public. Clinton's views did not satisfy the strongest of pro-choice advocates, but before the 1996 elections he had vetoed a controversial measure to outlaw so-called "partial birth abortions," because, he said, it did not include safeguards for the life and health of the mother. His appointments to the Supreme Court were strengthening the pro-choice end of the spectrum, and another four years might give him a sufficient number of appointments to all but end the possibility of reversing the *Roe v. Wade* decision. Dole struggled to win support among those on the pro-life side of the issue during the nomination campaign. Their skepticism of him was revitalized when he sought to weaken the Republican platform's pro-life planks by being more open to those who hold other views. He lost that fight but surely was considered the more palatable of the candidates (including Perot) by the pro-life camp.

TABLE 6-7 Distribution of the Electorate on the Net Balance of Issues Measure and Major-Party Vote, 1996 (in percentages)

| | Net balance of issues | | | | | | | | |
	Strongly Democratic	Moderately Democratic	Slightly Democratic	Neutral	Slightly Republican	Moderately Republican	Strongly Republican	Total	(N)
A. Distribution of Responses									
	5	6	11	29	18	15	15	99	(1,713)
B. Major-Party Voters Who Voted for Clinton									
Percent	97	94	87	72	56	39	14		
(N)	(61)	(63)	(99)	(280)	(159)	(174)	(201)		

Note: Numbers are weighted.

The second reason for examining this issue is that it offers another salient and contentious policy question about which respondents were asked not only their own views but also what they thought Dole and Clinton's positions were. Respondents were provided the following four alternatives:

1. By law, abortion should never be permitted.
2. The law should permit abortion only in the case of rape, incest, or when the woman's life is in danger.
3. The law should permit abortion for reasons *other than* rape, incest, or danger to the woman's life, but only after the need for the abortion has been clearly established.
4. By law, a woman should always be able to obtain an abortion as a matter of personal choice.

The electorate's responses were clearly toward the pro-choice end of the measure. Among the 1,019 major-party voters who chose among these four alternatives, 43 percent said that abortion should be a matter of personal choice. Sixteen percent were willing to allow abortions for reasons other than rape, incest, or danger to the woman's life, and 30 percent said abortion should be allowed only under those conditions. Only 11 percent said that abortion should never be permitted.

Among major-party voters, there was a strong relationship between a voter's opinion and the way he or she voted. Table 6-8 presents the percentage of major-party voters who voted for Clinton according to their view on the abortion issue. Whereas seven in ten of those who believed that abortion should be a matter of personal choice supported Clinton, six in ten who thought it should never be permitted voted against him.

Because the survey asked respondents what they thought Clinton and Dole's positions were, we can see if the basic issue-voting criteria apply. If they do, we can expect to find a very strong relationship between the respondents' positions and how they voted if they met three additional conditions, beyond having an opinion on this issue themselves. First, they would have to have an opinion about where the candidates stood on the issue. Second, they would have to see a difference between the positions of Clinton and Dole. Third, to cast a policy-related vote reflecting the actual positions of the candidates, they would have to recognize that Clinton held a more pro-choice position than Dole. Two out of three respondents met all of these conditions.

Among voters who met all of these conditions, there was a very strong relationship between policy preferences and voting. We see this relationship by reading across the second row of Table 6-8. Among major-party voters who thought that abortions should never be allowed, only one in seven supported Clinton. Among those who thought that the decision to have an abortion should be a matter of personal choice, four out of five voted for him. The final row of Table 6-8 shows the relationship of issue preferences and the vote among voters who did *not* see Clinton as more pro-choice than Dole. Among such voters, there is a much weaker

TABLE 6-8 Percentage of Major-Party Voters Who Voted for Clinton, by Opinion about Abortion and What They Believed Dole and Clinton's Positions to Be, 1996

	Respondent's position on abortion							
	Abortion should never be permitted		Abortion should be permitted only in the case of rape, incest, or health of the woman		Abortion should be permitted for other reasons, but only if a need is established		Abortion should be a matter of personal choice	
	%	(N)	%	(N)	%	(N)	%	(N)
All major-party voters	40	(110)	42	(306)	58	(162)	72	(441)
Major-party voters who placed both candidates, who saw a difference between them, and who saw Clinton as more "pro-choice" than Dole	15	(63)	26	(205)	58	(98)	81	(304)
Major-party voters who did not meet all three of these conditions	73	(47)	75	(101)	58	(64)	50	(137)

Note: Numbers in parentheses are the totals on which the percentages are based. The numbers are weighted.

relationship. In fact, voters who were pro-choice were more likely to vote for Dole than those who held a right-to-life position.

These results do not prove that policy preferences shape voting decisions. Some voters may project the position they favor themselves onto the candidate they favor. But it does appear that unless all the basic conditions for issue voting are present, issue voting does not occur. When the conditions are present, there can be a strong relationship between the position voters hold and their choice between the major-party candidates.

THE ISSUE PREFERENCES OF PEROT VOTERS

Our discussion of issue preferences has focused on the major-party vote. Because the NES survey stopped asking respondents to place Perot on the issue scales during the course of the campaign, we cannot examine where the electorate saw Perot as standing on the issues. We can, however, compare the issue preferences of those who voted for Perot with those who voted for Clinton or Dole. Because there were relatively few Perot voters, however, our comparisons must be broad.

Perot voters were similar to major-party voters in regard to the problems that concerned them. All voters, that is, had a broad range of concerns, especially in comparison with previous elections, as we discussed earlier in this chapter. Like those who supported Clinton or Dole, those who voted for Perot were roughly evenly divided between selection of an economic or a social concern.

Perot voters saw clear differences between the two major-party nominees, but they typically saw slightly less discrepancy between the two on the 7-point issue scales. The reason Perot voters saw fewer differences than major-party voters appears to be due less to Perot voters than to major-party voters, however. That is, on most issues, those who voted for Clinton placed Dole at a more conservative position than either Dole or Perot voters, while Perot voters' perceptions of Dole were usually, but not always, fairly similar to Dole voters' perceptions of their candidate. Clinton voters saw Dole as, on average, about a half point more conservative than Dole voters saw him, with Perot voters in between but closer to Dole voters (except on the women's rights scale, where their average perceptions of Dole were slightly more conservative than those of Clinton voters). Conversely, Dole voters saw Clinton as much more liberal than Clinton voters saw him—with differences ranging from one-half to more than one full point (except in regard to women's rights, where the differences were very small). Perot voters typically placed Clinton in between, as more liberal than Clinton voters and as more conservative than Dole voters. On average, they saw Clinton as about a quarter point more liberal than did Clinton voters and about a half point more conservative than Dole voters. The result is that Perot voters saw clear differences between Clinton and Dole, but less differentiation than that seen by the typical major-party voter.

Finally, Perot voters were themselves less liberal than Clinton voters and less conservative than Dole voters. Perot voters, however, were on average similar to Clinton voters on the scales concerning jobs and standard of living guarantees, aid to minorities, regulation and the environment, and women's rights. On the remaining issue scales, they were approximately half-way between the positions of the voters for the major-party candidates. Thus, they were typically closer to neither candidate on issues that tapped the role of the government in the economy, but they were more like Clinton voters on other issues. This conclusion is reinforced by looking at Perot voters' positions on the 4-point abortion scale. Perot voters reported preferences similar to those of Clinton voters, and thus leaned more to the pro-choice end of the scale than did Dole voters. Sixty-five percent of Perot voters selected one of the two most pro-choice positions, as opposed to 70 percent of Clinton voters but only about 45 percent of Dole voters. Conversely, about one-third of both Perot and Clinton voters chose one of the two most pro-life options (and 8 percent of each chose the most pro-life position), while over half of Dole's voters chose a pro-life position (and 15 percent elected the most pro-life position).

CONCLUSION

The findings suggest that for major-party voters prospective issues were quite important in the 1996 election. Even so, the electorate's interest in prospective issues alone cannot account for Clinton's victory. Those for whom prospective issues gave a clear choice voted consistently with those issues. Most people, however, were located between the candidates as the electorate saw them. Indeed, on most issues, most people were relatively moderate, Clinton was seen as more liberal, and Dole was viewed as more conservative. In fact, Dole had a slight edge overall on prospective issues, so if they were the sole determinant of voting choices, he would have won a close contest, at least in the popular voting.

This line of reasoning suggests that voters took prospective issues into account in 1996, but that they also took other factors into consideration. In the next chapter, we shall see that the second form of policy voting, that based on retrospective evaluations, was among those other factors, as it has been in all six of the previous presidential elections.

Chapter 7

Presidential Performance
and Candidate Choice

Republicans in the 1994 congressional elections used President Bill Clinton as a favored campaign target, often "morphing" the image of the Democratic congressional candidate into the apparently disliked incumbent president. And yet, by the presidential election, Clinton had reversed his fortunes. According to the National Election Studies (NES) data, his was the most approved incumbency in two decades, topping even that of Ronald Reagan in 1984. One of the major factors in his high approval ratings in 1996, as in Reagan's in 1984, was the strength of the economy. After a brief downturn that hurt George Bush's support in 1992, the economy rebounded (probably even before the actual voting in 1992), and by 1996 inflation was low, employment was up, and the economy was growing.[1]

This cursory glance suggests that voters may have concluded in 1996, as they had in 1984, that "one good term deserves another." In 1992, in contrast, voters concluded that it was time to "throw the rascals out," voting against Bush as incumbent and electing Clinton. Such appeals to the performance of the incumbent administration, appeals about the successes or failures of earlier administrations, and assessments of what previous performance indicates about the future are attempts to benefit from retrospective evaluations.

Retrospective evaluations are concerns about policy, but they differ significantly from the prospective evaluations we considered in the last chapter. Retrospective evaluations are, as the name suggests, concerned about the past. While the past may be prologue to the future, retrospective evaluations also focus on outcomes, with what actually happened, rather than on the policy means for achieving outcomes—the heart of prospective evaluations.

In this chapter we focus on the same kinds of concerns as the candidates did, looking primarily at prosperity and the public's approval of the incumbent. We shall see that these assessments, in particular, played a powerful role in shaping not only the candidates' strategies but also voters' attitudes toward the candidates and the parties and their choices on election day.

WHAT IS RETROSPECTIVE VOTING?

An individual who voted for the incumbent party's candidate because the incumbent was, in the voter's opinion, a successful president is said to have cast a retrospective vote. A voter who votes for the opposition because, in the voter's opinion, the incumbent has been *un*successful has also cast a retrospective vote. In other words, retrospective voting decisions are based on evaluations of the course of politics over the last term in office and on evaluations of how much the incumbent should be held responsible for what good or ill occurred. V. O. Key, Jr., popularized this argument by suggesting that the voter might be "a rational god of vengeance and of reward."[2]

Obviously, the more closely the candidate of one party can be tied to the actions of the incumbent, the more likely it is that voters will decide retrospectively. The incumbent president cannot escape such evaluations, and the incumbent vice president is usually identified with (and often chooses to identify himself with) the administration's performance. In twenty-one of the twenty-five presidential elections since 1900 (all but those in 1908, 1920, 1928, and 1952), an incumbent president or vice president stood for election.

The perspective offered by Key has three aspects. First, retrospective voters are oriented toward outcomes rather than the policy means to achieve them. They also evaluate the performance of the incumbent only, all but ignoring the opposition. Finally, the retrospective voter evaluates what has been done, paying little attention to what the candidates promise to do in the future.

Anthony Downs presents a different picture of retrospective voting.[3] He argues that voters look to the past to understand what the incumbent party's candidate will do in the future. According to Downs, parties are basically consistent in their goals, methods, and ideologies over time. Therefore, the past performance of both parties' candidates, but especially that of the incumbent, may prove relevant for predicting their future conduct. Because it takes time and effort to evaluate campaign promises and because promises are just words, voters find it faster, easier, and safer to use past performance to project the administration's actions for the next four years. Downs also emphasizes that retrospective evaluations are used to make comparisons between the alternatives standing for election. Key sees a retrospective referendum on the incumbent's party alone. Downs believes that retrospective evaluations are used to make comparisons between the candidates as well as to provide a guide to the future. In 1996, for example, Clinton attempted to tie Bob Dole to the performance of congressional Republicans since they had assumed the majority in 1994 (an attempt made easier because Dole served as majority leader in the Senate throughout most of the preceding two years). Clinton pointedly referred to the 104th Congress as the "Dole-Gingrich" Congress.

Another view of retrospective voting is advanced by Morris P. Fiorina. His view is in many respects an elaboration and extension of Downs's thesis. For our purposes, Fiorina's major addition to the Downsian perspective is his argument that party identification plays a central role. He argues that "citizens monitor party promises and performances over time, encapsulate their observations in a summary judgment termed 'party identification,' and rely on this core of previous experience when they assign responsibility for current societal conditions and evaluate ambiguous platforms designed to deal with uncertain futures."[4] We return to Fiorina's views on partisanship in the next chapter.

Retrospective voting and voting according to issue positions, as analyzed in Chapter 6, differ significantly. The difference lies in how concerned people are with societal outcomes and how concerned they are with the means to achieve desired outcomes. For example, everyone prefers economic prosperity. The disagreement among political decision makers lies in how best to achieve it. At the voters' level, however, the central question is whether people care only about achieving prosperity or whether they care, or even are able to judge, how to achieve this desired goal. Perhaps they looked at high inflation and interest rates in 1980 and said, "We tried Carter's approach, and it failed. Let's try something else—anything else." Or they noted the long run of relative economic prosperity from 1983 to 1988 and said, "Whatever Reagan did, it worked. Let's keep it going by putting his vice president in office." Or, perhaps, they agreed with Clinton that he had presided over a successful economic program and they therefore were sufficiently convinced that they should remain with Clinton's programs.

Economic policies and foreign affairs issues are especially likely to be discussed in these terms because they share several characteristics. First, the outcomes are clear, and most voters can judge whether they approve of the results. Inflation and unemployment are high or low; the economy is growing or it is not. The country is at war or peace; the world is stable or unstable. Second, there is often near-consensus on what the desired outcomes are; no one disagrees with peace or prosperity, with world stability or low unemployment. Third, the means to achieve these ends are often very complex, and information is hard to understand; experts as well as candidates and parties disagree about the specific ways to achieve the desired ends.

As issues, therefore, peace and prosperity differ sharply from policy areas such as abortion and gun control, in which there is vigorous disagreement about the desired ends among experts, leaders, and the public. On still other issues, people value both ends *and* means. The classic cases often involve the question of whether it is appropriate for government to take action in that area at all. Reagan was fond of saying, "Government isn't the solution to our problems, government *is* the problem." For instance, should the government provide national health insurance? Few disagree with the end of better health care, but they do disagree over the appropriate means to achieve it. The choice of means involves some of the basic philosophical and ideological differences that have divided the Republicans from the Democrats for decades.[5] For example, in 1984 and 1988 the Democratic nominees acknowledged that we were in a period of economic prosperity and that prosperity is desirable. In 1984 Walter F. Mondale emphasized that Reagan's policies were unfair to the disadvantaged. Mondale, like Michael S.

Dukakis in 1988, and Clinton and Perot in 1992, also claimed that the policies of Reagan and Bush, by creating such large deficits, were sowing the seeds for future woes. Disagreement was not about the ends, but about the means and the consequences that would follow from using different means to achieve them.

Two basic conditions must occur before retrospective evaluations can affect voting choices. First, individuals must connect their concerns (for example, the problem they feel to be the most important) with the incumbent and the actions he took in office. One might blame earlier administrations with sowing the seeds that grew into the huge deficits of the 1980s, blame a profligate Congress, or even believe that the problems are beyond anyone's control. Second, individuals, in the Downs-Fiorina view, compare their evaluations of the incumbent's past performance with what they believe the nominee of the opposition party would do. For example, even if voters thought Clinton's performance on the economy was weak, they might conclude that Dole's programs either would not be any better or might even make things worse. It is more difficult, however, for a challenger to convince voters who think the incumbent's performance has been strong that the challenger would be even stronger. This asymmetry that had given the advantage to Republican candidates in the 1980s worked, as we shall see, to Dole's disadvantage in 1996.

We examine next some illustrative retrospective evaluations and study their effect on voter choice. In Chapter 6 we looked at issue scales designed to measure the public's evaluations of candidates' promises. Of course, the public can evaluate not only the promises of the incumbent party but also its actions. We compare promises with performance in this chapter, but one must remember that the distinctions are not as sharp in practice as they are in principle.[6] Of course, the Downs-Fiorina view is that past actions and projections about the future are necessarily intertwined.

EVALUATIONS OF GOVERNMENTAL PERFORMANCE

What do you consider the most important problem facing the country? How do you feel the government in Washington has been handling the problem? These questions are designed to measure retrospective judgments. Table 7-1 compares the respondents' evaluations of governmental performance on the problem that each respondent identified as the single most important one facing the country. We are able to track such evaluations for the past seven elections.[7] The most striking findings in Table 7-1A are that in 1996 few thought the government was doing a good job, but a nearly even division existed between those who thought the government was doing poorly and those who felt it was doing only fairly. This makes the 1996 election look most like those of 1976 and 1984—one that (barely) did not return the incumbent party and one that did. In contrast, the elections of 1980 and 1992 saw even more negative opinions, and the incumbent party was defeated.[8]

TABLE 7-1 Evaluation of Governmental Performance on Most Important Problem and Major-Party Vote, 1972–1996

Governmental performance	1972[a]	1976	1980	1984	1988	1992	1996[a]
A. Evaluation of Governmental Performance on Most Important Problem (in percentages)							
Good job	12	8	4	16	8	2	7
Only fair job	58	46	35	46	37	28	44
Poor job	30	46	61	39	56	69	48
Total	100	100	100	101	101	99	99
(N)	(993)	(2,156)[b]	(1,319)	(1,797)	(1,672)	(1,974)[b]	(752)[b]

B. Percentage of Major-Party Vote for Incumbent Party's Nominee

	Nixon	Ford	Carter	Reagan	Bush	Bush	Clinton
Good job	85	72	81	89	82	70	93
(N)	(91)	(128)[b]	(43)	(214)	(93)	(27)[b]	(38)[b]
Only fair job	69	53	55	65	61	45	68
(N)	(390)	(695)[b]	(289)	(579)	(429)	(352)[b]	(238)[b]
Poor job	46	39	33	37	44	39	44
(N)	(209)	(684)[b]	(505)	(494)	(631)	(841)[b]	(242)[b]

Note: Numbers in parentheses are the totals on which percentages are based.

[a]These questions were asked of a randomly selected half of the sample in 1972 and 1996. In 1972 the question wording and responses were different. Respondents were asked whether the government was being (a) very helpful, (b) somewhat helpful, or (c) not helpful at all in solving this most important problem.
[b]Numbers are weighted.

If the voter is a rational god of vengeance and reward, we can expect to find a strong relationship between the evaluation of government performance and the vote. We find one in all elections, as seen in Table 7-1B. Seven to nine out of ten major-party voters who thought the government was doing a good job on the most important problem voted for the incumbent party's nominee. In 1996 those who thought the government was doing a good job with the most important problem stayed with Clinton even more strongly than in previous elections. Clinton was supported about as well as Nixon (1972) and Reagan (1984) among those who thought the government was doing only a fair or a poor job with their chief concern.

According to Downs and Fiorina, it is important to know not just how things have been going but also to assess how that evaluation compares with the alternative. In recent elections, respondents have been asked which party would do a better job of solving the problem they named as the most important. Table 7-2A shows the responses to this question.[9] This question is clearly future-oriented, but it may call for judgments about past performance, consistent with the Downs-Fiorina view. It does not ask the respondent to evaluate policy alternatives, and thus responses are most likely based on a retrospective comparison of how the incumbent party had handled things with a prediction about how the opposition would fare. We therefore consider this question to be a measure of comparative retrospective evaluations.

By comparing Tables 7-1A and 7-2A, we can see that in 1996 about one in five of the respondents thought the Democratic party would be better at handling the most important problem, but this was a far larger proportion of respondents than thought the government was already doing a good job with it. Over half thought neither party would do a better job than the other, while about one in four thought the Republicans would be better at handling the most important problem. Indeed, responses in 1996 were very similar to those in 1988, a year in which the incumbent Republican won a solid, but not landslide, victory. But there is one similarity across all seven elections. The most frequent answer is that *neither* party would do a better job than the other in handling the most important problem.

As Table 7-2B reveals, the relationship between the party seen as better on the most important problem and the vote is very strong—stronger than that found in Table 7-1B, which examines voters and their perception of the government's handling of the problem. Clinton won more than nineteen out of twenty votes from those who thought his party would do better. He won only one in seven votes from those who thought the opposition party would do better, although this was a better showing than that of previous incumbents. It appears that one way of winning a vote is to convince the voter that your party will be better at handling whatever issue it is that concerns the voter the most. If neither candidate convinces the voter that his party is better, the voter apparently looks to other factors, although in all seven elections voters who saw no difference were more likely to stay with the incumbent party.

TABLE 7-2 Evaluation of Party Seen as Better on Most Important Problem and Major-Party Vote, 1972–1996

Party better	1972[a]	1976	1980	1984	1988	1992	1996[a]
A. Distribution of Responses on Party Better on Most Important Problem (in percentages)							
Republican	28	14	43	32	22	13	22
No difference	46	50	46	44	54	48	54
Democratic	26	37	11	25	24	39	24
Total	100	101	100	101	100	100	100
(N)	(931)	(2,054)[b]	(1,251)	(1,785)	(1,655)	(1,954)[b]	(746)[b]
B. Percentage of Major-Party Voters Who Voted Democratic for President							
Republican	6	3	12	5	5	4	15
(N)	(207)	(231)[b]	(391)	(464)	(295)	(185)[b]	(137)[b]
No difference	32	35	63	41	46	45	63
(N)	(275)	(673)[b]	(320)	(493)	(564)	(507)[b]	(250)[b]
Democratic	75	89	95	91	92	92	97
(N)	(180)	(565)[b]	(93)	(331)	(284)	(519)[b]	(133)[b]

Note: Numbers in parentheses are the totals on which percentages are based.

[a]These questions were asked of a randomly selected half of the sample in 1972 and 1996. In 1972 respondents were asked which party would be more likely to get the government to be helpful in solving the most important problem.
[b]Numbers are weighted.

The data presented in Tables 7-1 and 7-2 have two limitations. First, as we saw in Chapter 6, there was considerable diversity in what problems most concerned respondents. It is therefore hard to make comparisons and interpret the findings. Are those voters who expressed concern about the budget deficits, for example, similar to those who were concerned about drugs, about health care, or about some other problem? Second, the first survey question refers to "the government" and not to the incumbent president (is it the president, Congress, both, or even others—such as the bureaucracy or the courts—who are handling the job poorly?); the second question refers to the "political party" and not the candidate. So we shall look more closely at the incumbent and at people's evaluations of comparable problems where there are data to permit such comparisons.

ECONOMIC EVALUATIONS AND THE VOTE FOR THE INCUMBENT

More than any other, economic issues have received attention as suitable retrospective issues. The impact of economic conditions on congressional and presidential elections has been studied extensively.[10] Popular evaluations of presidential effectiveness, John E. Mueller has pointed out, are strongly influenced by the economy. Edward R. Tufte suggests that because the incumbent realizes his fate may hinge on the performance of the economy, he may attempt to manipulate it, leading to what is known as a "political business cycle."[11] A major reason for Carter's defeat in the 1980 election was the perception that economic performance was weak during his administration. Reagan's rhetorical question in the 1980 debate with Carter, "Are you better off than you were four years ago?" indicates that politicians realize the power such arguments have with the electorate. Reagan owed his sweeping reelection victory in 1984 largely to the very different and more positive perception that economic performance by the end of his first term had become, after a deep recession in the middle, much stronger.

If people are concerned about economic outcomes, they might start by looking for an answer to the sort of question Reagan asked. Table 7-3A presents respondents' perceptions of whether they were financially better off than they had been one year earlier. From 1972 to 1980 about a third of the sample felt they were better off. Over that period, however, more and more of the remainder felt they were worse off. By 1980 "worse now" was the most common response. But in 1984 many felt the economic recovery, and more than two in five said they were better off than in the previous year; only a little more than one in four felt worse off. Of course, 1984 was only two years after a deep recession. Therefore, many may have seen their economic fortunes improve considerably over the prior year or so. In 1988 that recovery had been sustained. So, too, were the responses to the question. The distribution of responses to this question in 1988 was very similar to that of 1984. By 1992 there was a return to the feelings of the earlier period, and responses were nearly evenly divided between better, the same,

TABLE 7-3 Assessments of Personal Financial Situation and Major-Party Vote, 1972–1996

Response	1972[a]	1976	1980	1984	1988	1992	1996
A. Distribution of Responses to the Question "Would you say that you (and your family here) are better off or worse off financially than you were a year ago?" (in percentages)							
Better now	36	34	33	44	42	31	46
Same	42	35	25	28	33	34	31
Worse now	23	31	42	27	25	35	24
Total	101	100	100	99	100	100	101
(N)	(955)	(2,828)[b]	(1,393)	(1,956)	(2,025)	(2,474)[b]	(1,708)[b]
B. Percentage of Major-Party Voters Who Voted for the Incumbent Party Nominee for President							
Better now	69	55	46	74	63	53	66
(N)	(247)	(574)[b]	(295)	(612)	(489)	(413)[b]	(462)[b]
Same	70	52	46	55	50	45	52
(N)	(279)	(571)[b]	(226)	(407)	(405)	(500)[b]	(348)[b]
Worse now	52	38	40	33	40	27	47
(N)	(153)	(475)[b]	(351)	(338)	(283)	(453)[b]	(225)[b]

Note: Numbers in parentheses are the totals on which percentages are based.

[a]These questions were asked of a randomly selected half of the sample in 1972.
[b]Numbers are weighted.

and worse off. But in 1996, the responses were like those of the 1984 and 1988 elections—and even slightly more favorable than in those years.

In Table 7-3B, responses to this question are related to the two-party presidential vote. We can see that the relationship between the respondents' financial situations and their vote is often not particularly strong. Even so, those who felt their financial status had become worse off in the last year were always the least likely to support the incumbent. Moreover, the relationship between this variable and the vote became considerably stronger in 1984. Although the relationship fell after 1984, it was stronger in 1988, 1992, and 1996 than in the 1972, 1976, and 1980 elections.

People may "vote their pocketbooks," but they are even more likely to vote retrospectively based on their judgments of how the economy as a whole has been faring. In 1980 about 40 percent thought their own financial situation was worse than the year before, but twice as many (84 percent) thought the national economy was worse off than the year before. In the first four columns of Table 7-4A, we see that there was quite a change in the perceptions of the fortunes of the national economy over the last four elections. In 1984 the improved status of personal finances almost matched perceptions of the status of the economy as a whole. In 1988 the personal financial situation was quite like that in 1984, but perceptions of the national economy were clearly more negative. In 1992 the public gave the nation's economy a far more negative assessment than they gave of their personal financial situations. Thus, one's perceptions of personal fortunes may be very different from those of the economy as a whole. But in 1996, respondents gave broadly similar assessments of their personal fortunes as those of the nation—making 1996 look most like 1984.

The next question is whether the respondents believe that the federal government and its policies have shaped these economic fortunes. The responses in 1996 suggest that respondents were less generous in crediting the government with the nation's good economic fortunes. Still, those attributions were more positive even than in 1988 and far more so than in 1992.

In Table 7-4B, we show the relationship between responses to these items and the two-party vote for president. As we can see, this relationship between these measures and the vote is always quite strong, somewhat more so in 1984 than in 1988, 1992, and 1996, but still robust in the later three surveys. Moreover, a comparison of the bottom halves of Tables 7-3B and 7-4B shows that, in general, the vote is more closely associated with perceptions of the nation's economy and the role the government has been seen to play in it than it is with perceptions of one's personal economic well-being.

To this point, we have looked at personal and national economic conditions and the role of the government in shaping them. We have not yet looked at the extent to which such evaluations are attributed to the incumbent. In Table 7-5, we report responses to the question of whether people approved of the incumbent's handling of the economy from the 1980 through the 1996 elections. Although a majority approved of Reagan's handling of the economy in

TABLE 7-4 Public's View of the State of the Economy, Government Economic Policies, and Major-Party Vote, 1984–1996

Response	Would you say that over the past year the nation's economy has gotten:				Would you say that the economic policies of the federal government have made the nation's economy:			
	1984	1988	1992	1996	1984	1988	1992	1996
A. Distribution of Responses (in percentages)								
Better [off]	44	19	4	40	38	20	4	24
Stayed same/not made much difference	33	50	22	44	40	57	51	58
Worse [off]	23	31	73	16	22	23	45	18
Total	100	100	99	100	100	100	100	100
(N)	(1,904)	(1,956)	(2,465)[a]	(1,700)[a]	(1,841)	(1,895)	(2,401)[a]	(1,700)[a]
B. Percentage of Major-Party Voters Who Voted for the Incumbent Party Nominee for President								
Better [off]	80	77	86	75	84	83	79	82
(N)	(646)	(249)	(62)[a]	(458)[a]	(544)	(258)	(61)[a]	(289)[a]
Stayed same/not made much difference	53	53	62	45	52	50	49	52
(N)	(413)	(568)	(318)[a]	(443)[a]	(457)	(606)	(671)[a]	(550)[a]
Worse [off]	21	34	32	33	23	30	29	32
(N)	(282)	(348)	(981)[a]	(130)[a]	(302)	(275)	(597)[a]	(170)[a]

Note: Numbers in parentheses are the totals on which percentages are based.

[a] Numbers are weighted.

TABLE 7-5   Evaluations of the Incumbent's Handling of the Economy and Major-Party Vote, 1980–1996

	Approval of incumbent's handling of the economy				
	1980[a]	1984[b]	1988[b]	1992[b]	1996[b]
A. Distribution of Responses (in percentages)					
Positive view	18	58	54	20	66
Balanced view	17	—	—	—	—
Negative view	65	42	46	80	34
Total	100	100	100	100	100
(N)	(1,097)	(1,858)	(1,897)	(2,425)[c]	(1,666)[c]

B. Percentage of Major-Party Voters Who Voted for the Incumbent Party Nominee for President

	1980[a]	1984[b]	1988[b]	1992[b]	1996[b]
Positive view	88	86	80	90	79
(N)	(130)	(801)	(645)	(310)[c]	(688)[c]
Balanced view	60	—	—	—	—
(N)	(114)				
Negative view	23	16	17	26	13
(N)	(451)	(515)	(492)	(1,039)[c]	(322)[c]

Note: Numbers in parentheses are the totals on which percentages are based.

[a]In 1980 the questions asked whether the respondent approved or disapproved of Carter's handling of inflation [unemployment]. A positive [negative] view was approve [disapprove] on both; balanced responses were approve on one, disapprove on the other.
[b]In 1984, 1988, 1992, and 1996 responses were whether the respondent approved of Reagan's [Bush's; Clinton's] handling of the economy.
[c]Numbers are weighted.

both 1984 and 1988, less than one in five held positive views of economic performance in the Carter years. Evaluations of Bush in 1992 were also very negative. Evaluations in 1996 of Clinton's handling of the economy were stronger than in any previous survey.

The key question is whether these views are related to voter choice. As the data in Table 7-5B show, the answer is yes. Those who held positive views of the incumbent's performance on the economy were very likely to vote for that party's candidate, and 79 percent of those voters backed Clinton in 1996, essentially comparable to the percentage that backed Bush, as a result of Reagan's incumbency, in 1988. Large majorities of those with negative views voted to change administrations. Bush's loss to Clinton among major-party voters in 1992, therefore, can be attributed primarily to the heavily negative views of his stewardship of the economy, just as Carter's loss to Reagan in 1980 could be. In 1996 Clinton benefited primarily from the positive assessments of his handling of the economy, even though he did worse among those who disapproved than any other incumbent.

EVALUATIONS OF THE INCUMBENT

Fiorina distinguishes between "simple" and "mediated" retrospective evaluations. By *simple,* Fiorina means evaluations of the direct effects of social outcomes on the person, such as one's financial status, or direct perceptions of the nation's economic well-being. Mediated retrospective evaluations are evaluations seen through or mediated by the perceptions of political actors and institutions. Approval of Clinton's handling of the economy or the assessment of which party would better handle the most important problem facing the country are examples.[12]

As we have seen, the more politically mediated the question, the more closely responses align with voting behavior. Perhaps the ultimate in mediated evaluations is the presidential approval question: "Do you approve or disapprove of the way [the incumbent] is handling his job as president?" From a retrospective voting standpoint, this evaluation is a summary of all aspects of his service in office. Table 7-6 reports the distribution of overall evaluations and their relationship to major-party voting in the last seven elections.[13]

As can be seen in Table 7-6A, incumbents Nixon, Ford, Reagan, and Clinton enjoyed widespread approval, whereas only two respondents in five approved of Carter's or of Bush's handling of his job.[14] This presented Carter in 1980 and Bush in 1992 with a problem. Conversely, incumbents highly approved of by voters, such as Reagan in 1984—and his vice president as beneficiary in 1988— had a major advantage. Clinton dramatically reversed any negative perceptions of his incumbency held in 1994, such that by 1996, he received the highest level of approval since Nixon's landslide reelection in 1972. As can be seen in Table 7-6B, there is a very strong relationship between approval of the incumbent and the vote for that incumbent. Clinton was as successful in winning the support of those who approved of his performance as other incumbents, although he won the backing of very few of those who disapproved. The key to his victory, therefore, was his ability to convince so many voters that he had done a good job in his first four years.

THE IMPACT OF RETROSPECTIVE EVALUATIONS

Our evidence strongly suggests that retrospective voting has been widespread in all recent elections. Moreover, as far as data permit us to judge, the evidence is clearly on the side of the Downs-Fiorina view. Retrospective evaluations appear to be used to make comparative judgments. Presumably, voters find it easier, less time consuming, and less risky to evaluate the incumbent party on what its presi-

TABLE 7-6 Distribution of Responses on President's Handling of His Job and Major-Party Vote, 1972–1996

Do you approve or disapprove of the way [the incumbent] is handling his job as president?	1972	1976	1980	1984	1988	1992	1996
A. Distribution of Responses (in percentages)							
Approve	71	63	41	63	60	43	68
Disapprove	29	37	59	37	40	57	32
Total percent	100	100	100	100	100	100	100
(N)	(1,215)	(2,439)[a]	(1,475)	(2,091)	(1,935)	(2,419)[a]	(1,692)[a]
B. Percentage of Major-Party Voters Who Voted for the Incumbent Party's Nominee							
Approve	83	74	81	87	79	81	84
(N)	(553)	(935)[a]	(315)	(863)	(722)	(587)[a]	(676)[a]
Disapprove	14	9	18	7	12	11	4
(N)	(203)	(523)[a]	(491)	(449)	(442)	(759)[a]	(350)[a]

Note: Question was asked of a randomly selected half-sample in 1972. Numbers in parentheses are the totals on which percentages are based.

[a]Numbers are weighted.

dent did in the most recent term or terms in office than on the nominees' promises for the future. But few base their vote on judgments of past performance alone. Most use past judgments as a starting point for comparing the major contenders. When the incumbent's performance in 1980 and 1992 was compared with the anticipated performance of the opponent, most felt the incumbent had not done very well, but a surprisingly large number of those did not believe that the opposition party would do any better (see Table 7-2). In 1972, 1984, 1988, and 1996, many felt the incumbent had done well, and few thought the challenger's party would do better. The 1996 election was most like the 1984 and 1988 elections. Evaluations were generally positive and, in the case of overall approval, unusually so. Even though few thought the government had done a good job handling the most important problem, many more thought the Democrats would do just as well as or better than the Republicans at solving it.

We can strengthen the overall assessment of retrospective voting in the last few elections by forming a combined index of retrospective evaluations common to the six most recent presidential election surveys. In Figures 7-1 and 7-2, we report the result of combining the presidential approval measure with the evaluation of the job the government has done on the most important problem and the assessment of which party would better handle that problem.[15] This creates a 7-point scale ranging from strongly opposed to the job the incumbent and his party have done to strongly supportive of that performance. For instance, those who approved of Clinton's job performance, thought the government was doing a good job, and thought the Democratic party would better handle the problem are scored as strongly supportive of the incumbent party's nominee in their retrospective evaluations in 1996.

In Figure 7-1, we report the distribution of responses on this combined measure. As these figures make clear, respondents had rather positive evaluations of the incumbent and his party in 1996. The most common category was slightly pro-incumbent, followed by neutral and then moderately pro-incumbent. A smaller percentage fell into the moderately and the slightly anti-incumbent categories than in any of the five earlier studies. The 1996 responses correspond most closely to 1984, although the 1984 responses were more uniformly distributed over the seven categories. The 1996 responses were also fairly similar to those in 1988 and most unlike those in 1980 and 1992. In short, evaluations in 1996 were like those in elections won by incumbents and unlike those in which they lost.

As Figure 7-2 shows, respondents who have positive retrospective evaluations of the incumbent party are much more likely to vote for that party than are those who disapprove of the incumbent party's performance. What is most striking about the figure is how similar and how very strong the relationship is in every election year. In this case, the support for Clinton in 1996 is even more strongly related to these retrospective evaluations than in past elections. Virtually no one in the two categories least favorable to the incumbent supported him, while all of the major-party voters in the most favorable two categories

FIGURE 7-1   Distribution of Electorate on Summary Measure of Retrospective Evaluations, 1976–1996

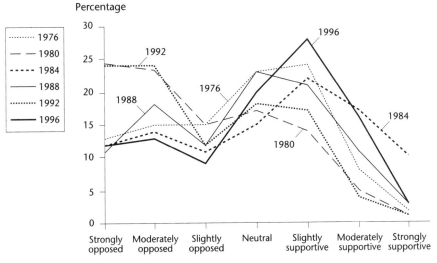

Note: The total number of cases: 1976 — 2,166 (weighted); 1980 — 1,325; 1984 — 1,814; 1988 — 1,409; 1992 — 1,987 (weighted); 1996 — 1,713 (weighted).

voted for him, and there was a sharp increase in going from slightly against to slightly in favor of the incumbent. As in all preceding elections, those in the neutral category were more likely to stay with, than to oppose, the incumbent's party (in 1996, seven in ten in the neutral category voted for Clinton).

In sum, it would seem reasonable to conclude that the 1980 election was a clear and strong rejection of Carter's incumbency. In 1984 Reagan won in large part because he was seen as having performed well and because Mondale was unable to convince the public that he would do better. In 1988 Bush won in large part because Reagan was seen as having performed well—and people thought Bush would stay the course. In 1992 Bush lost because of the far more negative evaluations of his administration and of his party than had been obtained in any other recent elections except 1980. In 1996 Clinton won reelection in large part for the same reasons that Reagan won in 1984—he was seen as having performed well on the job, and he was able to convince the public that his opponent would not do any better.

There is obviously more to the differences among these elections than retrospective evaluations alone. As you may recall from Chapter 6, prospective issues, especially our balance of issues measure, increasingly have been strongly related to the vote over the last few elections. Table 7-7 reports the impact of both types

FIGURE 7-2   Percentage of Major-Party Voters Who Voted for Incumbent, by
Summary Measure of Retrospective Evaluations, 1976–1996

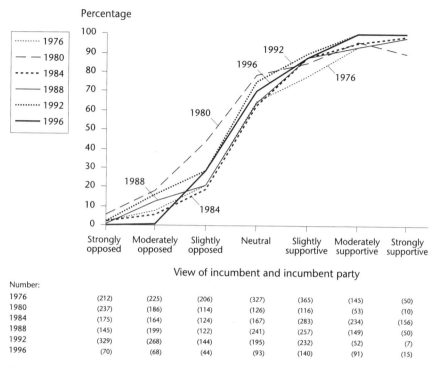

Note: Numbers in parentheses are the totals on which the percentages are based. Weighted *N*s were used for 1976, 1992, and 1996. Questions were asked of a randomly selected half-sample in 1996.

of policy evaluation measures on the major-party vote in 1996. Both policy measures were collapsed into three categories; pro-Democratic, neutral, and pro-Republican. Reading down each column, we see that retrospective evaluations are strongly related to the vote, even when one controls for prospective evaluations. Reading across each row, we see that prospective evaluations are clearly related to the vote among respondents with neutral retrospective evaluations, moderately related to the vote among those with pro-Republican evaluations, but not clearly related to the vote among those with pro-Democratic retrospective evaluations. Together, the two kinds of policy measures take us a long way toward understanding voting choices. Nearly nineteen in twenty of those with pro-Republican stances on the two measures, for example, voted for Dole, while an even larger proportion of those with pro-Democratic stances voted for Clinton. This accounting of voting choices is stronger when both forms of policy evaluations are considered than when either one is viewed individually. Analyses of the 1976 and 1980 elections, in contrast, showed little relationship

TABLE 7-7   Percentage of Major-Party Voters Who Voted for Clinton, by Balance of Issues and Summary Retrospective Measures, 1996

Summary retrospective[a]	Balance of Issues[b]							
	Republican		Neutral		Democratic		Total	
	%	(N)	%	(N)	%	(N)	%	(N)
Republican	3	(149)	20	(25)	[3]	(8)	7	(182)
Neutral	58	(38)	70	(33)	91	(22)	70	(93)
Democratic	93	(82)	89	(80)	98	(85)	93	(247)
Total	38	(269)	72	(138)	92	(115)	59	(522)

Note: Numbers in parentheses are the totals on which percentages are based. Numbers are weighted.

[a]The neutral category is the same as on the full scale, while the Republican [Democratic] category is the combination of all three Republican [Democratic] categories on the full scale.

[b]The neutral category is a score of –1, 0, or 1 on the full measure; the Republican [Democratic] category is any score greater than 1 [less than –1] on the full measure.

between prospective issues and the vote, once retrospective issues were taken into account. We found that in 1984 prospective issues had some effect (similar to but a bit weaker than that of 1996), and that the relationship in 1988 was stronger still.[16]

THE RETROSPECTIVE EVALUATIONS OF PEROT VOTERS

We have examined the effect of retrospective evaluations on major-party voters. In 1976, 1984, and 1988, over 98 percent of the voters supported either the Democratic or Republican presidential candidate. But Perot gained 19 percent of the total vote in 1992 and nearly half that in 1996, and we can ill afford to ignore the retrospective evaluations of his supporters. We shall examine those evaluations on the key measures that we use to construct our summary measure of retrospective evaluations.

Table 7-8 presents the percentage of Clinton, Dole, and Perot voters who approved of Clinton's performance as president, their views about the job the government was doing solving the most important national problem, and their beliefs about which party would do a better job solving that problem. Last, Table 7-8 shows the distribution of each candidate's voters on our summary measure of retrospective evaluations.

More than nineteen in twenty of Clinton voters approved of his handling of his job. Dole supporters were (as is usual for those voting for the challenger) split, with three who disapproved to every one who approved. Perhaps surprisingly, Perot voters approved of Clinton's job performance by a two-to-one margin. Few Clinton voters thought the government was doing a good job solving the most important problem, but far fewer Dole or Perot voters were this positive. Half of Clinton's voters said the government was doing "only fair," and a third thought it was doing a poor job. Perot voters, in this case, resembled Dole voters, with a third giving the government credit for doing "only fair" and two-thirds saying it was doing poorly with the most important problem. Clinton voters were likely to say the Democrats would handle that job better in the future, or neither party would be better; the Dole voters said the same but in favor of Dole's party. Seven in ten Perot voters said neither party would do better than the other.

Perot voters presented an unusual mixture of thinking the government had done poorly with the most important problem and thinking neither party would do a better job than the other. These responses for the major-party nominees in 1996 look much like they did in 1992.[17] While Perot voters in 1992 gave similar responses to the two questions concerning the most important problem facing the nation, as they did in 1996, in 1992 they disapproved of Bush by virtually the same two-to-one margin that they approved of Clinton's performance in 1996. It might well be the case, therefore, that one reason that Perot drew fewer votes in 1996 than in 1992 was because his potential supporters were not as dissatis-

TABLE 7-8   Retrospective Evaluations, by How Voted for President, 1996 (in percentages)

	Clinton	Dole	Perot
Approval of Clinton's job performance			
Approve	97	24	67
Disapprove	2	76	33
Don't know	1	0	0
Total	100	100	100
(*N*)	(590)	(442)	(85)
Job government is doing solving the most important problem			
Good	12	1	2
Only fair	53	35	31
Poor	34	64	67
Don't know	2	0	0
Total	101	100	100
(*N*)	(309)	(214)	(45)
Which party would do a better job solving problem			
Republican	7	55	8
Neither	51	43	71
Democratic	42	2	21
Don't know	0	0	0
Total	100	100	100
(*N*)	(307)	(214)	(43)
Summary measure of retrospective evaluations			
Strongly Republican	0	33	8
Moderately Republican	0	31	15
Slightly Republican	4	15	7
Neutral	21	13	35
Slightly Democratic	40	8	28
Moderately Democratic	30	0	6
Strongly Democratic	5	0	2
Total	100	100	101
(*N*)	(309)	(214)	(45)

Note: Numbers are weighted.

fied with Clinton as president as they were with Bush's incumbency. In any event, on the overall measure of retrospective voting, Clinton voters favored the Democratic incumbency, although not by as great a margin as Clinton voters in 1992 opposed the Bush-Republican incumbency. Dole voters were more negative toward Clinton than Bush voters had been positive toward the Bush-Republican incumbency. Perot voters were more nearly neutral on this measure in 1996, whereas in 1992 they were more heavily anti-incumbent.

CONCLUSION

In this and the previous chapter, we have found that both retrospective and prospective evaluations were strongly related to the vote. Indeed, in 1992 dissatisfaction with Bush's performance and with his and his party's handling of the most important problem—often an economic concern—goes a long way in explaining his defeat. In contrast, satisfaction with Clinton's performance and the absence of an advantage for the Republicans in being seen as able to deal with the most important concerns of voters go a long way in explaining his victory. It also appears that the role of issues was more consequential in 1996 than in many other recent elections but that its net impact was somewhat to Clinton's disadvantage, although less so than retrospective evaluations worked to his benefit. Still, our explanation remains incomplete. Most important, we have not accounted for why people hold the views they expressed on these two measures. We cannot provide a complete account of the origins of people's views, but there is one important source we can examine. Party identification, a variable we have used in previous chapters, provides a powerful means for the typical citizen to reach preliminary judgments. As we shall see, partisanship is strongly related to these judgments, especially to retrospective evaluations.

Moreover, party identification plays a central role in debates about the future of American politics. Will there be a partisan realignment? A dealignment? Or will the federal government continue under divided government, perhaps in a situation some have called a split-level realignment (albeit in a split different from the one originally considered, especially with Republican majorities in Congress)? Many political scientists believe that change of this magnitude in the political system can come only if there are changes in party loyalties in the electorate as well as in their voting behavior. Therefore, to understand voter choice better and to assess future partisan prospects, we must examine the role of party loyalties.

Chapter 8

Party Loyalties, Policy Preferences, and the Vote

Most Americans identify with a political party. Their party identification influences their political attitudes and, ultimately, their behavior. In the 1950s and 1960s the authors of *The American Voter,* along with other scholars, began to emphasize the role of party loyalties.[1] Although today few would deny that partisanship is central to political attitudes and behavior, many scholars question the interpretation of the evidence gathered during this period. We ask two questions: What is party identification? And how does it actually structure other attitudes and behavior? We then examine the role that party identification played in the 1996 presidential election.

PARTY IDENTIFICATION: THE STANDARD VIEW

According to the authors of *The American Voter,* party identification is "the individual's affective orientation to an important group-object in his environment," in this case the political party.[2] In other words, an individual sees that there are two major political parties that play significant roles in elections and develops an affinity for one of them. Partisanship, therefore, represents an evaluation of the two parties, but its implications extend to a wider variety of political phenomena. Angus Campbell and his colleagues measured partisanship by asking individuals which party they identified with and how strong that identification was.[3] If an individual does not identify with one of the parties, he or she may either "lean" toward a party or be a "pure" independent. Individuals who could not answer the party identification questions were classified as "apolitical."[4] Most Americans develop a preference for either the Republican or the Democratic party. Very few identify with any third party. The remainder are mostly independents, who are not only unattached to a party but also relatively unattached to politics in general. They are less interested, less informed, and less active than those who identify with a party.

Partisan identification in this view becomes an attachment or loyalty not un-like that observed between the individual and other groups or organizations in society, such as a religious body, a social class, or even a favorite sports team. As with loyalties to many of these groups, partisan affiliation often begins early. One of the first political attitudes children develop is partisan identification, and it develops well before they acquire policy preferences and many other political orientations. Furthermore, as with other group loyalties, once an attachment to a party develops, it tends to endure. Some people do switch parties, of course, but they usually do so only if their social situation changes, if there is an issue of overriding concern that sways their loyalties, or if the political parties them-selves change substantially.

Party identification, then, stands as a base or core orientation to electoral poli-tics. It is formed at an early age and endures for most people throughout their lives.[5] Once formed, this core orientation, predicated on a general evaluation of the two parties, affects many other specific orientations. Democratic loyalists tend to rate Democratic candidates and officeholders more highly than Repub-lican candidates and officeholders, and vice versa. In effect, one is predisposed to evaluate the promises and performance of one's party leaders relatively more favorably. It follows, therefore, that Democrats are more likely to vote for Demo-cratic candidates than are Republicans, and vice versa.

PARTY IDENTIFICATION: AN ALTERNATIVE VIEW

In *The Responsible Electorate,* published in 1966, V. O. Key, Jr., argued that party loyalties contributed to electoral inertia, and that many partisans voted as "standpatters" from election to election.[6] That is, in the absence of any informa-tion to the contrary, or if the attractions and disadvantages of the candidates are fairly evenly balanced, partisans are expected to vote for the candidate of their party. Voting for their party's candidates is their "standing decision," until and unless voters are given good reasons not to. More recently, scholars have reex-amined the bases of such behavior. In this new view, citizens who consider them-selves Democrats have a standing decision to vote for the Democratic nominee because of the past positions of the Democrats and the Republicans and because of the parties' comparative past performances while in office. In short, this view of partisan identification presumes that it is a "running tally" of past experiences (mostly in regard to policy and performance), a sort of summary expression of political memory, according to Morris P. Fiorina.[7]

Furthermore, when in doubt about what, for example, a Democratic candi-date is likely to do on civil rights in comparison to the Republican opponent, it is reasonable to assume the Democrat would be more liberal than the Republi-can—at least unless the candidates indicate otherwise. Because the political par-ties tend to be consistent on the basic historical policy cleavages, summary judgments of parties and their typical candidates do not change radically or of-ten.[8] As a result, a citizen's running tally serves as a good first approximation, changes rarely, and can be an excellent device for saving time and effort that would be spent gathering information in the absence of this "memory."

Many of the major findings used in support of the conventional interpretation of party identification are completely consistent with this more policy-oriented view. We do not have the evidence to assert that one view is superior to the other. Indeed, the two interpretations are not mutually exclusive. Moreover, they share the important conclusion that party identification plays a central role in shaping voters' decisions.

Both views agree that partisan identifications are long-term forces in politics. Both agree that such identifications are formed early in life for most of us; children often develop a partisan loyalty, which they usually learn from their parents, although these loyalties are seldom explicitly taught. Partisan identifications are also often closely associated with social forces, as discussed in Chapter 5, especially when a social group is actively engaged in partisan politics. An important illustration of this point is the support of many labor unions for the New Deal Democratic coalition, which often reinforced the tendency of those who were in labor unions to identify with the Democratic party. Finally, both views agree that partisanship is closely associated with more immediate evaluations, including prospective and retrospective issue evaluations and evaluations of the candidates, as analyzed in Chapters 6 and 7.

The two views disagree about the nature of the association between partisanship and other attitudes such as those toward the candidates and on issues. The standard view argues that partisanship, as a long-term loyalty, affects the evaluations of issues and candidates by voters, but that it in turn is largely unaffected by such evaluations, except in such dramatic circumstances as realigning elections. In this sense, partisanship is a "filter" through which the concerns relevant to the particular election are viewed. In the alternative view, partisanship as a running tally may affect, but is also affected by, more immediate concerns. Indeed, Fiorina's definition of partisanship makes clear that the running tally includes current as well as past assessments. Distinguishing empirically between these two views is therefore quite difficult. Although the alternative view may see partisan identification as being open to the impact of retrospective and prospective evaluations and assessments of the candidates in the current election, such assessments typically change an individual's identification relatively little, because of the accumulation of past experiences and the effect of initial socialization. We analyze the role of partisan identification in 1996 and other recent elections in ways consistent with both major views of partisan identification.

PARTY IDENTIFICATION IN THE ELECTORATE

If partisan identification is a fundamental orientation for most citizens, then the distribution of partisan loyalties is of crucial importance. The National Election Studies (NES) have monitored the party loyalties of the American electorate since 1952. In Table 8-1 we show the basic distributions of partisan loyalties in presidential election years from 1980 through 1996. As the table shows, most Americans identify with a political party. In 1996 more than two voters in three claimed to think of themselves as a Democrat or as a Republican, and an additional one-quarter, who initially said they were independent or had no partisan preference, nonetheless said they felt closer to one of the major parties than to the other.[9] About one in twelve was purely independent of party, and barely one in a hundred was classified as "apolitical." One of the largest changes in partisanship in the electorate began in the mid-1960s, when more people claimed to be independents.[10] This growth stopped, however, in the late 1970s and early 1980s. There was very little change in partisan loyalties between the 1984 and 1988 surveys, and there was only slightly more change by 1992, when the percentage of independents increased modestly.

These modest changes in 1992 did not continue. Indeed, there were signs in 1996 of reversals of the trends in party identification toward greater independence. All partisan groups increased slightly in 1996 compared with 1992, and the total percentage of partisans was higher in 1996 than in *any* of the six elections that preceded it. The 8 percent of "pure" independents (that is, those with no partisan leanings) was the lowest percentage since 1968, and this decline in independence appears to have begun in 1994 (when 10 percent were "pure" independents). These changes are small. Still, it is a reversal of patterns that had held for a generation and thus might presage more dramatic changes and perhaps a strengthening of partisan ties among the electorate.

Table 8-1 also shows that more people think of themselves as Democrats than as Republicans. Over the past forty years, the balance between the two parties

TABLE 8-1 Party Identification in Presidential Year, Preelection Surveys, 1980–1996 (in percentages)

Party Identification	1980	1984	1988	1992	1996
Strong Democrat	18	17	18	17	18
Weak Democrat	24	20	18	18	20
Independent, leans Democratic	12	11	12	14	14
Independent, no partisan leanings	13	11	11	12	8
Independent, leans Republican	10	13	14	13	12
Weak Republican	14	15	14	15	16
Strong Republican	9	13	14	11	13
Total	100	100	101	100	101
(*N*)	(1,577)	(2,198)	(1,999)	(2,450)[a]	(1,696)[a]
Apolitical	2	2	2	1	1
(*N*)	(35)	(38)	(33)	(23)	(14)

[a]Numbers are weighted.

has favored the Democrats by a range of about 55/45 to about 60/40. While the results from the last five presidential election years still fall within that range, they show a clear shift toward the Republicans. By recalculating the results in Table 8-1, we find that in 1980, 35 percent of partisans were Republicans; in 1984, 42 percent were; by 1988, 44 percent were; and in 1992 and in 1996, 43 percent of partisans were Republicans. Including independents who lean toward a party would increase the percentage of Republicans from 38 percent in 1980, to 45 percent in 1984, 47 percent in 1988, and then to 44 percent in the last two elections. Thus, the Democratic advantage in loyalties in the electorate has narrowed, an edge made even smaller in practice by the tendency of the Republicans to have higher turnout than Democrats (see Chapter 4).

The partisan loyalties of the American electorate can also be analyzed through other surveys. Among these, the most useful are the General Social Surveys (GSS), conducted by the National Opinion Research Council (NORC). These surveys are usually based on about 1,500 respondents who are interviewed in person, and they employ the standard party identification questions developed by the authors of *The American Voter* to measure long-term attachments to the political parties. The GSS surveys have been carried out annually since 1972.[11] Like the NES surveys, the GSS surveys reveal some Republican gains. According to our calculations based on the GSS codebooks, from 1972 through 1982, the percentage of party identifiers supporting the Republicans never rose above 37 percent. Even if independent leaners (relatively more of whom were Republicans) are included as partisans, support for the GOP never rose beyond 38 percent. The GOP made gains in 1983, and in 1984 the percentage of party identifiers who were Republican rose to 40 percent. Republican strength peaked in the 1990 GSS survey. Forty-eight percent of all party identifiers were Republicans, and if independents who lean toward a party are included, 49 percent were Republicans. But the Republicans made no further gains, even in the 1991 survey, conducted during and shortly after the Persian Gulf War. In the most recent GSS survey, based on 2,900 respondents and conducted in February, March, and April of 1996, 45 percent of all party identifiers were Republican, and the figure drops to 44 percent if independent leaners are included. Unlike the 1996 NES survey, the most recent GSS survey does not reveal gains in partisan strength among the electorate. Only 24 percent were strong party identifiers, and only 62 percent were strong or weak party identifiers. Sixteen percent were independents who leaned toward neither political party.

Our analysis of the NES surveys reveals that the shift toward the Republican party is concentrated among white Americans. As we saw in Chapter 5, the sharpest social division in U.S. electoral politics is race, and this division has been reflected in partisan loyalties for decades. Moreover, the gap appears to be widening. Although the distribution of partisanship in the electorate as a whole has changed only slightly since 1984, this stability masks a growth in Republican identification among whites and, of course, a compensating growth of already strong Democratic loyalties among African-Americans. In Table 8-2 we report the party identification of whites between 1952 and 1996, and in Table 8-3 we report the identification of blacks. As the tables show, black and white patterns in partisan loyalties have been very different throughout this period. There was a sharp shift in black loyalties in the early 1960s. Before 1962, about 50 percent of African-Americans were strong or weak Democrats; since that time, 60 percent, 70 percent, and even more blacks have considered themselves Democrats.

The party loyalties of whites have changed more slowly. Still, the percentage of self-professed Democrats among whites declined during the Reagan years, while the percentage of Republicans increased. In the last four elections partisanship by race has changed with shifts among whites. In 1984 an even balance existed between the two parties among whites, if independent leaners are included. By 1988 the shift continued. This time, the number of strong and weak Democrats and strong and weak Republicans was almost the same, with more strong Republicans than strong Democrats for the first time. Adding in the two independent-leaning groups gave Republicans a clear advantage in identification among whites. In 1992, however, this advantage disappeared. There were slightly more strong and weak Democrats than strong and weak Republicans. Thus, in 1992, the two parties had essentially the same proportions of white identifiers. In 1996, all four of the partisan categories were slightly larger than in 1992. The result was that the balance of Republicans to Democrats changed very slightly, and the near parity of identifiers with the two parties among whites remained.

Although the increased Republicanism of the white electorate is partly the result of long-term forces, such as generational replacement, the actual movement between 1964 and 1988 appears to result from two shorter-term increases in Republican identification. There was a 5 percentage point movement toward the GOP from 1964 through 1968, and a 10-point movement toward the GOP between 1982 and 1988. This movement waned modestly in the 1990s, as we saw.

Party identification among blacks is very different. In 1996 there were very few black Republicans. Ninety-four percent of strong and weak identifiers among blacks are Democrats (as opposed to 52 percent of whites), and, adding in leaners, 92 percent of blacks are Democrats (as opposed to 51 percent of whites)—all of these proportions are unchanged from 1992.

These racial differences in partisanship are of long standing, and over time, changes have increased this division. Between 1952 and 1960, blacks were primarily Democratic, but about one in seven supported the Republicans. Black partisanship shifted massively and abruptly even further toward the Democratic party in 1964. In that year, over half of all blacks considered themselves *strong* Democrats. Since then, well over half have identified with the Democratic party. Black Republican identification fell to barely a trace in 1964 and has edged up only very slightly since then.

The abrupt change in black loyalties in 1964 reflects the two presidential nominees of that year. President Lyndon B. Johnson's advocacy of civil rights legislation appealed directly to black voters, and his Great Society and War on Poverty

TABLE 8-2   Party Identification among Whites, 1952–1996 (in percentages)

Party identification[a]	1952	1954	1956	1958	1960	1962	1964	1966	1968	1970
Strong Democrat	21	22	20	26	20	22	24	17	16	17
Weak Democrat	25	25	23	22	25	23	25	27	25	22
Independent, leans Democratic	10	9	6	7	6	8	9	9	10	11
Independent, no partisan leaning	6	7	9	8	9	8	8	12	11	13
Independent, leans Republican	7	6	9	5	7	7	6	8	10	9
Weak Republican	14	15	14	17	14	17	14	16	16	16
Strong Republican	14	13	16	12	17	13	12	11	11	10
Apolitical	2	2	2	3	1	3	1	1	1	1
Total	99	99	99	100	100	101	99	101	100	99
(N)	(1,615)	(1,015)	(1,610)	(1,638)[b]	(1,739)[b]	(1,168)	(1,394)	(1,131)	(1,387)	(1,395)

[a]The percentage supporting another party has not been presented; it usually totals less than 1 percent and never totals more than 1 percent.
[b]Numbers are weighted.

TABLE 8-3   Party Identification among African-Americans, 1952–1996 (in percentages)

Party identification[a]	1952	1954	1956	1958	1960	1962	1964	1966	1968	1970
Strong Democrat	30	24	27	32	25	35	52	30	56	41
Weak Democrat	22	29	23	19	19	25	22	31	29	34
Independent, leans Democratic	10	6	5	7	7	4	8	11	7	7
Independent, no partisan leaning	4	5	7	4	16	6	6	14	3	12
Independent, leans Republican	4	6	1	4	4	2	1	2	1	1
Weak Republican	8	5	12	11	9	7	5	7	1	4
Strong Republican	5	11	7	7	7	6	2	2	1	0
Apolitical	17	15	18	16	14	15	4	3	3	1
Total	100	101	100	100	101	100	100	100	101	100
(N)	(171)	(101)	(146)	(161)[c]	(171)[c]	(110)	(156)	(132)	(149)	(157)

[a]The percentage supporting another party has not been presented; it usually totals less than 1 percent and never totals more than 1 percent.
[b]Less than 1 percent.
[c]Numbers are weighted.

1972	1974	1976	1978	1980	1982	1984	1986	1988	1990	1992	1994	1996
12	15	13	12	14	16	15	14	14	17	14	12	15
25	20	23	24	23	24	18	21	16	19	17	19	19
12	13	11	14	12	11	11	10	10	11	14	12	13
13	15	15	14	14	11	11	12	12	11	12	10	8
11	9	11	11	11	9	13	13	15	13	14	13	12
14	15	16	14	16	16	17	17	15	16	16	16	17
11	9	10	9	9	11	14	12	16	11	12	17	15
1	3	1	3	2	2	2	2	1	1	1	1	1
99	99	100	101	101	100	101	101	99	99	100	100	100
(2,397)	(2,246)[b]	(2,490)[b]	(2,006)	(1,405)	(1,248)	(1,931)	(1,798)	(1,693)	(1,663)	(2,702)[b]	(1,510)[b]	(1,451)[b]

1972	1974	1976	1978	1980	1982	1984	1986	1988	1990	1992	1994	1996
36	40	34	37	45	53	32	42	39	40	40	38	43
31	26	36	29	27	26	31	30	24	23	24	23	22
8	15	14	15	9	12	14	12	18	16	14	20	16
12	12	8	9	7	5	11	7	6	8	12	8	10
3	—[b]	1	2	3	1	6	2	5	7	3	4	5
4	—[b]	2	3	2	2	1	2	5	3	3	2	3
4	3	2	3	3	0	2	2	1	2	2	3	1
2	4	1	2	4	1	2	2	3	2	2	3	0
100	100	99	100	100	100	99	99	101	101	100	100	100
(267)	(224)[c]	(290)[c]	(230)	(187)	(148)	(247)	(322)	(267)	(270)	(317)[c]	(203)[c]	(200)[c]

programs made an only slightly less direct appeal. Sen. Barry M. Goldwater, the Republican nominee, voted against the 1964 Civil Rights Act, a vote criticized even by many of his Republican peers. Party stances have not changed appreciably since then, although the proportion of blacks who were strong Democrats declined somewhat after 1968.

The proportion of blacks considered "apolitical" dropped in 1964 as well, from the teens to very small proportions, similar to those among whites. This shift resulted from the civil rights movement, the contest between Johnson and Goldwater, and the passage of the Civil Rights Act. The civil rights movement stimulated many blacks, especially in the South, to become politically active. Furthermore, the 1965 Voting Rights Act enabled many of them to vote for the first time.

PARTY IDENTIFICATION AND THE VOTE

As we saw in Chapter 4, partisanship is related to turnout. Strong supporters of either party are more likely to vote than weak supporters, and independents who lean toward a party are more likely to vote than independents without partisan leanings. Republicans are somewhat more likely to vote than Democrats. Although partisanship influences whether people go to the polls, it is more strongly related to *how* people vote.

Table 8-4 reports the percentage of white major-party voters who voted for the Democratic presidential candidate across all categories of partisanship since 1952.[12] Clearly, there is a strong relationship between partisan identification and choice of candidate. In every election except that in 1972, the Democratic nominee has received more than 80 percent of the vote of strong Democrats and majority support from both weak Democratic partisans and independent leaners. In 1996 these figures were even higher than in the Democratic landslide of 1964, and higher than in any other election in this period. Since 1952, strong Republicans had given the Democratic candidate less than one vote in ten. In 1988 more of the weak Republicans and independents who leaned toward the Republican party voted for Michael S. Dukakis than had for Walter F. Mondale in 1984, but, even so, only about one in seven voted Democratic. In 1992 Clinton won an even larger percentage of the two-party vote from these Republicans, and he increased his support among Republicans again in 1996. The pure independent vote, which fluctuates substantially, has tended to be Republican. John F. Kennedy won 50 percent of that vote in 1960, but Clinton won nearly two-thirds of the pure independents' two-party votes in 1992, short only of Johnson's three in four in 1964. Although his support among independents dropped substantially in 1996, this was a small group with low turnout. Thus, at least among major-party voters, Bill Clinton won because he held his own party identifiers and did better than usual among independents who lean toward the GOP and among weak Republican identifiers. Still, the strength of the association between partisanship and the votes cast by major-party voters was as strong as usual.

TABLE 8-4   Percentage of White Major-Party Voters Who Voted Democratic for President, by Party Identification, 1952–1996

Party identification	1952	1956	1960	1964	1968	1972	1976	1980	1984	1988	1992	1996
Strong Democrat	82	85	91	94	89	66	88	87	88	93	96	98
Weak Democrat	61	63	70	81	66	44	72	59	63	68	80	88
Independent, leans Democratic	60	65	89	89	62	58	73	57	77	86	92	91
Independent, no partisan leanings	18	15	50	75	28	26	41	23	21	35	63	39
Independent, leans Republican	7	6	13	25	5	11	15	13	5	13	14	26
Weak Republican	4	7	11	40	10	9	22	5	6	16	18	21
Strong Republican	2	—[a]	2	9	3	2	3	4	2	2	2	3

Note: To approximate the numbers on which these percentages are based, see Table 8-2. Actual *N*s will be smaller than those that can be derived from Table 8-2 because respondents who did not vote (or voted for a non-major-party candidate) have been excluded from these calculations. Numbers also will be lower because the voting report is provided in the postelection interviews, which usually contain about 10 percent fewer respondents than the preelection interviews in which party identification is measured.

[a]Less than 1 percent.

Among whites, then, partisanship leads to loyalty in voting. Between 1964 and 1980 the relationship between party identification and the vote was declining, but in 1984 the relationship between party identification and the presidential vote was higher than in any of the five elections from 1964 through 1980. The relationship remained strong in 1988 and continued to be quite strong in the two Clinton elections, at least among major-party voters. Nonetheless, the partisan basis of the vote in congressional elections, while strengthening somewhat, remained weaker than it had been in the 1950s and early 1960s. Thus, the question of whether the parties are gathering new strength cannot be answered definitively from the 1996 election data, but these data suggest some resurgence of partisanship in influencing the vote.

Partisanship is related to the way people vote. The question, therefore, is why do partisans support their party's candidates? As we shall see, party identification affects behavior because it helps structure (and, according to Fiorina, is structured by) the way voters view both policies and performance.

POLICY PREFERENCES AND PERFORMANCE EVALUATIONS

In their study of voting in the 1948 election, Bernard R. Berelson, Paul F. Lazarsfeld, and William N. McPhee discovered that Democratic voters attributed to their nominee, incumbent Harry S. Truman, positions on key issues that were consistent with their beliefs—whether those beliefs were liberal, moderate, or conservative.[13] Similarly, Republicans tended to see their nominee, Gov. Thomas E. Dewey of New York, as taking whatever positions they preferred. Not only has research since then emphasized the role of party identification in the projection onto the preferred candidate of positions similar to the voter's own views but also its role in shaping the policy preferences in the public.[14] We use four examples to illustrate the strong relationship between partisan affiliation and perceptions, preferences, and evaluations of candidates.

First, most partisans evaluate the job done by a president of their party more highly than do independents and, especially, more highly than those who identify with the other party. Figure 8-1 shows the percentage of each of the seven partisan groups that approves of the way the incumbent has handled his job as president (as a proportion of those approving or disapproving) in the last seven presidential elections. Strong Republicans have given overwhelming approval to all Republican incumbents, just as strong Democrats overwhelmingly approved of Clinton's handling of the presidency in 1996. In 1980, in contrast, "only" three strong Democrats in four approved of Carter. In 1996 the other two Democratic categories gave Clinton very high marks as well, far higher than the comparable Republicans gave Bush in 1992, and even modestly higher than Republicans gave Reagan in 1988. In all elections but those in 1980 and 1992, independents approved of the incumbent. Until 1996 that meant they approved of the Republican incumbent, but in 1996 a Democratic incumbent gained their approval. In

FIGURE 8-1   Approval of Incumbent's Handling of Job by Party Identification, 1972–1996

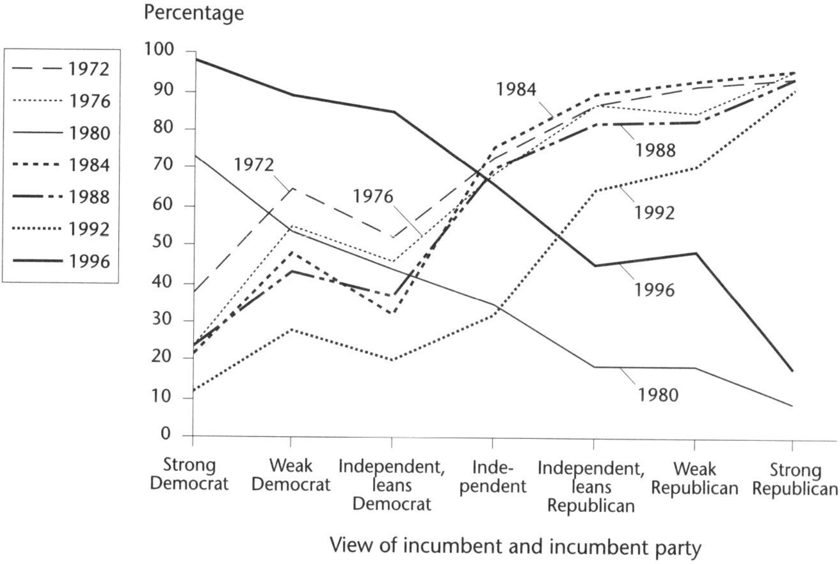

Number:

	Strong Democrat	Weak Democrat	Independent, leans Democrat	Independent	Independent, leans Republican	Weak Republican	Strong Republican
1972	(151)	(323)	(127)	(142)	(137)	(177)	(137)
1976[a]	(359)	(608)	(282)	(325)	(253)	(358)	(235)
1980	(214)	(291)	(148)	(163)	(144)	(193)	(119)
1984	(307)	(360)	(200)	(188)	(242)	(281)	(254)
1988	(338)	(146)	(225)	(189)	(266)	(270)	(278)
1992[a]	(418)	(441)	(334)	(269)	(305)	(354)	(273)
1996[a]	(312)	(329)	(226)	(136)	(197)	(266)	(215)

[a] Numbers are weighted.

1996 slightly under half of the Republican-leaning independents and the weak Republicans approved of Clinton, which is not unlike the percentages received by popular Republican incumbents from weak Democrats and Democratic-leaning independents (in 1972, 1984, 1988, and even 1976). Strong partisans, however, rarely approve of an incumbent from the other party, and 1996 was no exception. Thus, there is clearly a strong relationship between partisanship and presidential approval. Clinton's advantage over Dole, therefore, lay in large part in reversing the relatively low approval ratings he had held in 1994 that had made him the major target of Republican candidates in that year's congressional elections. Still, the relationship is not complete, as illustrated by the relatively high approval ratings weak Republicans gave Clinton.

Our second illustration extends the connection we have drawn between partisanship and approval of the incumbent. In this case, we examine the relationship between partisanship and approval of the incumbent's handling of the economy, in particular. Table 8-5 shows the relationship between all seven partisan categories and the approval of the handling of the economy by Reagan in 1984 and 1988, Bush in 1992, and Clinton in 1996.[15]

In 1984 and 1988, over three-quarters of each of the three Republican groups approved of Reagan's handling of the economy, while over half—and often over two-thirds—of the three Democratic groups disapproved. Independents generally approved of Reagan's economic efforts, albeit more strongly so in 1984 than in 1988. The 1992 election was dramatically different; the three Democratic groups and the pure independents overwhelmingly disapproved of Bush's handling of the economy. Even two-thirds of the weak and independent-leaning Republicans disapproved. Only strong Republicans typically approved, and even then one in three did not. The relationship in 1996 is most like that of 1984. In part this is because approval of Reagan's handling of the economy was high that year—even if voters approved even more highly of Clinton's handling of the economy. The relationship in 1996, while strong, is not quite as strong as in 1984, most notably because Democrats gave Reagan lower marks in 1984 than Republicans gave Clinton in 1996. This may be a result of the higher saliency of economic issues in 1984 and to Walter F. Mondale's emphasis on the uneven and, he claimed, unfair impact of that year's economic improvement. This claim that the Republicans' policies helped the better off more than the less well off likely triggered long-held partisan beliefs even more strongly than usual.

The third example of the effect of partisanship on attitudes and beliefs is its relationship to positions on policy issues. In Table 8-6 we report this relationship between the seven partisan categories and our balance of issues measure developed in Chapter 6, collapsed into a threefold grouping (pro-Democratic, neutral, pro-Republican).[16] As we saw, these issues favored the Republicans in 1972, 1976, and 1980, worked slightly to the Democratic advantage in 1984, 1988, and 1992, but reversed to favor the Republicans again in 1996.

As the table shows, there has regularly been a clear and moderately strong relationship between partisanship and the balance of issues measure, but it is one that, by 1996, had strengthened considerably. Until 1984 the relationship had been stronger among Republicans than among Democrats. In 1984 and 1988 (and also 1992, but recall that that measure depends on only three issues and is therefore less useful) the relationship was, if anything, stronger among Democrats than Republicans. The reason for that change very likely was the changing political context. In 1980, for example, more people, Democrats as well as Republicans, were closer to the median position of Reagan than of Carter on such important issues as defense spending and cutting income taxes. Reagan pushed increases in defense spending and cuts in income taxes through Congress in his first term, and he slowed the increases in spending for many domestic programs as well. By 1984, therefore, the electorate no longer favored as great an increase in defense spending and was more amenable to increased spending on some domestic issues. Thus, in the next three elections, issues tended to divide the electorate along party lines, with Democrats closer to their

TABLE 8-5 Approval of Incumbent's Handling of the Economy among Partisan Groups, 1984–1996 (in percentages)

	Party identification							
	Strong Democrat	Weak Democrat	Independent, leans Democrat	Independent	Independent, leans Republican	Weak Republican	Strong Republican	Total
1984								
Approve	17	41	32	68	84	86	95	58
Disapprove	83	59	68	32	16	14	5	42
Total	100	100	100	100	100	100	100	100
(N)	(309)	(367)	(207)	(179)	(245)	(277)	(249)	(1,833)
1988								
Approve	19	35	32	57	76	79	92	54
Disapprove	81	65	68	43	24	21	8	46
Total	100	100	100	100	100	100	100	100
(N)	(337)	(332)	(229)	(185)	(262)	(262)	(269)	(1,876)
1992								
Approve	3	9	6	9	31	34	66	20
Disapprove	97	91	94	91	69	66	34	80
Total	100	100	100	100	100	100	100	100
(N)[a]	(425)	(445)	(340)	(267)	(310)	(347)	(266)	(2,401)
1996								
Approve	96	82	76	58	46	49	30	66
Disapprove	4	18	24	42	54	50	70	34
Total	100	100	100	100	100	100	100	100
(N)[a]	(310)	(325)	(228)	(131)	(188)	(263)	(209)	(1,655)

[a]Numbers are weighted.

TABLE 8-6   Balance of Issues Positions among Partisan Groups, 1976–1996 (in percentages)

| | Party identification | | | | | | | |
Issue positions closer to:[a]	Strong Democrat	Weak Democrat	Independent, leans Democrat	Independent	Independent, leans Republican	Weak Republican	Strong Republican	Total
1976								
Democratic candidate	28	27	22	15	12	9	3	18
Neutral[b]	32	26	37	29	27	23	27	29
Republican candidate	39	47	40	55	61	67	69	53
Total	99	100	99	99	100	99	99	100
(N)	(422)	(655)	(336)	(416)	(277)	(408)	(254)	(2,778)
1980								
Democratic candidate	26	23	27	20	12	10	9	19
Neutral	34	37	33	43	40	43	31	37
Republican candidate	40	40	40	37	48	48	60	43
Total	100	100	100	100	100	101	100	99
(N)	(245)	(317)	(161)	(176)	(150)	(202)	(127)	(1,378)
1984								
Democratic candidate	57	49	59	35	23	29	14	39
Neutral	32	37	28	48	46	40	39	38
Republican candidate	11	14	13	17	32	32	47	23
Total	100	100	100	100	101	101	100	100
(N)	(331)	(390)	(215)	(213)	(248)	(295)	(256)	(1,948)

1988

Democratic candidate	49	36	50	33	21	21	11	32
Neutral	34	40	38	48	46	43	35	40
Republican candidate	17	24	12	19	33	36	53	29
Total	100	100	100	100	100	100	99	101
(N)	(355)	(359)	(240)	(215)	(270)	(281)	(279)	(1,999)

1992

Democratic candidate	40	36	30	26	13	13	9	25
Neutral	55	57	65	70	74	77	74	67
Republican candidate	5	7	4	5	13	11	17	9
Total	100	100	99	101	100	101	100	101
(N)[b]	(380)	(389)	(313)	(235)	(283)	(335)	(238)	(2,192)

1996

Democratic candidate	44	27	35	17	13	9	1	22
Neutral	27	36	34	43	27	23	14	29
Republican candidate	30	37	31	40	60	68	85	49
Total	100	100	100	100	100	100	100	100
(N)[b]	(313)	(333)	(229)	(140)	(195)	(268)	(217)	(1,696)

[a]The neutral category consists of scores of –1, 0, or 1 on the full measure; the Republican [Democratic] category is any score greater than 1 [less than –1] on the full measure.
[b]Numbers are weighted.

party's nominee. The result was a sharper and more balanced relationship between partisanship and the balance of issues measure. The increased polarization of the parties in Congress and among candidates generally accelerated in the 1994 congressional elections. This division between the two parties appears to have translated to partisan affiliation in the public as well. In 1996, although the balance of issues measure favored the Republicans, its relationship to party identification was stronger than ever.

Finally, we find a strong relationship between party identification and our measure of retrospective evaluations in the last six presidential elections.[17] Table 8-7 shows the basic relationship from 1976 through 1996, collapsing the summary retrospective measure into the three categories of pro-Democratic, neutral, and pro-Republican. In all years except 1992, a majority in the Republican category tended to evaluate Republican performance favorably. In all years but 1980, more than three in five Democratic identifiers assessed the Democratic party favorably. Even in the unfavorable years of 1980 for the Democrats and 1992 for the Republicans, those parties' identifiers were far more likely than the rest of the public to favor their party. In 1996 the relationship was, once again, very strong, with large majorities of partisan identifiers favoring their party on retrospective evaluations. This relationship, therefore, has consistently been among the strongest, and it suggests that Clinton was victorious in 1996 in large part because the public thought he and the Democrats had done well and were at least as good a bet as the Republicans to do well in the future.

We have seen that both party identification and retrospective evaluations have been consistently and strongly related to the vote, but these two measures are also strongly related to each other in every election. Do they both still contribute independently to the vote? The answer, as can be seen in Table 8-8, is yes. In this table, we have examined the combined impact of party identification and retrospective evaluations on voting choices in the last six presidential elections. To simplify the presentation, we have used the threefold grouping of the summary retrospective evaluations measure, and we have also regrouped party identification into the three groups of strong and weak Republicans, all three independent categories, and strong and weak Democrats.

Table 8-8 shows the percentage of major-party voters who voted Republican by both party identification and retrospective evaluations. Reading across the rows reveals that for all elections, retrospective evaluations are strongly related to the vote, regardless of the voter's party identification. Reading down each column shows that in all elections, party identification is related to the vote, regardless of the voter's retrospective evaluations. Moreover, party identification and retrospective evaluations have a combined effect on how people voted. For example, in 1996, among Republicans with pro-Republican evaluations, 96 percent voted for Dole; among Democrats with pro-Democratic identification, only 2 percent did. Note also the overall similarity, especially among the last four elections. The most important reason that the Republicans won a smaller victory in 1988 than in 1984 appears to be the less positive retrospective evalua-

TABLE 8-7 Retrospective Evaluations among Partisan Groups, 1976–1996 (in percentages)

Summary measure of retrospective evaluations[a]	Party identification							
	Strong Democrat	Weak Democrat	Independent, leans Democrat	Independent	Independent, leans Republican	Weak Republican	Strong Republican	Total
1976[b]								
Democratic	80	53	62	39	16	19	6	42
Neutral	11	23	24	28	28	25	23	23
Republican	10	24	15	33	56	57	71	35
Total	101	100	101	100	100	101	100	100
(N)	(314)	(535)	(249)	(293)	(238)	(314)	(206)	(2,149)
1980								
Democratic	45	29	18	11	8	7	4	20
Neutral	26	21	25	22	8	9	2	17
Republican	29	50	57	68	85	84	93	62
Total	100	100	100	101	101	100	99	99
(N)	(299)	(294)	(157)	(160)	(144)	(197)	(123)	(1,304)
1984								
Democratic	77	54	65	27	9	9	5	37
Neutral	12	17	13	22	15	18	5	14
Republican	12	29	21	52	76	73	90	49
Total	101	100	99	101	100	100	100	100
(N)	(303)	(356)	(197)	(181)	(241)	(270)	(239)	(1,787)

(Table continues)

TABLE 8-7 (continued)

Summary measure of retrospective evaluations[a]	Party identification							
	Strong Democrat	Weak Democrat	Independent, leans Democrat	Independent	Independent, leans Republican	Weak Republican	Strong Republican	Total
1988								
Democratic	79	61	64	32	20	17	6	42
Neutral	11	19	24	34	32	28	19	23
Republican	10	20	12	35	48	55	75	36
Total	100	100	100	101	100	100	100	101
(N)	(287)	(305)	(199)	(167)	(228)	(239)	(245)	(1,670)
1992[b]								
Democratic	90	80	85	72	39	32	12	61
Neutral	7	12	8	16	28	29	26	17
Republican	3	9	7	12	32	39	62	21
Total	100	101	100	100	99	100	100	99
(N)	(339)	(340)	(267)	(207)	(245)	(268)	(221)	(1,886)
1996[b]								
Democratic	77	72	59	37	25	19	3	47
Neutral	20	19	28	29	13	25	10	20
Republican	3	9	13	35	62	56	87	33
Total	100	100	100	101	100	100	100	100
(N)	(162)	(150)	(91)	(50)	(79)	(130)	(93)	(756)

[a]The neutral category is the same as that on the full scale; the Democratic [Republican] category is the combination of all three Democratic [Republican] categories on the full scale.
[b]Numbers are weighted.

TABLE 8-8   Percentage of Major-Party Voters Who Voted for the Republican Candidate, by Party Identification and Summary Retrospective Measures, 1976–1996

Party identification[a]	Summary retrospective[b]							
	Republican		Neutral		Democratic		Total	
	%	(N)	%	(N)	%	(N)	%	(N)
A. Voted for Ford, 1976[c]								
Republican	96	(269)[d]	90	(98)	35	(54)	87	(421)
Independent	85	(183)	73	(133)	16	(187)	56	(503)
Democratic	53	(111)	30	(96)	5	(404)	18	(611)
Total	84	(563)	65	(327)	11	(645)	49	(1,535)
B. Voted for Reagan, 1980								
Republican	100	(217)	75	(12)	33	(12)	95	(241)
Independent	82	(183)	36	(36)	24	(25)	69	(244)
Democratic	51	(135)	6	(78)	7	(140)	24	(353)
Total	81	(535)	21	(126)	11	(177)	58	(838)
C. Voted for Reagan, 1984								
Republican	99	(344)	86	(42)	39	(18)	95	(404)
Independent	91	(230)	77	(62)	10	(110)	67	(402)
Democratic	72	(97)	32	(62)	5	(333)	22	(492)
Total	93	(671)	63	(166)	8	(461)	59	(1,298)

(Table continues)

TABLE 8-8 (continued)

	Summary retrospective[b]							
	Republican		Neutral		Democratic		Total	
Party identification[a]	%	(N)	%	(N)	%	(N)	%	(N)
D. Voted for Bush, 1988								
Republican	97	(277)	93	(84)	46	(37)	91	(398)
Independent	86	(124)	64	(94)	15	(131)	54	(349)
Democratic	67	(54)	27	(63)	5	(296)	16	(413)
Total	91	(455)	64	(241)	11	(464)	53	(1,160)
E. Voted for Bush, 1992								
Republican	99	(187)	89	(87)	57	(61)	89	(335)
Independent	86	(72)	83	(56)	15	(233)	40	(362)
Democratic	58	(24)	32	(41)	4	(422)	9	(487)
Total	92	(283)	75	(184)	12	(717)	41	(1,184)
F. Voted for Dole, 1996								
Republican	96	(121)	74	(27)	45	(20)	86	(168)
Independent	91	(47)	29	(28)	9	(47)	45	(122)
Democratic	50	(12)	0	(43)	2	(175)	4	(230)
Total	92	(180)	29	(98)	7	(242)	40	(520)

Note: The numbers in parentheses are the totals on which percentages are based.

[a]Democratic [Republican] identifiers were those classified as strong and weak Democrats [Republicans]. Independents include those who lean toward either party and "pure" independents.

[b]The neutral category is the same as that on the full scale; the Democratic [Republican] category is the combination of all three Democratic [Republican] categories on the full scale.

[c]Numbers are weighted.

tions. Clinton's victory in 1992 appears to be due to the decidedly negative assessments of the Republican performance, and his victory in 1996 seems to be due to the positive assessments of him and his party. Thus, partisanship is a key component for understanding the evaluations of the public and their votes, but the large changes in outcomes over time must be traced to retrospective and prospective evaluations, simply because partisanship does not change substantially between elections.

In sum, partisanship appears to affect the way voters evaluate incumbents and their performance. Positions on issues have been a bit different. Although partisans in the 1970s and early 1980s were likely to be closer to their party's nominee on policy, the connection was less clear than that between partisanship and retrospective evaluations. In recent years, this relationship has strengthened, perhaps reflecting the increasingly sharp cleavages between the parties among candidates and officeholders.[18] Still, policy-related evaluations are influenced partly by history and political memory and partly by the candidates' campaign strategies. Partisan attachments, then, limit the ability of the candidates to control their fate in the electorate, but they are not entirely rigid. Candidates may, however, be more tightly constrained by prior performance, especially that of the incumbent, as seen in partisan terms by the electorate.

THE PEROT CANDIDACY

Perot differed from the other third-party and independent candidates who enjoyed appreciable success in this century. Theodore Roosevelt in 1912, Robert M. LaFollette in 1924, J. Strom Thurmond in 1948, George C. Wallace in 1968, and John B. Anderson in 1980 had all been notable figures within the two-party system before they launched their presidential candidacies. Perot was not. In 1992 he was known to the public primarily for his success in business, and in 1996 he was known in addition because of his candidacy in 1992 and his attempts to create a viable third party since then. In both elections, he also differed from his predecessors in 1968 and 1980, the two election years for which survey evidence is available, in that he did not lose support as his campaign progressed. Of course, he was supported in 1992 by more than twice as many voters as in 1996. Still, he received what would otherwise have been considered an unusually large proportion of the vote in 1996, were it not for his surprising strength in 1992. We therefore consider briefly the basis of his appeal.

In Table 8-9 we report how whites voted for the three candidates in 1996 (recall that very few African-Americans voted for Perot) according to their partisan identification, along with comparisons among comparable data for the 1968, 1980, and 1992 races. Support for Wallace, Anderson, and Perot has one basic characteristic in common. In all four elections, the third-party or independent candidate drew most strongly from independents, and Wallace and Perot did best among pure independents. Anderson in 1980 drew most strongly from in-

TABLE 8-9   How Whites Voted for President among the Three Major
Candidates in 1968, 1980, 1992, and 1996, by Party Identification
(in percentages)

	Candidate				
Party identification	Democrat	Independent	Republican	Total	(*N*)
A. 1968	Humphrey	Wallace	Nixon		
Strong Democrat	80	10	10	100	(164)
Weak Democrat	55	17	28	100	(212)
Independent, leans Democrat	51	18	31	100	(89)
Independent, no partisan leanings	23	20	57	100	(84)
Independent, leans Republican	4	14	82	100	(101)
Weak Republican	9	8	83	100	(163)
Strong Republican	3	2	96	101	(117)
B. 1980	Carter	Anderson	Reagan		
Strong Democrat	84	3	12	99	(129)
Weak Democrat	54	9	38	101	(173)
Independent, leans Democrat	44	23	33	100	(93)
Independent, no partisan leanings	20	13	67	100	(79)
Independent, leans Republican	11	10	78	99	(106)
Weak Republican	5	9	87	101	(151)
Strong Republican	4	4	93	101	(110)
C. 1992	Clinton	Perot	Bush		
Strong Democrat	90	6	4	100	(228)[a]
Weak Democrat	65	20	16	101	(238)[a]
Independent, leans Democrat	68	26	6	100	(203)[a]
Independent, no partisan leanings	37	41	22	100	(125)[a]
Independent, leans Republican	10	29	60	99	(193)[a]
Weak Republican	14	26	61	101	(240)[a]
Strong Republican	2	11	87	100	(210)[a]

D. 1996	Clinton	Perot	Dole		
Strong Democrat	94	4	2	100	(178)[a]
Weak Democrat	83	6	11	100	(177)[a]
Independent, leans Democrat	74	18	7	99	(107)[a]
Independent, no partisan leanings	29	24	47	100	(49)[a]
Independent, leans Republican	23	11	66	100	(112)[a]
Weak Republican	19	10	71	100	(171)[a]
Strong Republican	3	1	96	100	(188)[a]

[a]Numbers are weighted.

dependents who leaned toward the Democratic party and then from the pure independents. In 1968, 1980, and 1992, the third-party candidate also drew greater support from the party of the incumbent president than from the opposition party, but there was no such tendency in 1996. The difference is due to voters' approval of the incumbent. In the first three election years, the incumbent president was quite unpopular, and identifiers with his party appeared to be more willing to "defect" to a third-party or independent candidate instead of defecting to the nominee of the opposing major party. One reason that Wallace, Anderson, and Perot in 1992 did as well as they did, while Perot was less successful in 1996, was that the first candidacies were aided (indeed, attracted to compete in the first place) by a seemingly failed incumbency. Clinton's greater approval ratings in 1996 not only meant that Democrats were less likely to defect than in the earlier cases but also that this third-party candidacy would not attract as much support overall as four years earlier.

In Table 8-10 we report the percentage of support from whites for each of the three candidates in 1996 according to their partisanship.[19] The figures for the two major-party nominees are exaggerated versions of those in 1992. That is, in both cases all partisan groups, but especially strong partisans, made up an even larger proportion of the support for Clinton and Dole than they had for Clinton and Bush four years earlier. Over two-thirds of their votes came from their (strong and weak) partisans, less than one in ten came from partisans of the other party. In both elections, Perot drew primarily from the center categories. In 1992 his support was fairly even across the middle five partisan groups, but it was tilted so that he drew more from the Republican than the comparable Democratic categories. In 1996 he drew almost exactly the same proportion from those groups, but the largest block of support (one in four of his votes) were from independents who leaned Democratic, followed by the weak Republicans.

TABLE 8-10   Party Identification among Whites, by How Voted for President, 1996 (in percentages)

Party identification	How Voted for President		
	Dole	Clinton	Perot
Strong Democrat	1	36	8
Weak Democrat	5	31	13
Independent, leans Democratic	2	17	25
Independent, no partisan leanings	5	3	14
Independent, leans Republican	17	6	15
Weak Republican	28	7	22
Strong Republican	42	1	3
Total	100	101	100
(*N*)	(429)	(470)	(81)

Note: Numbers are weighted.

The most important characteristics of Perot voters in both 1992 and 1996 were their relative independence of party, their dissatisfaction with the government's handling of the most important problem, and their belief that neither party would be better than the other at solving that problem. The decline in Perot's support from 1992 to 1996 therefore rests on two major differences. First, Perot supporters, as we saw in Chapter 7, were relatively satisfied with Clinton's job performance in 1996, and since that satisfaction was far more common among the general electorate in 1996 than was approval of Bush's job performance in 1992, it seems that there was simply a smaller pool of potential third-party votes. Second, other retrospective evaluations were more positive in 1996 than in 1992. At bottom, it appears that the public perceived the economy to have improved considerably by 1996, and thus it was no longer of major concern. We previously argued that the Perot voter in 1992 was unpredictable: "Weakly or not at all loyal to a major party, apparently standing closer to neither party on the issues, and having been dissatisfied with the previous administration, this large bloc of voters could be wooed to Clinton's side if they view him as successful, could be wooed by the Republican nominee if they do not—or could remain with Perot if he were to run in 1996."[20] Clinton was widely viewed as successful, and he won substantial support among those who supported Perot in 1992; Dole also gained substantial support among 1992 Perot voters. According to the 1996 NES survey, among respondents who said that they voted for Perot in 1992 (*N* = 208), 26 percent voted for Clinton, 24 percent voted for Perot, 32 percent voted for Dole, and 15 percent did not vote.[21]

CONCLUSION

Party loyalties affect how people vote, how they evaluate issues, and how they judge the performance of the incumbent president and his party. In recent years, research has suggested that party loyalties not only affect issue preferences, perceptions, and evaluations, but that these may also affect partisanship. There is good reason to believe that the relationship between partisanship and these factors is more complex than any model that assumes a one-way relationship would suggest. Doubtless, evaluations of the incumbent's performance may also affect party loyalties.[22]

As we saw in this chapter, there was a substantial shift toward Republican loyalties among whites during the 1980s. The clear advantage Democrats have enjoyed during the past four decades appears to be gone. To some extent, this shift in party loyalties must have reflected Reagan's appeal and his successful performance in office, as judged by the electorate. It also appears that he was able to shift some of that appeal in Bush's direction in 1988 directly, by the connection between performance judgments and the vote, and also indirectly, through shifts in party loyalties among white Americans. Bush lost much of the appeal he inherited, primarily because of negative assessments of his performance in office in regard to the economy, and he was also not able to hold on to the high approval ratings he had held in 1991 after the success in the Gulf War. In 1996 Clinton demonstrated that a president could rebound from what the electorate judged to be a weak early performance and could benefit from a growing economy.

The increase in independence of the electorate over the 1970s and through to 1992 suggested that there was room for a third-party or independent candidate to win considerable support, and Perot demonstrated that potential handsomely. Many expected that these long-term trends toward independence would be accelerated by Perot and his new party. As we have seen, however, in both 1994 and 1996, the trend toward independence appears to have stopped, and partisanship in the public seems to be reflecting the deep cleavages that have appeared between Republicans and Democrats in campaigns and in office. Thus, not only is it still as true today as it was four decades ago that most Americans have a sense of identification with one or the other of the major parties, but the degree of attachment may have recently increased, at least marginally. This identification therefore continues to stand as a major force that connects the social affiliations of Americans with electoral politics, and it is closely related to the evaluations most Americans make of the candidates, the issues, and the performance of the incumbent party in office. Partisanship thus plays a major role in the voting choices of most Americans.

The 1996 election is comparable to the reelection campaigns of other recent, successful incumbents. Clinton received as high or higher marks for his overall performance and for his handling of the economy as Nixon in 1972 and Reagan in 1984. With strong retrospective judgments, the electorate basically decided that one good term deserved another. Still, these assessments also included expectations about the major-party opponent. Dole and the Republicans were burdened by the weak assessments of Bush's incumbency and by the negative evaluations of the new Republican majority in Congress. Thus, while Dole had the advantage, on balance, of being closer to more of the public on issues than Clinton, these judgments and the legacy of recently being the leader of the Republican majority in the Senate were too great to overcome. Except for the Republican advantage on the balance of issues measure, the surprise in these data was the relatively close outcome. Clinton failed to win the outright majority he sought, whereas his successful predecessors had won with overwhelming landslides.

The political landscape after the 1996 election is dramatically different from the time just before the 1992 elections. While the proportion of Democrats to Republicans in the electorate has been quite close for more than a decade, the general impression was that Republicans had a "lock" on the White House, and the forty-year Democratic majority in the U.S. House was thought to be unbreakable. The 1992 election demonstrated that a party has a "lock" on the presidency only when the public believes its candidate will handle the office better than its opposition. The 1994 elections so reversed conventional thinking that some now consider Congress a stronghold for the Republican party. It would be wise to remember two things. First, while party loyalties are a fundamental force, the balance between the two parties is quite close; thus, if no other forces are at work, a very close race should be expected. Second, even though there may be somewhat fewer independents in 1996 than there were in 1992, there are still more independents and there are weaker loyalties among the rest of the voters today than when the Democratic House majority was first forged. As a result, a strong performance by an incumbent, an extreme stance by a candidate or party, or a convincing claim that one party will be better able to solve pressing problems than the other can shift electoral fortunes considerably. Clinton benefited from both the improving economy and from the perceived extremity of the Republican congressional majority, two major liabilities that Dole faced and was unable to overcome. Republicans, however, held on to their successes in Congress. The effect of partisanship is important not only in presidential voting but also in voting for members of Congress. Events of the 1990s provide compelling documentation of the dramatic differences it makes if Congress is controlled by a Democratic or by a Republican majority.

PART 3

The 1996 and 1998
Congressional Elections

So far we have focused on the presidential election, but in 1996 the congressional elections were also of great importance. Indeed, some have argued that they were even more important than the contest between Bill Clinton and Bob Dole. "While most of the focus of the political coverage and commentary of 1996 was on the Presidential race," Elizabeth Drew writes, "for virtually all of the powerful groups behind the Republican Party their overriding goal of keeping control of the House stemmed from their view that that was where the real power—near- and long-term—lay." "The House," Drew continues, "was where the political realignment of the country in favor of the Republicans would be nailed down or lost."[1] Having concluded our analysis of Clinton's reelection, we now turn to the selection of the Congress that governs with him. In Part 3 we consider the selection of the 105th and 106th Congresses in 1996 and 1998.

There were many elections in 1996. In addition to the presidential election, there were eleven gubernatorial elections, elections for thousands of state and local offices, thirty-four elections for the U.S. Senate, and elections for all 435 members of the U.S. House of Representatives.[2] Unlike the 1980 elections, in which the Republicans won control of the Senate, and the 1994 midterm elections, in which the Republicans gained both the House and the Senate, the 1996 election held no major surprises. Although the Republicans lost 9 seats in the House, they still held partisan control, winning 227 seats to the Democrats' 207, with one seat going to an independent. In the Senate, the Republicans gained 2 seats, and held a 55-to-45 seat margin over the Democrats.

Although these results were not surprising, they were remarkable in a broader historical context. As Gary C. Jacobson writes, "The idea that the Democrats could win the White House by eight million votes without winning control of Congress would have been unthinkable only a few years ago."[3] Indeed, the Democrats had won the presidency in nineteen of the forty-two presidential elections

191

between 1828 and 1992, and in all nineteen of their victories they also won control of the House of Representatives. Republican presidential candidates were not nearly as successful. The Republicans had won the presidency twenty-one times between 1860 and 1988, but the Democrats had won control of the House in seven of these elections (1876, 1958, 1968, 1972, 1980, 1984, and 1988).

By returning Bill Clinton to the White House and by returning control of Congress to the Republicans, voters continued divided government. In 1994 the Republicans gained control of the House of Representatives for the first time since the 1952 election, ending a Democratic winning streak of twenty consecutive general elections for control of the House, by far the longest winning streak in U.S. electoral history. The 1996 Republican House victory marked the first time since 1928 that the GOP had held control of the House in two consecutive elections.

Despite the GOP congressional victories, the Republican edge in the House was very narrow. In fact, the party held the House by the narrowest margin of any party since the GOP won the House by a 221-to-213 margin in Eisenhower's 1952 landslide.

Why did the Democrats fail to regain control of the House, despite Clinton's impressive reelection victory? Did Clinton's likely victory actually aid the GOP in retaining control of the House? What will continued divided government mean for U.S. public policy? What are the prospects that the Republicans will build on their narrow majority and become a clear majority party in national legislative elections?

Chapter 9 attempts to answer these questions by examining the election results. Part of the Republicans' success came from their ability to field more incumbents. A total of 384 incumbents sought reelection, and 361 were successful. Even though Republican incumbents were somewhat less successful than Democratic incumbents, 92 percent were reelected. Despite the lower success rate of GOP incumbents, the Republicans did better at winning open seats previously held by Democrats than the Democrats did at winning open seats held by Republicans. Republican open-seat victories were concentrated in the South. Since World War II, regional support for the congressional parties has undergone a major change. We examine the geographic basis of party support and show that there has been a significant transformation, paralleling—though not quite as striking as—the change we observed in presidential elections.

In recent years there have been legal conflicts about the way congressional districts are drawn, especially the creation of oddly drawn districts to increase the chances of a black or Hispanic being elected. We discuss these conflicts, noting that the impact of recent court decisions is still difficult to evaluate.

We also discuss the 1996 congressional campaign, noting that the battle for control was shaped by the public's reaction to the Republican-controlled 104th Congress. By the summer of 1996 controversy had turned to compromise as Republicans began to worry about continued partisan conflict undermining their chances of controlling Congress. We examine Clinton's muted efforts to help the

Democrats win the Congress and note that in the last weeks of the campaign congressional Republican leaders tacitly abandoned Dole in order to increase their chances of retaining control of the House.

We examine the reasons that most incumbents are successful. Incumbency itself is a major political resource, and challengers to House incumbents usually lack the experience and money necessary to launch an effective campaign. All the same, we find that challengers who have held elective office and those who can raise substantial amounts of money are more successful than challengers who lack these assets. We note that during the 1980s there was an increase in the margin of victory for incumbents, although this trend was reversed in the 1990s. We examine alternative explanations for the increasing success of incumbents, as well as explanations that account for the declining victory margins in the 1990s.

Compared with the 1994 election, which swept the Democrats from majority control, the impact of the 1996 elections on Congress was relatively modest, but we will see how the elections reinforced the ideological divisions between the Republicans and the Democrats. We will also see how the narrow Republican majority in the House contributed to the problems of GOP House leaders. This narrow majority forced the GOP leadership to make substantial concessions to Clinton in regard to the budget and tax reform, despite the opposition of conservative Republicans in the House.

Finally, we speculate on the future of congressional elections through the beginning of the twenty-first century from the post-1996 perspective. The party controlling the White House lost strength in thirty-eight of the thirty-nine midterm elections between 1842 and 1994, so it seemed likely that the Democrats would lose House seats in 1998.[4] All the same, we expected those losses to be small. We discuss several academic models that give us insight about the likely outcome of midterm congressional elections. Given the relatively small number of Senate races, it is usually more difficult to predict Senate outcomes than House outcomes. Still, given the actual contests that were to be held in 1998, Democratic prospects for gaining control of the Senate seemed poor, although many observers expected the GOP to gain a few seats. The Democratic prospects for regaining control of Congress seemed better for 2000. Beyond that, as we will see, the reapportionment and redistricting that will occur after the 2000 census will bring changes that will first be seen in the 2002 midterm elections.

Chapter 10 explores how voters make congressional voting decisions—one of the most exciting and growing areas of research since the National Election Studies (NES) survey introduced questions in 1978 to study congressional voting behavior. Because only about a third of the Senate seats are contested in each election, our analysis focuses on the House. Chapter 10 examines how social factors influence voters' choices and compares the relationship of these factors in congressional and presidential voting. The effects of issues, party loyalties, and incumbency on voters' choices will also be assessed. We examine the ways that congressional voting can be seen as a referendum on the performance of a particular member, and show how it can be viewed as a referendum on the president's performance. We attempt to discover whether Clinton had "coattails," that is to say, whether Democrats were elected to Congress because of his presidential victory. Our analyses suggest that the presidential vote exerted some influence on the congressional vote, although it did not have as strong an influence as partisanship and congressional incumbency. As we will see, the conditions that led to the long-term Democratic advantage in congressional elections have changed, but because there are still more Democrats than Republicans among the electorate, the overall balance of partisan forces in Congress is highly competitive.

In Chapter 11 we discuss the 1998 congressional elections, reporting on the unexpected Democratic gains in the House and their success in holding on to 45 Senate seats. Although the Republicans retained control of both chambers, their loss of 5 House seats was a major disappointment, especially in light of historical patterns. The GOP won 223 seats to the Democrats' 211, with 1 seat taken by an independent, the Republican margin being only slightly larger than that after Eisenhower's election in 1952. On the other hand, the Republicans won twenty-three of the thirty-six gubernatorial elections, with the Democrats winning eleven. The victory of Democrat Gray Davis in California over Republican Dan Lungren, however, may give the Democrats control of the redistricting process in a state with 52 House seats.

Our analysis begins by considering the pattern of outcomes, comparing them to the previous results we discussed in Chapter 9. The vast majority of House incumbents who ran were reelected, although Democratic incumbents fared better than Republican incumbents, and the Democrats did slightly better in open-seat races. There was very little change in the party shares of the regional delegations for either the House or the Senate. Although the election brought little change in the partisan distribution in the House and no change in the Senate, the Republicans had expected substantial gains in both chambers. On the other hand, Democratic successes were consistent with academic models of congressional voting behavior that emphasize the state of the economy and presidential approval.

We then consider the impact of various factors on the election results. We examine the public's views of the economy and the failure of the Monica Lewinsky scandal to reduce Clinton's job approval ratings. We discuss the Republican strategy of attempting to capitalize upon the scandal, and conclude that these efforts may have been counterproductive. Both parties and their allies devoted great efforts to get their supporters to the polls, and the Democrats appear to have been more successful than the GOP in their mobilization efforts. We examine the attempts by both national parties to recruit strong congressional candidates and show how the national parties are playing a growing role in recruiting candidates, especially in potentially competitive races. The national parties are also increasingly involved in financing congressional campaigns, with money channeled largely into potentially competitive districts. But most House races are not competitive, and in 1998 a large number of races were not contested by both major parties. Many other races with candidates from both parties were "financially uncontested."

We next consider the impact of the 1998 elections on Congress. As a result of the election, Newt Gingrich was forced to resign as Speaker, and in the course of the impeachment debate Robert L. Livingston (R-La.), the designated Speaker-to-be, withdrew from contention. In the Senate, however, the election brought little change. Unlike the many reforms in House procedures following the GOP landslide in 1994, organizational changes in response to the 1998 election were few. Given the intense partisan conflicts over the impeachment debate at the end of the 105th Congress, it is difficult to anticipate major legislative achievements during the 106th.

In the final section we offer some ideas about congressional elections in 2000 and beyond. The 2000 elections may be affected by the impeachment vote, which was opposed by most Americans. At least in the short term, the impeachment vote has eroded public support for the Republican party, and it may harm GOP chances in 2000 if it encourages strong Democratic candidates to run for Congress and discourages strong Republicans. Based upon the 1998 results, however, there are relatively few House incumbents who won by a narrow margin, and there will probably be relatively few open seats in 2000. Thus, the battle for control of the House in 2000 may be focused on a small number of relatively close seats, and given the narrow Republican margin in the current House, the Democrats clearly have the potential of winning control. In the Senate there are more GOP seats at risk than Democratic seats, although most observers think that Democrats are less likely to win control of the Senate than they are of the House. After the 2000 census and the ensuing congressional reapportionment, redistricting will occur in every state with more than one House seat. As western and southern states are expected to gain House seats, and as most losses will be in the Northeast, reapportionment may somewhat benefit the Republicans. But neither party seems well positioned to make major gains from redistricting. On balance, the 1998 elections did relatively little to alter the political landscape. Rather, they underscored the close balance between the two major parties.

Chapter 9

Candidates and Outcomes in 1996

The congressional elections of 1996 were shaped by the electoral earthquake of 1994. In that year the Republicans unexpectedly won control of both chambers of Congress, the first time the GOP had won the House since the election of 1952. The 1996 election would determine whether they could hold the House for two consecutive elections (something they had not done since the 1920s) and thus continue their efforts to transform federal government policies. As it turned out, they succeeded in holding both chambers, continuing divided control of the federal government between the parties. In the House, they ended up with a somewhat narrower margin, winning 227 seats to the Democrats' 207, with one seat going to an independent.[1] This was a net loss of nine seats for the GOP. In the Senate, however, the Republicans gained two seats, resulting in a 55-45 seat division of the chamber.

In this chapter, we examine the pattern of congressional outcomes for 1996 and how they compared with outcomes of previous years. We seek to explain why the 1996 results took the shape they did—what factors affected the success of incumbents seeking to return and what permitted some challengers to run better than others. We also discuss the likely impact of the election results on the politics of the 105th Congress. Finally, we consider the implications of the 1996 results for the 1998 midterm elections and for subsequent elections through the beginning of the next century.

ELECTION OUTCOMES IN 1996

Patterns of Incumbency Success

Most races involve incumbents and most incumbents are reelected. This generalization has been correct for every set of congressional elections since World War II, although the degree to which it has held has varied somewhat from one

197

election to another. Table 9-1 presents information on election outcomes for House and Senate races involving incumbents between 1954 and 1996.[2] During this period, an average of 93 percent of the House incumbents and 83 percent of the Senate incumbents who sought reelection were successful.

In 1996 the proportion of representatives reelected (94 percent) was very close to the House average for the last twenty-two elections, while the success rate for senators (95 percent) was considerably better than the Senate average since 1954. The reelection rate in the House was higher than both of the two previous elections. Success was depressed in 1992 by rates of defeat that were higher than usual both in primaries and general elections. The large number of losses occurred in part because the election followed a census (when redistricting changed many district lines and forced many representatives to face one another in the same district), and in part because of a major scandal involving many House incumbents. In 1994 the lower rate of reelection was due almost entirely to the general election defeat of an unusually large number of Democrats, causing the turnover of partisan control of the House. In contrast, the 1996 elections saw very few primary defeats of incumbents (only one in each party), and the proportion that lost in the general election was very close to the long-term average (5.7 percent). In the 1996 Senate races, the number of incumbents seeking reelection was lower than in any other year in the table, and only one incumbent lost. (We discuss this point more below.)

During the period covered by Table 9-1, House and Senate outcomes have sometimes followed different patterns. For example, in most years between 1968 and 1988, House incumbents were substantially more successful than their Senate counterparts. In the three elections between 1976 and 1980, the success of incumbent representatives averaged over 93 percent, while that of senators averaged only 62 percent. In contrast, the success rates of House and Senate incumbents in the last four elections were very similar to each other.

It appears that the variation in the comparative results between the two bodies results from at least two factors. The first is primarily statistical: House elections routinely involve about 400 incumbents, while Senate contests usually have fewer than 30. A comparatively small number of cases is more likely to produce volatile results over time. Thus, the proportion of successful Senate incumbents tends to jump around more than that of successful House incumbents. Second, Senate races during the earlier period were more likely to be vigorously contested than House races. Many years saw a substantial number of representatives who had no opponent at all, or had one who was inexperienced or underfunded or both. Senators, in contrast, often had strong, well-financed opponents. Thus, representatives had more of an advantage than senators. In the 1990s the competitiveness of House elections has increased, reducing the relative advantage for representatives. We consider this issue in more detail later in the chapter.

We next turn from the consideration of incumbency to party. Figure 9-1 portrays the proportion of seats in the House held by the Democrats after each election since 1952. It graphically demonstrates how large a departure from the

TABLE 9-1   House and Senate Incumbents and Election Outcomes, 1954–1996

Year	Incumbents running (N)	Primary defeats (N)	Primary defeats (%)	General election defeats (N)	General election defeats (%)	Reelected (N)	Reelected (%)
House							
1954	(407)	(6)	1.5	(22)	5.4	(379)	93.1
1956	(410)	(6)	1.5	(15)	3.7	(389)	94.9
1958	(394)	(3)	0.8	(37)	9.4	(354)	89.8
1960	(405)	(5)	1.2	(25)	6.2	(375)	92.6
1962	(402)	(12)	3.0	(22)	5.5	(368)	91.5
1964	(397)	(8)	2.0	(45)	11.3	(344)	86.6
1966	(411)	(8)	1.9	(41)	10.0	(362)	88.1
1968	(409)	(4)	1.0	(9)	2.2	(396)	96.8
1970	(401)	(10)	2.5	(12)	3.0	(379)	94.5
1972	(392)	(13)	3.3	(13)	3.3	(366)	93.4
1974	(391)	(8)	2.0	(40)	10.2	(343)	87.7
1976	(383)	(3)	0.8	(12)	3.1	(368)	96.1
1978	(382)	(5)	1.3	(19)	5.0	(358)	93.7
1980	(398)	(6)	1.5	(31)	7.8	(361)	90.7
1982	(393)	(10)	2.5	(29)	7.4	(354)	90.1
1984	(411)	(3)	0.7	(16)	3.9	(392)	95.4
1986	(393)	(2)	0.5	(6)	1.5	(385)	98.0
1988	(409)	(1)	0.2	(6)	1.5	(402)	98.3
1990	(407)	(1)	0.2	(15)	3.7	(391)	96.1
1992	(368)	(20)	5.4	(23)	6.3	(325)	88.3
1994	(387)	(4)	1.0	(34)	8.8	(349)	90.2
1996	(384)	(2)	0.5	(21)	5.5	(361)	94.0
Senate							
1954	(27)	(0)	—	(4)	15	(23)	85
1956	(30)	(0)	—	(4)	13	(26)	87
1958	(26)	(0)	—	(9)	35	(17)	65
1960	(28)	(0)	—	(1)	4	(27)	96
1962	(30)	(0)	—	(3)	10	(27)	90
1964	(30)	(0)	—	(2)	7	(28)	93
1966	(29)	(2)	7	(1)	3	(26)	90
1968	(28)	(4)	14	(4)	14	(20)	71
1970	(28)	(1)	4	(3)	11	(24)	86
1972	(26)	(1)	4	(5)	19	(20)	77
1974	(26)	(1)	4	(2)	8	(23)	88
1976	(25)	(0)	—	(9)	36	(16)	64

(Table continues)

TABLE 9-1 (continued)

Year	Incumbents running (*N*)	Primary defeats (*N*)	Primary defeats (%)	General election defeats (*N*)	General election defeats (%)	Reelected (*N*)	Reelected (%)
1978	(22)	(1)	5	(6)	27	(15)	68
1980	(29)	(4)	14	(9)	31	(16)	55
1982	(30)	(0)	—	(2)	7	(28)	93
1984	(29)	(0)	—	(3)	10	(26)	90
1986	(27)	(0)	—	(6)	22	(21)	78
1988	(26)	(0)	—	(3)	12	(23)	88
1990	(30)	(0)	—	(1)	3	(29)	97
1992	(27)	(1)	4	(3)	11	(23)	85
1994	(26)	(0)	—	(2)	8	(24)	92
1996	(20)	(0)	—	(1)	5	(19)	95

past were the elections of 1994 and 1996. In House elections before 1994, high rates of incumbent participation, coupled with high rates of incumbent success, led to fairly stable partisan control. Most important, the Democrats had won a majority in the House in every election since 1954 and had won twenty consecutive national elections. This was by far the longest period of dominance of the House by the same party in American history.[3] This victory string was terminated by the cataclysm of 1994, when the GOP made a net gain of fifty-two representatives, winning 53 percent of the total seats. They held their majority in 1996, although there was a small shift back to the Democrats. In the Senate, the last Republican control was much more recent. Republicans had taken the Senate in the victory of Ronald Reagan in 1980 and then retained it in the next two elections. When the class of 1980 faced the voters in 1986, however, the Democrats made significant gains and won back the majority. They held it until the GOP regained control in 1994, and then the Republicans expanded their margin in 1996. In fact, the 55 percent of the seats they achieved was the highest Republican percentage in either House during this forty-four-year period.

The combined effect of party and incumbency in the general election of 1996 is shown in Table 9-2. Overall, the Republicans won 52 percent of the races for House seats, and 62 percent of the Senate contests. Despite the sharp partisanship of both the presidential and congressional races, incumbents of both parties in both chambers did very well. Ninety-two percent of House and Senate Republican incumbents in the general election won reelection, and 98 percent of House Democrats and 100 percent of Senate Democrats were successful. We can see that a significant part of the Democrats' failure to do better in the 1996 congressional races was their lower rate of success in open-seat contests. In those races, the Democrats lost about a third of their own open seats in each House (with losses concentrated in

FIGURE 9-1   Democratic Share of Seats in the House and Senate, 1953–1997

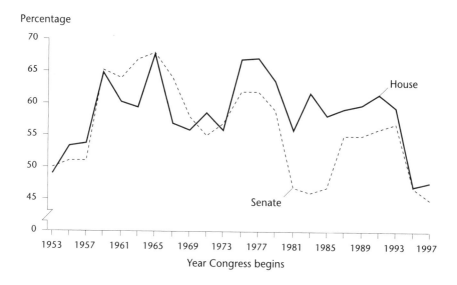

the South), and they were unable to win an equivalent proportion of Republican open seats. Indeed, the Democrats' 1996 performance in Republican open seats was virtually identical to 1994, although fortunately for them the success rate in Democratic open seats was considerably higher.[4]

TABLE 9-2   House and Senate General Election Outcomes, by Party and Incumbency, 1996 (in percentages)

| | Democratic incumbent | No incumbent | | Republican incumbent | Total |
		Democratic seat	Republican seat		
House					
Democrats	98	69	17	8	48
Republicans	2	31	83	92	52
Total	100	100	100	100	100
(*N*)	(169)	(29)	(24)	(213)	(435)
Senate					
Democrats	100	63	0	8	38
Republicans	0	38	100	92	62
Total	100	101	100	100	100
(*N*)	(7)	(8)	(6)	(13)	(34)

The important point in these results is that in 1996 the GOP was able to fight the Democrats to an outcome that virtually maintained the status quo. Furthermore, this was done in the election following their best showing in forty years. We would surely expect (all other things being equal) a legislative party to be more vulnerable to losses in an election after such a high point than in one after their electoral achievements had been more modest.[5] The 1996 election should have offered the Democrats a relatively positive context in which to regain control of the House. (Expectations regarding the Senate are less clear because the same seats are not contested in consecutive elections.) That they failed to do so may mean that in the future they may well need additional compensating advantages to win.

Regional Bases of Power

The geographic pattern of 1996 outcomes in the House and Senate can be seen in the partisan breakdowns by region in Table 9-3.[6] For comparison, we also present corresponding data for 1981 (after the Republicans took control of the Senate in Reagan's first election) and for 1953 (the last Congress until 1995 in

TABLE 9-3   Party Shares of Regional Delegations in the House and Senate, 1953, 1981, and 1997

	1953			1981			1997		
Region	Democrats (%)	Republicans (%)	(N)	Democrats (%)	Republicans (%)	(N)	Democrats (%)	Republicans (%)	(N)
House									
East	35	65	(116)	56	44	(105)	61	39	(89)
Midwest	23	76	(118)[a]	47	53	(111)	47	53	(96)
West	33	67	(57)	51	49	(76)	45	55	(93)
South	94	6	(106)	64	36	(108)	43	57	(125)
Border	68	32	(38)	69	31	(35)	41	59	(32)
Total	49	51	(435)	56	44	(435)	48	52	(435)
Senate									
East	25	75	(20)	50	50	(20)	50	50	(20)
Midwest	14	86	(22)	41	59	(22)	59	41	(22)
West	45	55	(22)	35	65	(26)	39	61	(26)
South	100	0	(22)	55	45	(22)	32	68	(22)
Border	70	30	(10)	70	30	(10)	50	50	(10)
Total	49	51	(96)	47	53	(100)	45	55	(100)

[a]Includes one independent.

which the Republicans controlled both chambers). Comparing 1997 to 1981, we see that in the House the GOP stayed the same in the Midwest, lost ground in the East, and increased its share of seats in the other three regions. Overall, the Republicans won a majority of seats in all regions but the East in the 1996 elections. The pattern is somewhat more varied when we consider the Senate. Between 1981 and 1997, GOP gains were limited to two regions (the South and the Border states); the Republicans lost slightly in the West and noticeably in the Midwest. The East stayed the same. Only in the West and South did the Republicans have a majority of seats after 1996.

The 1997 results are more interesting when viewed from the longer historical perspective. In 1953 there were sharp regional differences in party representation in both houses. In the intervening years these differences have greatly diminished. The most obvious changes occurred in the South. The percentage of southern seats in the House held by the Democrats declined from 94 percent in 1953 to 43 percent in 1997. In 1953 the Democrats held all twenty-two southern Senate seats, but in 1997 they controlled only seven of those seats. The regional shift was less dramatic for congressional representation than for presidential elections (see Chapter 3), but in both instances there has been a change from Democratic dominance in the South to a distinct GOP advantage.

This change in the partisan share of the South's seats in Congress has had an important effect on that region's influence within the two parties. The South used to be the backbone of Democratic congressional representation. This, and the tendency of southern members to build seniority, gave southerners disproportionate power within the Democratic party in Congress. Because of declining Democratic electoral success in the region, the numerical strength of southern Democrats in Congress has waned. In 1953, with the Republicans in control of both chambers, southerners accounted for about 45 percent of Democratic seats in the House and Senate. By the 1970s southern strength had declined, to stabilize at between 25 and 30 percent of Democratic seats. In 1997, southerners accounted for 26 percent of Democratic representatives and only 16 percent of Democratic senators.

A consideration of the South's share of Republican congressional representation presents the reverse picture. Minuscule at the end of World War II, it steadily began to grow, reaching about 20 percent in 1980 and 31 percent in 1996. As a consequence of these changes, southern influence has declined in the Democratic party and grown in the GOP. Because southerners of both parties tend to be more conservative than their colleagues from other regions, these shifts in strength have tended to make the Democratic party in Congress more liberal and the Republican party more conservative.[7]

Other regional changes since 1953, while not as striking as those in the South, are also significant. In the House in 1953 the Republicans controlled the East and West by margins of two to one, and the Midwest by three to one; in 1997 they held only a narrow advantage in the West and Midwest, and the Democrats had a majority of eastern seats. The Senate also exhibited substantial shifts away from Republican dominance of the East and Midwest. On balance, we might refer to these changing patterns of geographic representation as the "deregionalization" of congressional elections. The Congress of 1997 is notably more regionally homogeneous with regard to partisan representation than the Congress of 1953.

Legal Conflicts Concerning the Structure of Congressional Elections

The patterns of outcomes discussed above were shaped by a variety of influences. As with most congressional elections, the most important among these influences were the resources available to individual candidates and how those resources were distributed between the parties. Before discussing those matters, however, we consider some of the influences that were particular to 1996, including the continuing conflict over the constitutional and legal framework governing congressional elections.

One aspect of this conflict involved the rules governing the drawing of congressional districts. After each census, a formula is applied to determine the number of representatives each state is entitled to. By federal law, all states with more than one House seat must establish districts, one for each seat. According to the Supreme Court's "one-person, one-vote" rulings, the population of all the districts within a state must be as equal as possible. State legislatures, with the approval of the governor, usually draw the lines, although if there is deadlock, the courts can take control of the process. Before 1992, Republicans had long believed that district lines in many states had been drawn to their party's disadvantage, but because they had gained some strategic advantages, they had hopes that they would fare better after districts were redrawn based on the 1990 census.

Chief among these advantages was that the party had gained control of additional governorships and state legislative houses, so there were comparatively few states in which the Democrats completely controlled the districting process. In some states the two parties reached agreement on a compromise plan; in others failure to agree passed the districting task to the judiciary. Another advantage to the GOP was conferred by the Voting Rights Act, which was originally passed in 1965 to protect the right of minorities to vote. When the act was renewed in 1982, amendments were included that were intended to foster the creation of legislative districts that had black or Latino majorities. (Such districts are termed *majority-minority* districts.) As interpreted by the federal Justice Department, the law required that where it was possible to create or retain a majority-minority district, that had to be done. These rules applied to the South and to a few other states with large Latino populations. In those states, the Justice Department had to approve new districting plans before they could take effect. The requirement to create majority-minority districts was supported by most leaders of minority groups, who wanted more members of Congress from their racial or ethnic group. It was also supported by the Republican party, which believed that by concentrating minority voters who usually supported Democrats within a few districts, many Democratic incumbents whom those voters had supported in the past would be undermined. Because of the pressures from the Justice Department, the districting process resulted in a number of districts with very convoluted lines.

There have been various views about the effect of districting in general and about the post-1990 set of plans in particular; we will not try to reproduce that discussion here.[8] It seems clear that the plans that took effect in 1990 disrupted many established patterns of political support, and that that disruption (coupled with the large number of freshmen representatives elected in 1992) played some role in the GOP gains of 1994. Still, our previous analyses indicated that the creation of majority-minority districts had only a modest impact on the relative fortunes of the two parties in 1992, or (in a delayed reaction) in 1994.[9] Regardless, however, of the overall effects of the redistricting that occurred after the 1990 census, politicians may perceive advantage or disadvantage for groups or individuals in particular instances, and they are always aware of the potential for such advantage or disadvantage from a new plan. Thus, there is often incentive to search for grounds to overturn the existing order and to impose a substitute, and this was true before and after the 1994 elections.

Despite the perception that the Republican party benefited electorally from the creation of majority-minority districts, many conservatives had ideological objections to the practice, which some dubbed "affirmative-action districting." Legal challenges resulted, on the grounds that such plans were discriminatory on the basis of race and so violated the federal Constitution. In 1993, in the case of *Shaw v. Reno,* the Supreme Court expressed concern about "bizarrely-shaped" districts that had been drawn for racial purposes and indicated that such districting plans could violate the equal protection clause of the Fourteenth Amendment. In 1995 the Court went much further. By a vote of five to four in *Miller v. Johnson,* the justices declared Georgia's districting plan unconstitutional because it had responded to the Justice Department's pressure to create three majority-minority districts without constitutional justification.[10] This was true even though the third district created was not particularly irregular in shape. Indeed, the majority said that any plan in which race was "the predominant factor" was seriously suspect.

The same day as the Georgia ruling, the Court accepted two more cases (from North Carolina and Texas) involving the same issue. In addition, other cases were initiated in other states in the lower courts. In June 1996 the Supreme Court reinforced the decision in *Miller v. Johnson* by declaring unconstitutional four majority-minority districts in North Carolina and Texas. While most of the justices acknowledged that race could be taken into account under some circumstances in drawing districts, a majority asserted that the states had gone too far in these cases. Meanwhile, the district lines in Louisiana and Florida were declared unconstitutional by lower federal courts based on the earlier *Miller v. Johnson* precedent.

New district lines were drawn for Florida, Louisiana, and Texas before the

November 1996 elections; North Carolina was permitted to delay its new plan until 1997. After the Supreme Court decisions discussed above, many observers—particularly minority political leaders—expressed the expectation that minority representatives would lose their seats because of them. At least in 1996, however, this did not happen. One representative from a majority-minority district (Cleo Fields [D-La.]) chose not to seek reelection because of the changes, but no minority representative who ran in the affected states lost, even in instances where the composition of their districts was massively altered. In Georgia, for example, the black percentage of the voting-age population in the district of Sanford Bishop was reduced from 52.3 to 35.1, while that of Cynthia McKinney dropped from 60.4 to 32.8. Nonetheless, Bishop and McKinney were reelected despite strong challenges, with 54 and 58 percent of the vote, respectively. Whether minority candidates will be able to win in these revised districts without the benefit of incumbency will not be known for some time. It is sure, however, that the conflict concerning the role of race in drawing districts will continue, and we return to the topic below.

Another legal challenge affecting districting involved the census. As we noted, after each census, the population numbers are used to determine how many House seats each state will receive. This process is called reapportionment, and it is extremely sensitive politically. The total number of House seats has been fixed at 435 since early in this century, and thus during reapportionment, some states gain seats and some lose them. Changes in the number of seats affect the power of each state in Congress, as well as its influence in presidential elections (because the number of House seats is the main determinant of the state's electoral votes).

The legal issue in this dispute was which census numbers to use. It is well known that censuses have disproportionately undercounted minorities and city residents. The secretary of commerce, in 1991, considered using a statistical adjustment to the census count to reflect this undercount but decided against it. His choice was challenged in court and although it was upheld by a federal district court judge, an appeals court said that the lower court should reconsider the matter using a stricter standard of judgment. That ruling was appealed to the U.S. Supreme Court by the Clinton administration, and the Court accepted the case. The case was of potentially great consequence because a ruling requiring the use of adjusted census figures could have forced a new reapportionment and wholesale redistricting in the states. That was avoided, however, when the Court ruled unanimously that the decision was within the power of the Commerce Department.[11] But the decision did not dispose entirely of the controversy, as we shall see below.

A final legal issue involving congressional elections was settled before the 1996 vote, although here, too, controversy lingered. That issue involved term limits for members of Congress. In the early 1990s, dissatisfaction with government fueled a nationwide movement to impose term limits on politicians, and by 1995, twenty-three states had adopted some form of limits on congressional terms. These laws were challenged in a case originating in Arkansas, in which a federal district court ruled the state's law unconstitutional. The Supreme Court agreed in a close five-to-four ruling. The majority said that the Constitution spelled out the qualifications for office for U.S. representatives and that states were without power to add to them.[12] Only an amendment to the U.S. Constitution could reverse this ruling. The Republican majority in Congress tried to pass such an amendment early in 1997, but they could not muster the required two-thirds majority.

Reacting to the Revolution: The 104th Congress and the 1996 Elections

Setting the Stage: The Politics of the 104th Congress. Probably the most important set of issues in 1996 involved the public's reactions to the 104th Congress—its policies, its leadership, and its incumbents. The GOP, led by Speaker of the House Newt Gingrich (R-Ga.), promised a "revolution" when they took control of the House and Senate after the 1994 elections. The public relations centerpiece of the revolution was the "Contract with America," a ten-point agenda that yielded a set of more than twenty legislative proposals that the House Republicans promised to bring to a vote during the first 100 days of the 104th Congress. They met this promise with days to spare, and, moreover, all but one of the items on the agenda passed the House. (The sole exception was the proposed constitutional amendment to impose term limits on members of Congress.)[13] While the Senate was left to consider the items of the Contract, the House moved on to what was the heart of the revolution—the rearrangement of governmental priorities through the budget and appropriations process. GOP conservatives intended to use these fiscal vehicles to reduce the level of federal spending on programs favored by liberals. More than that, however, they also intended to change policy itself, abolishing or substantially altering the structure of programs through those measures to an extent unprecedented in earlier congresses.

In the early days of the 104th Congress, the Democrats—particularly those in the House—were left almost entirely on the defensive. Still stunned by the 1994 results, President Bill Clinton was reduced to asserting that he was still "relevant" in the legislative process, while the Democrats in Congress were largely bystanders to the juggernaut that the House GOP spearheaded. They were unable to block any significant measure on the House GOP's agenda, and they were seldom able even to make significant amendments because of Republican solidarity. By the second half of 1995, however, things began to change. The Democrats began to rally their troops within and outside Congress through vigorous opposition to (and hyperbolic claims about) Republican plans to change the Medicare program. The more moderate Senate, with procedural rules that made minorities more able to slow or block legislation they objected to, resisted many items in the Contract with America. Even in the House, Democrats had some success exploiting divisions within the GOP on a few issues (particularly the environment) and using them to force some changes in the majority's proposals.

Clearly, the Democrats' most significant procedural advantage was the presidential veto. Indeed, Clinton promised early on to veto any Medicare cut as large as the $270 billion included in the Republican budget proposal, and he threatened to use the power against numerous other initiatives contained in the appropriations and budget reconciliation proposals as they moved through Congress.[14] The real turning point for the 104th Congress came late in 1995 when, during a five-week period, the president vetoed the reconciliation bill, a proposal to increase the debt ceiling (required for the federal government to continue borrowing money), and four appropriations bills. Because congressional Republicans were unable to muster the votes to override any of these vetoes, and because they persisted in trying to force the president to accept their legislative priorities, these conflicts resulted in two partial federal government shutdowns, because authority for it to operate and spend money had not been passed.[15]

During these budgetary conflicts and the accompanying shutdowns, public opinion crystallized behind Clinton and the Democrats. A Gallup poll in November showed that 47 percent of the respondents believed that the first shutdown was mainly the fault of GOP leaders in Congress, while only 25 percent put the primary blame on Clinton. Perhaps even worse for the GOP, the survey showed the public siding with Clinton on substantive grounds as well, with 58 percent favoring his veto of the reconciliation bill.[16] The public also blamed the Republicans when the government closed the second time. The government reopened, but the dispute continued into January, when Clinton presented his annual State of the Union address. In the speech, the president tilted strongly toward the moderate side of issues, seeking to distinguish his positions from the Democrats' liberal past, but also trying to portray the GOP as too extreme. He declared, "The era of big government is over. But we cannot go back to the time when our citizens were left to fend for themselves."[17] Surveys following the speech showed that public opinion was holding behind the president. For example, an ABC News follow-up poll indicated that 75 percent of those who watched approved of the speech, and by 59 to 25 percent, viewers said that they wanted the United States to go in the direction Clinton favored as opposed to that desired by Republicans. In response, the GOP leadership moved to compromise with Clinton on the budget, although a final agreement was not reached until April 1996.

Policy conflict continued in 1996 on other matters. The Republicans claimed success on one of the items in the Contract with the passage of the Welfare Reform bill, but Clinton used his veto to force the GOP to move the final bill significantly in his direction. The Democrats were even able to go on the offensive in some instances, rather than just reacting to Republican proposals. For example, the Clinton administration proposed and secured passage of a bill increasing the minimum wage. The Republican leadership in both houses had used procedural devices to prevent the issue from coming to a vote, but in the end they were unable to resist the public's unequivocal support for an increase. Finally, as the 1996 elections approached, Congress faced another round of budgeting and appropriations, just as the previous year's conflicts were finally resolved. Disagreements between the branches and between the parties were again prominent, but the GOP was concerned about undermining their chances of maintaining control of Congress. Therefore, they compromised with the administration on many items (with the president winning the dominant share of the concessions) in order to permit adjournment with ample time for Republican incumbents to campaign.

During these policy conflicts, as public opinion shifted against them, congressional Republicans moved from the euphoria they felt in the wake of the 1994 elections to progressively greater concern about holding on to their majority. Some of the opinion change had to do with the policy issues discussed above. Clinton sought to portray himself as moderate and the GOP as extreme, and he was generally successful, at least until the Republicans decided to compromise as the elections approached. For example, by March of 1996, 50 percent of the public indicated that they disagreed with most of what the Republicans in Congress were trying to do, while only 34 percent said they agreed.[18] Some of the negative shift among the public, however, was due to personalities, particularly a reaction to Newt Gingrich. In January of 1995, 53 percent of respondents with an opinion approved of the job Gingrich was doing as Speaker; by January of 1996, approval had fallen to 36 percent.[19] Whatever the reasons, the changes in public opinion from the pro-Republican tilt of 1994 convinced participants and analysts that the partisan control of Congress was in doubt in the 1996 elections.

Party Efforts. Because both parties could legitimately believe that they had a chance to win control of Congress in 1996, they had strong incentives to be active in the months leading up to the elections. One prime area of party activity was in candidate recruitment. As we shall see, the quality of challengers and of candidates in open seats is an important determinant of victory. Recruitment was especially important in 1996 because there were many potentially vulnerable incumbents (mainly as a result of the narrow victories won in 1994 by many GOP freshmen in the House), and because there were many open seats.

Some seats were open for routine or idiosyncratic reasons. For example, some senior members had reached normal retirement age, while Democratic representative Blanche Lincoln of Arkansas quit because she was pregnant with twins. Some members who might not otherwise have departed, however, did so because of the politics of the 104th Congress. In particular, the bitter partisan conflict made congressional service unpalatable for some members, especially ideological moderates. As Sen. William Cohen (R-Me.) said after announcing his retirement, "I suspect . . . we [retirees] share a common level of frustration over the absence of political accord and the increase in personal hostilities that now permeate our system and our society."[20] Additional incentives to leave were provided by the increasingly hectic pace of Congress, both in the legislative process and in campaigning, which disrupted normal family life. Due to the combination of these forces, the number of open House seats was a substantial fifty-three (virtually the same number as in 1994), while in the Senate it reached a record fourteen.

It was generally acknowledged that the GOP had a better chance of defending the Senate than the House. As a consequence, they had little trouble with candidate recruitment. The Democrats, however, had particular difficulty. Many strong potential contenders, like state office holders or U.S. representatives, passed up the chance to run. Sen. Bob Kerrey of Nebraska, chairman of the Democratic Senatorial Campaign Committee, resorted to focusing his efforts on encouraging wealthy businessmen to run, almost without regard to their political views. (Wealth was a particular advantage, because the Democrats did not have large amounts of money to provide to candidates.) One of his recruits, for example, was Walt Minnick of Idaho, a business executive who had been an aide in the Nixon White House. This strategy did not bear fruit. All six of the new Democratic senators elected in 1996 were experienced officeholders; four were sitting representatives.

Efforts to entice strong candidates to run for seats in the House were particularly aggressive. Early in the process, especially before public opinion began to shift, the advantage lay with the GOP. This was partly a result of the attractions of their newly secured majority status but also of the increased fund-raising ability that went with that status. In 1993 the National Republican Congressional Committee (NRCC) was not able to promise funding to candidates. In the fall of 1995, in contrast, Ed Brookover—the political director of the NRCC—estimated that the organization would be able to make the maximum party contribution ($70,000) to more than one hundred candidates. Beginning in November 1995, the group started offering training courses for prospective candidates.[21] Newt Gingrich's "National Strategic Plan for 1996" called for winning a net of sixteen additional seats in 1996, while Rep. Bill Paxon, chairman of the NRCC, predicted a gain of thirty seats as late as April 1996.[22] As public attitudes changed, however, GOP efforts failed in some instances. A Republican state representative in Connecticut, for example, passed up a chance to run against the Democratic representative Sam Gejdenson, who had barely survived in 1994. She said: "I am reluctant to throw my hat into the ring because of the Republican position coming out of Washington. . . . It's going to be an uphill battle for anyone who decides to run."[23]

For the Democrats, efforts at recruiting candidates focused especially on finding strong challengers for GOP incumbents, in particular, opponents for the freshmen. In October 1995, seventy potential candidates were invited to Democratic National Committee Headquarters, where Minority Leader Richard Gephardt (D-Mo.) urged them to run, saying, "This is the group that will take back the people's house in 1996."[24] The recruits were told to make the unpopular Speaker of the House a centerpiece of their campaigns. As Martin Frost of Texas, chairman of the Democratic Congressional Campaign Committee, said, "one thing I want you to take away from this, it's that your opponent's middle name is Gingrich."[25] Another part of the Democratic effort involved fund-raising; as the election approached, Gephardt urged his party's incumbents to contribute up to $20,000 to help fund challenges in other districts.[26]

The President's Role in Congressional Races. As we shall see later in this chapter, the public's attitude toward the president apparently can have a prominent role in their evaluation of congressional candidates. It has certainly been the case historically, as candidates of one party sought to tie their opponents to the image of an unpopular president of the opposite party. Such an effort by the Republicans was readily apparent in 1994. Bill Clinton's approval ratings were relatively low by historical standards, hovering between 40 and 45 percent during most of the second half of 1994. As we saw in Chapter 7, the performance of the economy is closely related to presidential approval. Although objective numbers indicated an improving economy in 1994, the public's subjective evaluation did not reflect that, and Clinton was not getting any credit for what improvement was recognized. As a consequence of Clinton's perceived weakness, most Democratic candidates in the midterm elections went to great lengths to distance themselves from the president. Indeed, even the Speaker of the House, Tom Foley of Washington, passed up an appearance with Clinton at a fund-raiser in his state (to little avail; he lost his seat anyway).[27]

Circumstances were quite different in 1996. We saw in Chapter 2 that Clinton had strong approval ratings, peaking at 60 percent in September and registering even higher in the National Election Study (NES) preelection survey (see Table 7-6). Furthermore, the public's view of the economy was much more positive than in 1994; in the exit polls conducted by the Voter News Service (VNS) on election day, 57 percent of voters said the national economy was excellent or good, compared with only 42 percent four years earlier.[28] The consequence of these changes in context was that Democratic congressional candidates were far more willing to connect their campaigns to the president. Even in Virginia, a GOP presidential stronghold since 1968, one Democratic candidate for Congress sent out a flyer with a picture of himself and Clinton at the White House, while another used the campaign slogan "Re-Elect Bill and take back the Hill." On the other side of the partisan divide, many Republican candidates were reluctant to link themselves to Bob Dole. One GOP House candidate in Indiana (also a strong Republican state in presidential races) "said it 'would be counterproductive' to have Mr. Dole campaign on her behalf . . . adding that 'I need to stay with my race and keep it isolated' from the national ticket."[29]

Clinton responded to these changed circumstances by being much more active in congressional races than he had been in the preceding midterm. He began calling for the election of a Democratic Congress during the summer, and he was active in appearing at fund-raisers for his party's candidates for the House and Senate. As the campaign went into its later stages, the president made some decisions about where to campaign based on a desire to influence the congressional races, appearing both in southern states to stave off some GOP victories and in strongly Democratic eastern states where boosting turnout might help win some close races.[30] Clinton's appeals were, however, mostly indirect—calling for people to go to the polls rather than urging them to give him a Democratic Congress. He chose this strategy because poll data showed that the electorate had considerable ambivalence about restoring Democratic majorities to Congress to serve with a Democratic president. For example, a *New York Times*/CBS News survey in mid-October showed that 48 percent of respondents said it would be better to elect a Republican Congress to "limit the power of President Clinton," while 41 percent said it would "be better to elect a Democratic Congress to increase the power" of the president.[31] Similarly, the Voter News Service (VNS) exit poll indicated that 56 percent of 1996 voters said that it was better if party control of Congress and the White House were split, while 44 percent thought it was better if one party controlled both branches.[32]

This is, of course, not the same thing as saying that individual voters with a preference for divided government would choose candidates in order to achieve that end. But the data do show that the congressional Republicans had a basis for making an appeal to the electorate to try to save their majorities, and they did so—even though it meant tacitly admitting that Dole was going to lose the presidential race. On October 22, Haley Barbour (chairman of the Republican National Committee) said at a news conference: "If Clinton is re-elected, heaven forbid, the last thing the American people want is for him to have a blank check in the form of a liberal Democratic Congress."[33] This "blank check" theme was repeated frequently by GOP leaders and candidates over the next two weeks. The Republicans began running TV ads that began with an announcer saying: "What would happen if the Democrats controlled Congress and the White House? Been there, done that." The ads then showed newspaper headlines from Clinton's first two years relating to fights over taxes and health care, and then they went on to link individual Democratic House candidates to unpopular features of their party's agenda. Whether because of this campaign tactic, public reactions to questions raised in the closing weeks about Democratic fund-raising tactics in the presidential race, or something else, the Democrats' lead in the polls faded to the near dead-heat result on election day.

CANDIDATES' RESOURCES AND ELECTION OUTCOMES

Seats in the House and Senate are highly valued posts for which candidates compete vigorously. In contests for these offices, candidates draw on whatever resources they have available. To explain the results of congressional elections we must consider the comparative advantages and disadvantages of the various candidates. In this section we discuss the most significant resources available to candidates and the effect of those resources on the outcomes of congressional elections.

Candidate Quality

One major resource that candidates can draw on is the set of personal abilities that foster electoral success. Few constituencies today offer a certain victory for one of the two major parties, so election outcomes usually depend heavily on candidate quality. A strong, capable candidate is a significant asset for a party; a weak, inept one is a liability that is difficult to overcome. In his study of the activities of House members in their districts, Richard F. Fenno, Jr., described how members try to build support within their constituencies, establishing bonds of trust between constituents and their representative.[34] Members attempt to convey to their constituents a sense that they are qualified for their job, a sense that they identify with their constituents, and a sense of empathy with constituents and their problems. Challengers of incumbents and candidates for open seats must engage in similar activities to win support. The winner of a contested congressional election is usually the candidate who is better able to establish these bonds of support among constituents and to convince them that he or she is the person for the job.

One indicator of candidate quality is previous success at winning elective office. The more important the office a candidate has held, the more likely it is that he or she had to overcome significant competition to obtain it. Moreover, the visibility and reputation for performance that usually accompany the holding of public office can also be a significant electoral asset. For example, a state legislator who is running for a House seat can appeal to the electorate by pointing out that the previous office prepared him or her for congressional service because of the similarities of tasks facing all legislators. A state legislator would also have built a successful electoral organization that could be useful in conducting a congressional campaign. Finally, previous success in an electoral arena suggests that experienced candidates are more likely to be able to run strong campaigns than candidates without previous success or experience. Less adept candidates are likely to have been screened out at lower levels of competition for office. For these and other reasons, an experienced candidate tends to have an electoral advantage over a candidate who has never held elective office.[35] Moreover, the higher the office previously held, the stronger the candidate will tend to be in the congressional contest.

In Table 9-4 we present data that show which candidates were successful in 1996, controlling for elective-office background, party, and incumbency.[36] The vast majority of candidates who challenged incumbents lost regardless of their office background or party, but generally, House challengers with experience in elective office were more successful than those who had none. In Senate races, only one incumbent was defeated, so it is not surprising that there is no visible relationship to challenger quality. Candidate quality also has a noticeable effect in races without incumbents. Among Democrats, candidates with stronger elective-office experience were much more successful than those with lesser or no experience. Among Republicans, however, the relationship was reversed. Part of the reason for this is that eighteen of these races were in the South, and the GOP won twelve of them. Because of the historical Democratic dominance in the South, Republicans still often do not have potential candidates with experience in elective office, but they have been successful in recruiting strong nonexperienced candidates, especially in recent years.

TABLE 9-4   Success in House and Senate Elections, Controlling for Office
Background, Party, and Incumbency, 1996

Candidate's last office	Candidate is opponent of				No incumbent in district			
	Democratic incumbent		Republican incumbent		Democratic candidate		Republican candidate	
	(%)	(N)	(%)	(N)	(%)	(N)	(%)	(N)
House								
State legislature or U.S. House	8	(13)	30	(27)	63	(19)	27	(15)
Other elective office	0	(8)	7	(15)	42	(7)	25	(4)
No elective office	1	(140)	6	(160)	35	(26)	55	(33)
Senate								
U.S. House	0	(1)	50	(2)	75	(4)	80	(5)
Statewide elective office	0	(2)	0	(1)	33	(6)	50	(2)
Other elective office	—	(0)	0	(1)	0	(1)	50	(4)
No elective office	0	(4)	0	(9)	0	(3)	67	(3)

Note: Percentages show proportion of candidates in each category who won; numbers in parentheses are the totals on which percentages are based.

Given the importance of candidate quality, it is worth noting that during the 1980s there was a decline in the proportion of House incumbents that faced challengers who had previously won elective office and that this decline was reversed in 1992. In 1980, 17.6 percent of incumbents faced such challenges; in 1984, 14.7 percent did; in 1988, only 10.5 percent did; but in 1992, the proportion rose to 23.5 percent only to fall to 16.6 percent in 1996.[37] It is also important to note that in races against incumbents, Democrats were slightly more likely than Republicans to field candidates with elective-office experience (19.8 percent versus 12.5 percent). In open-seat races, the Democrats ran experienced candidates in 49 percent of the contests, whereas Republicans ran such candidates in 36 percent of these races.[38] We return to this partisan contrast in candidate quality later in the chapter.

Whether experienced politicians actually run for the House or Senate is, of course, not accidental. These are significant strategic decisions made by politicians, and they have much to lose if they make the wrong choice. The choices are governed by a host of factors, relating to the perceived chance of success, the potential value of the new office relative to what will be lost if the candidate fails, and the costs of running.[39] The chances of success of the two major parties vary from election to election, both locally and nationally. Therefore, each election offers a different mix of experienced and inexperienced candidates from the two parties for the House and Senate.

The most influential factor in the choice of a potential candidate is whether there is an incumbent in the race. High reelection rates tend to discourage potentially strong challengers from running, which in turn makes it more likely that the incumbents will win. In addition to the general difficulty of challenging incumbents, factors related to specific election years (both nationally and in a particular district) affect decisions to run. For example, the Republican party had particular difficulty recruiting strong candidates in 1986 because of fears about a potential backlash from the Iran-contra scandals. Recent research indicates, however, that potential House candidates are most strongly influenced in their decision by their perceived chances of winning their party's nomination.[40] Moreover, the actions of incumbents may influence the choices of potential challengers. For example, building up a large reserve of campaign funds between elections may dissuade some possible opponents, although analysis of Senate contests (which usually involve experienced challengers) indicates that this factor does not have a systematic impact in those races.[41]

As we have seen, most congressional races do not involve challengers who have previous experience in elective office. Given their slight chance of winning, why do challengers without experience run at all? As Jeffrey S. Banks and D. Roderick Kiewiet pointed out, although the chances of success against incumbents may be small for such candidates, such a race may be their best chance of ever winning a seat in Congress.[42] If inexperienced challengers put off their candidacies until a time when there is no incumbent, their opposition is likely to include multiple experienced candidates from both parties. Moreover, as David Canon demonstrated, previous elective-office experience is an imperfect indicator of candidate quality, because some candidates without such experience can still have significant political assets and be formidable challengers.[43] For example, four former television journalists who had never held elective office won seats in the House in 1992, and three of them defeated incumbents. They were able to build on their substantial name recognition among voters to win nomination and election.[44]

Incumbency

One reason most incumbents win is that incumbency itself is a significant resource. Actually, incumbency is not a single resource but rather a status that usually gives a candidate a variety of benefits. In some respects, incumbency works to a candidate's advantage automatically. For example, incumbents tend to be more visible to voters than their challengers.[45] Less automatic, but very important, is the tendency for incumbents to be viewed more favorably than challengers. Moreover, at least a plurality of the electorate in most districts will identify with the incumbent's political party. Incumbents can also use their status to gain advantages. Incumbents usually raise and spend more campaign funds than challengers, and they usually have a better-developed and more experienced campaign organization. They also have assets (such as staffs and franked mail), provided at public expense, that both help them perform their jobs and provide electoral benefits.

Increasing Electoral Margins. From the mid-1960s through the late 1980s, the margins by which incumbents were reelected increased (the pattern was less clear and more erratic in Senate elections than in House elections).[46] These changing patterns have interested analysts both for their own sake and because it was believed that the disappearance of marginal incumbents would mean less congressional turnover and a locking in of current members.

An early explanation for the increased incumbent margins was offered by Edward R. Tufte, who argued that redistricting had protected incumbents of both parties.[47] This argument seemed plausible, because the increase in margins occurred about the same time as the massive redistrictings required by Supreme Court decisions of the mid-1960s. But other analysts showed that incumbents had won by larger margins both in states that had redistricted and in those that had not, as well as in Senate contests.[48] Thus, redistricting could not be the major reason for the change.

Another explanation for the increase in incumbents' margins was the growth in the perquisites of members and the greater complexity of government. Morris P. Fiorina noted that in the post-New Deal period the level of federal services and the bureaucracy that administers them have grown tremendously.[49] More complex government means that many people will encounter problems in receiving services, and people who have problems frequently contact their representative to complain and seek help. Fiorina contended that in the mid-1960s new members of Congress placed greater emphasis on such constituency problem solving than had their predecessors. This expanded constituency service was translated into a reservoir of electoral support. Although analyses of the impact of constituency services have produced mixed conclusions, it is likely that the growth of these services offers a partial explanation for the changing incumbent vote margins and for the incumbency advantage generally.[50]

The declining impact of party loyalties offers a third explanation for the growth in incumbent vote margins, either alone or in interaction with other factors. Until the mid-1960s there was a very strong linkage between party identification and congressional voting behavior: most people identified with a political party, many of them strongly, and most voters supported the candidate of their chosen party. Subsequently, however, the impact of party identification decreased, as we shall see in Chapter 10. John A. Ferejohn, drawing on data from the NES surveys, showed that the strength of party ties generally weakened and that within any given category of party identification the propensity to support the candidate of one's party declined.[51] An analysis by Albert D. Cover revealed that between 1958 and 1974 those voters who did not identify with the party of a congressional incumbent were increasingly more likely to defect from their party and support the incumbent, whereas there was no increase in defections from party identification by voters of the same party as incumbents.[52] Thus, weakened party ties produced a substantial net benefit for incumbents.

The Trend Reversed. Whatever the relative importance of these factors, and the others we discuss later, in explaining the increase in incumbents' victory margins, the increase continued through the 1980s, as the data in Table 9-5 show. The average share of the vote for all incumbents was 61.7 percent in 1974; in 1982 it was 64.1. The share then continued to grow, peaking at 68.2 percent in 1986 and 1988.[53] These data are only for races in which both parties ran candidates. Thus, they exclude contests in which an incumbent ran unopposed. Such races were also increasing in number during this period; therefore, the data actually understate the growth in incumbents' margins.

Then, in 1990, something changed. The average share of the vote for incumbents declined by nearly 5 percentage points. The decline was, moreover, not a result of a shift of voters toward one party, as with the decline from 1980 to 1982; both parties' incumbents suffered. Rather, the shift in incumbents' electoral fortunes was apparently the result of what was called the anti-incumbent mood among the voters. Early in 1990, pollsters and commentators began to perceive stronger anti-Congress sentiments within the electorate.[54] For the first time, analysts began to question whether incumbency remained the asset it used to be.

There was, of course, nothing new about Congress being unpopular; Congress had long suffered ups and downs in approval, just as the president had. Indeed, Fenno had noted long before that candidates for Congress often sought election by running against Congress. They sought to convince voters that while most members of Congress were untrustworthy, they themselves were different and deserved the voters' support.[55] What changed in 1990 was that Congress's

TABLE 9-5   Average Vote Percentages of House Incumbents, Selected Years, 1974–1996

Year	Democrats	Republicans	All incumbents
1974	68.5	55.2	61.7
1980	64.0	67.9	65.5
1982	67.9	59.9	64.1
1984	64.2	68.2	65.9
1986	70.2	65.6	68.2
1988	68.8	67.5	68.2
1990	65.8	59.8	63.5
1992	63.3	62.9	63.1
1994	60.0	67.6	62.8
1996	66.6	60.7	63.3

unpopularity appeared to be undermining the approval of individual members by their own constituents. Yet, as the data presented in Table 9-1 showed, even though there was a drop in the average percentage of the vote received by incumbents in 1990, the rate of reelection still reached 96 percent. The decline in vote margins was not great enough to produce a rash of defeats. Many observers wondered, however, whether 1990 was the beginning of a new trend: Would incumbents' electoral drawing power continue to decline?

In 1992 scandals swirled around a large number of representatives of both parties, and the public's evaluation of Congress was very low. Opponents of incumbents emphasized that they were "outsiders" and not "professional politicians" (even when they had substantial political experience). The results from 1992 show that incumbents' share of the vote dropped a bit more. Republicans rebounded a little from their bad 1990 showing, but Democrats fell more than 2 percentage points. Again, however, the casualty rate among incumbents who ran in the general election was lower than many expected; 93 percent were reelected. (Still, it is important to note that a substantial number of incumbents had already been made casualties in the primaries.) Then, in 1994, although there was only a slight additional drop in incumbents' share of the vote overall, the drop was greater (and concentrated) for Democrats, and their casualty rate was high. The result was the loss of their majority. Finally, in 1996, the vote share of incumbents rebounded slightly; that of the Democrats increased sharply while that of the GOP fell. We have seen how that vote shift translated into the defeat of eighteen Republican incumbents but only three Democrats.

This discussion illustrates that the vote margins and reelection success of incumbents are related but distinct phenomena. When—as was true in the 1980s—the average share of the vote received by incumbents is very high, they can lose a lot of ground before registering a large number of defeats. What appears to have occurred in 1990 is that many incumbents were subjected to vigorous contests for the first time in many years. Such challenges were then often repeated or extended to additional incumbents in the elections of 1992 through 1996. Potential candidates apparently looked at the political situation and concluded that incumbents who had previously seemed immovable could now potentially be defeated, and thus the number of candidates for Congress increased substantially. These vigorous contests by challengers who were stronger than usual resulted in a decrease in the share of the vote received by many incumbents. In most cases in 1990, the decrease was not large enough to bring the challenger victory; in later years, however, the increased competition caught up with a greater number of incumbents.

Campaign Spending

A third resource that has an important impact on congressional elections is campaign spending. The effects of campaign spending have received a great deal of attention in the last two decades because researchers gained access to more dependable data than had previously been available.[56] The data on spending have consistently shown that incumbents generally outspend their challengers, often greatly, and that through the early 1990s, the disparity grew wider.[57] In 1990 incumbent spending averaged about $401,000, while challengers spent approximately $116,000—a ratio of 3.45 to 1. In 1992 challenger spending increased to an average of $160,000, but the stronger challenges of that year also stimulated the incumbents to keep pace, and their spending rose to $560,000. This was a ratio of 3.50 to 1, which left challengers and incumbents in about the same relative position as they had been in two years earlier.[58]

Disparities in campaign spending are linked to the increase in incumbents' election margins. In the 1960s, congressional campaigns began to rely more heavily on campaign techniques that cost money—for example, media advertising, campaign consulting, and direct mailing—and these items have become more and more expensive. At the same time, candidates were progressively less likely to have available pools of campaign workers from established party organizations or from interest groups, making expensive media and direct mail strategies relatively more important. Most challengers are unable to raise significant campaign funds. Neither individuals nor the groups who are interested in the outcomes of congressional elections like to throw money away; before making contributions they usually need to be convinced that the candidate has a chance. Yet we have seen that few incumbents have been beaten. Thus, it is often difficult to convince potential contributors that their money will produce results, and contributions are often not forthcoming. Most challengers are therefore at a strategic disadvantage, unable to raise sufficient funds to wage a competitive campaign.

It is the ability to compete, rather than the simple question of relative amounts of spending, that is at the core of the issue. We have noted that incumbents have many inherent advantages that the challenger must overcome if he or she hopes to win. But often the money is not there to overcome them. In 1990, for example, over 47 percent of the challengers spent $25,000 or less. With so little money available, challengers are unable to make themselves visible to the electorate or to convey a convincing message. Under such circumstances, most voters—being unaware of the positions, or perhaps even the existence, of the challenger—vote for the incumbent.

Data from 1996 on campaign spending and election outcomes seem consistent with this argument, but they also show changes in the political landscape.[59] The increased competitiveness that was shown by the data on incumbents' vote share is reflected in the spending figures. Challenger spending, averaging about $262,000, was up sharply in relation to the 1990–1992 figures presented above. Incumbent spending was up also (averaging $684,000), but the incumbent-to-challenger ratio was nevertheless reduced to 2.61 to 1. Two reasons for this shift were a substantial effort by organized labor, which provided direct contributions to challengers of thirty-two targeted Republican incumbents, and independent anti-incumbent advertising.[60] Linking spending to outcomes, Table 9-6

TABLE 9-6   Incumbents' Share of the Vote in the 1996 House Elections, by Challenger Campaign Spending (in percentages)

Challenger spending[a]	Incumbents' share of the two-party vote				Total	(N)
	70% or more	60–69%	55–59%	Less than 55%		
0–25	52.2	44.9	2.9	0.0	100.0	(69)
26–75	22.5	67.6	7.0	2.8	99.9	(71)
76–199	14.8	66.7	14.8	3.7	100.0	(54)
200–399	4.5	29.5	40.9	25.0	99.9	(44)
400 or more	0.0	6.5	32.3	61.3	100.1	(93)
All	18.7	40.5	19.0	21.8	100.0	(331)

[a]In thousands of dollars.

shows the relationship between the incumbent's share of the vote in the 1996 House elections and the amount of money spent by the challenger. It is clear that there is a strong negative relationship between how much challengers spend and how well incumbents do. In races where challengers spent less than $26,000, 97 percent of the incumbents received 60 percent or more of the vote. At the other end of the spectrum, in races where challengers spent $400,000 or more, 93 percent of the incumbents received less than 60 percent of the vote, and over three-fifths got less than 55 percent. These results are consistent with those in earlier House elections for which comparable data are available.[61]

These findings are reinforced by other research, which shows that challenger spending has a much greater influence on election outcomes than does incumbent spending.[62] This generalization has been questioned on methodological grounds, but further research by Gary C. Jacobson reinforced his earlier findings.[63] Using both aggregate and survey data, he found that "the amount spent by the challenger is far more important in accounting for voters' decisions than is the amount of spending by the incumbent."[64] Parallel results have been found for Senate elections.[65]

It is true, of course, that challengers who appear to have good prospects will find it easier to raise money than those whose chances seem slim. Thus, one might wonder whether these data are simply a reflection of the fulfillment of expectations, in which money flows to challengers who would have done well regardless of spending. Other research, however, indicates that that is probably not the case. In an analysis of the 1972 and 1974 congressional elections, Jacobson concluded, "Our evidence is that campaign spending helps candidates, particularly non-incumbents, by bringing them to the attention of the voters; it is not the case that well-known candidates simply attract more money; rather money buys attention."[66] From this perspective, adequate funding is a necessary but not a sufficient condition for a closely fought election contest, a perspective consistent with the data in Table 9-6. Heavily outspending one's opponent is not a guarantee of victory; the evidence does not support the conclusion that elections can be bought. If an incumbent outspends the challenger, the incumbent can still lose if the challenger is adequately funded and runs a campaign that persuades the voters. The 1996 elections offer clear evidence of this. In eleven of the twenty-one races in which incumbents lost, the loser outspent the winner. In these contests, incumbents outspent challengers by 60 percent to 40 percent on average, and in three instances the loser spent more than twice as much. Most important, no victorious challenger spent less than $600,000. That may be a rough estimate of the amount needed to have a chance to win against an incumbent.

A spending advantage, however, is not any kind of guarantee to a challenger. In an extreme example from 1986, the Republican Marc Holtzman, in the Eleventh Congressional District of Pennsylvania, spent $1.35 million in his race against the Democratic incumbent Paul E. Kanjorski, who spent about $714,000. Holtzman received only 29 percent of the vote. Based on this analysis, our view can be summarized as follows: if a challenger is to attain visibility and get his or her message across to the voters—neutralizing the incumbent's advantages in name recognition and perquisites of office—the challenger needs to be adequately funded. If both sides in a race are adequately funded, the outcome will tend to turn on factors other than money, and the relative spending of the two candidates will not matter very much.

This argument carries us full circle back to our earlier discussion and leads us to bring together the three kinds of resources that we have been considering—candidate experience, incumbency, and campaign spending. Table 9-7 presents data about these three factors in the 1996 House elections. We have categorized challenger experience as strong or weak depending on previous elective-office experience; challenger spending was classified as low or high depending on whether it was below or above $200,000.[67] The data show that each of the elements exerted some independent effect, but that spending seems to have exerted the greatest effect, perhaps reflecting the growing attractiveness of "outsider" candidates. When challengers had weak experience and low spending (over 60 percent of the races), all incumbents won, and 92 percent won with more than 60 percent of the vote. In the opposite situation, where the challenger had both strong experience and substantial spending, over 90 percent of the races were relatively close. The combined results for the two intermediate categories fall between the extremes. Table 9-7 also reveals that it is very rare for a challenger with strong experience not to be able to raise substantial funds.

This combination of factors also helps to explain the greater volatility of outcomes in Senate races. Previous analysis has shown that data on campaign spending in Senate contests are consistent with what we have found true for House races: if challenger spending is above some threshold level, the election is likely to be quite close; if it is below that level, the incumbent is likely to win by a large

TABLE 9-7   Incumbents' Share of the Vote in the 1996 House Elections, by Challenger Campaign Spending and Office Background (in percentages)

| Challenger experience/ challenger spending | Incumbents' share of the two-party vote | | | | | | Percentage of incumbents defeated |
	70% or more	60–69%	55–59%	Less than 55%	Total	(N)	
Weak/low	38.3	54.1	6.2	1.4	100.0	(209)	0.0
Strong/low	0.0	60.0	40.0	0.0	100.0	(5)	0.0
Weak/high	2.2	16.9	32.6	48.3	100.0	(89)	12.4
Strong/high	0.0	8.3	41.7	50.0	100.0	(36)	27.8

Note: Percentages read across. Strong challengers have held a significant elective office (see note 66). High-spending challengers spent more than $200,000.

margin.[68] In Senate races, however, the mix of well-funded and poorly funded challengers is different. Senate challengers are more likely than their House counterparts to be able to raise significant amounts of money. Senate challengers, moreover, are also more likely to possess significant elective-office experience. Thus, in Senate contests incumbents often will face well-funded and experienced challengers, and the stage is then set for their defeat if other circumstances work against them. The lesson from the evidence presented in this section appears to be captured by the statement made by David Johnson, the director of the Democratic Senatorial Campaign Committee, to Rep. Richard C. Shelby of Alabama, who was challenging the Republican senator Jeremiah Denton in 1986. Shelby, who eventually won, was concerned that he did not have enough campaign funds, since Denton was outspending him two to one. Johnson responded: "You don't have as much money, but you're going to have enough—and enough is all it takes to win."[69]

THE 1996 ELECTIONS: THE IMPACT ON CONGRESS

Compared with the electoral avalanche of 1994, which swept the Democrats from majority control, the impact of the 1996 elections was comparatively modest. In some ways they reinforced the results of 1994, and in some ways they adjusted them, but there was little movement in either direction. One of the reinforcements of 1994 (and of 1992) was the continuation of the membership turnover that had marked the partisan transition. We saw earlier that the move to impose term limits on congressional membership by law had failed. The choices of voters at the ballot box and of members in their decisions not to seek reelection, however, achieved the result that many supporters of term limits were seeking: bringing to Congress a large number of new members. The "class of 1996" included seventy-four new representatives (17 percent of the body) and fifteen new senators (15 percent). Cumulatively, the results of the last three elections yielded even more impressive totals. In the House, nearly two-thirds of the Republicans and almost half of the Democrats had come to the body in the 1992 election or later. In the Senate, twenty-seven of the fifty-five Republicans and thirteen of the forty-five Democrats had had less than six years of service. For an institution that was seen by the public to be dominated by aging career politicians, the Congress had a lot of new blood.

The new members of 1996 reinforced another trend of recent years: ideologically, the 105th Congress witnessed a decline in the ranks of moderate members and an increase in the number of conservative Republicans and liberal Democrats. Twenty or thirty years ago there was considerable ideological "overlap" between the parties. The Democrats had a substantial contingent, mostly from the South, that was as conservative as the right wing of the Republican party. Similarly, the GOP had a contingent (primarily from the Northeast) that was as liberal as northern Democrats. In addition, each party had members who held the positions between the two ends of the political spectrum. During the intervening years, however, because of changes in the electorate and in Congress, this overlap between the parties began to disappear.[70] The result was that by the mid-1980s, each party in both houses of Congress had become more politically homogeneous, and in each chamber there was little departure from a complete ideological separation of the two parties. The election of 1996 merely continued this trend. In both the House and the Senate, departing members came disproportionately from the ranks of moderates (especially southern Democrats and Republicans from the Northeast), and the new members were characteristic of their respective partisan contingents.

Because of differences in the partisan distribution of the new members and in the operating characteristics of the two chambers, the membership changes had different implications for the House and Senate. The new representatives were disproportionately Democrats, which narrowed the margin of control for the GOP. The House is a "majoritarian" institution, where the side with the most votes in any instance can largely work its will. With a narrower majority, the Republican leadership could not afford to have many defections to the opposition before they would lose control of the chamber's decision making. As we discuss below, because of increased conflict between their factions and because of political troubles within their leadership, the close numerical balance was to cause the House Republicans considerable problems in the first six months of the 105th Congress. In the Senate, in contrast, Republican ranks were strengthened by two additional seats, and there were fewer internal conflicts within the majority than in the previous Congress. Yet, because the Senate vests considerable power in individual members and in cohesive minorities, the GOP was not able simply to roll over the Democrats. At crucial points, the minority party was able to compel the majority to compromise in order to pass legislation.

In 1995 the new Republican majorities instituted major institutional changes, especially in the House.[71] By comparison, the changes in organization for the 105th Congress were decidedly modest. In fact, the most important events involved previously made changes whose effects had been delayed until the next Congress, particularly the new rules governing committee and subcommittee leadership among Senate Republicans. The Senate GOP had adopted rules that prohibited (with a few exceptions) full committee chairmen from also chairing subcommittees. These new restrictions were confirmed at the beginning of 1997, and as a result several senior committee chairs had to give up control of subcommittees. This further accentuated the dispersal of power to more junior members that had long been developing in the Senate; all eleven of the GOP senators that had been elected in 1994, and five of the eight newly elected in 1996 became subcommittee chairs. In the House, little was done organizationally beyond ordering the Speaker and the minority leader to draw up a policy for random drug testing of members and staff and prohibiting the distribution of campaign donations on the House floor. There was little sentiment for further major rearrangement of committee jurisdictions of the kind done in 1995. The report of a

Republican task force on committee review indicated that such change was unnecessary because the GOP leadership had sufficient capability to induce responsiveness from committees or to pass legislation through the use of ad hoc task forces.[72]

The electorate's confirmation of divided government prompted calls for bipartisanship from both parties. However, many aspects of the political situation in 1997 demonstrated the difficulties of achieving this end. Right at the beginning of the 105th Congress, the House faced the task of voting on the reelection of Newt Gingrich as Speaker in the midst of serious charges from Democrats regarding his ethics. After investigations by the House Ethics Committee, Gingrich admitted that he had failed to manage the finances of his political operations properly and that he had provided misleading information to the committee. He was only narrowly reelected Speaker (with six GOP representatives voting "present"—that is, effectively abstaining—and four voting for other Republicans), and later in January the House voted overwhelmingly for a formal reprimand of Gingrich. These events weakened Gingrich's leadership position and led some in the GOP to think that he should be replaced.

The effort to promote bipartisanship was also challenged by the Republicans use of their majority status. Both the House and the Senate launched investigations of fund-raising practices in the 1996 elections. They mainly focused on Clinton's reelection campaign and the possibility of the infiltration of illegal foreign money, although the Senate investigation also devoted some time to questionable Republican practices. The activities of these two panels were a continued source of friction between the White House and the GOP majority, although the hearings did not seem to have much negative impact on Clinton's public approval. Two other investigations amplified the conflict between the congressional parties. They involved challenges to the 1996 elections of two Democrats, Sen. Mary Landrieu of Louisiana and Rep. Loretta Sanchez of California. Both women had won narrow victories, and the Republicans initiated investigations of possible vote fraud. Democrats in both Houses charged that the claims of fraud were without merit and that the investigations had strictly partisan motives. Indeed, the Democrats on the Senate Committee on Rules and Administration, which was conducting the Louisiana investigation, walked out in protest against continuation of the probe, calling it a "partisan witch hunt."[73]

Another occasion for partisan conflict was the continuing issue of presidential appointments to executive departments, independent regulatory agencies, and the judiciary, which require Senate approval. As of August 1997, over 40 percent of the 109 positions in regulatory agencies requiring Senate confirmation were vacant, awaiting either nominations or Senate action.[74] Among the factors slowing the process were political differences between the parties, the administration's desire for racial and ethnic diversity, and the need for extensive background checks to avoid embarrassing revelations during Senate consideration. Political differences were even more prominent in the delays of appointments to lifetime judicial posts. In March there were ninety-three vacancies in federal judgeships. Sen. Orrin Hatch (R-Utah), chairman of the Judiciary Committee had pledged to "personally do my best" to see that nominees "who are, or will be judicial activists" would not be nominated or confirmed by the Senate.[75]

The partisan strains from these and other causes permeated the two major legislative battles of early 1997, although we can also see that they did not entirely foreclose the possibility of bipartisan agreement and that there were also internal party problems. One bill seemed straightforward on the surface. It was an appropriations measure designed primarily to provide emergency relief to victims of major flooding in the Midwest. However, in a virtual replay of the strategy that led to the government shutdowns in the 104th Congress, the House Republicans thought that they could use this apparently "must pass" bill as a vehicle to accomplish some of their other policy objectives, although this strategy was opposed by Gingrich. They therefore included in the bill one provision that would have automatically kept the government operating in the event of another budget impasse (thus sharply reducing the president's bargaining leverage), and another provision that would have blocked the use of statistical sampling to adjust the results of the 2000 census. (We discuss the significance of the latter issue in the next section.) Clinton vetoed the bill nineteen minutes after he received it, and public reaction (as with the shutdowns) sided with the president and blamed the GOP. Three days later the Republicans capitulated and passed a bill without the disputed provisions, although it was opposed by conservatives, including almost all of the Republican leadership in the House.

The other major bill was one of the most notable achievements of recent years: an agreement to balance the budget by 2002. In early May the White House and the Republican leadership reached an agreement in principle to cut Medicare and Medicaid spending, reduce taxes, and provide new money for Clinton's priorities, while also balancing the budget. Demonstrating that the GOP was not the only party with internal divisions, a number of liberal Democrats—led by House Minority Leader Richard Gephardt of Missouri—attacked the plan for betraying Democratic principles. Gephardt called the plan "a budget of many deficits—a deficit of principle, a deficit of fairness, a deficit of tax justice, and, worst of all, a deficit of dollars."[76] Translating the agreement to specific legislative language took more than two months of frequently bitter partisan conflict. In the Senate, Majority Leader Trent Lott (R-Miss.) said that the president was acting like a "spoiled brat" in the tax-cut negotiations.[77] There was also discord within the House GOP, where Majority Leader Dick Armey (R-Texas) contended that he was not bound by the agreement that Gingrich had negotiated (although he later relented).[78] In the midst of the final negotiations, a group of mostly conservative Republican representatives (with the complicity of some in the leadership) went so far as to attempt—unsuccessfully—a coup to remove Gingrich as Speaker. As a result, Clinton seemed to get the best of the final bargaining, and the legislation (with much bipartisan self-congratulation) passed in July. With the apparent resolution of one of the main sources of interparty conflict, Clinton and the Congress were left trying to define their new agendas for the remainder of the 105th and for subsequent Congresses.

The Elections of 1998

Expectations about midterm elections are usually shaped by a strong historical pattern: the party of the president lost strength in the House in twenty-three of the twenty-four midterm elections in this century. The first column in Table 9-8 shows the magnitude of these losses in midterms since World War II. They average 27.5 seats for the president's party. There was, however, considerable variation in the outcomes, from the 55-seat loss by the Democrats in 1946 to the 4-seat Democratic loss in 1962. Another consideration related to the president, however, clarifies the context for judgment somewhat. During the first midterm election of his presidency, the president may be able to make a plausible appeal that he has not had enough time to bring about substantial change or to solidify many achievements. Moreover, even if things are not going very well, voters may not place the blame on a president who has served for such a short time. But four years later (if the president is fortunate enough to face a second midterm), appeals of too little time are likely to be unpersuasive. After six years, if the economy or foreign policy is not going well, voters may seek a policy change by reducing the number of the president's partisans in Congress.

The second and third columns in Table 9-8 indicate that this is what has happened in the past. Losses by the president's party in the first midterm election of a presidency have tended to be much smaller than losses in subsequent midterms.[79] Indeed, with the exception of the results in 1986 and 1994, the two categories yield two fairly homogeneous sets of outcomes that are sharply different from one another. In the six midterm elections before 1994 that took place during a first term, the president's party lost between four and twenty-six seats, with an average loss of fourteen. In the five elections after the first term (excluding 1986), the range of losses was between twenty-nine and fifty-five seats, with an average loss of forty-four.

Models of House Elections. In the last two decades, many scholars have constructed and tested models of congressional election outcomes, focusing especially on midterms, seeking to isolate the factors that most strongly influence the results. The first models, constructed by Tufte and by Jacobson and Samuel Kernell, focused on two variables: presidential approval and a measure of the state of the economy.[80] Tufte hypothesized a direct influence by these forces on voter choice and election outcomes. The theory was that an unpopular president or a poor economic situation would cause the president's party to lose votes and, there-

TABLE 9-8   House Seat Losses by the President's Party in Midterm Elections, 1946–1996

All elections			First term of administration			Later term of administration		
1946:	55	Democrats	1954:	18	Republicans	1946:	55	Democrats
1950:	29	Democrats	1962:	4	Democrats	1950:	29	Democrats
1954:	18	Republicans	1970:	12	Republicans	1958:	47	Republicans
1958:	47	Republicans	1978:	11	Democrats	1966:	47	Democrats
1962:	4	Democrats	1982:	26	Republicans	1974:	43	Republicans
1966:	47	Democrats	1990:	9	Republicans	1986:	5	Republicans
1970:	12	Republicans	1994:	52	Democrats			
1974:	43	Republicans				Average: 37.7		
1978:	11	Democrats	Average: 18.9					
1982:	26	Republicans						
1986:	5	Republicans						
1990:	9	Republicans						
1994:	52	Democrats						
Average: 27.5								

fore, seats in the House. In essence, the midterm elections were viewed as a referendum on the performance of the president and his party. Jacobson and Kernell, in contrast, saw more indirect effects of presidential approval and the economy. They argued that these forces affected election results by influencing the decisions of potential congressional candidates. If the president is unpopular and the economy is in bad shape, potential candidates will expect the president's party to perform poorly. As a consequence, strong potential candidates of the president's party will be more inclined to forgo running until a better year, and strong candidates from the opposition party will be more inclined to run because they foresee good prospects for success. According to Jacobson and Kernell, this mix of weak candidates from the president's party and strong opposition candidates will lead to a poor election performance by the party occupying the White House. To measure this predicted relationship, their model relates the partisan division of the vote to presidential approval and the economic situation early in the election year. This, they argued, is when decisions to run for office are being made, not at the time of the election, so it is not appropriate to focus on approval and the economy at that time. This view has come to be called the "strategic politicians hypothesis."[81]

More recent research has built from this base. One model, developed by Alan I. Abramowitz, Albert D. Cover, and Helmut Norpoth, considered a new variable: short-term party evaluations.[82] They argued that voters' attitudes about the economic competence of the political parties affect the impact of presidential approval and economic conditions on voting decisions. If the electorate judges that the party holding the presidency is better able to deal with the problems voters regard as most serious, the negative impact of an unpopular president or a weak economy will be reduced. The authors concluded from their analysis of both aggregate votes and responses to surveys in midterm elections that there is evidence for their "party competence" hypothesis.

All of these models used the division of the popular vote as the variable to be predicted, and they focused only on midterm elections. More recent work has merged midterm results with those of presidential years, contending that there should be no conceptual distinction between them. These efforts have sought to predict changes in seats without reference to the division of the vote. For example, a study by Bruce I. Oppenheimer, James A. Stimson, and Richard W. Waterman argued that the missing piece in the congressional election puzzle is the degree of "exposure," or "the excess or deficit number of seats a party holds measured against its long-term norm."[83] If a party wins more House seats than normal, those extra seats will be vulnerable in the next election, and the party is likely to suffer losses. Indeed, the May 1986 article by Oppenheimer and his colleagues predicted only small Republican losses for 1986 because Reagan's large 1984 victory was not accompanied by substantial congressional gains for his party. The actual result in 1986 was consistent with this prediction, for the GOP lost only five seats.

Another model of House elections was constructed by Robin F. Marra and Charles W. Ostrom, Jr.[84] They developed a "comprehensive referendum voting model" of both presidential year and midterm elections, and included factors such as foreign policy crises, scandals, unresolved policy disputes, party identification, and the change in the level of presidential approval. The model also incorporated measures reflecting hypothesized relationships in the models we discussed earlier: the level of presidential approval, the state of the economy, the strategic politicians hypothesis, exposure, and party competence. The model was tested on data from all congressional elections from 1950 through 1986.

The Marra-Ostrom analysis showed significant support for most of the predicted relationships. The results indicated that the most powerful influences affecting congressional seat changes were presidential approval (directly and through various events) and exposure. The model was striking in its statistical accuracy; the average error in the predicted change was only four seats. The average error varied little whether presidential or midterm years were predicted, and the analysis demonstrated that the usually greater losses for the president's party in second midterm years resulted from negative shifts in presidential approval, exposure, and scandals.

Drawing on the insights of these various models, we can see how these factors may influence outcomes in the 1998 House elections. How well the economy is doing and what proportion of the voters approve of Clinton's performance early in the year may encourage or discourage high-quality potential challengers. The same variables close to election time may lead voters to support or oppose Democratic candidates based on their judgments of the job the Clinton administration is doing. In the summer of 1997, Clinton's approval was around the high point for his entire presidency, and the economy has continued to perform well. If Clinton remains popular and the economy remains strong, the Democrats' chances would be much better than we would normally expect. Furthermore, Democratic exposure is not high, perhaps the only positive benefit to them of the catastrophe of 1994. Thus, there are not a lot of vulnerable Democratic seats in this category. Finally, unforeseeable events like crises and scandals in the Marra-Ostrom model may influence the 1998 congressional election results.

Some Additional Considerations. Other issues related to the points raised in the previous section in connection with the models or to our earlier discussion are worth noting. First, it is not only Clinton's approval rating that is potentially relevant; the public's reaction to Congress in general and to the GOP and its leadership in particular could influence the 1998 contests. In June 1997 (after the budget deal was made public) approval of Congress was balanced at 44 percent each for approval and disapproval. While hardly a ringing endorsement, this was better than the 39 to 50 percent negative balance in January during Gingrich's ethics problems and much better than that in the depths of 1994.[85] If, however, approval of Congress takes another nose dive, it is not clear who would bear the brunt; it might hurt the majority party or it might damage the president's party.

The potentially vulnerable target is clearer in the case of the public's reaction to Newt Gingrich and congressional Republicans. The electorate's evaluation of Newt Gingrich continues to be remarkably negative. In August 1996, leading into the election, survey data showed that the public's opinion was 32 percent positive and 56 percent negative. By June 1997, the Speaker's standing had fallen even further, to 25 percent favorable and 61 percent unfavorable. Nor were the GOP's worries only tied to one person. When asked if the Republicans in Congress were "out of touch with the American people," 61 percent of respondents said yes and only 35 percent said no.[86] Some analysts have raised particular concerns that continued internecine war within the House GOP could undermine its majority status, both directly and indirectly. As Stuart Rothenberg said (reflecting the "strategic politicians hypothesis"), Republican divisions "could make potential GOP Congressional candidates think twice about running next November."[87]

Another thing to take into account is that the vulnerability of individual members varies across parties and across other attributes, and we should not expect those distributions to be similar from election to election. For example, in one year a party may have a relatively high percentage of freshmen or of members who won by narrow margins in the preceding election, while in another year the party's proportion of such potentially vulnerable members may be low. As Table 9-9 shows, both parties have a substantial (and relatively similar) number of

TABLE 9-9   Percentage of the Vote Received by Winning House Candidates, by Party and Type of Race, 1996

Percentage of the vote	Republicans			Democrats		
	Reelected incumbent	Successful challenger	Open seat	Reelected incumbent	Successful challenger	Open seat
55 or less	34	3	14	18	15	11
55.1–60.0	33	0	7	30	2	4
60.1–70.0	90	0	6	57	1	5
70–100	38	0	2	61	0	4
Total	195	3	29	166	18	24

members who won with 55 percent of the vote or less. Fifty-one Republicans and forty-four Democrats fell into this marginal category. It is in the districts of such members that potentially strong challengers are most likely to come forward and where the challengers who do run are most able to raise adequate campaign funds. Thus, previously close districts could yield almost 100 "hot contests" in 1998.

As the remarks on marginal districts—as well as our earlier analysis—indicate, the parties' respective success in recruiting strong candidates for open seats and to oppose the other party's incumbents can be expected to play a significant role in shaping outcomes for 1998. Both Democratic and Republican campaign organizations were actively pursuing recruits during 1997. Of particular note here is the potential impact of term limits in the states. Although the term limits movement failed to impose restrictions on members of Congress, it succeeded in getting limits adopted for state legislators in twenty states, and those limits are beginning to take effect. One potential outlet for a state legislator who cannot run for reelection is to seek a congressional seat. For example, California state senator Mike Thompson (a Democrat who had declined to try for the House in 1996) was barred from running again in 1998, so he announced his candidacy against Rep. Frank Riggs, a marginal GOP incumbent. Thompson's chief of staff said, "The term limits law played a central role in the process that led to his decision."[88] (A subsequent court decision overturned the California term limits law, at least for the 1998 elections.)

Also related to the questions of candidate recruitment and district vulnerability is the potential number of open seats. We have seen that parties are more likely to be switched in open-seat contests than in contests that include an incumbent and that both parties are more likely to field strong candidates for open seats. As of the summer of 1997 it appeared that there would be many fewer retirements from the House than we have seen in the last few election cycles and that there also would not be a great number of incumbents seeking other offices.

If this picture does not change, the chances of a large shift in seats either way in 1998 will be reduced.

Another factor that assumed great prominence in our analysis earlier in this chapter was the relevance of adequate campaign funding. The degree of success that challengers for 1998 have in raising campaign money will play a large role in the results in competitive districts. Where challengers are perceived to have a good chance, they can do well in this realm. For example, state senator Mike Thompson, whose candidacy we noted above in connection with term limits, had as much cash on hand ($105,000) at the end of June 1997 as did the incumbent. He is running in a highly competitive district in which party control has switched three times in the last five elections.[89] Also probably relevant will be the fund-raising success of vulnerable incumbents, even though it appears that challenger spending is generally more consequential. Of the thirty freshmen who won less than 53 percent of the vote in 1996, and for whom money data are available, thirteen had more than $100,000 on hand at the end of June 1997, and eight had less than $50,000.[90]

Finally, the targeting decisions of the two parties and of other groups may affect the 1998 outcomes. The organizations of both parties will try to calculate which of their districts and which of the other party's districts are most vulnerable. Each will then try to "shore up" their own districts and attack the latter. As noted above, the parties will try to recruit strong candidates, and they will try to provide campaign funds for their priority districts. As the majority party, the GOP will have an advantage in fund-raising, although it is too early to tell how great it will be. Besides the parties, other organizations will seek to influence the process, as organized labor did in 1996 when it targeted thirty-two GOP incumbents. Following up on that effort, labor has already started spending on critical issue-oriented messages regarding "corporate welfare" in nineteen districts.[91] What is different this year is that the targeting has not been confined to Republicans; seven of the districts selected for the initial ads were represented by conservative Democrats. Moreover, the AFL-CIO indicated that a much larger number of Democratic districts would later be included, provoking a sharp reaction from moderate and conservative Democrats.[92]

Senate Races in 1998. Because there are few Senate contests and because they are more independent of one another, we have focused the discussion of 1998 on House races to this point, but it is appropriate that we say a few words about the other chamber's contests. The Democrats' prospects for making gains appear to be poor; indeed, at this early point many observers expect the GOP to gain a seat or two. One reason is that of the four incumbents who are retiring, three are Democrats, and two of those are in the South or Border states (Arkansas and Kentucky). We have seen that open seats are more vulnerable to party switching and that Democrats have had particular trouble in the two regions mentioned. In addition, Democrats appear to have as many or more vulnerable incumbents as the GOP. Beyond those considerations, it is clear that there will be many strongly contested and expensive races and that incumbents are preparing for that with greater than ever fund-raising efforts. Probably the most extreme case will be the seat of Alfonse D'Amato (R-N.Y.); as of June 30, the incumbent had $8.6 million on hand, and one potential Democratic opponent had more than $6.5 million.[93]

To summarize, then, it appears that in House races 1998 may see a blunting of the usual shift against the party that holds the White House. Coupled with fewer than usual open seats, the chances of a large net switch in party representation do not seem great. Given, however, that the size of the GOP majority is so small, the struggle for control of the House may still be in doubt. The same is not true in the Senate, where a continued (and perhaps expanded) Republican majority seems very probable.

Beyond 1998: Continued Uncertainty of House Control?

The greater uncertainty about future patterns of Senate elections applies even more strongly to contests beyond the current cycle, so we focus this concluding section on a few factors related to House races. Probably the most important of these involves the reapportionment and redistricting that will follow the 2000 census. As we write this, the battle over using statistical sampling to adjust the census results continues. Democrats want to adjust the census count to compensate for the undercount of minorities and urban residents. Republicans are resisting this plan, partly because they distrust the accuracy or fairness of the adjustment and partly because they fear that it will cost them House seats. This could happen in two ways: first, the effects of sampling would not touch every state equally. States with large urban centers would probably gain relatively more population than smaller states, potentially affecting the reapportionment of seats among the states. Second, sampling could also affect redistricting within the states by adding urban and minority residents to some (probably Democratic) districts, thus permitting current Democratic voters to be spread around to surrounding districts.

As always, the first political impact of the new census would be in the process of reapportionment. Estimates by the Congressional Research Service in early 1997 indicated that nine states (mostly in the Northeast and industrial Midwest) were likely to lose House seats, while eight states (generally in the South and the mountain states) would gain.[94] These shifts would continue the pattern of the last few decades of shifting representation from the "rust belt" to the "sun belt." Following reapportionment, the states will have to redistrict before the elections in 2002. That process will be profoundly affected by the 1998 elections (and, to a much lesser extent, those in 2000) in which many governors and state legislatures will be elected. Currently, party control is divided in many states, especially the large ones with the lion's share of House seats. If that pattern persists, the parties will be forced to compromise on redistricting in many instances, or risk deadlock, which would transfer control of this important task to the federal or state courts.

Two other factors that may figure in future elections are worth noting. First, while the effort legally to impose term limits on members of Congress has failed so far, a significant number of members elected since 1992 have pledged to voters that they would limit their own terms. For example, of the eighty-six representatives first elected in 1994, thirty-nine (or 45 percent) promised to leave the House after a specified number of years, ranging from six to twelve. Of the seventy-four members of the class of 1996, seventeen (23 percent) chose self-imposed limits.[95] Of course, these members could change their minds or leave their seats before the limits are relevant (nine of the thirty-nine from 1994 have already gone), but the effect could still be consequential over time. This is particularly true because those adopting limits are disproportionately Republican. Indeed, this policy has already affected one member: Bob Inglis (R-S.C.). First elected in 1992, he promised to serve only six years. As a consequence, he announced that he would challenge Democratic senator Fritz Hollings in 1998. As we can see, term limits do not necessarily mean leaving Congress.

Finally, one event that would be potentially very important if it occurred would be campaign finance reform. In the wake of finance scandals touching both parties, there has been a renewed bipartisan effort at reform, spearheaded by Sen. John McCain (R-Ariz.) and Sen. Russell Feingold (D-Wis.). Their bill seeks to ban so-called "soft money" (raised by parties outside the limits that otherwise apply to direct donations to candidates) and ban contributions from Political Action Committees (PACs).[96] Such changes could substantially alter the process of raising and spending campaign funds. There is, however, also bipartisan resistance to these or any other major changes, so a significant revamping of the current finance system does not seem likely at this time. Rather, the elections of 2000 and in the near term thereafter will probably take place under the pattern of rules and incentives we have described in this chapter.

Chapter 10

The Congressional Electorate in 1996

In the preceding chapter we viewed congressional elections at the district and state level and saw how those outcomes came together to form a national result. In this chapter we consider congressional elections from the point of view of the individual voter, using the same National Election Studies (NES) surveys we employed to study presidential voting. We discuss how social forces, issues, partisan loyalties, incumbency, and evaluations of congressional and presidential performance influence the decisions of voters in congressional elections. We also try to determine the existence and extent of presidential coattails.

SOCIAL FORCES AND THE CONGRESSIONAL VOTE

In general, social forces relate to the congressional vote the same way they do to the presidential vote (Table 10-1).[1] But in 1996, Democratic congressional candidates did not run as well as their presidential candidate, Bill Clinton, in many of the categories used in the presidential vote analysis (see Table 5-1).[2] This is true mainly because Clinton was a relatively popular incumbent, whereas most Democratic House candidates were opposing incumbents or running in open seats.

Consider, for example, the relationship between voting and Hispanic identification. Among white voters who identify as Hispanic, Democratic House candidates ran 42 percentage points ahead of Republicans, while the comparable figure for Clinton versus Bob Dole was 60 points. Similarly, among whites who do not identify as Hispanic, Democratic House candidates ran 16 points behind Republicans, while Clinton and Dole ran dead even within that group. (As Table 10-1 shows, the vast majority of blacks voted Democratic; therefore, except for the discussion of voting and race, the analysis here, as in Chapter 5, is limited to white voters.)

Keeping in mind this difference in relative support, we find that presidential

TABLE 10-1   How Social Groups Voted for Congress, 1996 (in percentages)

Social group	Democratic	Republican	Total	(N)
Total electorate	47	53	100	(1,027)
Electorate, by race				
African-American	86	14	100	(94)
White	44	56	100	(900)
Whites, by Hispanic identification				
Identify as Hispanic	71	29	100	(62)
Do not identify	42	58	100	(836)
Whites, by gender				
Females	47	53	100	(458)
Males	40	60	100	(441)
Whites, by region				
New England and Mid-Atlantic	46	54	100	(183)
North Central	46	54	100	(247)
South	38	62	100	(232)
Border	39	61	100	(49)
Mountain and Pacific	46	54	100	(190)
Whites, by birth cohort				
Before 1924	46	54	100	(90)
1924–1939	48	52	100	(188)
1940–1954	46	54	100	(264)
1955–1962	32	68	100	(194)
1963–1970	46	54	100	(123)
1971–1978	47	53	100	(38)
Whites, by social class				
Working class	47	53	100	(289)
Middle class	42	58	100	(501)
Farmers	42	58	100	(26)
Whites, by occupation of head of household				
Unskilled manual	53	47	100	(60)
Skilled, semiskilled manual	46	54	100	(229)
Clerical, sales, other white collar	49	51	100	(115)
Managerial	37	63	100	(195)
Professional and semiprofessional	42	58	100	(190)

Social group	Democratic	Republican	Total	(N)
Whites, by level of education				
Eight grades or less	75	25	100	(20)
Some high school	66	34	100	(47)
High school graduate	48	52	100	(249)
Some college	41	59	100	(250)
College graduate	36	64	100	(217)
Advanced degree	38	62	100	(116)
Whites, by annual family income				
Less than $10,000	63	37	100	(49)
$10,000 to $14,999	50	50	100	(42)
$15,000 to $19,999	68	32	100	(47)
$20,000 to $24,999	60	40	100	(53)
$25,000 to $29,999	48	52	100	(61)
$30,000 to $34,999	54	46	100	(69)
$35,000 to $39,999	34	66	100	(53)
$40,000 to $49,999	40	60	100	(100)
$50,000 to $59,999	33	67	100	(103)
$60,000 to $74,999	31	69	100	(114)
$75,000 to $89,999	36	64	100	(56)
$90,000 and over	36	64	100	(104)
Whites, by union membership[a]				
Member	54	46	100	(182)
Nonmember	41	59	100	(717)
Whites, by religion				
Jewish	77	23	100	(26)
Catholic	48	52	100	(273)
Protestant	36	64	100	(502)
None, no preference	59	41	100	(86)
White Protestants, by whether born again				
Not born again	42	58	100	(244)
Born again	31	69	100	(256)
White Protestants, by religious commitment				
Medium or low	45	55	100	(216)
High	33	67	100	(156)
Very high	19	81	100	(91)

(Table continues)

TABLE 10-1 (continued)

Social group	Democratic	Republican	Total	(N)
White Protestants, by religious tradition				
Mainline	36	64	100	(230)
Evangelical	38	62	100	(197)
Whites, by social class and religion				
Working-class Catholics	59	41	100	(85)
Middle-class Catholics	45	55	100	(159)
Working-class Protestants	38	62	100	(167)
Middle-class Protestants	34	66	100	(267)

Note: Numbers are weighted. Respondents for whom direction of vote was not ascertained or who voted for candidates who were neither Republicans nor Democrats have been excluded from these analyses.

^aWhether respondent or family member in union.

and congressional voting patterns are similar not only with respect to Hispanic heritage, but also within many other social categories, including race, gender, social class, education, income, union membership, and Protestant and Catholic categories of religion. For both the presidential and the congressional vote, African-Americans were substantially more likely to vote Democratic. Among major-party voters, the difference was 47 points for the presidential race and 42 points in House contests. Members of union families were 13 percentage points more likely to vote Democratic for the House than voters from nonunion families; working-class voters were 5 points more Democratic than middle-class voters. Catholics were 12 points more likely to vote Democratic than Protestants, and among Protestants, those who did not claim to be "born again" were 11 points more Democratic than those who claimed that status. Religious commitment was also related to congressional voting preferences, and the relationship was almost as strong as that between religious commitment and presidential voting choices. About a third of the white Protestants who had very high levels of religious commitment voted Democratic, while Protestants who did not score very high split their vote more evenly between the two major parties.

There are some differences in the ways the presidential and congressional vote relate to income categories, but it is likely that these differences reflect the small number of cases in those categories. The overall patterns are similar and consistent: the propensity to vote Democratic is considerably greater in lower categories of income.

Of particular interest is the relationship between House voting and gender. In 1988 there was a small gender gap in the presidential vote (about 3 points), with women more likely to vote Democratic than men, but there was no gap in the

House vote. Then, in 1992, there was a 9-point gap in the presidential vote for the Democrats, and a 5-point gap in the House vote. In 1996 the gender gap was more pronounced in the vote both for the president and for representatives; the major-party share of the vote was 12 points more Democratic for women in the former case and 7 points more Democratic in the latter.

There are, however, some differences worth noting in the way social forces relate to the two types of votes. One is with respect to region; for Clinton the best regions were the New England and Mid-Atlantic states, and the mountain and Pacific states, while the South and North Central states were the worst for him. In the House vote, Democrats ran noticeably behind in the South and the Border states, while their showing in the other three regions was essentially identical. This is a shift from 1988, when the South was the worst region for the Democrats in the presidential race, but not for Democrats in the congressional contests. (The 1996 pattern by region was, however, more similar to that in 1992.) Overall, then, the relationship of social forces to the 1996 congressional vote was quite similar to their relationship to the 1996 presidential vote.

ISSUES AND THE CONGRESSIONAL VOTE

In Chapter 6 we analyzed the impact of issues on the presidential vote in 1996. Any attempt to conduct a similar analysis for congressional elections is hampered by limited data. One interesting perspective on issues in the congressional vote is gained by asking whether voters are affected by their perceptions of where candidates stand on the issues. Previous analysis has demonstrated a relationship between a voter's perception of House candidates' positions on a liberal-conservative issue scale and the voter's choice.[3] Unfortunately, the 1996 NES survey does not contain questions that would permit an analysis parallel to the one we offered on issues in the presidential race. We can, however, draw on other research to shed further light on this question. In two articles, Alan I. Abramowitz used NES surveys to demonstrate a relationship between candidate ideology and voter choice in both House and Senate elections.[4] For the 1978 Senate election, Abramowitz classified the contests according to the clarity of the ideological choice the two major-party candidates offered to voters. He found that the higher the ideological clarity of the race, the more likely voters were to perceive some difference between the candidates on a liberalism-conservatism scale, and the stronger the relationship was between voters' positions on that scale and the vote. Indeed, in races with a very clear choice, ideology had approximately the same impact on the vote as party identification. In an analysis of House races in 1980 and 1982, Abramowitz found that the more liberal the voter was, the more likely the voter was to vote Democratic; but the relationship was statistically significant only in 1982.

Another point of view was offered in an analysis by Robert S. Erikson and Gerald C. Wright.[5] They examined the positions of 1982 House candidates on a variety of issues (expressed in response to a CBS News/*New York Times* poll) and found that, on most issues, most of the districts were presented with a liberal Democrat and a conservative Republican. They also found that moderate candidates did better in attracting votes than more extreme candidates. In a more recent study, involving the 1994 House elections, Erikson and Wright show that both the issue stands of incumbents (measured by positions on roll-call votes) and the district's ideology (measured by the district's average propensity to vote Democratic in the previous two presidential elections) are strongly related to the congressional vote.[6]

Despite the data restrictions we mentioned, we conducted a limited analysis of the relationships between issues and congressional voting choices in 1996, analyzing the issues we studied in Chapter 6. For the most part, the relationship between issue preferences and congressional vote choices were weak and inconsistent, and these relationships were even weaker when we controlled for the tendency of Democratic party identifiers to have liberal positions on these issues and of Republicans to have conservative issue preferences. However, partisan loyalties clearly affect congressional voting, even when we take issue preferences into account. Therefore, before considering the effects of other factors we provide more information about the effects of party identification on House voting.

PARTY IDENTIFICATION AND THE CONGRESSIONAL VOTE

As our discussion in the preceding chapters demonstrates and data presented here indicate, party identification has a significant effect on voters' decisions.

TABLE 10-2   Percentage of White Major-Party Voters Who Voted Democratic for the House, by Party Identification, 1952–1996

Party identification	1952	1954	1956	1958	1960	1962	1964	1966	1968
Strong Democrat	90	97	94	96	92	96	92	92	88
Weak Democrat	76	77	86	88	85	83	84	81	72
Independent, leans Democrat	63	70	82	75	86	74	78	54	60
Independent, no partisan leanings	25	41	35	46	52	61	70	49	48
Independent, leans Republican	18	6	17	26	26	28	28	31	18
Weak Republican	10	6	11	22	14	14	34	22	21
Strong Republican	5	5	5	6	8	6	8	12	8

Notes: To approximate the numbers on which these percentages are based, see Table 8-2. Actual Ns will be smaller than those that can be derived from Table 8-2 because respondents who did not vote (or who voted for a minor party) have been excluded from these calculations. Numbers also will be lower for the presidential election years because the voting report is provided in the postelection interviews that usu-

Table 10-2, which corresponds to Table 8-4 on the presidential vote, reports the percentage of whites voting Democratic for the House across all categories of partisanship from 1952 through 1996. Even a casual inspection of the data reveals that the proportion of voters who cast ballots in accordance with their party identification has declined substantially over time through the 1980s. During the 1990s, however, there has been some resurgence of party voting for the House, especially among Republican identifiers.

Consider first the strong identifier categories. In every election from 1952 through 1964, at least nine strong party identifiers out of ten supported the candidate of their party. After that, the percentage dropped, falling to four out of five in 1980, then fluctuating through 1992. But in the last two elections, strong Republicans showed levels of loyalty similar to those in the late 1950s and early 1960s. The relationship between party and voting among weak party identifiers shows a more erratic pattern, although in most years before 1994 defection rates tend to be higher since the 1970s than earlier. Because we present the percentage of major-party voters who voted Democratic, the defection rate for Democrats is the reported percentage subtracted from 100 percent. Among Republicans, the percentage reported in the table is the defection rate. Note that the tendency to defect was stronger among Republicans, which reflected the Democrats' greater number of incumbents, as discussed in Chapter 9. Here too, however, there has been some recent change. In 1994 and 1996, the tendency to defect rose among Democrats, whereas among Republicans it fell. We consider this further in the next section.

1970	1972	1974	1976	1978	1980	1982	1984	1986	1988	1990	1992	1994	1996
91	91	89	86	83	82	90	87	91	86	91	87	87	87
76	79	81	76	79	66	73	66	71	80	80	81	73	70
74	78	87	76	60	69	84	76	71	86	79	73	65	70
48	54	54	55	56	57	31	59	59	66	60	53	55	42
35	27	38	32	36	32	36	39	37	37	33	36	26	19
17	24	31	28	34	26	20	33	34	29	39	35	21	19
4	15	14	15	19	22	12	15	20	23	17	16	6	2

ally contain about 10 percent fewer respondents than the preelection interviews in which party identification was measured. The 1954 survey measured voting intention shortly before the election. Except for 1954, the off-year election surveys are based on a postelection interview.

Despite this increase in defections from party identification since the mid-1960s, strong party identifiers continue to be notably more likely to vote in accord with their party than weak identifiers. In most years, weak Republicans were more likely to vote Republican than independents who leaned toward the Republican party, although in 1996 these groups were equally likely to vote Republican. Weak Democrats were more likely to vote Democratic than independents who leaned Democratic in most of the elections from 1952 through 1978, although in the 1980s this pattern was reversed, and in 1996 the two groups were equally likely to vote Democratic. In general, then, the relationship between party identification and the vote was strongest in the 1950s and early 1960s, less strong thereafter, and shows some recent rebound.

As we saw in Chapters 4 and 8, however, the proportion of the electorate that strongly identifies with a political party has declined. Thus, strong Democrats, for example, not only became less likely to vote Democratic than before, but also fewer voters identify themselves as strong Democrats. Even with some resurgence of party loyalty, therefore, the impact of party on voting is weaker than it was decades ago.

If party identifiers have been defecting more frequently in House elections, to whom have they been defecting? As one might expect from the preceding chapter, the answer is: to incumbents.

INCUMBENCY AND THE CONGRESSIONAL VOTE

In Chapter 9 we mentioned Albert D. Cover's analysis of congressional voting behavior from 1958 through 1974.[7] Cover compared the rates of defection from party identification among voters who were of the same party as the incumbent and those who were of the same party as the challenger. The analysis showed no systematic increase over time in defection among voters who shared identification with incumbents, and the proportions defecting varied between 5 percent and 14 percent. Among voters who identified with the same party as challengers, however, the rate of defection—that is, the proportion voting for the incumbent instead of the candidate of their own party—increased steadily from 16 percent in 1958 to 56 percent in 1972, then dropped to 49 percent in 1974. Thus, the decline in the strength of the relationship between party identification and House voting appeared to be due in large measure to increased support for incumbents. Because there were more Democratic incumbents, this tendency was consistent with the higher defection rates among Republican identifiers, as seen in Table 10-2.

Controlling for party identification and incumbency, we present in Table 10-3 data on the percentage of respondents who voted Democratic for the House and Senate in 1996 that confirm this view. In House voting we find the same relationship as Cover did. As we present the percentage of major-party voters who voted Democratic, the defection rate for Democrats is the reported percentage subtracted from 100 percent. Among Republicans, the percentage reported in

TABLE 10-3 Percentage of Respondents Who Voted Democratic for the House and Senate, by Party Identification and Incumbency, 1996

| | Party identification | | | | | |
| | Democrat | | Independent | | Republican | |
Incumbency	(%)	(N)	(%)	(N)	(%)	(N)
House						
Democrat	96	(189)	61	(111)	29	(87)
None	91	(45)	63	(27)	11	(18)
Republican	59	(164)	30	(132)	2	(232)
Senate						
Democrat	93	(54)	41	(37)	18	(50)
None	91	(85)	53	(61)	11	(61)
Republican	79	(86)	41	(68)	13	(86)

Note: Numbers in parentheses are totals on which percentages are based. Numbers are weighted.

the table is the defection rate. (By definition, independents cannot defect.) The proportion of voters defecting from their party identification is low when that identification is shared by the incumbent: 4 percent among Democrats and 2 percent among Republicans.[8] When, however, the incumbent belongs to the other party, defection rates are much higher: 41 percent among Democrats and 29 percent among Republicans. Note also that the support of the independents is skewed sharply in favor of the incumbent. When an incumbent Democrat was running, 61 percent of the independents voted Democratic; when an incumbent Republican was running, 70 percent of the independents voted Republican.

The analogous pattern is weaker or nonexistent in the data on Senate voting. When given the opportunity to support a Republican House incumbent, 41 percent of the Democratic identifiers defected. Faced with the opportunity to support an incumbent Republican senator, only 21 percent defected, and among Republican identifiers the tendency to defect remains low across categories of incumbency. Because the proportion of the electorate that has the chance to vote for Democratic and Republican senatorial candidates varies greatly from election to election, it is difficult to make generalizations about the overall effects of incumbency in Senate contests. But the results in Table 10-3 show that in the House elections represented in the 1996 NES survey, the Republicans were the clear beneficiaries of the tendency to support incumbents. About two-thirds of all Republican identifiers lived in a district in which a Republican incumbent was seeking reelection. In contrast, just about one-fourth of the Republican identifiers lived in a district in which a Democratic incumbent was running. Democratic identifiers were more evenly distributed between districts with Democratic and Republican incumbents, as were independents. In the remainder of this chapter we explore this relationship among party identification, incumbency, and congressional voting.

In Chapter 7 we analyzed the effect of perceptions of presidential performance on the vote for president in 1996, more or less viewing that election as a referendum on Clinton's job performance, especially about the economy. A similar conception can be applied here, employing different perspectives. On the one hand, a congressional election can be considered as a referendum on the performance of a particular member of Congress in office; on the other hand, it can be viewed as a referendum on the performance of the president. We will consider both possibilities here.

As we noted in Chapter 9, for some time, public opinion surveys have shown that the approval ratings of congressional incumbents are very high, even when judgments on the performance of Congress as an institution are not. While traveling with House incumbents in their districts, Richard F. Fenno, Jr., noted that the people he met overwhelmingly approved of the performance of their own representative, although at the time the public generally disapproved of the job Congress was doing.[9] Data in the 1996 NES survey again indicate widespread approval of House incumbents: among respondents who had an opinion, an average of 84 percent endorsed their member's job performance. Approval was widespread, regardless of the party identification of the voter or the party of the incumbent. Indeed, an examination of all combinations of these two variables shows that the lowest approval rate for incumbents is the 62 percent level achieved by Democratic members among Republican party identifiers.

Further evidence indicates, moreover, that the level of approval has electoral consequences. Table 10-4 shows the level of proincumbent voting among voters who share the incumbent's party and among those who are of the opposite party, controlling for whether they approve or disapprove of the incumbent's job performance. If voters approve of the member's performance and share his or her partisanship, support is overwhelming. At the opposite pole, among voters from the opposite party who disapprove, support is negligible. In the mixed categories, the incumbents' receive intermediate levels of support. Because approval rates are very high even among voters of the opposite party, most incumbents are reelected by large margins even in a difficult year (for Democrats) like 1994.

In Chapter 9 we pointed out that midterm congressional elections were influenced by public evaluations of the president's job performance. Voters who think the president is doing a good job are more likely to support the congressional candidate of the president's party. Less scholarly attention has been given to this phenomenon in presidential election years, but the 1996 NES survey provides us with the data needed to explore the question.

TABLE 10-4   Percentage of Voters Who Supported Incumbents in House Voting, by Party and Evaluations of Incumbent's Performance, 1996

| | Voters' evaluation of incumbent's job performance | | | |
| | Approve | | Disapprove | |
	(%)	(N)	(%)	(N)
Incumbent is of same party as voter	99	(373)	78	(18)
Incumbent is of opposite party	41	(148)	2	(66)

Note: Numbers in parentheses are totals on which percentages are based. Numbers are weighted. The total number of cases is markedly lower than for previous tables because we have excluded respondents who did not evaluate the performance of the incumbent and those who live in a district that had no incumbent running.

On the surface at least, there would appear to be a strong relationship. Among voters who approved of Clinton's job performance, 66 percent voted Democratic for the House; among those who disapproved of the president's performance, only 12 percent supported Democrats. In 1980 there was a similar relationship between the two variables, but when controls were introduced for party identification and incumbency, the relationship all but disappeared.[10] Approval of Carter increased the Democratic House vote by a small amount among Democrats, but had virtually no effect among independents and Republicans. In 1996, however, the results are very different. Table 10-5 presents the relevant data on House voting, controlling for party identification and incumbency. We found that even with these controls, evaluations of the president's job had a noticeable impact on

TABLE 10-5   Percentage of Respondents Who Voted Democratic for the House, by Evaluation of Clinton's Performance, Party Identification, and Incumbency, 1996

	Evaluation of Clinton's job							
	Incumbent is Republican				Incumbent is Democrat			
Party identification	Approve		Disapprove		Approve		Disapprove	
	(%)	(N)	(%)	(N)	(%)	(N)	(%)	(N)
Democrat	61	(150)	18	(11)	97	(178)	80	(10)
Independent	42	(85)	9	(47)	74	(69)	38	(42)
Republican	5	(64)	0	(166)	50	(34)	15	(53)

Note: Numbers in parentheses are totals on which percentages are based. Numbers are weighted.

House voting. To be sure, Republicans were still more likely both to disapprove of Clinton and to vote Republican than were Democrats. Yet even after we control for the pull of incumbency, within each party identification category, those who approved of Clinton's job performance were noticeably more likely to vote Democratic for the House than were those who disapproved, and the difference in all six categories was larger than the corresponding difference in 1980. The results for 1996 are similar to those for the 1984 through the 1992 elections. Further research is necessary to reconcile these conflicting findings.

PRESIDENTIAL COATTAILS AND THE CONGRESSIONAL VOTE

Another perspective on the congressional vote, somewhat related to the presidential referendum concept we have just considered, is the impact of the voter's presidential vote decision, or the length of a presidential candidate's coattails. That is, does a voter's decision to support a presidential candidate make him or her more likely to support a congressional candidate of the same party, so that the congressional candidate, as the saying goes, rides into office on the president's coattails?

Expectations regarding presidential coattails have been shaped in substantial measure by the period of the New Deal realignment. Franklin D. Roosevelt won by landslide margins in 1932 and 1936 and swept enormous congressional majorities into office with him. Research has indicated, however, that such strong pulling power by presidential candidates may have been a historical aberration, and in any event, that candidates' pulling power has declined in recent years.[11] In an analysis of the coattail effect since 1868, John A. Ferejohn and Randall L. Calvert pointed out that the effect is a combination of two factors: how many voters a presidential candidate can pull to congressional candidates of his party and how many congressional seats can be shifted between the parties by the addition of those voters.[12] (The second aspect is called the seats/votes relationship, or the swing ratio.)

Ferejohn and Calvert discovered that the relationship between presidential voting and congressional voting from 1932 through 1948 was virtually the same as it was from 1896 through 1928 and that the impact of coattails was strengthened by an increase in the swing ratio. In other words, the same proportion of votes pulled in by a presidential candidate produced more congressional seats in the New Deal era than in the past. After 1948, they argued, the coattail effect declined because the relationship between presidential and congressional voting decreased. Analyzing data from presidential elections from 1956 through 1980, Calvert and Ferejohn reached similar conclusions about the length of presidential coattails.[13] They found that although every election during the period exhibited significant coattail voting, over time the extent of such voting probably declined. More recently, James E. Campbell and Joe A. Sumners concluded from an analysis of Senate elections that presidential coattails exert a modest but significant influence on the Senate vote.[14]

TABLE 10-6   Percentage of Respondents Who Voted Democratic for House and Senate, by Party Identification and Presidential Vote, 1996

Presidential vote	Party identification					
	Democrat		Independent		Republican	
	(%)	(N)	(%)	(N)	(%)	(N)
House						
Clinton	84	(349)	64	(129)	40	(35)
Dole	45	(20)	18	(94)	5	(281)
Perot	45	(20)	53	(36)	8	(13)
Senate						
Clinton	91	(201)	66	(76)	53	(19)
Dole	23	(13)	18	(61)	8	(164)
Perot	88	(8)	36	(22)	33	(9)

Note: Numbers in parentheses are totals on which percentages are based. Numbers are weighted.

In Table 10-6 we present data on the percentage of respondents who voted Democratic for the House and Senate in 1996 according to their presidential vote, controlling for their party identification. For both houses, a strong relationship is apparent. Within each party identification category, the proportion of Dole voters who supported Democratic congressional candidates is substantially lower than the proportion of Clinton voters who supported Democratic candidates. Moreover, the proportion of Perot voters who voted Democratic falls between the proportions for the supporters of the two major-party candidates in five of the six comparisons.

Because we know that this apparent relationship could be just a consequence of the distribution of different types of voters among Democratic and Republican districts, in Table 10-7 we present the same data on House voting in 1996, but this time also controlling for the party of the House incumbent. Despite this additional control, the relationship holds up very well. Within every category for which comparisons are possible, Dole voters supported Democratic candidates at substantially lower rates than did Clinton voters. In three of the four cases for which we find more than ten respondents reporting voting for Perot, the Perot voters fell between Clinton and Dole voters. These data are consistent with the interpretation that the presidential vote exerted some influence on the congressional vote, although not as strong an influence as partisanship and congressional incumbency. The results in both tables are very similar to the corresponding data for 1980 through 1992: within the various categories of party identification and congressional incumbency, the relationship between presidential voting and congressional voting seems to be substantially the same in these five elections.[15]

TABLE 10-7   Percentage of Respondents Who Voted Democratic for the House, by Presidential Vote, Party Identification, and Incumbency, 1996

Party identification	Voted for Dole (%)	Voted for Dole (N)	Voted for Clinton (%)	Voted for Clinton (N)	Voted for Perot (%)	Voted for Perot (N)
			Incumbent is Democrat			
Democrat	—	(7)	97	(171)	—	(3)
Independent	33	(40)	81	(53)	69	(13)
Republican	18	(71)	91	(11)	—	(2)
			Incumbent is Republican			
Democrat	0	(10)	66	(140)	15	(13)
Independent	6	(47)	43	(63)	50	(16)
Republican	0	(196)	14	(22)	9	(11)

Note: Numbers in parentheses are totals on which percentages are based. Numbers are weighted. No percentage is reported where the total *N* is less than 10.

CONCLUSION

In this chapter we have considered a variety of possible influences on voters' decisions in congressional elections. We found that social forces have some impact on that choice. There is evidence from the work of other researchers that issues also have an effect. Incumbency has a major and consistent impact on voters' choices. It solidifies the support of the incumbent's partisans, attracts independents, and leads to defections by voters who identify with the challenger's party. Incumbent support is linked to a positive evaluation of the representative's job by the voters. The tendency to favor incumbents currently appears to benefit the Republican party in House races. Within the context of this incumbency effect, voters' choices also seem to be affected by their evaluations of the job the president is doing and by their vote for president. Partisanship has some direct impact on the vote, even after we control for incumbency. The total effect of partisanship is, however, larger, because most incumbents represent districts that have more partisans of their party than of the opposition. The long-term advantage of Democrats in congressional elections was built on a three-part base: there were more Democrats than Republicans in the electorate; most incumbents of both parties achieved high levels of approval in their constituencies; and the incumbents had resources that made it possible for them to create direct contacts with voters. With the GOP now in the majority in Congress, their members may continue to benefit from the last two factors while they try to ameliorate their deficit on the first.

Chapter 11

The 1998 Congressional Elections

In Chapter 9 we focused on the Republicans' reversal of the patterns of recent history in 1994 by ending the Democrats' unparalleled dominance over elections to the House. We also considered how the GOP retained its new majority in 1996, despite some negative reactions to the party's governance during the 104th Congress, and despite Bill Clinton's reelection. In this chapter we will discuss the pattern of outcomes in the 1998 congressional races to determine whether there is any collective message in the individual results and to assess the implications of these outcomes for future elections.

The magnitude of the shift in electoral results from 1996 was small. The Republicans won sixteen of the thirty-four Senate contests, for a total of fifty-five seats in the 106th Congress—exactly the same total they held before the election. In the House the GOP won 223 seats to the Democrats' 211, with one seat taken by an independent.[1] The Democrats gained five seats, leaving them six seats short of the majority control they sought. Despite what may justly have been termed a "status quo" result, many observers were shocked by the GOP's failure to make gains, and, as we shall see below, the Republicans themselves were mightily disappointed. Our attempt to discover the patterns underlying these results begins with a closer examination of the congressional outcomes.

THE PATTERN OF OUTCOMES

The data on incumbency and electoral success in Table 11-1 provide an update of the information found in Table 9-1. They show that the success of incumbents was great; indeed for the House it was at a historic level—the 98.3 percent reelected tied the highest proportion (in 1988) since 1954. Only seven House incumbents lost, one Democrat and six Republicans (one of the latter in a primary). Moreover, the number of incumbents seeking reelection (401) was also high. The combination of these factors—many incumbents with a high success

TABLE 11-1 House and Senate Incumbents and Election Outcomes, 1998

Chamber	Incumbents running (N)	Primary defeats (%)	Primary defeats (N)	General election defeats (%)	General election defeats (N)	Reelected (%)	Reelected (N)
House	401	0.2	(1)	1.5	(6)	98.3	(394)
Senate	29	—	(0)	10.3	(3)	89.7	(26)

rate—resulted in one of the smaller freshman classes in the postwar era, only 40 newly elected members. In the Senate contests, incumbents' success was somewhat lower than it was in the House, but still high at about 90 percent, with no primary defeats and only three losses in the general elections. Only six elections since 1954 registered higher rates of incumbent success in the Senate.

Table 11-2 shows the combined effects of party and incumbency in 1998. Given the overall results, the pattern for both parties basically reflects what we have just seen for the two houses. In both House and Senate contests involving incumbents, Democrats did slightly better than Republicans. The same was true for open House seats, while that pattern was reversed in open Senate seats. All in all, there was little variation by party.

Not surprisingly, the slight partisan shifts translated into small changes in the party shares of regional delegations. Compared to the divisions in 1997 (listed in

TABLE 11-2 House and Senate General Election Outcomes, by Party and Incumbency, 1998 (in percentages)

	Democratic incumbent	No incumbent — Democratic seat	No incumbent — Republican seat	Republican incumbent	Total
House					
Democrats	99	71	35	2	49
Republicans	1	29	65	98	51
Total	100	100	100	100	100
(N)	(190)	(17)	(17)	(211)	(435)
Senate					
Democrats	93	33	50	14	53
Republicans	7	67	50	86	47
Total	100	100	100	100	100
(N)	(15)	(3)	(2)	(14)	(34)

Table 9-3), the Democrats were just slightly better off in the House in the East, the Midwest, and the West, while they stayed the same in the South and in Border states.[2] In the Senate the regional shifts were even smaller. After the election the Democrats found themselves one seat better off in the East and the South, while the Republicans had a net gain of one seat in both the Midwest and the Border states.[3]

ASSESSING VICTORY AND EXPLAINING THE RESULTS

After every election, one question that is always of interest is: Which party won and which party lost? This question is of real consequence to politicians and citizens because the public interpretation of election outcomes can have an effect on the calculations of politicians and their ability to advance their policy agendas, and it can also affect their relationships with each other. Those politicians use their interpretations of the results, and those of other observers, to infer (rightly or wrongly) the political desires of the voters. For example, in 1980 Ronald Reagan's convincing electoral vote victory over President Jimmy Carter and the substantial gains made by the Republicans in the congressional elections were interpreted as a wholesale endorsement of the Republican agenda of tax cuts, reductions of social spending, and increases in defense expenditures. As a consequence, all of these measures were enacted into law in the subsequent Congress.

To evaluate a party's success we must apply some standard—a "yardstick"—to measure victory. The standard provides us with a set of expectations against which the actual results can be compared. In addition, as we saw in Chapter 9, expectations or hypotheses about election outcomes can be combined in models of the electoral process that can provide explanations as well as predictions. We will, in turn, consider the historical pattern, the expectations of participants and observers, and the insights from academic models as yardsticks by which to measure the relative success of each party.

Historical Trends

In Chapter 9 we presented data on seat changes in midterm House elections (see Table 9-8). Recall that the party that held the White House has lost strength in all but one midterm this century, and in every one since World War II. Thus, based on this trend alone, one would have expected Democratic losses in 1998. The question was how great would those losses be? The historical results showed that a party's losses were larger in the second or later midterm of an administration than in the first midterm. In fact, we can see an even clearer picture of the historical trends by introducing an additional variable: whether the president's party held a majority in the House before the election. Remember that the "exposure" hypothesis discussed in Chapter 9 argued that the more seats a party held (rela-

TABLE 11-3 Average Seat Losses by the President's Party in Midterm Elections, 1946–1994

President's party in the House	First term of administration	Later term of administration	Total
Majority	21.3 $(N = 4)$[a]	43.7 $(N = 3)$[b]	30.9 $(N = 7)$
Minority	15.7 $(N = 3)$[c]	31.7 $(N = 3)$[d]	23.7 $(N = 6)$
Total	18.9 $(N = 7)$	37.7 $(N = 6)$	27.5 $(N = 13)$

[a] 1954, 1962, 1978, and 1994.
[b] 1946, 1950, and 1966.
[c] 1970, 1982, and 1990.
[d] 1958, 1974, and 1986.

tive to the recent historical pattern), the more vulnerable it would be to losses. Similarly, we might expect that a majority party would be more vulnerable than a minority. Table 11-3 reconfigures the data from Table 9-8 and shows that this expectation is correct. On average, minority parties lost fewer seats than majority parties in postwar midterm elections, both overall and when we control for first or later midterms of an administration. Note, however, that the impact of first versus later midterms also continues to hold, and appears to be more substantial than this new variable.

In light of these historical patterns, the actual showing of the Democrats in the House races was quite remarkable. The only previous gain by the president's party in a midterm this century was by the Democrats in 1934 in Franklin D. Roosevelt's first midterm, when the GOP was still suffering from the public's negative reaction to the Great Depression. While we did not previously discuss in detail similar data for the Senate, we can draw similar conclusions. In general in the postwar period the party that controlled the White House did better in first midterms (averaging a net loss of only one seat per election) than in later midterms.[4] In the latter circumstance, the parties have lost an average of eight seats, as compared to the Democrats' actual showing in 1998 of no loss at all. Thus, in both chambers the Democrats did considerably better than would have been expected from the historical pattern for midterm elections.

Observers' Expectations

The pre-election expectations of politicians and media analysts provide another standard for judging election outcomes. Even if a party loses ground, it may try to claim victory (at least a "moral victory") if it performs notably better than was anticipated. These publicly-stated expectations are shaped in part by the historical standards we just discussed, but they are also influenced by polls and by recent political events.

Of course, the anticipations voiced by politicians during election campaigns are a mixture of predictions, hopes, and public-relations statements. They cannot be taken entirely at face value. In the year leading up to the 1998 elections, however, estimates of the likely outcome were probably more variable over time than usual. Late in 1997 Republican party strategists confidently predicted that their candidates would fare well in the upcoming election, although no one indicated that they expected gains in the historical twenty-five-plus range. On the other hand, surveys at that time showed somewhat more respondents planning to vote for Democratic candidates than for Republicans, which would not portend GOP gains.[5] Republican conservatives also voiced concerns that lack of action on a conservative agenda would leave core GOP voters without incentives to turn out on election day. Rep. David McIntosh (R-Ind.) said: "The reality is that in an off-year election your base matters and you have to energize it. We haven't."[6]

By mid-1998 Republican leaders still predicted significant gains. John Linder, the chairman of the National Republican Congressional Committee (NRCC), said: "We'll lose no more than five open and incumbent seats combined . . . and we'll end up with a net gain of 10 to 15 seats."[7] Speaker Newt Gingrich went even further, predicting that his party's gains could reach as high as forty seats.[8] Predictions about the Senate were less variable. With only a few open seats, and with general agreement that the Democrats had more vulnerable incumbents than the GOP, both politicians and journalists generally agreed that Republican gains (of from one to five seats, depending on the evaluator) were likely. A five-seat gain was something the Republicans really wanted, because it would give them sixty seats total, enough votes in the Senate to block any Democratic filibuster if all GOP members stuck together.

By September, Republican hopes were even stronger. A bipartisan survey indicated that moral issues had moved to the top of voter concerns, which many observers saw as evidence of an impact from President Clinton's sex scandal. One of the designers of the poll, Republican Ed Goeas, contended that "the scandal's having an impact both in terms of the issue agenda for this fall and a tremendous dampening effect on Democratic turnout."[9] If this trend continued, Republicans felt that they had a realistic chance of gaining more than twenty seats in the House, and seven or eight Senate seats. Indeed, Gingrich told a closed-door meeting of House Republicans that 250 GOP seats were in reach (a 22-seat gain), and Linder decided to shift party funds from defending GOP incumbents to challengers of Democrats.[10] Yet by late September, Democratic strategists were arguing that they detected a growing backlash to Independent Counsel Kenneth Starr's and the Republicans' handling of the investigation of Clinton, and that this was activating their core constituents. (We will address the impact of the scandal in some detail below.)

As election day grew closer, surveys continued to indicate that while many individual races in the House could go either way, there was no indication of a strong trend for either party. In a front-page article in the *Washington Post* on the Sunday before the election, the headline indicated "Upset in Power Balance Unlikely," followed by "Democrats May Slip in Senate; Few House Seats Appear Vulnerable." [11] Indeed Campaign '98, a web site devoted to covering the elections, compiled the predictions of thirty-one journalists, pundits, and campaign professionals about the House races. While only one anticipated a gain for the Democrats, seventeen predicted only single-digit gains for the GOP, and six more anticipated an eleven-seat surge. Only one observer saw more than a fifteen-seat gain for the Republicans. Thus while the 1998 House results were historically atypical, they have to be regarded as only a mild surprise based on predictions shortly before election day.

Academic Insights

In looking forward to the election of 1998 in Chapter 9, we discussed a number of academic models of House elections. In the next section we include a detailed discussion of a number of the variables that were employed in these models. At this point we want only to consider the collective picture they offered regarding Republican prospects. Most of these models include variables that measure the performance of the economy and the level of approval for the president. In 1998 the economy was doing remarkably well in objective terms (which, perhaps more importantly, was also reflected in strongly positive subjective evaluations of the economy by the public), and Clinton's approval ratings were very strong, both by comparison to previous presidents at the same point in their terms and compared to earlier periods in the Clinton presidency. [12] Regarding "exposure," or the number of seats held by the president's party relative to a historical trend, the Democrats were in the minority, which was for them an unusual status, and as a consequence the number of seats they held was noticeably below the average for their party over the previous four decades.

Thus most of the variables that had been judged to be important in predicting the level of partisan success in congressional elections indicated that the Democrats should have been expected to perform better than the historical pattern in 1998. There was, however, at least one important countervailing variable: scandal. Many politicians, as well as more neutral observers, had expected all through 1998 that the president's sex scandal would finally damage his standing with the public, and that the negative reaction would spill over to his party in the congressional elections. Yet as we shall see shortly in more detail, such a negative reaction did not show up in Clinton's job approval ratings. Short of this development, a good Democratic performance in 1998 would have been expected from academic models of elections, and so from this perspective as well the outcome of little change in seats could not be judged to be much of a surprise.

NATIONAL AND LOCAL INFLUENCES IN CONGRESSIONAL ELECTIONS

Thomas P. "Tip" O'Neill, the former Democratic Speaker of the House, was well known for asserting that "all politics is local." Yet, as our previous discussion indicates, this characterization is not entirely correct with regard to congressional elections. National-level factors, such as the state of the economy, can also influence the results. Thus every election is affected by both local and national forces, although the relative impact of each will vary from one election to the next. We now turn to a consideration of some factors that were relevant to the 1998 congressional elections.

President Clinton in 1998: The Economy, Job Approval, and Scandal

Two factors that previous analyses of congressional elections have generally shown to have an important impact on outcomes are the economy and evaluations of the president. Indeed, as we showed in Chapter 7, the two tend to be closely related because the president is usually held accountable if the economy is going badly. As we indicated above, the performance of the U.S. economy in 1998 was very good by objective standards, with unemployment and inflation at low levels. Of course, objective reality is not as important as the subjective evaluation of voters. In 1994 the economy had been doing pretty well, but many people did not reflect those trends in their personal judgment. In exit polls that year, the proportion of voters who said that the national economy was not so good or poor outnumbered those who said it was good or excellent by 58 to 42 percent. Moreover, only 24 percent said that their family financial situation was better than it had been two years earlier.[13] These attitudes had played a role in the enormous congressional losses suffered by Democrats and in the GOP takeover of Congress.

In 1998, on the other hand, objective economic numbers and subjective evaluations were in much better alignment, probably because the economy's expansion had continued virtually without break over the intervening four years. In the 1998 Voter News Service (VNS) exit poll, the proportion of respondents who said that their family's economic situation had improved over the two previous years was 41 percent, while only 13 percent said it was worse.[14]

The connection between good economic performance and positive evaluations of the president's job appeared to continue in 1998, despite the breaking of the Monica Lewinsky scandal and the various congressional and independent counsel investigations of the administration. Among the public, positive ratings of Clinton in the Gallup Poll had moved ahead of negative evaluations in January of 1996, during the battles with Congress over the budget and the partial shutdown of the federal government. From that time through the 1998 elections, the president's approval ratings remained in the positive range, and after late January of 1998, they never fell below 60 percent.[15]

The failure of the administration's scandals to have an impact on Clinton's job approval ratings and on Democratic electoral fortunes was both surprising and frustrating for the GOP, for it had expected otherwise. In April of 1998, the NRCC head Linder claimed that the impact of the scandals at that time on Democratic recruitment and fundraising was "discouragement" (although a Democratic spokesperson disagreed). Yet the party's election strategists were reluctant to advise their candidates to highlight the issue in their campaigns, hoping that the investigations and ensuing media coverage would do the job.[16] Of course, Clinton's troubles were not without effect as far as the public's evaluations of the president as a person were concerned. Analysis by Richard A. Brody indicates that during 1998 the proportion of poll respondents who said Clinton was "honest and trustworthy" dropped about nine points (from 42 to 33 percent), and the proportion that said he had high moral and ethical standards dropped seventeen points (from 42 to 25 percent).[17]

As election day approached, the Republicans' wait for the scandal to damage the president's approval rating and the Democrats' election prospects continued to be in vain, and new concerns arose among GOP strategists about turnout. Most observers expected turnout in 1998 to be low, and traditionally this would be expected to benefit the Republicans, but party leaders feared that their conservative base might not be sufficiently motivated to turn out. This could, in turn, cost them in a number of close races. To forestall this possibility, the Republicans decided to try to stimulate their conservative activists who detested the president and his behavior by directly (albeit subtly) raising the scandal issue in a substantial number of media markets during the last week of the campaign. They devised three thirty-second commercials. One showed two mothers discussing how they would explain the events to their children, while another had a narrator asking: "Should we reward not telling the truth? That is the question of this election. Reward Bill Clinton or vote Republican."[18]

The Republicans recognized that this strategy was a gamble. By mid-October the proportion of survey respondents who said they disapproved of the way Congress was handling impeachment had reached 62 percent, and the proportion that approved of the way Congress was doing its job had fallen seven points (from 52 to 45 percent) in two weeks.[19] But they felt they had no good alternative. As Republican campaign consultant Tony Marsh (who created one of the three commercials) said: "We couldn't connect on other issues."[20] When word of the new GOP campaign strategy leaked out, Democrats responded quickly. The Democratic National Committee developed a response commercial that they planned to run in ten to fifteen of the congressional districts in which they thought the Republicans' ads might be most successful. President Clinton directly appealed to voters to ignore the GOP commercials, saying they were an effort to "distract you and divert your attention."[21] The Democrats' counterattack was reinforced by substantial media coverage of the new Republican ad campaign, and the president's party found new ammunition when it was revealed that Speaker Gingrich had devised the campaign, which had been tested before more than three dozen groups of likely voters.[22] As we noted in Chapter 9, Gingrich had long been unpopular with the American public, and this status continued into 1998.

Did the Republicans' efforts to gain political advantage from the scandal backfire on election day? It is difficult to say with assurance at this point, before dependable survey data are available for academic analysis. We will take up the question of the impact on voter turnout in the next section. Here we will only note a few races where the scandal issue figured prominently. Sen. Lauch Faircloth (R-N.C.) was the only incumbent who openly tried to use the scandal issue. His campaign ran commercials showing his opponent John Edwards and Clinton with elongated noses, along with the description as "two tobacco-taxing lawyers who have a habit of stretching the truth."[23] Faircloth was one of the two GOP senators who lost their reelection bids. In Washington State, Democratic challenger Jay Inslee ran ads in his campaign against Republican House incumbent Rick White that attacked the impeachment effort. They stated: "Rick White's vote on impeachment will drag us through months and months of mud and politics. . . . Enough is enough. It's time to get on with the nation's business."[24] Inslee won.

Meanwhile, on the other coast, Democratic challenger Rush Holt used incumbent New Jersey Republican Michael Pappas's own words against him. A few days after Independent Counsel Kenneth Starr sent his report to the House, Pappas went to the House floor and sang the following song (set to the tune of "Twinkle, Twinkle, Little Star"):

Twinkle, twinkle, Kenneth Starr,
Now we see how brave you are.
We could not see which way to go
If you did not lead us so,
Twinkle, twinkle, Kenneth Starr,
Now we see how brave you are.

Holt's campaign repeatedly ran ads showing Pappas's performance, followed by the tagline: "Congressman Pappas: Out of tune, out of touch." Holt won by over five thousand votes, becoming "the first Democrat to be elected from the district in modern memory."[25] Of course, a few examples cannot demonstrate a systematic effect, but coupled with the other evidence it seems safe to at least conclude that the Republicans' strategy at the end of the 1998 campaign was not an asset to their aims.

Turnout in 1998

Chapter 4 discussed declining turnout among American voters in the postwar era, and expectations about a continuation of that trend figured prominently in the parties' strategies for 1998. We have already noted the Republicans' concern about turnout among their core voters. However, worries about who would vote were not confined to the GOP, especially earlier in the campaign. Traditionally, analysts have concluded that lower rates of turnout favored the Republican party because the demographic factors that were linked to voting in low turnout elections (like higher levels of income or education) were also linked to voting for the GOP. Such expectations were reinforced by indications that those voters who reacted negatively to the president because of the scandal would be more inclined to vote. For example, Republican surveys in the late summer showed that respondents who identified as religious conservatives or who said their more important concern was moral values were also more likely than other people to say that the election was important to them.[26] Those respondents were also substantially more likely to say they intended to vote for Republicans for the House.

Given this context, the parties and their allies in interest groups devoted a great deal of effort to try to ensure that *their* supporters actually voted. For example, the Christian Coalition manned voter registration tables in thousands of churches on Sunday, September 27, and then distributed millions of their voter guides in churches on the Sunday before the election. On the pro-Democratic side, organized labor switched its strategy from the large-scale media advertising campaign they had pursued in 1996 to grass-roots organizing aimed at union families.[27] As the election approached, party efforts intensified. First Lady Hillary Rodham Clinton made a four-state tour in mid-October accompanied by nearly a dozen female Democratic House candidates to shore up support among women. Democratic polls had raised some concerns that women might be less likely to turn out than usual because of the scandal.[28]

The president also went to considerable effort to stimulate Democratic constituencies. For example, on the Sunday before the election Clinton spoke at a black church in Baltimore, and the next day he appeared on a radio show with a largely African-American audience, and then gave an interview to a group of four Hispanic journalists. He argued that electing Democrats to office was particularly important to minorities because the Democrats supported policies that were valuable to those communities.[29] The Republicans also stepped up their efforts at the end of the campaign, with Gingrich appearing in fifteen states in the last week alone. During those efforts he accused the president and Mrs. Clinton of resorting to "the rhetoric of fear."[30]

On election day, the expectations of analysts who anticipated further decline in turnout were justified, as only 36 percent of the voting-age population voted. This was the lowest level since World War II, and down from 39 percent in 1994.[31] Yet the traditional views of the effect of low turnout were countered, because the Democrats did not suffer as a result. It appears that in 1998 the Democrats benefited from asymmetric turnout effects, just as the Republicans apparently did in 1994.[32] That is, the decline in turnout did not fall equally on all places and all contests, and the result was a net benefit to the Democrats.

First, the Democratic efforts to stimulate black voters appeared to have been successful in some areas, and those were places that counted for the Democrats.

TABLE 11-4 Union Proportion of Voters and Vote Choice, 1992–1998

Year	Proportion of electorate	Vote Choice Democrat	Vote Choice Republican
1992	19%	67%	33%
1994	14%	60%	40%
1996	23%	63%	37%
1998	22%	64%	36%

Source: Exit polls conducted by the Voters News Service (1994–1998) and Voters Research and Surveys (1992).

Although black turnout declined significantly in five populous states, it was up in eight states. "In those eight states, black voters proved critical in electing or re-electing four Democratic governors and two Senators."[33] In Georgia, blacks had accounted for 19 percent of the vote in 1994; that jumped to 29 percent in 1998. That may have been the consequence of a particularly vigorous get-out-the-vote effort by the Democratic party that was designed to exploit anger among African-Americans over the impeachment effort. The campaign included a mailing sent to black voters that pictured Gingrich and Starr, and read: "They couldn't win at the ballot box, so now they want to overturn your choice."[34] An additional motivation in Georgia was the presence of three black Democratic candidates on the state-wide ticket, two of whom won.

Another turnout success appears to have been the campaign by organized labor. In the end, the AFL-CIO spent only $5 million on broadcast ads, while spending $15 million on turnout-related activities like leaflets, phone banks, and the salaries of four hundred coordinators working full time for a month before the election.[35] Table 11-4 presents data from exit polls on the share of the electorate that came from union households, and the vote choice for the House of Representatives among those voters.[36] Unfortunately these numbers are not open to a simple interpretation because the polling organization changed the way that it asked the question about union membership in the household in 1996, thus rendering the results not completely comparable across the surveyed years (and, worse, probably inflating the proportion in the later period relative to the former).[37] Despite that problem, they still shed some light on the issue. Note that while the proportions of the vote choice do not vary a great deal across the elections (especially if we exclude the down year of 1994), the proportions of the electorate change quite a bit. A comparison of 1992 and 1994 (which use the same question format) show a noticeable fall off in the latter year while 1996 to 1998 (both of which used the altered format) do not show such a decline. This provides some support for the view that labor's campaign was successful and beneficial to the Democrats, and that view is endorsed by Representative Linder of the NRCC, who said: "They (labor) had a huge turnout with phone banks in regions across the country, and I've got to congratulate them.[38]

Finally, there is some evidence that the GOP's concern about a possible fall off in turnout among conservative voters may have been justified. The exit polls cited above show that the proportion of respondents who identified themselves as conservatives in 1998 was 31 percent, which was down from 36 percent in 1994 and 34 percent in 1996. One possibility here is that the change is due merely to a declining proportion of conservatives in the population as a whole, but that appears not to be the case. In 1996 and 1998 the proportion of conservatives in the exit polls was lower than the proportion in the final Gallup Poll, but this had not been true in 1994.[39] Thus overall the Democrats appear to have benefited from the pattern of voter turnout, and this was in turn at least partly due to the success of the strategies they and their allies pursued.

Candidate Resources

In Chapter 9 we focused on candidates' resources in each district—specifically incumbency, candidate quality, and campaign spending—to explain outcomes in House elections. We will conclude our analysis of 1998 by returning to these factors, paying particular attention to the increased role of the national parties in marshaling them.[40]

Incumbency. We have already discussed incumbency at a number of points in this chapter, noting particularly that incumbents had an extremely high success rate. Incumbent success is not an immutable fact of nature. Reelection rates for incumbents vary over time, as we have seen, and they vary between the parties. In the Republican landslide of 1994, for example, 15 percent of Democratic incumbents were beaten in House races while not a single GOP incumbent lost. This was a very one-sided election in which the voters punished the incumbents of a single party.[41] In the 1992 House races, on the other hand, defeats of incumbents were less one-sided. The elections occurred in the context of a financial scandal in the House and of national redistricting after the 1990 census. Sixteen Democrats and eight Republicans lost their seats to the opposition party in the general election, while an additional fourteen Democrats and five Republicans had lost in the primaries.[42]

Incumbent success was higher in 1998 than in 1992 or 1994 simply because the underlying political conditions were more favorable to incumbents. As we have noted previously, the economy was performing very well, and the voters perceived this to be the case. In addition, while the approval rating of Congress did not match the president's, it was considerably higher than it had been earlier in the decade. Perhaps most important for incumbent success was the positive evaluation by voters of their own incumbent, which we discussed in the last chapter. In the spring of 1998, 64 percent of respondents to a national survey by the Gallup organization said that their own representative should be reelected. Moreover, 56 percent said that most members of the House should be reelected. The comparable figure in a 1992 poll had been 29 percent.[43]

This very positive environment for incumbents was reflected in the election, not only in their high reelection rates but also in increased margins of victory. In 1998 the average share of the vote for all incumbents in races contested by both parties was 65.2 percent; for Republican incumbents the figure was 62.9 percent, while for Democrats it was 67.5 percent.[44] This is the highest average figure since 1988 (see Table 9-5), and it is even more impressive when we remember that it includes only contested races. Another indicator of the strong position of incumbents is that the number of safe seats in which one major party chose not to field a candidate was at a postwar high: ninety-four incumbents (fifty-five Republicans and thirty-nine Democrats) were unopposed. Had these seats been contested, and thus the vote results included in our calculations, the average incumbents' share of the vote would surely have been higher.

Candidate Quality. Table 11-5 shows data on the success of candidates in 1998, controlling for office background, party, and incumbency.[45] This corresponds to the 1996 evidence listed in Table 9-4. We see that both for challengers to House Republican incumbents and open House seats, there is a link between previous office experience and candidate success. (With only a single Democratic incumbent loss, there is no variation to explain there.) In general, candidates with of-

TABLE 11-5   Success in House and Senate Elections, Controlling for Office Background, Party, and Incumbency, 1998

Candidate's last office	Candidate is opponent of				No incumbent in district			
	Democratic incumbent		Republican incumbent		Democratic candidate		Republican candidate	
	(%)	(N)	(%)	(N)	(%)	(N)	(%)	(N)
House								
State legislature or U.S. House	0	(16)	7	(14)	64	(11)	75	(8)
Other elective office	0	(8)	13	(15)	57	(7)	33	(3)
No elective office	1	(127)	2	(127)	44	(16)	39	(23)
Senate								
U.S. House	0	(5)	100	(1)	50	(2)	100	(2)
Statewide elective office	0	(1)	0	(1)	100	(1)	100	(1)
Other elective office	100	(1)	—	(0)	0	(1)	0	(2)
No elective office	0	(8)	8	(12)	0	(1)	—	(0)

Note: Percentages show proportion of candidates in each category who won; numbers in parentheses are the totals on which percentages are based.

fice experience were more likely to win than those with none, and in open seats candidates with the highest level of experience had the greatest success. In the Senate races, there are few cases, but here too the candidates with the highest levels of experience were more likely to win.

As we discussed in Chapter 9, decisions by politicians on whether to run for office are important strategic choices. In particular, we discussed the argument offered by Gary C. Jacobson and Samuel Kernell that these decisions would be shaped by potential candidates' evaluations of the national electoral context. In 1998 observers raised questions about whether Clinton's difficulties would lead potential Democratic candidates to pass up the chance to run because they concluded that it would not be a good year for their party's candidates. Moreover, some officials of both parties were concerned that what had happened to the president might deter candidates generally because they would not want their private life opened up to public scrutiny. For instance, Illinois state Democratic chair Gary LaPaille said: "I think people who are highly qualified will simply say it is not worth embarrassing myself, my family and my children and be opened up like a can of sardines." [46]

We do not have systematic data for this election or for previous ones about which candidates considered running and chose not to. To be sure there are various examples of the two parties trying to recruit candidates in 1998, succeeding in some instances and failing in others. Moreover, observers early in the season evaluated the success of both parties as below average.[47] One might be tempted to presume that the data in the previous section showing the record number of uncontested seats is evidence of candidate reluctance, but virtually all of these were safe seats where the opposition would have no chance. Moreover, parties may not always want to recruit candidates in districts where they have little chance, for fear that a contested race will stimulate supporters of the dominant party to turn out, thereby negatively affecting other races. For example, late in 1997 there were reports that the Republicans in Georgia were considering not fielding candidates against Democrats Cynthia McKinney and John Lewis, who represented black majority districts and were certain to win reelection. GOP leaders feared "that a large turnout of black voters . . . could swing" state races to the Democrats. NRCC chair Linder said, "I am not going to discourage anyone from running against them, but I am not eager to see it happen." [48] There is evidence that indicates that the Republicans' concern was justified. In the end, both McKinney and Lewis had GOP opponents, neither of whom received more than 39 percent of the vote. Meanwhile, the Democrats carried the governorship and a number of other state-wide races.

A rough, but better, indicator of party success at recruitment is the number of experienced candidates that chose to run against incumbents. The data in Table 11-5 show that there were fifty-three candidates with office experience who opposed incumbents in 1998, twenty-nine of them Democrats opposing Republicans and twenty-four of them Republicans opposing Democrats. This number falls short of the eighty experienced candidates (fifty-three of them Republicans) who ran in 1992, which as we noted could have been expected to be a good year for the GOP due to redistricting and the House financial scandal.[49] It was also fewer than the sixty-three who ran in 1996, forty-two of them Democrats, when there was a large number of Republican freshmen who had won in 1994 by narrow margins and the Democrats thought they had a good chance to retake control of the House. On the other hand, the number of experienced candidates in 1998 was more than the thirty-nine who ran in 1990 or the forty-three who sought House seats in 1988, both of which were years in which incumbents were expected to do well, and was very close to the fifty-two who ran in 1994. Thus there is no reason, at least from these data, to conclude that party efforts to re- cruit candidates in the last election were noticeably less successful than normal because of concerns that 1998 would not be a good year for challengers gener- ally or for Democrats specifically.

The national parties' involvement in candidate recruitment has been expand- ing in recent years. These parties each want to win majority control of the House, and thus have strong incentives to want the strongest possible candidates to run. They now have, moreover, considerable resources at their disposal that can provide incentives for potential candidates. First, as we shall see in the next sec- tion, the national party organizations play a significant and increasing role in fund raising. In addition, they can provide expertise, advice, and political con- tacts that can be very useful in campaigns. In the past, however, they would nor- mally not have become involved if there was possible competition for the party's nomination.[50]

Increasingly, though, national officials have sought to influence the choice in potentially competitive situations. For example, in 1998 in a special election caused by the death of incumbent California Democrat Walter Capps, Newt Gingrich backed moderate (and wealthy) state legislator Brooks Firestone for the GOP nomination against Capps's widow, Lois. The district had given both Clinton and Dole 44 percent of the vote in 1996, but it had chosen Capps over a very conservative GOP incumbent even though he had been outspent. (He was the first Democrat to carry the district since World War II.) Gingrich and other national party officials concluded that a moderate Republican would have a bet- ter chance, but this brought them into conflict with conservative activists in California. Those activists (including a number of other GOP representatives from California) backed another state legislator, Tom Bordonaro, for the nomi- nation. Bordonaro was also supported by independent ads from national con- servative organizations. He ran second to Capps in the three-candidate race, securing a place in the runoff. (Because it was a special election, candidates from both parties ran together in a common first-round election, which would be followed by a runoff between the top two if no one got a majority.) Rep. John Doolittle (R-Calif.) said, "The Speaker's candidate was soundly defeated. . . . Despite the efforts of the leadership to impose the most liberal Republican on the Conference, we ended up with a strong Reagan conservative and someone who will win in the runoff."[51] This was not, however, to be the case. Capps won the runoff by eight points, and she was reelected (again over Bordonaro) by twelve points in November. It is likely that future efforts by national party leaders to engineer the choice of the most electable candidate will run into similar ideological resistance.

Campaign Spending. In Chapter 9 we argued that a principal reason for both the frequency of incumbents being reelected and the growth in their margins of reelection through the 1980s was that challengers found it increasingly difficult to raise the money necessary to compete effectively. Our evidence, and that of other analysts such as Jacobson, showed that when challengers could raise an adequate amount of money, much of the incumbency advantage could be neutralized and competitive elections would usually result. The preliminary evidence from 1998 seems to reinforce that conclusion, but it also shows major changes from previous years.

Federal Election Commission data indicate that overall spending by House and Senate candidates dropped slightly in 1998 relative to 1996, from $626.3 million to $617.1 million.[52] Spending in Senate races increased by eleven percent, from $220.0 million to $244.4 million, while in House races, on the other hand, spending dropped eight percent, from $405.6 million to $372.9 million. A closer look at the House data illustrates how the Republicans' consolidation of their hold on majority status has produced a financial advantage for them, but it also shows vividly that this financial advantage was no guarantee of success. Between 1996 and 1998, median spending by both Democratic and Republican incumbents declined by 10 percent and 29 percent, respectively. This is not surprising, given that in 1998 there were fewer sharply contested races involving incumbents and that in 1996 the GOP freshman class from 1994 was defending itself for the first time.

Much more striking is what happened to challengers and in open races. Median spending by Democratic challengers declined by 28 percent (from $127,000 to $99,000), but GOP challengers' spending increased 63 percent (from $98,000 to $160,000). Similarly, in open-seat contests Republican spending increased by 41 percent ($588,000 to $828,000), while Democrats' spending increased only 8 percent ($580,000 to $628,000). Yet as we have seen, these shifts in spending were not matched by corresponding shifts in candidate success, particularly in open-seat races where Democrats were slightly more successful in 1998 than two years earlier. This is mainly because the aggregate figures cited above mask considerable district variation. Specifically, in open-seat races both Republican and Democratic winners tended to outspend their opponents by considerable margins. Median spending by winning Democrats was $789,000, while losing GOP candidates spent $419,000. Similarly, victorious Republicans spent $864,000, while the median for their Democratic opponents was $357,000.

Despite the continued high levels of aggregate campaign spending, one of the most salient features of the 1998 elections was that so many of the House races had no real contests. In addition to the large number of races with only one major-party candidate, which we discussed above, approximately 260 other House contests saw incumbents with ten-to-one spending advantages over their challengers in contributions from Political Action Committees (PACs). This same ratio held for the twenty-nine incumbent senators of both parties seeking re-election.[53] As a consequence of these imbalances in money raising, many races with two candidates could be termed "financially uncontested."

One reason for improving Republican funding has been the continuation of growth in various sources of party funding. The GOP has used its majority status to improve its financial position, both relative to the past and compared to the Democrats. In the summer of 1998, it was anticipated that the NRCC would be able to give the full $70,000 in direct donations to as many as one hundred of its candidates, while the corresponding Democratic committee would be able to similarly fund only about thirty candidates.

Probably more important than these direct donations, however, is the growth in "soft money," the unregulated funds parties can raise from corporations and other sources to spend on activities that do not specifically advocate the election of a particular candidate. The Republicans launched a $37 million set of issue ads called "Operation Breakout" late in the campaign. (The amount for the effort was later scaled back to $25 million. The ads raising the Clinton scandal, which we discussed above, were part of this effort.) In addition to private sources, the GOP sought funds from its own candidates who were not seen to be in political jeopardy. For example, Sen. Mitch McConnell (R-Ky., the chairman of the National Republican Senatorial Committee) sought $9 million in donations from GOP senators.[54] Furthermore, party officials were much more likely than in the past to put pressure on their own members who were reluctant to provide money to the party cause. For example, Rep. Philip A. Crane (R-Ill., second-ranking Republican on the Ways and Means Committee) sent a $25,000 check to the party after Speaker Gingrich and Linder of the NRCC privately criticized him.[55] With all of their efforts, party committees on both sides produced a flood of soft money. Early estimates of the totals for the 1998 election cycle were $94 million for the Republicans (up 144 percent from the 1994 elections) and $79 million for the Democrats (up 84 percent).[56]

THE 1998 ELECTIONS: THE IMPACT ON CONGRESS

We turn now to what is surely the most remarkable aspect of the 1998 elections: that an election with such a small change in the aggregate membership of Congress could serve as the springboard for such large-scale and momentous events within the Congress, and in such a short time. Only forty freshman House members joined that institution, and only eight new senators. These additions altered the political balance within or between the parties in Congress scarcely at all. Yet as we write this, only two months after the election, we have already seen the resignation of the Speaker and other House leaders, then the fall of the Speaker-to-be, followed by the impeachment of the president of the United States.

The Fall of Gingrich (et. al.)

The post-election reaction by House Republicans was decidedly negative and had a number of sources. One was the disappointing results themselves. As late as election day, the Speaker had predicted double-digit GOP gains, and as the pro-Democratic returns rolled in he continued to assert that they would get better. After the rosy expectations of the fall campaign, House Republicans regarded their loss as inexplicable and unacceptable. As one source close to the NRCC said: "You've got the President facing impeachment, you have a huge money advantage, and an incumbency advantage, and you lose five seats—that's borderline disaster. . . ." [57] The blame for the outcome was generally placed on the Speaker and on his ally, Linder. The negative reaction was exacerbated when Gingrich, speaking on morning talk shows the day after the election, tried to blame the media and pollsters, and claimed that he had had little to do with the GOP's late ad campaign. [58] From outside the Congress, conservative leaders also blamed the Republican leadership, saying that they erred by trying to make Clinton the only issue instead of focusing on social issues that would have motivated GOP core voters. Prospects also did not look good for Republican consensus on an agenda for the new 106th Congress.

On the day after the election, conservative representative Matt Salmon (R-Ariz.), a frequent Gingrich critic in the 105th Congress, announced that he would not vote for Gingrich as Speaker, and he had similar pledges from six other House Republicans. That would have been enough votes to deprive the Speaker of a majority on the selection vote for the new Congress and deadlock the choice. Meanwhile, Steve Largent (R-Okla.), a leader of the revolutionaries of the class of 1994, and Bob Livingston (R-La.), chairman of the Appropriations Committee, began calling colleagues to ascertain the prospects for a challenge of one or more of the members of the GOP leadership. Two days later, on Friday morning, Livingston sent a letter to Gingrich that was nothing short of an ultimatum. It listed sixteen points that Gingrich was to agree to "without exception." [59] Later in the morning, Largent announced he would challenge Majority Leader Dick Armey (R-Tex.), and Livingston announced for Speaker.

Gingrich saw the handwriting on the wall and issued a statement in which he said he would not run again for Speaker, and would resign from the House. The statement said that the "Republican Conference needs to be unified and it is time for me to move forward." [60] In a conference call the day before, however, he was more acerbic when he told his closest allies he would not run: "I'm willing to lead but I'm not willing to preside over people who are cannibals." [61] Livingston quickly lined up support, and other potential candidates for Speaker decided to pass up the race. There were, however, other leadership contests. In addition to Largent versus Armey, two other candidates were involved in the race for majority leader. Also, J. C. Watts (R-Okla.), the only black GOP member, launched a challenge to John Boehner (R-Ohio), chairman of the Republican Conference. Members additionally talked about replacing Linder as chair of the NRCC, but to force the change they would also have to alter the conference rules because the job was appointive. When the Republicans convened in mid-November, Livingston won the GOP designation as Speaker unopposed. Boehner lost to Watts, and the conference chose to replace Linder with moderate Tom Davis of Virginia, but Armey survived his challenge, winning on the third ballot. Among House Democrats, by contrast, the election aftermath was relatively uneventful. The two top leaders were reelected, and Martin Frost (D-Tex.), the successful chairman of the Democratic Congressional Campaign Committee, was rewarded by his selection as chairman of the House Democratic Caucus.

In the Senate the election did not bring substantial changes. Among Republicans there was also disappointment about the election results, but the blame was not placed at the door of Majority Leader Trent Lott (R-Miss.). Lott's second in command, conservative majority whip Don Nickles (R-Okla.), did voice some dissatisfaction, but he focused his attention on a set of rules changes (mainly involving the budget process) that he was drafting to offer early in the 106th Congress.[62] More displeasure was focused on NRSC chair McConnell, and he actually drew a formal challenge for his post, but he survived easily.

Organizational Developments for the 106th Congress

Unlike the major institutional changes made by the House GOP after gaining the majority in 1994, large-scale alterations were avoided by the party when it gathered to elect its leaders late in November after the 1998 voting. It was not that there were no members who desired rules reforms, but rather a lack of consensus within the narrow majority. As Joe Barton (R-Tex.) asked, "Why anger 10 or 15 members when the whole purpose of this week is to provide unity?"[63] Instead, they decided to postpone discussion of possible changes until the new Congress convened. Among the issues that were left for later was the possibility of repealing the six-year term limits for committee chairs that had been enacted four years earlier. There was obvious sentiment for this among some senior members, but resistance among the more junior group. Another issue demonstrated that the 1998 results did not herald a decline in the determination of the majority party to run the House. Sonny Callahan (R-Ala.) indicated that he planned "to offer a rules change that would permit the Speaker to punish committee chairmen and other high-ranking members who go against the party line on key procedural votes."[64]

Livingston quickly demonstrated that while he did not covet the national limelight that his predecessor had, he intended to be the leader of his party and the institution. As he put it, "I am not going to shy away but I am going to make sure to run the House."[65] One place where he asserted his leadership was in the committee assignment process. In his letter to Gingrich after the election, Livingston had indicated his disagreement with the Speaker's strategy of putting junior members with narrow margins of victory on the top committees. (Gingrich's aim was to facilitate the members' ability to raise campaign funds.) Livingston had said that "fragile members are afraid to cast tough votes, and that inhibits the passage of credible legislation." [66] Reflecting this view, only one of the GOP freshmen elected in 1998 was assigned to one of the top four committees. Another potential leadership use of committee assignments is to reward one's personal supporters. Along this line, Livingston secured the appointment of an ally of his from Pennsylvania to a vacant Appropriations seat, instead of a supporter of Dick Armey (with whom Livingston had frequently clashed) who had also sought the appointment. [67]

Another indicator of the continued high level of partisanship within the House also involved committee assignments. One of the first things that the majority party must do in each Congress is to establish the number of seats that will be allocated to each party on each committee. These party ratios usually approximate the party division in the chamber, but there have often been departures from this standard for particular committees or in particular Congresses. More specifically, the majority party has often allocated additional seats above the chamber ratio on the set of top committees (usually Appropriations, Commerce, Rules, and Ways and Means) that are most important to the majority's agenda. There has also been the propensity for the majority to take "bonus seats" more generally on committees when the party division in the House is very close. [68] In organizing for the 106th Congress, despite the Democrats' seat gain in the election, the GOP leadership decided to grant the other party only seven total additional committee seats. Moreover, only one of these new seats was on a top committee. Minority Leader Richard Gephardt (D-Mo.) objected strenuously, saying, "Our problem . . . is one of both quality and quantity of slots." [69] Such committee allocations limit both the minority's ability to influence the content of legislation in committee and its ability to use desirable assignments to reward its members. There was, however, little the Democrats could do to block the GOP plan given their minority status.

In the Senate there was also little organizational change. The only significant development was the decision of the chairman of the Republican Policy Committee (Sen. Larry Craig of Idaho) to expand the committee's membership to include junior members. Previously only the elected party leaders and committee chairmen formed the Policy Committee's membership. Observers speculated that the reason for the move was to reduce the likelihood of any potential revolt against the leadership as occurred in the House. In explaining his decision, Craig said: "I want to be more inclusive. . . . I want to open the process up." [70]

The House Republicans Impeach the President and Lose Another Leader

After the strong Democratic showing in the elections, many observers within and outside the Congress expected that the issue of the president's impeachment would just fade away, but this was not to be. The Republicans on the House Judiciary Committee (who were more conservative than GOP members generally) and Minority Whip Tom DeLay of Texas (also a strong conservative) kept the issue on the agenda and pushed toward a decision. To be sure, House Republicans and their allies worried about the possible political impact of their decisions. An NBC News–*Wall Street Journal* poll in early December showed that 68 percent of the respondents opposed impeachment. As Ralph Reed, former director of the Christian Coalition, remarked: "This is a delicate and potentially vulnerable time for the party." [71]

Despite these concerns, the Judiciary Committee voted for four impeachment resolutions along party lines, sending the matter to the House floor. The partisan exploitation of majority status was again illustrated as the GOP leaders prepared for the votes on impeachment. A number of moderate Republicans, as well as almost all Democrats, favored having the option of voting to censure the president instead of impeaching him. However, Speaker-designate Livingston, DeLay, and other leaders decided that such an option would not be offered. Moreover, "DeLay and Livingston have said publicly that they would take a dim view of any Republican who refused to back up the leadership in blocking a floor vote on censure." [72] The leadership wanted to restrict its members to a stark choice of supporting impeachment or letting the president off completely, without the option of the middle ground of censure. Once the procedural resolution on the voting agenda passed, 230–204 (with only two Republicans defecting), the outcome on impeachment was determined, and two of the four Judiciary Committee resolutions were adopted.

The impeachment debate produced some additional drama, and another casualty, when Livingston decided to reveal to the Republican Conference two days before the floor vote that he had been unfaithful to his wife a number of times over the years of their marriage. He had learned that media people were investigating his background, and concluded that the information would come to light. Most GOP members quickly rallied around their choice for Speaker, and Democrats refrained from criticism, with Gephardt saying to the House: "The politics of slash-and-burn must end." [73] A few conservative Republican members, however, spoke out negatively, and the morning of the impeachment vote one colleague informed Livingston that at least eighteen GOP representatives were having second thoughts about supporting him for Speaker. [74] This presented Livingston with the same problem that had faced Gingrich, because fewer than half that many defectors would have deadlocked the Speaker election. He concluded that he "would not have been effectively leading 100 percent of the Republicans," and announced to an astonished House that he would not seek election to the speakership and would resign from the House in six months, calling on Clinton to resign as well. [75]

Seeking to avoid complete chaos, and with the opening of the 106th Congress less than three weeks away, the Republicans quickly rallied around Dennis Hastert of Illinois, the chief deputy whip, to be Speaker. Thus came to an end the remarkable series of events that flowed from an election that was very close to a draw. We will defer a discussion of the likely electoral impact of these happenings until the concluding section of this chapter. In terms of their impact on the legislative activity and political interactions of the 106th Congress, it seems plausible that the partisan conflict and personal animosities in the House will be reinforced. The very conservative majority of the House Republican Conference, reflecting the activist base of the party, intensely favored impeachment. On the Democratic side, there is anger over what they perceive as the partisan character of the process, particularly the GOP leadership's blocking of a censure option. As Minority Whip David Bonior of Michigan said: "This just frays the ability of both parties to get along and reach reasonable solutions to proceed. . . . This will be a very difficult Congress."[76] Certainly these events will further undermine the working relationship between the White House and the Republican congressional majority. Of course one should not overestimate the marginal impact of elections and these subsequent developments. On the one hand, quite independent of 1998 there will be pressure from members up for reelection to achieve some legislative results. On the other hand, the likelihood of significant legislative accomplishments in a Congress with a lame-duck president and an oncoming presidential election, given divided party control of government and deep ideological divergence between the parties, would have been low in any event. This just makes any major achievements even less likely.

THE 2000 ELECTIONS AND BEYOND

We will conclude this chapter with a look forward to the congressional elections of 2000 and beyond, and a discussion of the factors likely to influence them.

General Considerations for 2000

In Chapter 9 we emphasized that—looking ahead to 1998—approval of the president, the performance of the Congress, and the public's evaluation of the Republican congressional majority would all be important in shaping the outcomes of the upcoming elections. The same is at least as true for 2000, and the most prominent factor relating to those considerations may be the electorate's response to Congress's actions in the impeachment process.

As we noted previously, before the House votes the respondents to surveys had indicated that they opposed impeachment. At the time most polls showed that they also opposed Clinton's resignation in the event of impeachment, but there were some conflicting findings, and some observers also expected the public's views to shift negatively after the House acted. Surveys after the House vote, however, did not show the tide of opinion moving against the president. The Pew Research Center for the People and the Press conducted a survey after the House acted in which they reinterviewed respondents they had surveyed the week before. Among those people, Clinton's approval rating actually rose ten points, from 61 to 71 percent. This jump was likely, at least in part, a temporary surge based on sympathy for the president, but it at least showed that there was no negative shift. Moreover, 67 percent of respondents indicated that they thought that members of Congress who had voted for impeachment had done so for political reasons, while only 25 percent thought they had done so because Clinton's behavior warranted removal from office.[77]

Other polls confirmed the public's response. A *New York Times*–CBS News survey immediately after impeachment showed Clinton's approval at 72 percent, and 60 percent against the House action. Looking ahead, 65 percent opposed resignation and 68 percent were against the Senate's removing the president. Sixty-two percent of those polled thought the Republican members of Congress were out of touch with what Americans wanted to happen with the impeachment. Perhaps most worrisome for the GOP's political future, the results showed that 58 percent viewed the Republican party unfavorably. This was the lowest level for the party in the fourteen years that the *Times* and CBS had been asking the question—even lower than it had been after the government shutdown in 1995.[78]

There is, moreover, little question that the negative public response was linked to impeachment. The Gallup Poll also asked its respondents questions about favorable or unfavorable opinions of the two parties in two surveys just before and after the House action. Regarding the Democrats, there was little change; the response was 58 percent favorable to 32 percent unfavorable before, and 57 percent to 30 percent after. Regarding the GOP, however, opinion went from 43 percent favorable and 47 percent unfavorable before to 31 percent favorable and 57 percent unfavorable after.[79] Perhaps most remarkable of all, in late December Gallup reported that Bill Clinton was again cited by respondents to a national poll as the man most admired by Americans. He was chosen by 18 percent, up from 14 percent in 1997 and well ahead of the Pope, who was in second place at seven percent.[80]

This is clearly a dangerous state of affairs for the Republican party. Of course, as we noted, opinion may change before the next election. Moreover, GOP strategists argue that the saliency of the impeachment issue will decline over time and that the public will forget. While that is also true, the point may be less relevant for 2000 than it seems. First, the public will not have to remember all by itself. There will be Democratic candidates, other participants, and the news media to remind them as the election approaches. Second, the threat comes less from the impeachment issue alone and more from the ability of Democrats to sell the ideas that impeachment was part of a pattern in which Republicans are out of touch with what most Americans want, and that they are controlled by extremist elements in the party's right wing.

Finally, the impeachment may have the kind of indirect effect on Democratic fortunes that is hypothesized in the analysis by Jacobson and Kernell that we discussed earlier. That is, strong potential Democratic candidates may expect that voters will punish the GOP for its actions (or may be motivated by personal anger about them) and decide to run for office. Then, because a stronger group of Democratic candidates is in the field, the party may be more successful than it would otherwise have been, even if the impeachment issue does not actually affect the choices of voters in 2000. (Correspondingly, these expectations could produce a weaker field of Republican candidates.) Similarly, public reaction to the issue may generate additional financial contributions to Democratic candidates, also indirectly improving the party's success rate. This propensity could be reinforced by other factors, like gridlock over policy in the Congress.

House Races in 2000

In addition to the general context of the election, we contended in Chapter 9 that one important thing to focus on is the potential vulnerability of individual incumbents. Table 11-6 shows the distribution of winning percentages in 1998 across the parties and types of races. Probably reflecting the disparity in the number of highly contested races, the number of close races (outcome of 55 percent or less) was down sharply from ninety-five in 1996 to only fifty-nine in 1998. These potentially vulnerable members are relatively evenly distributed across the parties: thirty-three Republicans and twenty-six Democrats. These previously close contests are likely to dominate the efforts of the respective parties in 2000.

Another source of strong contests is open seats. Given the large number of retirements in recent years, it is not likely that the departure of members with long service will be the source of a large number of open seats in the next election. A second potential reason for open seats is representatives seeking higher office; some may do that in 2000. A third source of open seats is the self-term-limited members we discussed at the end of Chapter 9. There are ten of these with limits that run out in 2000, all but one of them Republicans. While some are entertaining the possibility of changing their minds, six (all GOP) have confirmed their departures. This adds a measure of asymmetric vulnerability to the Republicans.

TABLE 11-6 Percentage of the Vote Received by Winning House Candidates, by Party and Type of Race, 1998

Percentage of the vote	Republicans			Democrats		
	Reelected incumbent	Successful challenger	Open seat	Reelected incumbent	Successful challenger	Open seat
55 or less	22	1	10	13	5	8
55.1–60.0	28	0	3	35	0	2
60.1–70.0	81	0	3	47	0	5
70.1–100	75	0	0	94	0	3
Total	206	1	16	189	5	18

We have repeatedly emphasized the importance of candidate quality in determining the results of congressional races. Both parties are already at work trying to recruit candidates for 2000's House races. Seeking to build on the momentum from their party's good 1998 showing, Democratic leaders quickly began urging losing candidates who came close to try again, and began the search for new contenders. A spokeswoman for Minority Leader Gephardt said: "Our goal is to keep people interested in running in 2000. . . . The political landscape looks rich and our candidates perform better in a presidential year." [81] Republicans, on the other hand, are seeking to stave off any negative effects from 1998, and they contend that there are few. As the NRCC political director said: "We are still in the majority, and candidates still want to run." [82]

Senate Races in 2000

Unlike the House, where all seats are up for election every two years, the Senate offers quite a different set of contests each time. The thirty-three seats up in 2000 have a particular distinction: they are the set that produced the Republican majority in 1994 when the party gained eight seats. Thus, unlike recent election years, this time there will be more GOP seats at risk than Democratic ones (nineteen versus fourteen). Moreover, nine of the Republicans (and none of the Democrats) are freshmen who will be facing reelection for the first time. Because of this context, Democrats argue that they will have a chance to take back the Senate in the next election, but it appears that the six-seat gain necessary for a majority (or five seats for control if the Democrats retain the presidency) will be very difficult to achieve. Indeed, it is not even certain that the Democrats are favorites to gain any seats at all.

Even more than with regard to our discussion of the House, party prospects for gains or losses in the Senate will depend on who chooses to seek office and what seats are open. At this point only one incumbent (Democrat Daniel Patrick Moynihan of New York) has announced his retirement, but there appear to be more possibilities among the Democrats than the GOP. On the other hand, the only announced strong challenger is popular Democratic governor Mel Carnahan of Missouri against John Ashcroft, although Democrat Chuck Robb of Virginia is almost certain to face former Governor George Allen. As candidate decisions are made over the next year or so, Senate prospects will become clearer.

Beyond 2000: Continued Uncertainty of House Control?

We chose the same title for this concluding section as we used for the corresponding one in Chapter 9 because the issues of interest remain the same. The battle over whether to use statistical sampling in the 2000 census continues, and the matter reached the U.S. Supreme Court. Lower courts ruled in two separate cases that sampling was unconstitutional, agreeing with Republicans that the Constitution's call for an "actual enumeration" required a count of all individuals. The cases were then appealed, but when the Court heard arguments, the justices appeared reluctant to get involved in what they regarded as a partisan political dispute between the president and Congress. Justice Antonin Scalia indicated that he thought the other two branches should just "duke it out." [83] When the Court decided the case in January of 1999, it upheld the lower courts, but in a narrow ruling. It ruled out the use of sampling for the purposes of apportionment of House seats, but apparently left open the possibility of its use for other purposes, like drawing district lines or allocating federal spending. Thus the battle over the census will likely continue.

When the 2000 census is completed, the numbers will first be used to reapportion the 435 House seats among the states in preparation for the election in 2002. Based on estimates through 1998 announced by the Census Bureau, 9 House seats would be gained by seven growing states in the South and West, while that number would be lost mostly by northeastern states. [84] As a result, three states (California, Florida, and Texas) would elect 25 percent of the House, and they would control 43 percent of the electoral votes necessary to elect a president in 2004. These are, however, preliminary estimates, and the actual census could yield different results. Indeed, the number of seats involved and the states affected are somewhat different from those on the list announced two years ago (see Chapter 9, note 94), although the general pattern of shifting seats from the "rust belt" to the "sun belt" continues.

After reapportionment comes redistricting in every state with more than one representative. The picture of the strategic context of redistricting is a bit clearer after the elections of 1998, although the races of 2000 will still shape the balance in many states because nearly all will hold elections for the lower house of their legislature, and some will elect a governor or the upper house. Party control of a number of states shifted in 1998. Overall, in the fourteen states that currently have ten or more representatives (and are thus most consequential with regard to redistricting), the Democrats control the governor and legislature in four, the Republicans in five, and five are split. [85] Gaining new control in Florida and Michigan was consequential for the Republicans, but the big prize of 1998 was won by the Democrats when they captured the California governor's office while retaining control of the legislature. It is expected that the Democrats will be able to add minority voters to the districts of some marginal Republicans and thereby endanger their chances for holding on to their seats.

Beyond the matter of reapportionment and redistricting, the future political context will be affected by the same patterns of public opinion we discussed as relevant to 2000: how the public reacts to the impeachment issue and governmental performance, and how that reaction in turn shapes attitudes toward the two parties. In addition, as we previously discussed, the advent of significant campaign finance reform could have a major impact on the political balance, although the prospect seems no more likely now than it did after 1996. All in all, the 1998 elections did relatively little to alter the political landscape, and it seems likely that control of the House—and now the Senate too—will hang in the balance for the near political future.

PART 4

The 1996 and 1998 Elections in Perspective

A careful analysis of past voting patterns provides evidence for speculating about future elections. But winning in politics is partly a question of luck, as Niccolò Machiavelli reminded us more than four centuries ago. "Fortune," Machiavelli conceded, "is the ruler of half of our actions." [1] Bill Clinton was fortunate in his 1992 nomination campaign and in his general election campaign against George Bush.

In 1996 Clinton's luck was born out of adversity. After the unexpected Republican landslide in the 1994 midterm election, many political pundits viewed Clinton as critically wounded. But in many respects, the Republican leadership, especially in the U.S. House of Representatives, proved to be an asset for Clinton. The Republicans had proclaimed a "revolution" in 1994, and perhaps they took this rhetoric seriously. But because Republicans pushed for greater cuts in public spending than the public wanted, Clinton was able to move to the political center by resisting reforms demanded by the Republicans in the 104th Congress. His vetoes of congressional spending bills led to two partial shutdowns of the government in 1995, and in both these confrontations the public supported Clinton more than his GOP rivals. Out of necessity, Clinton abandoned some of his more ambitious reforms, especially establishing a national health plan, but he was willing to support more modest legislation, backed by both parties, to provide portability for health insurance. Although in early 1995 many Democrats hoped that Clinton would not seek reelection, by the end of the year no Democrat emerged to challenge his renomination. He was thus spared a potentially divisive contest within his own party and was able to spend money provided by federal funding to promote his general election.

Clinton was also fortunate to have a weak opponent. Although the Senate is a major recruiting ground for presidential candidates, no Senate leader had ever won his party's presidential nomination, and the skills that Bob Dole had honed as a successful insider were of little use in running a general election campaign. Moreover, even though he resigned from the Senate before the Republican presidential nomination convention, he could scarcely pass as a political outsider, and the Democrats were able to link him with the unpopular Republican House Speaker, Newt Gingrich. As we saw in Chapter 2, Dole was never able to zero in on a single campaign strategy and moved from issue to issue over the course of the general election campaign. And although Clinton also faced a challenge from H. Ross Perot, now running as head of the newly created Reform party, Perot's support had diminished since 1992. Perot's candidacy deprived Clinton of a popular vote majority, but it had no effect on the presidential election result. Perot did, however, make substantial gains during the last two weeks of his campaign, raising doubts about Clinton that may have helped the Republicans maintain a narrow majority in the U.S. House of Representatives.

But above all, Clinton was fortunate in running for reelection under favorable economic conditions. Granted, his policies of increasing taxes in 1993 may have contributed to reduced deficits and, as a result of decreased federal borrowing, lower interest rates. With low inflation and low unemployment, the public was less concerned about economic issues than in recent elections, and Clinton was clearly the beneficiary of improved economic conditions. In fact, most Americans did not directly credit Clinton for these improvements. Even so, two-thirds of the electorate approved of Clinton's handling of the economy, and among those who approved, Clinton won nearly four-fifths of the major-party vote.

Clinton's proverbial good luck seemed to desert him in January 1998, when revelations emerged suggesting that he had lied in a civil deposition in a sexual harassment case filed by a former Arkansas state employee, Paula Jones. Clinton's denial of a sexual relationship with a former White House intern, Monica S. Lewinsky, was investigated by Independent Counsel Kenneth Starr. Although Clinton strongly denied having such a relationship, he was unlucky enough to have provided DNA evidence demonstrating his involvement. In his testimony before a federal grand jury in August, he acknowledged an improper relationship with Lewinsky but denied having committed perjury in his earlier civil deposition. By October the U.S. House of Representatives had voted to authorize the House Judiciary Committee to determine whether to recommend articles of impeachment against Clinton. In the short term, the impeachment inquiry may have led to Democratic gains, for they gained five seats in the House in the 1998 midterm election, the first midterm election since 1934 in which the party holding the White House gained seats. In fact, the party controlling the presidency had lost strength in the House in thirty-eight of the thirty-nine midterm elections held between 1842 and 1994. Although most pundits also predicted Democratic losses in the U.S. Senate, the Democrats held their own.

As a result of the poor showings in the House elections, Gingrich announced that he would not serve as Speaker in the 106th Congress and further declared that he would resign from the House. Six weeks later, during the floor debate over the articles of impeachment, Bob Livingtson, who had been chosen to be the next Speaker by the House Republican Conference, announced that he would not run for Speaker, and that he, too, would resign from the House. But these short-term Democratic victories did not spare Clinton from impeachment. Despite the Republican losses, and despite public opinion polls showing that most Americans opposed impeachment, the Republican-controlled House Judiciary Committee recommended four articles of impeachment, and, by a vote cast overwhelmingly along party lines, the outgoing House approved two of them. Clinton became only the second president in U.S. history to be impeached and the only elected president ever to be impeached.

The remarkable events of 1998 remind us that politics is highly unpredictable. Some pundits argue that the Republicans will pay a price for impeaching a popular president, while others argue that by the fall of 2000 few politicians will be held to account for an impeachment vote cast in December 1998. Nor can we be sure of how the impeachment controversy will affect the 2000 presidential election.

Despite a great deal of uncertainty, the U.S. government has constitutional features that make its politics more predictable than the politics of most other democracies. Writing in 1984, Arend Lijphart classified the United States as the only established democracy with a pure presidential system.[2] Unlike parliamentary democracies, in which no one can predict when elections will be held, congressional elections and presidential elections are held at fixed intervals. Indeed, even if a president must be replaced, no election is held to fill the position.[3] Thus, we know that if Clinton were to leave office, Vice President Al Gore would become president, and, subject to the approval of the House and Senate, he could appoint a new vice president. We know that all 435 House seats will be filled in 2000 and that, after congressional reapportionment and redistricting, they will be filled again in 2002. In each of these years, a third of the Senate seats will be filled. Moreover, we know that Clinton's second term is scheduled to end on January 20, 2001. Although election dates are not constitutionally fixed, we can be confident that the next congressional and presidential elections will be held on November 7, 2000, and that midterm elections will be held on November 5, 2002.

Although political parties are not mentioned in the Constitution, the U.S. party system is the most stable in the democratic world, and we can safely predict that both the Republican and Democratic parties will field presidential candidates in 2000. Moreover, we know that these candidates will be selected by party nominating conventions to be held in the summer of 2000 and that most of the delegates to these conventions will be selected by the end of March 2000. Moreover, barring dramatic developments, either the Republican or Democratic presidential candidate will be elected. But what is the likelihood of either of these parties again becoming the clear majority party, and what is the likelihood of one or both of these parties being replaced?

In Chapter 12 we begin by examining the prospect of the Democrats once again becoming the majority party. We then explore Republican prospects, noting that internal divisions within the GOP may create problems in regaining the White House. We then weigh the prospects for a new political party, paying particular attention to the Reform party, created in 1996. Last, we consider the likelihood of continued electoral volatility, the pattern that has prevailed in postwar American politics.

Chapter 12

The 1996 and 1998 Elections and the Future of American Politics

In his classic study of political parties, Maurice Duverger argued that in some democracies there is a clearly dominant political party. Despite competitive elections, a single party is consistently at the center of political power. A party, Duverger wrote "is dominant when it holds the majority over a long period of political development." Although a dominant party may occasionally lose an election, it remains dominant because "it is identified with an epoch" and because "its doctrines, ideas, methods, its style, so to speak, coincide with those of the epoch." One reason a party dominates is because it is believed to be dominant. "Even the enemies of the dominant party, even citizens who refuse to give it their vote," Duverger wrote, "acknowledge its superior status and its influence; they deplore it but admit it." [1]

Duverger's concept of the dominant party provides insights about the decline of the Democratic party after 1964. Students of comparative politics provide at least four clear examples of dominant parties: Mapai in Israel (now the Labor party), the Christian Democratic Party (DC) in Italy, the Swedish Social Democratic Party, and the Liberal Democratic Party (LDP) in Japan.[2] But Duverger argued that if a country had free elections, a dominant party was always in peril. "The dominant party wears itself out in office, it loses its vigour, its arteries harden." And, he concluded, "every domination bears within itself the seeds of its own destruction." [3]

Duverger appears to be prophetic.[4] Mapai was the dominant party even before Israel attained statehood in 1948. Asher Arian writes,

In the years immediately following independence, Mapai epitomized the dominant party. The largest vote getter, the key ingredient of any government coalition, the standard-bearer of society's goals, and the articulator of its aspirations, Mapai also had the tremendous political advantages of a united and integrated leadership; a broad-based, well-functioning, and flexible political organization; no serious political opposition; and control over the major economic and human resources flowing into the country.[5]

Mapai remained dominant until 1977, when an electoral "upheaval" drove the Alignment (the successor to Mapai) from office, and it did not become the leading party in a political coalition again until 1992. Although Labor (the new name for the Alignment) was the largest party in the Knesset after the 1996 election, the Israeli electorate also voted directly for prime minister, and Labor again lost power. In Italy, the DC, with American support, won nearly half the vote in 1948, when Italy held its first postwar elections. It lost power more gradually than Mapai, but it suffered a major loss in the 1983 election, which brought Italy's first Socialist prime minister to power.[6] By 1994, with revelations of widespread corruption, the DC lost two-thirds of its remaining support, and a coalition of new political parties, led by media-magnate Silvio Berlusconi, came to power. By the 1996 election, the remnants of the DC lost even more strength, and a new left-center coalition of parties, known as the Olive Tree coalition, gained political power, to be replaced by a more leftist coalition headed by a former Communist, Massimo D'Alema, in October 1998. The Swedish Social Democrats came to power in 1932, and, although it was forced into opposition by elections in 1976 and 1979, it returned to power in 1982. But in 1991 the nonsocialist parties won an absolute majority of the votes. The Social Democratic party regained power in 1994, and although it won only a 36 percent of the vote, it narrowly held power in 1998. Clearly, it has lost its dominant position among the Swedish electorate. Since its formation in 1955, the Liberal Democratic party consistently held the most seats in the Japanese House of Representatives, but in 1993, in the face of mounting scandals, the LDP split, the prime minister dissolved the House of Representatives and called an election, the party lost its majority, and, although it was still the single largest party, it was excluded from the coalition formed after the election. The LDP won nearly half the seats in the House of Representatives in 1996, and it formed a government supported by several smaller parties. The LDP suffered major loses, however, in the upper-house elections in 1998, forcing the resignation of Prime Minister Ryutaro Hashimoto. Even though the Liberal Democrats retained control of the government, the LDP appears to have lost its electoral dominance.[7]

Writing in 1958, Duverger argued that the Democrats were the dominant party in the United States, even though Dwight D. Eisenhower, running as a Republican, had been elected president in both 1952 and 1956. Duverger viewed Eisenhower's election as a personal victory that did not change the balance of partisan power.[8] Indeed, scholars writing after the 1964 elections might have seen the Democrats as even more dominant. The Democrats won the White House under Franklin D. Roosevelt in 1932 and then won six of the next eight elections. In 1964, under Lyndon B. Johnson, the Democrats won by a landslide over the Republican Barry Goldwater and had gained thirty-eight seats in the

House. The only Republican victories had come under a former general, Eisenhower, who had been courted by both the Democratic and Republican parties. The Republicans, much like the Whigs, who ran William Henry Harrison in 1840 and Zachary Taylor in 1848, defeated the Democrats by choosing a war hero as their standard-bearer. Both of the generals elected by the Whigs died shortly after taking office, whereas Eisenhower served two full terms. However, like the Whigs, the Republicans seldom controlled Congress. Between the 73d Congress, elected in 1932, and the 89th Congress, elected in 1964, the Republicans held a majority for only four years (the 80th Congress, elected in 1946, and the 83d Congress, elected in 1952).

In retrospect, it is easy to see that the Democratic party had within it the "seeds of its own destruction," although the seeds for the party's decline may be found in the composition of the coalition that supported it.[9] The Democratic coalition drew support from northern blacks and from southern whites. This coalition was sustainable only as long as discrimination against African Americans in the South was not a major political issue. After the civil rights movement began in the mid-1950s, ignoring racial injustice in the South became untenable. By backing the Civil Rights Act of 1964 and the Voting Rights Act of 1965, Johnson chose a position that was morally correct, and he may well have had strategic goals in mind, too. However, his decision aggressively to seek African-American voters helped to end Democratic dominance in presidential elections. With hindsight, the seeds of future Democratic defeats can be seen in Johnson's landslide over Goldwater, for in addition to winning his home state of Arizona, Goldwater carried Alabama, Georgia, Louisiana, Mississippi, and South Carolina. By the end of the 1960s, African Americans in these states were able to vote, and, as Johnson expected, they voted heavily Democratic. Even so, in most subsequent presidential elections these states, as well as the remaining southern states, have voted Republican. Virginia has voted Republican in all eight presidential elections held since 1964.

It took the Republicans forty years to regain the House after losing control of it in 1954. But several political scientists, writing after the 1988 election, argued that the Republicans had become the dominant party in presidential elections.[10] From 1968 through 1988, the Republicans won five of six presidential elections, and the only victory for the Democrats came when they narrowly defeated Gerald R. Ford, the man who pardoned Richard M. Nixon after the Watergate scandal, which had resulted in Nixon's forced resignation.

But after the 1992 election it appeared that the coalition that supported Ronald Reagan and his successor, George Bush, also had within it the seeds of its own destruction. Reagan had created a coalition of social conservatives, for whom the fight against abortion and the right to hold prayers in public schools were important issues, and economic conservatives, who believed that less government was the key to economic growth. Although Reagan and Bush mainly paid lip service to conservative social values, they provided tangible benefits to social conservatives by a series of court appointments, especially to the Supreme Court, that put *Roe v. Wade* in jeopardy. When Republican economic policies no longer appeared to provide economic growth, a large number of economic conservatives, and some social conservatives, deserted Bush, although many turned to H. Ross Perot instead of to Bill Clinton. In 1994 two-thirds of the Perot voters who went to the polls voted for Republican congressional candidates, contributing to the GOP legislative landslide.

Despite Clinton's reelection in 1996, the Democrats did not return to electoral dominance, for they failed to regain control of Congress. Between 1828 and 1996, the Democrats had won the presidency twenty times in forty-three elections, but 1996 was the only time they won the White House without also winning control of the U.S. House of Representatives. And although the Democrats unexpectedly gained five House seats in the 1998 midterm election, the Republicans retained control of both the House and Senate. After the 1996 and 1998 elections there appeared to be no clear majority party in the United States, and it would be unwise to predict the future of the American party system. But we can rely on what we have already learned to evaluate alternative possibilities. First, we discuss the likelihood of a Democratic resurgence as the majority party. Next, we discuss Republican prospects for the future. We then look at the question of whether a new political party is likely to emerge, focusing mainly on the newly organized Reform party. Finally, we discuss prospects for continued electoral volatility.

PROSPECTS FOR THE DEMOCRATS

When Clinton assumed the presidency in January 1993, his party held a majority in both the House and the Senate, and twelve years of divided government came to an end. Although Clinton had won only 43 percent of the popular vote, he had, at least in principle, the opportunity to create a policy agenda that would transform the Democrats into the majority party for decades to come. Despite some early policy successes, the second year of his presidency was marked by major policy failures. The ambitious health care reforms that Clinton proposed received little legislative support, and Clinton abandoned his own reforms to back a proposal by Senate majority leader George Mitchell. Ultimately, no health care bill was passed in either the House or Senate. Clinton also failed to achieve significant welfare reform, another important policy goal.

Whatever prospects the Democrats had to seize control of the policy agenda ended with the Republican midterm victory of 1994. After the midterm defeat, many Democrats were hopeful that Clinton would not run for president in 1996, and many hoped that if he did he would be challenged for the party nomination. But, as Evan Thomas, a reporter for *Newsweek* wrote, "Bill Clinton, by shrewdness, luck and love of the game, came back from a near-death experience to win a second term." [11] Indeed, as we saw in Chapter 1, Clinton faced no opposition for the Democratic nomination, and 1996 was the first effectively uncontested

Democratic nomination since Johnson was nominated in 1964. After the 1994 midterm defeat, Clinton moved to the political center. In 1996 he signed legislation substantially changing the welfare system by transferring authority to the states, thus ending "welfare as we know it." He did not, however, entirely abandon some liberal Democratic goals. As we saw in Chapter 6, the electorate perceived major policy differences between Clinton and Bob Dole. And Clinton won approval for his efforts to restrain the Republican-controlled Congress, with the pubic blaming congressional Republicans more than Clinton for two partial government shutdowns in 1995. But ultimately it was the strong economy that proved to be Clinton's greatest asset, and, as we saw, his reelection resulted mainly from positive retrospective evaluation among the electorate.

But the 1996 elections continued divided government between the executive and legislative branches, and, despite Democratic gains in 1998, the government remained divided. That the Republicans control both the House and Senate may be an advantage for the Democrats in 2000. Just as the Republicans argued that electing a Democratic Congress in 1996 might give Clinton a "blank check," some voters may fear that electing a Republican president in 2000 would give the Republicans too much power. Still, a net gain of six seats would give the Democrats control of the House. The Democrats would need to win six seats to gain control of the Senate, and could control the Senate with a gain of five seats if they retained the vice presidency. Thirty-four Senate seats will be filled in 2000, and, as of this writing, the Republicans hold twenty of these seats and the Democrats hold only fourteen.

In many respects the Democrats seem well positioned to maintain control of the presidency, even though in early 1999 trial heats showed that the Republican front-runner, Governor George W. Bush of Texas, would narrowly defeat the Democratic front-runner, Vice President Al Gore. But early trial heats often prove to be poor guides about actual elections, and there are forces that may favor the Democrats. The Republican gains in party identification have eroded since the late 1980s, and the balance of forces in the electoral college seems fairly even. As James W. Ceaser and Andrew E. Busch write, "The striking similarity of the 1992 and 1996 presidential election results provide a clear warning that the Democrats may be in the process of constructing a new and durable presidential majority." But as they also remind us, "the balance today between the two parties remains quite close" with both parties having a "reasonable prospect" of building a winning electoral coalition.[12]

Before either the Democratic or the Republican party can win the 2000 general election, they will need to nominate presidential and vice presidential candidates. In many ways, the nomination contests will be conducted under very unusual conditions, for they will follow the impeachment of a sitting president. But in other ways the 2000 nomination contests will continue traditions and practices that are hallmarks of American democracy, and they will be especially influenced by practices introduced after the 1968 presidential elections.

The 2000 nominations may be affected in many ways by Clinton's impeachment trial in the Senate, by the aftermath of that trial, and by the public's reaction to these events. In 1868 the Radical Republicans, who strongly supported severe sanctions against the South, supported Andrew Johnson's impeachment and came within one vote of convicting him in the Senate. But the impeachment and the Senate trial had little effect on the 1868 presidential election. Johnson, a Democrat who became president after Abraham Lincoln's assassination in 1865, had joined a fusion ticket of Republicans and pro-war Democrats in 1864. He had no chance of winning the Republican presidential nomination and would have been rejected by the Democrats if he had tried to rejoin their ranks. Ulysses S. Grant, the commanding general of the Union armies, was the unanimous choice for president at the Republican nomination convention. He defeated Horatio Seymour, a former Democratic governor of New York, in the general election, and the Republicans easily retained control of both the House and the Senate.[13] Even if Johnson had been convicted, moving Benjamin F. Wade of Ohio, the president pro tem of the Senate, into the White House, it seems likely that the Republicans would have chosen Grant as their nominee. Clinton's Senate trial in 1999, however, seems likely to affect both the presidential and congressional elections in 2000, but in ways that are as yet unpredictable.

But given the American presidential system, many aspects of the 2000 elections can be predicted. First, there will be congressional and presidential elections on the first Tuesday following the first Monday in November (November 7, 2000). Second, as a result of the Twenty-second Amendment, Clinton will be ineligible to run for a third term. Third, an overwhelming majority of serious candidates and eventual winners will be Democrats and Republicans. An impeachment trial may determine who the strongest candidate for the Democratic party's presidential nomination will be. But it may also affect the House and Senate elections.

As we saw in Chapter 1, the system of primaries and caucuses used to select delegates to the Democratic and Republican party nominating conventions developed after the 1968 presidential elections. It developed mainly as a result of reforms initiated by the Democratic party after its disastrous convention in Chicago, and the subsequent loss by Vice President Hubert H. Humphrey to Richard M. Nixon in the general election. The broad outlines of that system were in place for the 1972 nomination campaigns. There were changes in campaign financing introduced in 1971, and they were revised in 1974 in the wake of the Watergate crisis. The Democrats in particular modified their rules in every contest between 1976 and 1988. In 2000 the Democrats will have two major rules different from those of the Republicans. In the first place, about one-fifth of the Democratic delegates will be chosen from elected Democratic officeholders and party officials, and these delegates will be free to support any presidential candidate they choose, regardless of the preferences of voters of their states. These delegates are commonly called "superdelegates." Second, all Democratic primaries and caucuses will use some form of proportional representation for selecting delegates, so that each presidential candidate who gains a 15 percent threshold of the vote will be entitled to a proportionate share of delegates to the party's nomination convention. By contrast, the Republicans do not specifically allocate a designated percentage of their convention delegates to elected officials, and the Republicans allow winner-take-all primaries in which the candidate with a plurality of the vote can win all of a state's delegates.

For the most part, however, the Democratic and Republican parties follow similar rules and follow a similar delegate selection schedule. As with all nomination campaigns since 1972, the campaign will be conducted in and to the public through the media with an attempt to win support among the electorate. It is mathematically possible that no candidate will emerge from the primary process with the support of a majority of delegates at the nominating conventions, although, as we explain in Chapter 1, it is likely that the eventual winner of both parties will be chosen before the nomination conventions begin. In 2000 it is possible that the contest will be resolved fairly early in the delegate selection season.

Perhaps the greatest change from 1996 to 2000 is that several more states, including California, are considering changing or already have changed the date of their primary by moving it close to the beginning of the primary season. This process of "frontloading" the primary season reflects an ongoing process that has been under way for several elections. Essentially, states are slowly adjusting to the realities of the new nomination system by recognizing that early primaries have more effect on the outcome than those held later in the season. The obvious response, therefore, has been to move their state delegate selections to earlier in the year and to capitalize on the resulting media attention that crucial events bring to the state.

California currently plans (via newly enacted legislation) to hold its primary on March 7, the same day as those of New York, several New England states, and possibly some other western states. The date is shortly after the New Hampshire primary and the Iowa caucuses, and a week before a series of primaries to be held in southern states, including Florida and Texas, as well as some states outside the South. These latter events, currently scheduled for March 14, arose from an agreement among these states to create a regional primary that would give southern states more leverage on the type of candidates likely to be nominated. In 1988 there were sixteen Democratic primaries on a single day, dubbed "Super Tuesday." But if the California primary is actually used to select delegates, March 7, 2000, promises to be even more "super," with a bicoastal primary creating nearly a national contest.[14] More to the point, candidates who hope to win their party's nomination will need to compete in many large states in every region of the country over an eight-day period. As a result, candidates will need a great deal of organization and resources, especially money, well before the primary season begins. Many pundits argue that to run an effective primary campaign, a candidate will have to raise $20 million by the end of 1999. Thus, the campaign is likely to be won by candidates who are well known before the campaign and who have access to a large amount of money before the election year begins.

On the Democratic side, about one out of five delegates will be superdelegates. Superdelegates were first introduced in 1984, although at that time only one Democratic delegate in seven was a superdelegate. In 1984 about 85 percent of these superdelegates backed the "insider" candidate, former vice president Walter F. Mondale, and very few backed the leading "outsider" candidates, Senator Gary Hart of Colorado and Reverend Jesse Jackson, Jr. The support of Democratic superdelegates played a crucial role in helping Mondale wrap up his delegate majority a month before the 1984 Democratic nomination convention.[15] In 2000 superdelegates are likely to support Al Gore, although some would have supported House Minority Leader Richard Gephardt of Missouri if he had run.

As we saw in the 1988 campaign, when there is no incumbent president eligible for nomination, both parties are likely to field a large number of strong contenders for their presidential nomination.[16] Gore may be the incumbent president when the election year begins. If so, we can expect relatively few Democrats to oppose him, even if his policies are unpopular. In 1976 Gerald Ford held office as the incumbent president, having succeeded Nixon, who as a result of the Watergate affair faced impeachment in the House and a likely conviction in the Senate. Ford had never been elected to national office (he had been appointed to the vice presidency in 1973 after Spiro T. Agnew was forced to resign), and he was a relatively unpopular incumbent. Even so, the power of incumbency deterred all Republicans except Ronald Reagan from contesting his nomination. If Gore were to become president, he might face little or no opposition.

Gore is very likely to be a strong contender in 2000, even if he does not become president. But if he remains vice president, he is likely to face opposition. Gephardt, who ran for president in 1988, might have been Gore's strongest opponent, but in February 1999 he announced that he would set his sights on being Speaker of the House. In early 1999 one current and one former senator were carefully investigating their prospects. John Kerry (Mass.) is a liberal Democrat who has begun the lengthy processes to consider running. So, too, has former senator Bill Bradley of New Jersey, a more moderate Democrat. There is continued speculation that Jesse Jackson might initiate a third campaign, having earlier run for the party's nomination in 1984 and 1988. Jackson might run primarily as a representative of African Americans within the Democratic party, and a race against Gore might be especially likely as a result of friction that developed between the Gore and Jackson campaigns in the 1988 nomination contest. Since World War II, many Democratic senators have run for their party's nomination, and, in addition to Kerry, Dianne Feinstein (Calif.) is commonly mentioned as a possible contender. In 1988 and 1992 Democratic governors won their party's nomination, but relatively few are being mentioned as likely contenders for 2000. Howard Dean of Vermont is considered to be a possibility, although he disavows any interest in running. The large amount of money required to mount an effective campaign, as well as the likelihood that a candidate's personal life will come under intense public scrutiny, may discourage some candidates from declaring.

Given their unexpected triumph in the 1994 midterm elections, the Republicans' failure to win the presidency in 1996 was a major disappointment. But the U.S. presidential nomination system makes it difficult for party leaders to control the process, and even more difficult for the party that does not hold the presidency. As the Republican nomination contest narrowed into a three-way fight among Bob Dole, Pat Buchanan, and Steve Forbes, Dole clearly appeared to be the most reasonable candidate to stave off a Republican debacle. Even though Buchanan had very little chance of winning the Republican presidential nomination, his first-place showing in the New Hampshire primary raised the specter of Republican leaders losing control of the party. South Carolina became a firewall at which Republican leaders united behind Dole to secure his nomination.[17]

Failing to win the 1996 presidential election was a disappointment, but losing House seats in the 1998 midterm was seen as a disaster. A few days after these unexpected losses, Newt Gingrich announced that he would not serve as Speaker in the 106th Congress and that he would resign his seat in the House. As we have argued, the Republican party has deep divisions between economic and social conservatives, and these divisions were highlighted by recriminations following the 1998 midterm results. Moderates argued that a focus on social issues had hurt the Republican party. "We still tend to focus on the well-known wedge issues," complained Eddie Mahe, a Republican party operative. "Once you become a governing majority, you've got to have some magnets." [18] Even conservatives, such as Senate Majority Leader Trent Lott of Mississippi, argued that the Republicans needed to emphasize economic issues. "We need to talk more as Republicans about our commitment to tax cuts and growth and local control of education." [19]

Social conservatives argued that the Republicans lost votes by failing to emphasize social issues. For example, according to Randy Tate, executive director of the Christian Coalition, "There was no clear conservative agenda coming out of the conservative leaders in Washington, D.C. . . . The Republicans tried to run a campaign solely on anti-Clinton sentiment." [20] And Gary Bauer, president of the Family Research Council, complained, "Dozens of candidates ran for the tall grass on values issues. And the result was they demoralized their own base." [21]

Even after their midterm losses, the Republicans may have other self-inflicted wounds. Many observers viewed the 1998 midterm elections as a clear sign that the electorate did not want Clinton to be impeached, and public opinion polls showed that most Americans opposed impeachment. But the Republican-controlled House nonetheless voted, on largely party-lines, to pass two articles of impeachment. As we saw in Chapter 11, polls conducted shortly after the House impeachment vote showed that nearly three out of five Americans had a negative view of the Republican party, the lowest level of support for the Republican party in fourteen years.

We cannot judge the long-term electoral consequences of the impeachment vote, although as we noted in Chapter 11, Democrats are likely to use the impeachment vote to argue that the Republican party is out of touch with the American people. But the impeachment vote will not necessarily affect Republican prospects for winning the presidential election. But before any Republican candidate can win the presidency, he or she must first win the party's presidential nomination. Whoever captures the Republican nomination will inherit major political assets. Although the Republicans clearly have no electoral vote lock, sixteen states, yielding 135 electoral votes, have voted Republican in all five of the last presidential elections.[22] In 1996 the national electorate appeared to be somewhat closer to where they saw Dole on the issues than to where they saw Clinton. And although the Republicans have lost some of the gains in party identification they made with the Reagan presidency, they are still close to parity with the Democrats, especially considering that Republicans are somewhat more likely to vote than Democrats.

Although we cannot predict who will win the Republican nomination contest, we know that when there is no incumbent president eligible for a party's nomination, many candidates are likely to emerge. The current leader in the polls is Governor Bush (Texas), who ran a strong reelection campaign in 1998 that drew substantial support from Hispanics and blacks. Former vice president Dan Quayle (Ind.) is planning to run, as are some of the surprises of the 1996 season—magazine publisher Steve Forbes and former Tennessee governor Lamar Alexander. Jack Kemp (former House representative from New York, secretary of Housing and Urban Development, and the 1996 vice presidential candidate) is another possible contender. Senator Bob Smith (N.H.) and Representative John R. Kasich (Ohio) are likely to run as well. Other possibilities are Senators Fred Thompson (Tenn.) and John McCain (Ariz.), and Governors George E. Pataki (N.Y.), Tom Ridge (Pa.), and John Engler (Mich.). Elizabeth Dole, who resigned as president of the American Red Cross in January 1999, may run, and many believe she would be a strong contender. Former general Colin L. Powell has consistently said that he does not plan to run, but many believe that he would have a good chance of wining both the nomination and the general election. Gary Bauer, who has long been active in the pro-life movement, might run as a "message" candidate to focus attention on a series of policies, rather than to actually win the nomination. In short, there is a long list of possible candidates. As with the Democrats, the large amount of money required to succeed may discourage some candidates. Moreover, the likelihood of having one's personal life subjected to public scrutiny may also discourage some candidates from declaring.

PROSPECTS FOR A NEW POLITICAL PARTY

For the past 130 years the Democratic and Republican parties have held a duopoly in American politics. Ever since the election of Franklin Pierce in 1852, either a Democrat or a Republican has won the presidency, and in the thirty-four elections from 1864 (in which Abraham Lincoln was reelected) through 1996, there have been only six contests in which a third-party or independent candidate has won the electoral vote of even a single state. The last election in which more than one out of ten members of the U.S. House of Representatives was affiliated with a third party was the 55th Congress (1897–1899). From the 76th Congress (1939–1941) through the 106th Congress (elected in 1998), the third-party representation in the House has never topped 1 percent, and from the 80th Congress (1945–1947) to the present there has been at most one House member who did not affiliate with either the Democratic or the Republican party. In his comparative study of electoral systems in twenty-seven democracies, Arend Lijphart classifies the United States as having the lowest number of "effective political parties" and the second lowest number of "effective parliamentary parties." [23]

Clearly, third parties in the United States face many obstacles, the most formidable of which are the rules by which candidates win office. With the exception of Maine and Nebraska, all the states and the District of Columbia have a winner-take-all electoral system for allocating their presidential electors. To win the electoral votes of these states, a presidential candidate (or, to be more specific, a slate of electors pledged to a presidential candidate) must win a plurality of the vote within the state. Perot did not win a single electoral vote in either 1992 or 1996. The only third parties actually to win electoral votes since World War II have been parties of the political right—the States' Rights Democrats in 1948 and the American Independent party in 1968, and all of their votes came from the states of the old Confederacy. Although there was some regional variation in Perot's vote in 1992, he had no regional base, and there was very little regional variation in Perot's support in 1996.

Third parties have a difficult time getting on the ballot, although recent court decisions have made access to the ballot much easier than it was before George C. Wallace's 1968 candidacy. Independent or third-party candidates also have financial problems, and the federal election laws place an additional burden on their ability to raise money. Democratic and Republican candidates are guaranteed federal funding, whereas third-party candidates receive funding only if they win 5 percent of the vote, and only after the general election. In 1992 Perot did not seek federal funding and spent $65 million of his own money. In 1996 he accepted $29 million in federal funding (based on what he was entitled to as a result of his 1992 popular vote totals), less than half of what he spent on his own four years earlier.

In 1992 Perot ran as an independent. But in 1995 he announced that he would help fund efforts to create a new political party. This required a petition effort, and ultimately the Reform party appeared on the ballot in all fifty states. As a result of votes won in 1996, the Reform party will be entitled to receive about $17 million in federal funding for the 2000 presidential election. Of course, this amount is negligible compared to the amounts that the major political parties are able to raise through "soft-money" contributions.

As a result of their 1996 votes, the Reform party was automatically qualified to run on the ballot in thirty-four states in 1998. But as a result of its poor show-ing in many of these states, it lost the right to qualify automatically for the ballot in seventeen states. It is still qualified for an automatic place on the ballot in seventeen states, and may regain its ballot access in California if it maintains 88,000 registered voters during 1999.[24]

Will the Reform party prove viable? Is it really a political party? In 1996 the Reform party fielded two candidates, Ross Perot for president and Pat Choate for vice president. In effect, the Reform party was little more than a vehicle for Perot's own candidacy.[25] As Joseph A. Schlesinger reminds us, a political party in a democracy is an organized attempt to gain public office by winning elections.[26] When the Republican party emerged in 1854, it ran candidates for office at every level in the nonslave states. Politically ambitious Whigs, as well as members of the Free Soil party and the Know-Nothing party, could become Republicans and seek office for state legislatures, Congress, and governorships. In the 34th Con-gress, the first elected after the Republican party was founded, 108 of the 234 House members were Republicans. The Republican party promised the collec-tive good of limiting slavery, but it also provided selective incentives for indi-viduals seeking elective office. Politically ambitious citizens today may want selective incentives, such as access to office for themselves, as well as the oppor-tunity of working for the collective good of electing Perot.[27]

In 1998 the Reform party had one notable success. A former professional wres-tler, Jesse Ventura was elected governor of Minnesota in a three-way contest in which he gained 37 percent of the vote. Mae Schunk was elected as his lieutenant governor. But not a single Reform candidate was elected to Congress or to a single seat in a state legislature. In fact, even though the Reform party had auto-matic ballot access in thirty-four states, relatively few Americans ran as Reform party candidates. According to the Reform party's web site, there were eight Re-form candidates for governor (out of thirty-six contests), ten candidates for the U.S. Senate (out of thirty-four contests), twenty-seven candidates for U.S. House seats, and only forty-nine candidates for state legislative seats.[28] Jesse Ventura's stunning victory should not overshadow the failure of the party to retain its automatic place on the ballot in seventeen out of thirty-four states.

In addition to problems of ballot access, the Reform party, as well as other third parties, may also face a fundamental difficulty in recruiting presidential candidates. The very openness of the major-party nomination process encour-ages strong candidates to seek either the Republican or Democratic presidential nomination. There are few restraints on entering the party primaries, and a ma-jor-party nomination will probably continue to attract far more votes than it repels. Strong candidates who actually have a chance of winning the presidency are likely to seek one of the major-party nominations.[29]

PROSPECTS FOR CONTINUED ELECTORAL VOLATILITY

For the moment *dealignment* seems to be a more accurate term to describe the American political scene. The old party system may be in disarray, but nothing has replaced it. Admittedly, the Democrats might be positioned to become the majority party if they can hold the presidency in 2000 and regain control of Congress. The Republicans may overcome their intraparty conflicts, hold on to Congress, and regain the presidency. But even if divided government ends in 2000, continued electoral volatility seems likely.

There are many reasons for predicting continued electoral volatility. The most obvious is the appeal of Perot. More than nineteen million Americans supported Perot in 1992, even though he had a negligible chance of winning. Even in 1996 Perot won eight million votes, and a total of 10 percent of the vote was cast for Perot and other minor-party candidates. The 1992 and 1996 elections mark the first time since the Civil War that the two major parties failed to win more than 90 percent of the vote in two consecutive elections. As in 1992, the 1996 Perot vote came from a broad spectrum of American society, although, as in 1992, relatively few African Americans, southern whites, or Jews voted for him. As we saw in Chapter 6, Perot voters did not have distinctive issue preferences, but, as we saw in Chapter 7, they were very likely to believe that neither the Republicans nor the Democrats could solve the nation's problems. In Chapter 8 we saw that over half of Perot's votes came from self-proclaimed independents.

Part of Perot's success in both 1992 and 1996 derived from the weak party loyalties of the American electorate. Although the strength of U.S. party attachments is somewhat greater than it was at its postwar low in 1978, it is considerably weaker than it was from 1952 through 1964, the years Philip E. Converse labeled the "steady-state" period in American politics.[30] During that period, 22 percent of the electorate were classified as independents. In the 1996 National Election Study (NES) survey, 34 percent were. Although some self-professed independents may be "hidden partisans," the claim of independence does in fact reveal a lack of strong commitment to a party.[31] Moreover, from 1952 through 1964, 36 percent of the electorate claimed to be strong party identifiers; in the 1996 NES survey, 31 percent did. In addition, the 1996 General Social Survey conducted by the National Opinion Research Center reveals weaker party identifications among the U.S. electorate. Thirty-seven percent were self-professed independents and only 24 percent were strong party identifiers. Weak partisans and self-professed independents are much more volatile in their voting choices than are individuals with strong party ties.

Moreover, as we saw in Chapters 5 and 10, with the exception of race, social forces have less and less influence on voting behavior—a trend that is likely to contribute to electoral volatility. Today, few voters feel bound to a political party by social class, ethnicity, or religion. This absence of affiliation increases the proportion of the electorate that is likely to switch its vote from one election to the next.

Finally, the very low turnout in 1996 may be seen as another indicator of dealignment. As we saw in Chapter 4, past realignments have been characterized by increases in electoral participation and the mobilization of new groups into the electorate. Of course, there is no necessary reason that a future party realignment, should one occur, must bear all of the hallmarks of previous realignments.

But it would be difficult to consider any alignment as stable when nearly half the politically eligible population does not vote.

In the late 1990s the party systems of many democracies appeared to be in disarray. But the U.S. electoral system, like that in Britain, provides a check against new political parties and considerable protection for the two major parties. Ultimately, however, the people can displace a major party, although this has not happened in the United States since the 1850s or in Britain since the 1920s. The ability of the Democratic and Republican parties to maintain their duopoly ultimately depends on the ability of their leaders to solve the nation's problems.

Notes

INTRODUCTION TO PART 1

1. See, for example, Benjamin Ginsberg and Martin Shefter, *Politics by Other Means: The Declining Importance of Elections in America* (New York: Basic Books, 1990).

2. See Benjamin Ginsberg and Alan Stone, eds., *Do Elections Matter?* 3d ed. (New York: Sharpe, 1996).

3. John H. Aldrich and Thomas Weko, "The Presidency and the Election Process: Campaign Strategy, Voting, and Governance," in *The Presidency and the Political System,* 2d ed., ed. Michael Nelson (Washington, D.C.: CQ Press, 1988), 251–267.

4. Phil Gailey, "Republicans Start to Worry about Signs of Slippage," *New York Times,* August 25, 1984, E5.

5. V. O. Key, Jr., "A Theory of Critical Elections," *Journal of Politics* 17 (February 1955): 4.

6. V. O. Key, Jr., "Secular Realignment and the Party System," *Journal of Politics* 21 (May 1959): 198.

7. These two states were, and still are, the most heavily Roman Catholic states. Both of these states voted Republican in seventeen of the eighteen presidential elections from 1856 through 1924, voting Democratic only when the Republican party was split in 1912.

8. V. O. Key, Jr., *Politics, Parties, and Pressure Groups,* 5th ed. (New York: Thomas Y. Crowell, 1964), 186.

9. James L. Sundquist, *Dynamics of the Party System: Alignment and Realignment of Political Parties in the United States,* rev. ed. (Washington, D.C.: Brookings Institution, 1983), 4; Lawrence G. McMichael and Richard J. Trilling, "The Structure and Meaning of Critical Realignment: The Case of Pennsylvania," in *Realignment in American Politics: Toward a Theory,* ed. Bruce A. Campbell and Richard J. Trilling (Austin: University of Texas Press, 1980), 25.

10. In addition to the eleven states that formed the Confederacy (Alabama, Arkansas, Florida, Georgia, Louisiana, Mississippi, North Carolina, South Carolina, Tennessee, Texas, and Virginia), Delaware, Kentucky, Maryland, and Missouri were also slave states. There were fifteen free states in 1848: Connecticut, Illinois, Indiana, Iowa, Maine, Massachusetts, Michigan, New Hampshire, New Jersey, New York, Ohio, Pennsylvania, Rhode Island, Vermont, and Wisconsin. By 1860, three additional free states (California, Minnesota, and Oregon) had been admitted into the Union.

11. Michael Nelson, "The Constitutional Aspects of the Election," in *The Elections of 1988,* ed. Michael Nelson (Washington, D.C.: CQ Press, 1989), 197.

12. Byron E. Shafer, "The Election of 1988 and the Structure of American Politics: Thoughts on Interpreting an Electoral Order," *Electoral Studies* 8 (April 1989): 11.

13. Ronald Inglehart and Avram Hochstein, "Alignment and Dealignment of the Electorate in France and the United States," *Comparative Political Studies* 5 (October 1972): 343–372; Russell J. Dalton, Paul Allen Beck, and Scott C. Flanagan, "Electoral Change in Advanced Industrial Democracies," in *Electoral Change in Advanced Industrial Democracies: Realignment or Dealignment?* ed. Dalton, Flanagan, and Beck (Princeton, N.J.: Princeton University Press, 1984), 14.

14. Russell J. Dalton and Martin P. Wattenberg, "The Not So Simple Act of Voting," in *Political Science: The State of the Discipline, II,* ed. Ada W. Finifter (Washington, D.C.: American Political Science Association, 1993), 204.

15. Bo Särlvik and Ivor Crewe, *Decade of Dealignment: The Conservative Victory of 1979 and Electoral Trends in the 1970s* (Cambridge: Cambridge University Press, 1983).

16. Harold D. Clarke et al., *Absent Mandate: Canadian Electoral Politics in an Era of Restructuring* (Toronto: Gage Educational Publishing, 1996).

17. Everett Carll Ladd, "1996 Vote: The 'No Majority' Realignment Continues," *Political Science Quarterly* 112 (Spring 1997): 2.

18. Walter Dean Burnham, "Bill Clinton: Riding the Tiger," in *The Election of 1996: Reports and Interpretations,* ed. Gerald M. Pomper et al. (Chatham, N.J.: Chatham House, 1997), 6, 8.

19. Michael Nelson, "The Election: Turbulence and Tranquility in Contempo-

rary American Politics," in *The Elections of 1996,* ed. Michael Nelson (Washington, D.C.: CQ Press, 1997), 64.

20. James W. Ceaser and Andrew E. Busch, *Losing to Win: The 1996 Elections and American Politics* (Lanham, Md.: Rowman and Littlefield, 1997), 18.

21. The Republicans won control of the House in eight consecutive elections between 1884 and 1908, far short of the twenty consecutive Democratic victories from 1954 through 1992.

22. The size of the voting-age citizen population is based on an estimate by Walter Dean Burnham. He estimates the population to be 189,396,000 (personal communication, July 1, 1997). Because we are usually analyzing responses to key questions measured only in the postelection interview (for example, how respondents said they voted for president or Congress), we often restrict our analysis to the 1,534 respondents in the 1996 NES postelection interview.

23. For a brief nontechnical introduction to polling, see Herbert Asher, *Polling and the Public: What Every Citizen Should Know,* 2d ed. (Washington, D.C.: CQ Press, 1992).

24. For a brief description of the procedures used by the SRC to carry out its sampling, see Paul R. Abramson, *Political Attitudes in America: Formation and Change* (San Francisco: Freeman, 1983), 18–23. For a more detailed analysis, see Survey Research Center, *Interviewer's Manual,* rev. ed. (Ann Arbor, Mich.: Institute for Social Research, 1976).

25. The magnitude of sampling error is greater for proportions near 50 percent and diminishes somewhat for proportions about 70 percent or below 30 percent. The magnitude of error diminishes markedly for proportions above 90 percent and below 10 percent. For the sake of simplicity, we report confidence levels for percentages near 50 percent.

26. For an excellent table that allows us to evaluate differences between two groups, see Leslie Kish, *Survey Sampling* (New York: Wiley, 1965), 580. Kish defines the difference between two groups to be significant if the results are two standard errors apart.

27. Seventy-seven percent of the 1996 respondents were originally interviewed as part of earlier NES surveys conducted in 1992 and 1994. In order to compensate for differential attrition among respondents originally interviewed as part of earlier surveys, a weighting factor must be employed to obtain a representative sample. Thus, the results for the 1996 NES survey (as well as the 1958, 1960, 1974, 1976, 1992, and 1994 NES surveys) report the "weighted" number of cases.

For the vast majority of this book, we employ weight V960003, which is designed to provide the most representative result for the 1996 survey. However, there is also a time-series weight (V960005) that is to be used when comparing the results of the 1996 NES with earlier NES surveys. We employ this time-series weight for our analysis of the decline of electoral participation in Chapter 4. We employ the weights originally released with the survey in April 1997. A memorandum issued by the NES in October 1997 reported that "Early analysis suggests that the weight variables included in the 1996 NES data file may not compensate sufficiently for panel attrition in the 1996 sample, especially when examining trends in voter turnout." The NES announced that it was introducing a new weight in December 1997, along with supporting documentation. This new weight was not available when our analyses were conducted.

1. THE NOMINATION STRUGGLE

1. See Paul R. Abramson, John H. Aldrich, and David W. Rohde, *Change and Continuity in the 1992 Elections,* rev. ed. (Washington, D.C.: CQ Press, 1995), 26–30.

2. Technically, Dornan simply retired from the field rather than actually withdrew. Indeed, he was not completely inactive in the primary season in 1996.

3. See Joseph A. Schlesinger, *Ambition and Politics: Political Careers in the United States* (Chicago: Rand McNally, 1966) and *Political Parties and the Winning of Office* (Ann Arbor: University of Michigan Press, 1991).

4. The Republican party has always used simple majority rule to select nominees. The Democratic party required that the nominee be selected by a two-thirds majority in every convention from its founding (except 1840) until 1936, when it changed to simple majority.

5. Since some states object to this feature or registration with a party at all, any Democratic delegates selected would not be recognized, therefore such state parties use other procedures for choosing their delegates.

6. Beginning with the 1980 campaign, the Democratic party requires that all its state parties select their delegates within a three-month "window," beginning in March. Designed to reduce the length of the primary season, they excepted Iowa and New Hampshire anyway, to respect their "traditions." The Republicans have no such rules, but many (although not all) states follow the Democratic example. Because primary elections are run by state governments and to reduce the considerable expense involved, both party primaries are held at the same time and thus are held within the confines of the Democratic window.

7. The importance of "momentum" and related dynamics is developed in John H. Aldrich, *Before the Convention: Strategies and Choices in Presidential Nomination Campaigns* (Chicago: University of Chicago Press, 1980). See also, Larry M. Bartels, *Presidential Primaries and the Dynamics of Public Choice* (Princeton: Princeton University Press, 1988).

8. He was aided in part by virtue of the one-third of the delegates who had been selected in 1967, before Johnson's renomination was opposed.

9. The Republican party does not require that its delegates be bound. Many states (especially those that hold primaries and write their laws following Democratic party rules) do bind Republican delegates.

10. Caucuses were held in seventeen of the fifty-two events on the Democratic side in 1996, with the larger number reflecting the requirement that primaries be restricted to party members and other specifically Democratic restrictions.

11. See his Table 1.1 and discussion about those data in William G. Mayer, "The Presidential Nominations," *The Election of 1996: Reports and Interpretations* (Chatham, N.J.: Chatham House 1997), 21–76. Table 1.1 is on page 23.

12. The most important adaption politicians have made to campaign finance is the acquisition and use of "soft money," that is, money that can be raised and spent without limit for party building and turnout efforts. Soft money became controversial in 1996 because of the increasingly vast sums raised, the sources of contributions, and of the alleged misuse of soft money for promoting election of candidates. Soft money is not, however, a major factor in intraparty competition, including presidential nomination campaigns.

13. *Time,* March 13, 1995, 80; see also the discussion in Mayer, *op cit.*

14. We believe the other important question is how Dole nearly lost the nomination at the outset. The answer to that question indicates the important roles relatively extreme and deeply committed activists play in nominations in both parties. Even so, we believe that his rapid recovery and victory tell us more about contemporary nomination politics and the increasing biases toward front-runners.

2. THE GENERAL ELECTION CAMPAIGN

1. See, for example, the data cited in *USA Today* from surveys done by the Gallup organization, November 4, 1997, 8A.

2. *USA Today,* September 4, 1996, 1A, 9A.

3. *New York Times,* September 6, 1996, A1.

4. Ibid., A11.

5. *USA Today,* August 9, 1996, 2A.

6. See Paul R. Abramson, John H. Aldrich, and David W. Rohde, *Change and Continuity in the 1992 Elections,* rev. ed. (Washington D.C.: CQ Press, 1995), 48–49.

7. Discussions of this conflict are presented in Elizabeth Drew, *Showdown: The Struggle between the Gingrich Congress and the Clinton White House* (New

York: Simon and Schuster, 1996); and David W. Rohde, "Parties, Institutional Control, and Political Incentives: A Perspective on Governing in the Clinton Presidency" (paper presented at the colloquium "The Clinton Years in Perspective," Université de Montréal, October 6–8, 1996).

8. *Congressional Quarterly Weekly Report,* January 27, 1996, 258.

9. The information for this account is drawn from a CNN analysis reported on the "All-Politics" Web site on April 2, 1996 (http://www.allpolitics.com).

10. *Washington Post,* April 20, 1996, A9.

11. Adam Nagourny and Elizabeth Kolbert, "Missteps Doomed Dole from the Start," *New York Times,* November 8, 1996, A1.

12. *New York Times,* September 6, 1996, A11.

13. *Newsweek,* November 18, 1996, 109.

14. *USA Today,* September 3, 1996, 4A.

15. *Hotline,* September 4, 1996. In addition, 18 percent thought that both campaigns had been too negative, whereas 40 percent said neither had been.

16. *Newsweek,* November 18, 1996, 109.

17. *New York Times,* September 3, 1996, A1.

18. Ibid., September 4, 1996, A12.

19. Ibid., September 13, 1996, A1.

20. Ibid., September 12, 1996, B9; *Washington Post,* September 12, 1996, A16.

21. Quoted in the *New York Times,* September 11, 1996, B9.

22. Quoted in the *Washington Post,* September 22, 1996, A1.

23. Ibid., September 7, 1996, A4.

24. *New York Times,* September 13, 1996, A1.

25. The text is reported in the *New York Times,* September 11, 1996, B9.

26. Ibid., November 7, 1996, B5.

27. Reported in *Newsweek,* November 18, 1996, 104. In fact, we believe that this claim is highly problematic; see Paul R. Abramson et al., "Third Party and Independent Candidates in American Politics," *Political Science Quarterly* 110 (Fall 1995): 349–367.

28. *Newsweek,* November 18, 1996, 105.

29. *New York Times,* September 19, 1996, A16.

30. *Newsweek,* November 18, 1996, 114.

31. Quoted in the *Congressional Quarterly Weekly Report,* October 12, 1996, 2934–2935.

32. *New York Times,* October 9, 1996, A1; ibid., October 10, 1996, A14.

33. Ibid., October 11, 1996, A11.

34. Quoted in ibid., October 14, 1996, A11; ibid., October 16, 1996, A13.

35. Ibid., October 22, 1996, A12.

36. Ibid., October 18, 1996, C20.

37. Ibid., October 23, 1996, A1, A12.

38. Ibid., October 19, 1996, 8.

39. *Washington Post,* October 25, 1996, A1.

40. *New York Times,* October 26, 1996, A1, A10.

41. Ibid., November 5, 1996, A15.

42. Ibid., November 4, 1996, A1, and November 5, 1996, A1.

43. Ibid.

44. Thomas M. Holbrook, "Did the Campaign Matter?" (paper presented at the annual meeting of the Midwest Political Science Association, Chicago, Ill., April 10–12, 1997, 20). See also Thomas Holbrook, *Do Campaigns Matter?* (Thousand Oaks, Calif.: Sage Publications, 1996).

45. For a discussion of the concept of party identification, see Chapter 8. For the questions used to measure party identification, see Chapter 4, note 52. The question used to measure the point at which the respondent decided how to vote was asked in the postelection interview and read as follows: "How long before the election did you decide that you were going to vote the way you did?" As with our subsequent analysis of the presidential vote, we exclude seventeen respondents who reported voting for other presidential candidates. It should be noted that the reported share of the vote for Clinton is somewhat higher than his actual share, and the proportions for Dole and Perot are somewhat lower. This issue is discussed in Chapter 5.

46. The five successful incumbents (and their average approval in Gallup surveys conducted in March, April, and May) were Eisenhower 1956 (70 percent), Johnson 1964 (76 percent), Nixon 1972 (56 percent), Reagan 1984 (54 percent), and Clinton 1996 (54 percent). The unsuccessful candidates were Johnson 1968 (36 percent), Ford 1976 (48 percent), Carter 1980 (40 percent), and Bush 1992 (40 percent). (Johnson's approval rating is only for March, because he withdrew from consideration at the end of that month.) The approval data are from Gallup polls, and for presidents through Reagan they were obtained from George C. Edwards III, ed., with Alec M. Gallup, *Presidential Approval: A Source Book* (Baltimore, Md.: Johns Hopkins University Press, 1990). For Bush and Clinton, the data were taken, respectively, from the August 1992 and the May 1996 issues of *Gallup Poll Monthly.*

3. THE ELECTION RESULTS

1. For the popular vote for president, by state, from 1824 through 1992, see *Presidential Elections, 1789–1992* (Washington, D.C.: Congressional Quarterly Inc., 1995), 89–128.

2. In the disputed election of 1876, records suggest that Samuel J. Tilden, the Democrat, won 51.0 percent of the popular vote and that Rutherford B. Hayes, the Republican and the declared winner, won 48.0 percent. In 1888 Grover Cleveland, the incumbent Democratic president, won 48.6 percent of the vote, but lost to the Republican challenger, Benjamin Harrison, who won 47.8 percent of the vote.

3. The twelve winners prior to Clinton were James K. Polk (Democrat) in 1844 with 49.5 percent; Zachary Taylor (Whig) in 1848 with 47.3 percent; James Buchanan (Democrat) in 1856 with 45.3 percent; Abraham Lincoln (Republican) in 1860 with 39.9 percent; James A. Garfield (Republican) in 1880 with 48.3 percent; Grover Cleveland (Democrat) in 1884 with 48.5 percent; Cleveland in 1892 with 46.1 percent; Woodrow Wilson (Democrat) in 1912 with 41.8 percent; Wilson in 1916 with 49.2 percent; Harry S. Truman (Democrat) in 1948 with 49.6 percent; John F. Kennedy (Democrat) in 1960 with 49.7 percent; and Richard M. Nixon (Republican) in 1968 with 43.4 percent.

4. Britain provides an excellent example of the effects of the plurality-vote win system on third parties. In Britain, like the United States, candidates for the national legislature run in single-member districts, and in all British parliamentary districts the plurality-vote winner is elected. Since the 1935 General Election, the Liberal party (and more recently the Alliance and the Liberal Democrats) has always received a smaller share of the seats in the House of Commons than it won by the popular vote.

5. The New England states include Connecticut, Maine, Massachusetts, New Hampshire, Rhode Island, and Vermont. Although the U.S. Bureau of the Census classifies several border states as well as the District of Columbia as southern, we use an explicitly political definition of the South: the eleven states that made up the old Confederacy, which are Alabama, Arkansas, Florida, Georgia, Louisiana, Mississippi, North Carolina, South Carolina, Tennessee, Texas, and Virginia.

6. The mountain states include Arizona, Colorado, Idaho, Montana, Nevada, New Mexico, Utah, and Wyoming.

7. Third-party candidates are not always underrepresented in the electoral college. In 1948 J. Strom Thurmond, the States' Rights Democrat, won only 2.4 percent of the popular vote, but he won 7.3 percent of the electoral votes. Thurmond won 55 percent of his total popular vote in the four states that he carried (Alabama, Louisiana, Mississippi, and South Carolina), all of which had very low turnout. He received no popular votes at all in thirty-one of the forty-eight states.

8. Maurice Duverger, *Political Parties: Their Organization and Activity in the Modern World,* trans. Barbara North and Robert North (New York: Wiley, 1963), 217. In the original, Duverger's formulation is, "le scrutin majoritaire à un seul

tour tend au dualism des partis." Duverger, *Les Partis Politiques,* 3d ed. (Paris: Armand Colin, 1958), 247; *Political Partis,* 218. For a discussion of Duverger's law, see William H. Riker, "The Two-Party System and Duverger's Law: An Essay on the History of Political Science," *American Political Science Review* 76 (December 1982): 753–766. For a more recent statement of Duverger's views, see Duverger, "Duverger's Law: Forty Years Later" in *Electoral Laws and Their Political Consequences,* ed. Bernard Grofman and Arend Lijphart (New York: Agathan Press, 1986), 69–84. For an extensive discussion of the effects of electoral rules on political outcomes, see Rein Taagepera and Matthew Soberg Shugart, *Seats and Votes: The Effects and Determinants of Electoral Systems* (New Haven, Conn.: Yale University Press, 1989).

9. William H. Riker, *The Art of Political Manipulation* (New Haven, Conn.: Yale University Press, 1986), 79.

10. Gerald M. Pomper, "The Presidential Election," in *The Election of 1992: Reports and Interpretations,* ed. Gerald M. Pomper et al. (Chatham, N.J.: Chatham House, 1993), 135.

11. For a comparison of the U.S. and French systems for electing presidents, see Paul R. Abramson et al., "Third-Party and Independent Candidates in American Politics: Wallace, Anderson, and Perot," *Political Science Quarterly* 110 (Fall 1995): 349–397. For an argument against runoff systems, see Mark P. Jones, *Electoral Laws and the Survival of Presidential Democracies* (Notre Dame, Ind.: Notre Dame University Press, 1995).

12. The Marquis de Condorcet (1743–1794) was a French philosopher. For a discussion of his principles of social choice, see Duncan Black, *The Theory of Committees and Elections* (Cambridge: Cambridge University Press, 1958). For evidence on the 1968, 1980, and 1992 elections, see Abramson et al., "Third-Party and Independent Candidates."

13. For a discussion of agenda setting during this period, see William H. Riker, *Liberalism against Populism: A Confrontation between the Theory of Democracy and the Theory of Social Choice* (San Francisco: Freeman, 1982), 213–232, and John H. Aldrich, *Why Parties? The Origin and Transformation of Political Parties in America* (Chicago: University of Chicago Press, 1995), 126–156.

14. Michael Nelson, "The Presidential Election," in *The Elections of 1988,* ed. Michael Nelson (Washington, D.C.: CQ Press, 1989), 195–196.

15. According to the U.S. Bureau of the Census, the West includes thirteen states: Alaska, Arizona, California, Colorado, Hawaii, Idaho, Montana, Nevada, New Mexico, Oregon, Utah, Washington, and Wyoming. But as Walter Dean Burnham has pointed out, for presidential elections the 96th meridian of longitude provides a dividing line. See Walter Dean Burnham, "The 1980 Earthquake: Realignment, Reaction, or What?" in *The Hidden Election: Politics and Econom-*

ics in the 1980 Presidential Campaign, ed. Thomas Ferguson and Joel Rogers (New York: Pantheon, 1981), 111. For our discussion in this chapter, we therefore consider Kansas, Nebraska, North Dakota, and South Dakota to be western. Even though Texas lies mainly to the west of the 96th meridian, we have classified it as southern, since it was a former Confederate state.

16. U.S. Department of Commerce, Bureau of the Census, *Statistical Abstract of the United States,* 101st ed. (Washington, D.C.: U.S. Government Printing Office, 1980).

17. See Paul R. Abramson, John H. Aldrich, and David W. Rohde, *Change and Continuity in the 1992 Elections,* rev. ed. (Washington, D.C.: CQ Press, 1994), 82–85.

18. Bill Schneider, "A New Sectionalism in American Politics," CNN "All-Politics" Web site, December 11, 1996 (http://www.allpolitics.com).

19. See Joseph A. Schlesinger, *Political Parties and the Winning of Office* (Ann Arbor: University of Michigan Press, 1991), Figure 5-1, 112. Schlesinger does not report the exact values, but he has provided them to us in a personal communication. Inclusion of the District of Columbia, which has voted since 1964, increases the standard deviation, since it always votes more Democratic than any state. We report only Schlesinger's results for the states, not the alternative results that include the District of Columbia.

20. V. O. Key, Jr., *Southern Politics in State and Nation* (New York: Alfred A. Knopf, 1949), 5.

21. There have been many excellent studies of change in the postwar South. For one that presents state-by-state results, see Alexander P. Lamis, *The Two Party South,* 2d expanded ed. (New York: Oxford University Press, 1990). For two others, see Earl Black and Merle Black, *Politics and Society in the Postwar South* (Cambridge, Mass.: Harvard University Press, 1987); and Black and Black, *The Vital South: How Presidents Are Elected* (Cambridge, Mass.: Harvard University Press, 1991).

22. Alabama, Georgia, Louisiana, Mississippi, and South Carolina are generally considered to be the five Deep South states. These are also the five southern states with the highest percentage of African-Americans.

23. Southern politicians also suffered additional setbacks at the 1948 Democratic presidential nominating convention. Their attempts to weaken the civil rights plank of the party platform were defeated. In addition, Hubert H. Humphrey, then mayor of Minneapolis, argued that the proposed civil rights platform was too weak and offered an amendment to the platform for a stronger statement. Humphrey's amendment was passed by a 651½ to 582½ vote margin.

24. Kennedy made a symbolic gesture that may have helped him with African-Americans. Three weeks before the election, Martin Luther King, Jr., was ar-

rested in Atlanta for taking part in a sit-in demonstration. Although all the other demonstrators were released, King was held on a technicality and sent to the Georgia State Penitentiary. Kennedy telephoned King's wife to express his concern, and his brother, Robert F. Kennedy, made a direct appeal to a Georgia judge, which led to King's release on bail. This incident received little notice in the press but had a great effect in the African-American community. For an account, see Theodore H. White, *The Making of the President, 1960* (New York: Atheneum, 1961), 321–323.

25. See Abramson, Aldrich, and Rohde, *Change and Continuity in the 1992 Elections,* rev. ed., Figure 2-1, 47.

26. Marjorie Randon Hershey, "The Campaign and the Media," in *The Election of 1988: Reports and Interpretations,* ed. Gerald M. Pomper et al. (Chatham, N.J.: Chatham House, 1989), 74.

27. Michael Nelson, "Constitutional Aspects of the Elections," in *The Elections of 1988,* 193–195; James C. Garand and Wayne T. Parent, "Representation, Swing, and Bias in U.S. Presidential Elections: 1872–1988," *American Journal of Political Science* 35 (November 1992): 1001–1031.

28. See Abramson, Aldrich, and Rohde, *Change and Continuity in the 1992 Elections,* rev. ed., 89.

29. For an interesting, if alarmist, discussion of this possibility, see David W. Abbott and James P. Levine, *Wrong Winner: The Coming Debacle in the Electoral College* (New York: Praeger, 1991).

INTRODUCTION TO PART 2

1. For an excellent collection of articles dealing with some of the major controversies, see Richard G. Niemi and Herbert F. Weisberg, eds., *Controversies in Voting Behavior,* 3d ed. (Washington, D.C.: CQ Press, 1993). For another excellent summary of research in this area, see Russell J. Dalton and Martin P. Wattenberg, "The Not So Simple Act of Voting," in *Political Science: The State of the Discipline II,* ed. Ada W. Finifter (Washington, D.C.: American Political Science Association, 1993), 193–218.

2. For an excellent summary of alternative theoretical perspectives to the study of political behavior, see Edward G. Carmines and Robert Huckfeldt, "Political Behavior: An Overview," in *A New Handbook of Political Science,* ed. Robert E. Goodin and Hans-Dieter Klingemann (New York: Oxford University Press, 1996), 223–254.

3. Paul F. Lazarsfeld, Bernard Berelson, and Hazel Gaudet, *The People's Choice: How the Voter Makes Up His Mind in a Presidential Campaign,* 2d ed. (New York:

Columbia University Press, 1948), 27. See also, Bernard R. Berelson, Paul F. Lazarsfeld, and William N. McPhee, *Voting: A Study of Opinion Formation in a Presidential Campaign* (Chicago: University of Chicago Press, 1954).

4. See Robert R. Alford, *Party and Society: The Anglo-American Democracies* (Chicago: Rand McNally, 1963); Richard F. Hamilton, *Class and Politics in the United States* (New York: Wiley, 1972); and Seymour Martin Lipset, *Political Man: The Social Bases of Politics,* expanded ed. (Baltimore: Johns Hopkins University Press, 1981). For a more recent book that uses this perspective, see Chandler Davidson, *Race and Class in Texas Politics* (Princeton, N.J.: Princeton University Press, 1990).

5. Angus Campbell et al., *The American Voter* (New York: Wiley, 1960).

6. For the single best essay summarizing Converse's views on voting behavior, see Philip E. Converse, "Public Opinion and Voting Behavior," in *Nongovernmental Politics,* ed. Fred I. Greenstein and Nelson W. Polsby, vol. 4 of *Handbook of Political Science* (Reading, Mass.: Addison-Wesley, 1975), 75–169. For an excellent summary of research from a social-psychological point of view, see Donald R. Kinder and David O. Sears, "Public Opinion and Political Action," in *Special Fields and Applications,* 3d ed., ed. Gardner Lindzey and Elliot Aronson, vol. 2 of *Handbook of Social Psychology* (New York: Random House, 1985), 659–741. For an alternative approach to the study of political psychology, see Paul M. Sniderman, Richard A. Brody, and Philip E. Tetlock, with others, *Reasoning and Choice: Explorations in Political Psychology* (Cambridge: Cambridge University Press, 1991). See also Sniderman, "The New Look in Public Opinion Research," in *Political Science: The State of the Discipline II,* ed. Ada W. Finifter (Washington, D.C.: American Political Science Association, 1993), 219–245. For another perspective, see John R. Zaller, *The Nature and Origins of Mass Opinion* (Cambridge: Cambridge University Press, 1992).

7. Warren E. Miller and J. Merrill Shanks, *The New American Voter* (Cambridge, Mass.: Harvard University Press, 1996). Although reemphasizing the importance of party identification, this work also demonstrates a shift away from the social-psychological tradition employed by Miller and his colleagues in *The American Voter.*

8. Anthony Downs, *An Economic Theory of Democracy* (New York: Harper & Row, 1957); William H. Riker, *A Theory of Political Coalitions* (New Haven, Conn.: Yale University Press, 1962).

9. See, for example, William H. Riker and Peter C. Ordeshook, "A Theory of the Calculus of Voting," *American Political Science Review* 62 (March 1968): 25–32; John A. Ferejohn and Morris P. Fiorina, "The Paradox of Not Voting: A Decision Theoretic Analysis," *American Political Science Review* 68 (June 1974): 525–536; and Morris P. Fiorina, *Retrospective Voting in American National Elec-*

tions (New Haven, Conn.: Yale University Press, 1981). For summaries of much of this research, see Melvin J. Hinich and Michael Munger, *Analytical Politics* (Cambridge: Cambridge University Press, 1997); and Kenneth A. Shepsle and Mark S. Bonchek, *Analyzing Politics: Rationality, Behavior, and Institutions* (New York: Norton, 1997). For an interesting perspective that combines rational choice and psychological perspectives, see Samuel L. Popkin, *The Reasoning Voter: Communication and Persuasion in Presidential Campaigns* (Chicago: University of Chicago Press, 1991).

10. The most important exception, at least in the study of elections, is Fiorina's *Retrospective Voting*, which we refer to extensively. For an interesting critique of the rational choice perspective, see Donald P. Green and Ian Shapiro, *Pathologies of Rational Choice Theory: A Critique of Applications in Political Science* (New Haven, Conn.: Yale University Press, 1994). For critiques of Green and Shapiro's work, see Jeffrey Friedman, ed., *The Rational Choice Controversy: Economic Models of Politics Reconsidered* (New Haven, Conn.: Yale University Press, 1996).

4. WHO VOTED?

1. For two excellent discussions of why electoral participation is lower in the United States than in other industrialized democracies, see G. Bingham Powell, Jr., "American Voter Turnout in Comparative Perspective," *American Political Science Review* 80 (March 1986): 17–43, and Robert W. Jackman, "Political Institutions and Voter Turnout in Industrialized Democracies," *American Political Science Review* 81 (June 1987): 405–423. For a discussion of the problem of low turnout in other democracies, see Arend Lijphart, "Unequal Participation: Democracy's Unresolved Dilemma," *American Political Science Review* 91 (March 1997): 1–14.

2. This chapter focuses on only one form of political participation, voting. For a discussion of other forms of political participation in the United States, as well as a different perspective on electoral participation, see M. Margaret Conway, *Political Participation in the United States,* 2d ed. (Washington, D.C.: CQ Press, 1991). For a major study of many forms of political participation in the United States, see Sidney Verba, Kay Lehman Schlozman, and Henry E. Brady, *Voice and Equality: Civic Voluntarism in American Politics* (Cambridge, Mass.: Harvard University Press, 1995).

3. It is difficult to calculate the total number of voters, and in most elections more people vote for president than for any other office. In 1996 there were eight states in which more voters cast their ballots for gubernatorial or senatorial candidates than for president. To maintain comparability through time, we estimate turnout based on the number of votes cast for president.

4. During the 1916 election women had full voting rights only in Arizona, California, Colorado, Idaho, Kansas, Montana, Nevada, Oregon, Utah, Washington, and Wyoming. Only 10 percent of the U.S population lived in these states. For a provocative discussion of the struggle for women's right to vote, see Alan P. Grimes, *The Puritan Ethic and Woman Suffrage* (New York: Oxford University Press, 1967).

5. See J. Morgan Kousser, *The Shaping of Southern Politics: Suffrage Restrictions and the Establishment of the One-Party South, 1880–1910* (New Haven, Conn.: Yale University Press, 1974). For a more general discussion of the decline of turnout in the late nineteenth century, see Paul Kleppner, *Who Voted? The Dynamics of Electoral Turnout, 1870–1980* (New York: Praeger, 1982), 55–82.

6. There has been a great deal of disagreement about the reasons for and the consequences of registration requirements. For some of the more interesting arguments, see Walter Dean Burnham, "The Changing Shape of the American Political Universe," *American Political Science Review* 59 (March 1965): 7–28; Philip E. Converse, "Change in the American Electorate," in *The Human Meaning of Social Change,* ed. Angus Campbell and Philip E. Converse (New York: Russell Sage, 1972), 266–301; and Walter Dean Burnham, "Theory and Voting Research: Some Reflections on Converse's 'Change in the American Electorate,'" *American Political Science Review* 68 (September 1974): 1002–1023. For another provocative discussion, see Frances Fox Piven and Richard A. Cloward, *Why Americans Don't Vote* (New York: Pantheon, 1988), 26–95.

7. For a rich source of information about the introduction of the Australian ballot and its effects, see Jerrold G. Rusk, "The Effect of the Australian Ballot on Split Ticket Voting: 1876–1908," *American Political Science Review* 64 (December 1970): 1220–1238.

8. For example, see Burnham's estimates of turnout among the voting-age population, which include results through 1984. These appear in Walter Dean Burnham, "The Turnout Problem," in *Elections American Style,* ed. A. James Reichley (Washington, D.C.: Brookings Institution, 1987), 113–114. Because Burnham's turnout denominator is smaller than ours, his estimates of turnout are somewhat larger. Although there are advantages to Burnham's calculations, we use the voting-age population as our base for two reasons. First, it is difficult to estimate the size of the noncitizen population, and official estimates by the U.S. Bureau of the Census use the voting-age population as the turnout denominator. Second, even though only citizens can vote in present-day U.S. elections, citizenship is not a constitutional requirement of voting. National legislation determines how long it takes to become a citizen, and state law imposes citizenship as a condition of voting. According to Burnham's estimates, turnout among the voting-age citizen population in

1988 was 52.7 percent, in 1992 it was 56.9 percent, and in 1996 it was 50.8 percent. (Based on personal communications, June 21, 1993, and July 1, 1997.)

9. The estimate of turnout among the politically eligible population is based on Burnham, "The Turnout Problem."

10. See Glenn Firebaugh and Kevin Chen, "Vote Turnout of Nineteenth Amendment Women: The Enduring Effects of Disfranchisement," *American Journal of Sociology* 100 (January 1995): 972–996.

11. Robert Toner, "Parties Pressing to Raise Turnout as Election Nears," *New York Times,* October 27, 1996, Y1, Y14.

12. For our analysis of the reasons for the increase in turnout in 1992, see Paul R. Abramson, John H. Aldrich, and David W. Rohde, *Change and Continuity in the 1992 Elections,* rev. ed. (Washington D.C.: CQ Press, 1995), 120–123. As we point out, it is difficult to demonstrate empirically that Perot's candidacy made an important contribution to the increase in turnout. For additional analyses, see Stephen M. Nichols and Paul Allen Beck, "Reversing the Decline: Voter Turnout in 1992," in *Democracy's Feast: Elections in America,* ed. Herbert F. Weisberg (Chatham, N.J.: Chatham House, 1995), 62–65; and Steven J. Rosenstone, Roy L. Behr, and Edward H. Lazarus, *Third Parties in America: Citizen Response to Major Party Failure,* 2d ed. (Princeton, N.J.: Princeton University Press, 1996), 254–257.

13. Toner, "Parties Pressing to Raise Turnout."

14. In our analyses of the 1980, 1984, 1988, and 1992 elections we also reported extensively on the Current Population Surveys conducted by the U.S. Census Bureau. Unfortunately, as a result of technical problems, only preliminary results from the 1996 survey were available when this chapter was written.

15. Eleven respondents who said they voted in the election but did not vote for president have been classified as nonvoters. When the time-series weight is employed (see the introduction to Part 1, note 27), 75.8 percent report voting for president. As with our analysis of the 1992 NES survey, we employ the time-series weight in our analysis of the decline of turnout in the section of this chapter entitled, "Why Did Turnout Decline?"

16. Respondents are asked the following question: "In talking to people about the elections, we often find that a lot of people were not able to vote because they weren't registered, they were sick, or they just didn't have time. How about you—did you vote in the elections this November?"

17. Vote validation studies were conducted after the 1964, 1976, 1980, 1984, and 1988 presidential elections and after the 1978, 1986, and 1990 midterm elections. Mainly for reasons of cost, these studies were discontinued after 1990. Fortunately, even though studies were not conducted in the most recent elections,

these past studies provide considerable information about the sources of bias in overreports of voting.

Most analyses that compare results of reported turnout with turnout as measured by the vote validation studies suggest that *relative* levels of turnout among most social groups can be measured using reported turnout. However, research also suggests that blacks are consistently more likely falsely to report voting than whites. As a result, turnout differences between the races are always greater when turnout is measured by the vote validation studies. For results between 1964 and 1988, see Paul R. Abramson and William Claggett, "Racial Differences in Self-Reported and Validated Turnout in the 1988 Presidential Elections," *Journal of Politics* 53 (February 1991): 186–187. For the results for 1990, see Abramson, Aldrich, and Rohde, *Change and Continuity in the 1992 Elections,* rev. ed., 382.

For an extensive discussion of the factors that contribute to false reports of voting, see Brian D. Silver, Barbara A. Anderson, and Paul R. Abramson, "Who Overreports Voting?" *American Political Science Review* 80 (June 1986): 613–624.

18. See Michael W. Traugott and John P. Katosh, "Response Validity in Surveys of Voting Behavior," *Public Opinion Quarterly* 43 (Fall 1979): 359–377; and Barbara A. Anderson, Brian D. Silver, and Paul R. Abramson, "The Effects of Race of the Interviewer on Measures of Electoral Participation by Blacks in SRC National Election Studies," *Public Opinion Quarterly* 52 (Spring 1988): 53–83.

19. These results are based on the Web site maintained by the U.S. Bureau of the Census (http://www.census.gov/population/socdemo/voting/history.vote. prn). According to the Current Population Survey conducted in November 1996, 54.2 percent of the voting-age population voted. Although this result is 5 points higher than the actual turnout among the voting-age population, it is far closer to the actual result than the NES survey figure. According to information provided by Martin O'Connell of the U.S. Bureau of the Census, the 1996 Current Population Survey is based on interviews conducted in 50,000 households and provides information on about 90,000 adults. For a discussion of the strengths and limitations of the Current Population Survey, see Abramson, Aldrich, and Rohde, *Change and Continuity in the 1992 Elections,* rev. ed., 105–106.

20. The vote validation studies are not free from error, for some true voters may be classified as validated nonvoters if no record can be found of their being registered to vote or if the voting records incorrectly fail to show that they voted. The voting records where blacks tend to live are not as well maintained as those where whites are likely to live. Still, it seems unlikely that the finding that blacks are more likely than whites falsely to report voting results from the poorer quality of black voting records. See Paul R. Abramson and William Claggett, "The Quality of Record Keeping and Racial Differences in Validated Turnout," *Journal of Politics* 54 (August 1992): 871–880.

21. See Katherine Tate, "Black Political Participation in the 1984 and 1988 Presidential Elections," *American Political Science Review* 85 (December 1991): 1159–1176. For a more extensive discussion, see Tate, *From Protest to Politics: The New Black Voters in American Elections,* enlarged ed. (Cambridge, Mass.: Harvard University Press, 1994).

22. As we explain in Chapter 3, we consider the South to include the eleven states of the old Confederacy. In our analyses of NES surveys, however, we do not classify residents of Tennessee as southern, because the University of Michigan Survey Research Center conducts samples in Tennessee to represent the border states. In this analysis, as well as analyses of regional differences using the NES surveys later in this book, we classify the following ten states as southern: Alabama, Arkansas, Florida, Georgia, Louisiana, Mississippi, North Carolina, South Carolina, Texas, and Virginia.

23. Hispanics may be of any race, but far more Hispanics are white than black. Among the 163 respondents classified as Hispanic in the 1996 NES survey, 85 percent were white and only 12 percent were black. Among Hispanics, respondents are classified as Mexican, Puerto Rican, Cuban, Latin American, Central American, Spanish, and other. However, the total number of Hispanics is too small to permit detailed analysis of their political behavior.

24. See Raymond E. Wolfinger and Steven J. Rosenstone, *Who Votes?* (New Haven, Conn.: Yale University Press, 1980), 93–94.

25. Ibid., 46–50.

26. We use this distinction mainly because it allows us to make comparisons over many elections, and is especially valuable for studying change over the entire postwar period, as we do in Chapter 5. However, since the 1988 presidential election survey, the NES surveys have not noted whether the respondent is the head of household. In all of our previous analyses, we classified respondents according to their head of household's occupation. Classification according to head of household's occupation is generally considered a more valid measure of a married woman's social class than her own occupation. Many women employed at relatively unskilled nonmanual jobs are married to manually employed men. Their social and political behavior appears to be affected more by their husband's occupation than by their own. In our analyses of the 1988, 1992, and 1996 surveys, we classified married women according to their husband's occupation. A reanalysis of the 1984 NES survey suggests that we came very close to reproducing our earlier measure, which was based directly on the head of household's occupation.

27. Our measure of family income is based on the respondent's estimate of his or her family's 1995 income before taxes. For respondents who refused to answer this question and for those whom the interviewers thought were answering dishonestly, we relied on the interviewer's assessment of family income.

28. See Wolfinger and Rosenstone, *Who Votes?* 13–36.

29. Protestants, Catholics, and other Christians were asked, "Would you call yourself a born-again Christian; that is, have you personally had a conversion experience related to Jesus Christ?"

30. David C. Leege and Lyman A. Kellstedt and others, *Rediscovering the Religious Factor in American Politics* (Armonk, N.Y.: Sharpe, 1993). We are grateful to Leege for providing us with detailed information about the procedures used to construct this variable. We constructed the measure as follows: respondents who prayed several times a day received 2 points, those who prayed less often received 1 point, and those who never prayed received 0 points; those who attended religious services at least once a week received 2 points, those who attended religious services less frequently received 1 point, and those who never attended received 0 points; those who said religion provided "a great deal" of guidance in their lives received 2 points, those who said it provided "quite a bit" of guidance received 1 point, and those who said it provided "some" or no guidance received 0 points; respondents who said the Bible was literally true or the "word of God" received 2 points, and those who said it "was written by men and is not the word of God" received 0 points. Respondents received a score of 1 point for each don't know, ambiguous, or not ascertained response, but those with more than two such responses were excluded from the analysis. Scores ranged from 0 to 8 points. In regrouping this variable into three categories, we classified respondents with 8 points as "very high," those with 6 to 7 points as "high," and those with a score below 6 as having "low or medium" religious commitment.

31. Kenneth D. Wald, *Religion and Politics in the United States,* 3d ed. (Washington, D.C.: CQ Press, 1997), 173.

32. R. Stephen Warner, *New Wine in Old Wineskins: Evangelicals and Liberals in a Small-Town Church* (Berkeley: University of California Press, 1988), 33, 34.

33. We are grateful to Leege for providing us with the specific NES codes used to classify Protestants into these religious traditions. These codes are based on the religious denomination variable in the codebook provided by the Inter-university Consortium for Political and Social Research. Categories 50, 60, 70, 100 through 109, 120 through 149, 160 through 219, 221, 222, 223, 231, 232, 233, 240, 250 through 269, 271 through 275, 280, 282, 289, 292, and 293 were classified as Evangelicals; categories 80, 90, 110, 150 through 159, 220, 229, 230, 249, 270, 276, 279, 281, 290, and 291 were classified as mainline.

34. Wolfinger and Rosenstone, *Who Votes?* 13–36.

35. Silver, Anderson, and Abramson's analysis of the 1964, 1976, and 1980 vote validation studies shows that respondents with higher levels of formal education do have very high turnout. However, their analysis also shows that persons with high levels of education who actually do not vote are more likely

falsely to claim to have voted than nonvoters with lower levels of formal education. (See Silver, Anderson, and Abramson, "Who Overreports Voting?") Our analysis shows a similar pattern with the 1978, 1984, 1986, 1988, and 1990 vote validation studies. We do not know if a similar pattern would be true in 1996, but if it is, the results in Table 4-3 may somewhat exaggerate educational differences in participation.

36. Richard A. Brody, "The Puzzle of Political Participation in America," in *The New American Political System,* ed. Anthony King (Washington, D.C.: American Enterprise Institute, 1978), 287–324.

37. Walter Dean Burnham, "The 1976 Election: Has the Crisis Been Adjourned?" in *American Politics and Public Policy,* ed. Walter Dean Burnham and Martha Wager Weinberg (Cambridge, Mass.: MIT Press, 1978), 24; Thomas E. Cavanagh, "Changes in American Voter Turnout, 1964–1976," *Political Science Quarterly* 96 (Spring 1981): 53–65.

38. Ruy A. Teixeira, *The Disappearing American Voter* (Washington, D.C.: American Enterprise Institute, 1992), 66–67. Teixeira is skeptical about the findings from NES surveys that show that turnout did not decline among college graduates.

39. Jan E. Leighley and Jonathan Nagler, "Socioeconomic Class Bias in Turnout, 1964–1988: The Voters Remain the Same," *American Political Science Review* 86 (September 1992): 728–730. For an analysis of congressional elections from 1968 through 1994 that supports Leighley and Nagler's conclusions, see Todd G. Shields and Robert K. Goidel, *American Journal of Political Science* 41 (April 1997): 683–691.

40. For estimates of the impact of generational replacement between 1956 and 1980, see Paul R. Abramson, *Political Attitudes in America: Formation and Change* (San Francisco: Freeman, 1983), 56–61.

41. This procedure assumes that overall educational levels were the same in 1996 as they were in 1960 but that reported turnout within each educational level was the same level actually observed in the 1996 survey.

42. Teixeira, *The Disappearing American Voter,* 46–47.

43. Steven J. Rosenstone and John Mark Hansen, *Mobilization, Participation, and Democracy in America* (New York: Macmillan, 1993), 214–215.

44. Teixeira, *The Disappearing American Voter,* 47.

45. Rosenstone and Hansen, *Mobilization, Participation, and Democracy,* 215.

46. Warren E. Miller, "The Puzzle Transformed: Explaining Declining Turnout," *Political Behavior* 14, no. 1 (1992): 1–43. See also, Warren E. Miller and J. Merrill Shanks, *The New American Voter* (Cambridge, Mass.: Harvard University Press, 1996), 95–114.

47. Teixeira, *The Disappearing American Voter,* 75–81. Rosenstone and Hansen,

Mobilization, Participation, and Democracy, 136–141. Teixeira provides an explicit critique of Miller's analysis.

48. George I. Balch, "Multiple Indicators in Survey Research: The Concept 'Sense of Political Efficacy,'" *Political Methodology* 1 (Spring 1974): 1–43. For an extensive discussion of feelings of political efficacy, see Abramson, *Political Attitudes in America,* 135–189.

49. Teixeira, *Why Americans Don't Vote: Turnout Decline in the United States, 1960–1984* (New York: Greenwood Press, 1987). In his more recent study, *The Disappearing American Voter,* Teixeira develops a measure of party-related characteristics that includes strength of party identification, concern about the electoral outcome, perceived differences between the parties, and knowledge of the parties and candidates (40–42).

50. Paul R. Abramson, John H. Aldrich, and David W. Rohde, *Change and Continuity in the 1980 Elections,* rev. ed. (Washington, D.C.: CQ Press, 1983), 85–87. For a more detailed analysis using probability procedures to estimate the impact of these attitudinal changes, see Abramson and Aldrich, "The Decline of Electoral Participation in America," *American Political Science Review* 76 (September 1982): 502–521.

51. Paul R. Abramson, John H. Aldrich, and David W. Rohde, *Change and Continuity in the 1984 Elections,* rev. ed (Washington, D.C.: CQ Press, 1987), 115–118; Abramson, Aldrich, and Rohde, *Change and Continuity in the 1988 Elections,* rev. ed. (Washington, D.C.: CQ Press, 1990), 103–106; and Abramson, Aldrich, and Rohde, *Change and Continuity in the 1992 Elections,* rev. ed., 117–120.

52. Respondents are asked, "Generally speaking, do you usually think of yourself as a Republican, a Democrat, an independent, or what?" Persons who call themselves Republicans or Democrats are asked, "Would you call yourself a strong (Republican, Democrat) or a not very strong (Republican, Democrat)?" Respondents who call themselves independents, answer "no preference," or name another party are asked, "Do you think of yourself as closer to the Republican Party or to the Democratic Party?" Respondents with no partisan preferences are usually classified as independents. They are classified as "apoliticals" only if they have low levels of political interest and involvement.

53. Angus Campbell et al., *The American Voter* (New York: Wiley, 1960), 120–167.

54. This expectation follows from a rational choice perspective. For the most extensive discussion of party identification from this point of view, see Morris P. Fiorina, *Retrospective Voting in American National Elections* (New Haven, Conn.: Yale University Press, 1981), 84–105. For a recent discussion of turnout from this perspective, see John H. Aldrich, "Rational Choice and Turnout," *American Journal of Political Science* 37 (February 1993): 246–278. For a comment on

Aldrich's essay, see Robert W. Jackman, "Rationality and Political Participation," *American Journal of Political Science* 37 (February 1993): 279–290. For an extensive critique of the rational choice approach to the study of electoral participation, see Donald P. Green and Ian Shapiro, *Pathologies of Rational Choice: A Critique of Applications in Political Science* (New Haven, Conn.: Yale University Press, 1994), 47–71.

55. Respondents who disagreed with both of these statements were scored as high in their feelings of political effectiveness; those who disagreed with one but agreed with the other were scored as medium; and those who agreed with both statements were scored as low. Respondents who scored "don't know" or "not ascertained" on one question were scored high or low depending on their responses to the remaining question, and those with "don't know" or "not ascertained" responses to both questions were excluded from the analysis. In 1988, 1992, and 1996 respondents were asked whether they strongly agreed, agreed, neither agreed nor disagreed, disagreed, or strongly disagreed with both statements. For all three years, we classified respondents who responded "neither agree nor disagree" to both statements as medium on this measure. This scoring decision has little effect on the results, because only 3 percent of the respondents in 1988, 2 percent in 1992, and 3 percent in 1996 answered "neither agree nor disagree" to both statements.

56. This finding is consistent with those of Bruce E. Keith and his colleagues that independents who feel close to one of the political parties are as politically involved as weak partisans are. See Bruce E. Keith et al., *The Myth of the Independent Voter* (Berkeley: University of California Press, 1992), 38–59.

57. This calculation is based on the assumption that each partisan strength category and each sense of political efficacy category was the same as that observed in 1960 but that reported turnout in each category was the same as that observed in 1996. For a full explanation of this technique, see Abramson, *Political Attitudes in America,* 296.

58. Our estimates are based on an algebraic standardization procedure. To simplify our analysis, we combined whites who had an eighth-grade education or less with those who had not graduated from high school, and combined weak partisans with independents who leaned toward a party.

59. See Abramson, *Political Attitudes in America,* 225–238.

60. Respondents are asked, "How much of the time do you think you can trust the government in Washington to do what is right—just about always, most of the time, or only some of the time?"

61. Respondents are asked, "Would you say the government is run for a few big interests looking out for themselves, or that it is run for the benefit of all the people?"

62. Rosenstone and Hansen, *Mobilization, Participation, and Democracy,* 215, 216.

63. Respondents are asked, "The political parties try to talk to as many people as they can to get them to vote for their candidate. Did anyone from one of the political parties call you up or come around to talk with you about the campaign this year?"

64. Bear in mind that reported turnout in the 1996 NES survey was the same as reported turnout in 1992. It is possible that in failing to register the decline in actual turnout, the survey also failed to capture the short-term forces that contributed to the decline of turnout.

65. Respondents are asked who they think will be elected president. Those who name a candidate are asked, "Do you think the election will be close or do you think that [the candidate named] will win by quite a bit?" Those who say they do not know who will win are asked, "Do you think the Presidential race will be close or will one candidate win by quite a bit?"

66. See John H. Aldrich, "Some Problems in Testing Two Rational Models of Participation," *American Journal of Political Science* 20 (November 1976): 713–733.

67. Orley Ashenfelter and Stanley Kelley, Jr., "Determinants of Participation in Presidential Elections," *Journal of Law and Economics* 18 (December 1975): 721.

68. James DeNardo, "Turnout and the Vote: The Joke's on the Democrats," *American Political Science Review* 74 (June 1980): 406–420.

69. Abramson, Aldrich, and Rohde, *Change and Continuity in the 1980 Elections,* rev. ed., 88–92; Abramson, Aldrich, and Rohde, *Change and Continuity in the 1984 Elections,* rev. ed., 119–124; Abramson, Aldrich, and Rohde, *Change and Continuity in the 1988 Elections,* rev. ed., 108–113.

70. Abramson, Aldrich, and Rohde, *Change and Continuity in the 1992 Elections,* rev. ed., 124–128.

71. The results we report for 1980, 1984, and 1988 are based on the responses of people whose voting was verified through a check of voting and registration records. However, the Republican turnout advantage was also found when reported electoral participation was studied.

72. In 1996 only a randomly selected half-sample was asked the questions about the most important problem facing the country, which accounts for the relatively small number of cases in the final part of Table 4-5.

73. See Wolfinger and Rosenstone, *Who Votes?* 108–114.

74. Piven and Cloward, *Why Americans Don't Vote,* 21. For similar arguments, see Walter Dean Burnham, "Shifting Patterns of Congressional Voting Participa-

tion," in *The Current Crisis in American Politics*, ed. Walter Dean Burnham (New York: Oxford University Press, 1981), 166–203.

75. See Seymour Martin Lipset, *Political Man: The Social Bases of Politics*, expanded ed. (Baltimore: Johns Hopkins University Press, 1981), 226–229. Lipset emphasizes the danger of sudden increases in political participation.

76. Gerald M. Pomper, "The Presidential Election," in *The Election of 1980: Reports and Interpretations*, Gerald M. Pomper et al. (Chatham, N.J.: Chatham House, 1981), 86.

5. SOCIAL FORCES AND THE VOTE

1. The basic social characteristics used in this chapter are the same as those used in Chapter 4. The variables are described in notes to that chapter. For similar tables showing voting by social groups in 1980, 1984, 1988, and 1992, see Paul R. Abramson, John H. Aldrich, and David W. Rohde, *Change and Continuity in the 1980 Elections*, rev. ed. (Washington, D.C.: CQ Press, 1983), 98–99; Abramson, Aldrich, and Rohde, *Change and Continuity in the 1984 Elections*, rev. ed. (Washington, D.C.: CQ Press, 1987), 136–137; Abramson, Aldrich, and Rohde, *Change and Continuity in the 1988 Elections*, rev. ed. (Washington, D.C.: CQ Press, 1990), 124–125; and Abramson, Aldrich, and Rohde, *Change and Continuity in the 1992 Elections*, rev. ed. (Washington, D.C.: CQ Press, 1995), 133–135.

2. Unless otherwise indicated our report of the results from this exit poll are from, "Portrait of the Electorate," *New York Times*, November 10, 1996, Y16. Exit polls have three main advantages. First, they are less expensive than the multistage probability samples conducted by the University of Michigan Survey Research Center. Second, partly because of their lower cost, a large number of people can be sampled. Third, because persons are selected to be interviewed shortly after they leave the voting stations, the vast majority have actually voted for president. Despite their large size, these surveys have three disadvantages. First, the questionnaires must be fairly brief. Second, it is difficult to supervise the field staff and to ensure that the interviewers are using the proper procedures to select respondents. Last, these surveys are of little use in studying turnout, since persons who do not go to the polls are not sampled. For a discussion of the procedures used to conduct exit polls, as well as some of their limitations, see Albert H. Cantril, *The Opinion Connection: Polling, Politics, and the Press* (Washington, D.C.: CQ Press, 1991).

3. This brief discussion cannot do justice to the complexities of black electoral behavior. For an important study based on the Black National Election

Study survey conducted by the Center for Political Studies of the University of Michigan, see Patricia Gurin, Shirley J. Hatchett, and James S. Jackson, *Hope and Independence: Blacks' Response to Electoral and Party Politics* (New York: Russell Sage Foundation, 1989). For two important studies that use both the 1984 Black National Election Study survey and the 1988 follow-up study, see Michael C. Dawson, *Behind the Mule: Race and Class in African-American Politics* (Princeton, N.J.: Princeton University Press, 1994), and Katherine Tate, *From Politics to Protest: The New Black Voter in American Elections,* enlarged ed. (Cambridge, Mass.: Harvard University Press, 1994).

4. Both our analysis of the 1996 NES survey and our recalculations based on the VNS exit poll show that 17 percent of Clinton's total vote came from black voters.

5. Although we have examined the results for blacks for all of the categories presented in Table 5-1, we do not present them. Given the relatively small number of blacks sampled, the number of blacks in some of these categories is too small to present meaningful results. No black Jews were sampled in the 1996 NES survey. Given the small number of African-Americans in the 1996 NES survey, and the very skewed results, our discussion of variation among black voters is based on the VNS exit poll.

6. For a review of political science research on Hispanics, as well as research on African-Americans, see Paula D. McClain and John D. Garcia, "Expanding Disciplinary Boundaries: Black, Latino, and Racial Minority Groups in Political Science," in *Political Science: The State of the Discipline II,* ed. Ada W. Finifter (Washington, D.C.: American Political Science Association, 1993), 247–279.

7. Gerald M. Pomper, "The Presidential Election," in *The Election of 1996: Reports and Interpretations,* Gerald M. Pomper et al. (Chatham, N.J.: Chatham House, 1997), 183.

8. James W. Ceaser and Andrew E. Busch, *Losing to Win: The 1996 Elections and American Politics* (Lanham, Md.: Rowman and Littlefield, 1997), 163.

9. For an extensive review of the research literature on women and politics, see Susan J. Carroll and Linda M. G. Zerilli, "Feminist Challenges to Political Science," in *Political Science: The State of the Discipline II,* 56–76. For a global comparison, see Barbara J. Nelson and Najma Chowdhury, eds., *Women and Politics Worldwide* (New Haven, Conn.: Yale University Press, 1994).

10. See Abramson, Aldrich, and Rohde, *Change and Continuity in the 1980 Elections,* rev. ed., 290.

11. The NES survey reports six types of marital status: married and living with spouse, never married, divorced, separated, widowed, and partners who are not married. In this paragraph we compare the first two of these groups.

12. Paul R. Abramson, "Generations and Political Change in the United States," *Research in Political Sociology* 4 (1989): 235–280. For a nuanced portrait of generational differences, see Warren E. Miller and J. Merrill Shanks, *The New American Voter* (Cambridge, Mass.: Harvard University Press, 1996), 151–185.

13. See Walter Dean Burnham, *Critical Elections and the Mainsprings of American Politics* (New York: Norton, 1970); Everett Carll Ladd, Jr., with Charles D. Hadley, *Transformations of the American Party System: Political Coalitions from the New Deal to the 1970s,* 2d ed. (New York: Norton, 1978).

14. For the best summary of religious differences in American political life, see Kenneth D. Wald, *Religion and Politics in America,* 3d ed. (Washington, D.C.: CQ Press, 1997).

15. The results for white Catholics are reported in Everett C. Ladd, "The 1996 Election and Postindustrial Realignment," in *America at the Polls, 1996,* ed. Regina Dougherty et al. (Storrs, Conn.: Roper Center, 1997), 14.

16. David C. Leege and Lyman A. Kellstedt, with others, *Rediscovering the Religious Factor in American Politics* (Armonk, N.Y.: Sharpe, 1993).

17. Robert Axelrod, "Where the Votes Come From: An Analysis of Electoral Coalitions, 1952–1968," *American Political Science Review* 66 (March 1972): 11–20. Axelrod continued to provide updates of his estimates through the 1984 election. For his update of the 1984 results, which includes the cumulative results from 1952 through 1964, see Robert Axelrod, "Presidential Election Coalitions in 1984," *American Political Science Review* 80 (March 1986): 281–284.

18. John R. Petrocik, *Party Coalitions: Realignment and the Decline of the New Deal Party System* (Chicago: University of Chicago Press, 1981).

19. Harold W. Stanley, William T. Bianco, and Richard G. Niemi, "Partisanship and Group Support over Time: A Multivariate Analysis," *American Political Science Review* 80 (September 1986). Stanley and his colleagues assess the independent contribution that group memberships make toward Democratic party loyalties after controls are introduced for membership in other pro-Democratic groups. For an update and extension through 1992, see Harold W. Stanley and Richard G. Niemi, "The Demise of the New Deal Coalition: Partisanship and Group Support, 1952–92," in *Democracy's Feast: Elections in America,* ed. Herbert F. Weisberg (Chatham, N.J.: Chatham House, 1995), 220–240. For an alternative approach, see Robert S. Erikson, Thomas D. Lancaster, and David W. Romero, "Group Components of the Presidential Vote, 1952–1984," *Journal of Politics* 51 (May 1989): 337–346.

20. For a discussion of the importance of the working class to the Democratic presidential coalition, see Abramson, *Generational Change in American Politics* (Lexington, Mass.: D. C. Heath, 1975).

21. See Axelrod, "Where the Votes Come From."

22. The NORC survey, based on 2,564 civilians, uses a quota sample that does not follow the probability procedures used by the University of Michigan Survey Research Center. Following quota procedures common at the time, southern blacks were not sampled. Because the NORC survey overrepresented upper-income groups and the middle and upper classes, it cannot be used to estimate the contribution of social groups to the Democratic and Republican presidential coalitions.

23. Abramson, *Generational Change in American Politics,* 65–68.

24. As we explained in Chapter 3, we consider the South to include the eleven states of the old Confederacy. Because we could not use this definition of the South with either the 1944 NORC survey or the 1948 University of Michigan Survey Research Center survey, we have not included these years in our analysis of regional differences among the white electorate.

25. Both the 1996 NES survey and the 1996 VNS exit poll show that 32 percent of Clinton's total vote in the South came from black voters.

26. See Robert R. Alford, *Party and Society: The Anglo-American Democracies* (Chicago: Rand McNally, 1963); Seymour Martin Lipset, *Political Man: The Social Bases of Politics,* expanded ed. (Baltimore: Johns Hopkins University Press, 1981); and Ronald Inglehart, *Modernization and Postmodernization: Cultural, Economic, and Political Change in 43 Societies* (Princeton, N.J.: Princeton University Press, 1997).

27. The variation in class voting is smaller if one focuses on class differences in the congressional vote, but the trend clearly shows a gradual decline in class voting between 1948 and 1992. See Russell J. Dalton, *Citizen Politics: Public Opinion and Political Parties in Advanced Western Democracies,* 2d ed. (Chatham, N.J.: Chatham House, 1996), 172.

28. See Mark N. Franklin, "The Decline in Cleavage Politics," in *Electoral Change: Responses to Evolving Social and Attitudinal Structures in Western Countries,* Mark N. Franklin, Thomas T. Mackie, and Henry Valen, with others (Cambridge: Cambridge University Press, 1992), 383–405. See also Ronald Inglehart, *Modernization and Postmodernization,* 237–266.

29. See *Statistical Abstract of the United States 1996,* 116th ed. (Washington, D.C.: U.S. Government Printing Office, 1996), 70. We list these states in descending order of the estimated number of Jews. The estimates of the number of Jews in each state are based mainly on estimates by local Jewish organizations.

30. Robert Huckfeldt and Carol Weitzel Kohfeld, *Race and the Decline of Class in American Politics* (Urbana: University of Illinois Press, 1989).

31. For evidence on this point, see Abramson, *Political Attitudes in America: Formation and Change* (San Francisco: Freeman, 1983), 65–68.

32. Edward G. Carmines and James A. Stimson, *Issue Evolution: Race and the Transformation of American Politics* (Princeton, N.J.: Princeton University Press, 1989). For a critique of their thesis, see Alan I. Abramowitz, "Issue Evolution Reconsidered: Racial Attitudes and Partisanship in the U.S. Electorate," *American Journal of Political Science* 38 (February 1994): 1–24.

33. James Ceaser and Andrew Busch, *Upside Down and Inside Out: The 1992 Elections and American Politics* (Lanham, Md.: Rowman and Littlefield, 1993), 168–171.

6. CANDIDATES, ISSUES, AND THE VOTE

1. This set of attitudes was first formulated and tested extensively in Angus Campbell, Philip E. Converse, Warren E. Miller, and Donald E. Stokes, *The American Voter* (New York: Wiley, 1960), using data from what are now called the National Election Studies (NES) surveys. They based their conclusions primarily on data from a survey of the 1956 presidential election, a rematch between the Democrat Adlai E. Stevenson and the Republican (and this time incumbent) Dwight D. Eisenhower.

2. For an analysis examining those components, see Wendy M. Rahn et al., "A Social-Cognitive Model of Candidate Appraisal," *Information and Democratic Processes,* ed. John A. Ferejohn and James H. Kuklinski (Urbana: University of Illinois Press, 1990), 136–159, and sources cited therein.

3. For explication of the theory and tests in various electoral settings, see Paul R. Abramson et al., "'Sophisticated' Voting in the 1988 Presidential Primaries," *American Political Science Review* 86 (March 1992): 55–69; Jerome H. Black, "The Multicandidate Calculus of Voting: Application to Canadian Federal Elections, *American Journal of Political Science* 22 (August 1978): 609–638; and Bruce E. Cain, "Strategic Voting in Britain," *American Journal of Political Science* 22 (August 1978): 639–655.

4. For a more detailed analysis of the 1980 election, see Paul R. Abramson, John H. Aldrich, and David W. Rohde, *Change and Continuity in the 1980 Elections,* rev. ed. (Washington, D.C.: CQ Press, 1983), 172–184. For a comparable analysis of the 1992 election, see Paul R. Abramson, John H. Aldrich, and David W. Rohde, *Change and Continuity in the 1992 Elections,* rev. ed. (Washington, D.C.: CQ Press, 1995), 216–219.

5. Black, "The Multicandidate Calculus of Voting"; Cain, "Strategic Voting in Britain."

6. See Abramson et al., "'Sophisticated' Voting in the 1988 Presidential Primaries."

7. For discussion, see Abramson, Aldrich, and Rohde, *Change and Continuity in the 1992 Elections*, 59, 167.

8. William H. Riker, *Liberalism Against Populism: A Confrontation Between the Theory of Democracy and the Theory of Social Choice* (San Francisco: Freeman, 1982), 85–88.

9. Ibid.

10. See Paul R. Abramson et al., "Third-Party and Independent Candidates in American Politics: Wallace, Anderson, and Perot." *Political Science Quarterly* 110 (Fall 1995): 349–367.

11. For more on the strategies of the candidates in the 1980, 1984, 1988, and 1992 elections, see Abramson, Aldrich, and Rohde, *Change and Continuity in the 1980 Elections*, rev. ed., chap. 2; Abramson, Aldrich, and Rohde, *Change and Continuity in the 1984 Elections*, rev. ed. (Washington, D.C.: CQ Press, 1987), chap. 2; Abramson, Aldrich, and Rohde, *Change and Continuity in the 1988 Elections*, rev. ed. (Washington, D.C.: CQ Press, 1991), chap. 2, and Abramson, Aldrich, and Rohde, *Change and Continuity in the 1992 Elections*, rev. ed., chap. 2.

12. For an analysis of how the candidates' campaign strategies in 1996 shaped the voters' decisions, see Thomas Weko and John H. Aldrich, "The Presidency and the Election Campaign: Framing the Choice in 1996," in *The Presidency and the Political System*, 5th ed., ed. Michael Nelson (Washington, D.C.: CQ Press, 1998).

13. Each respondent in the survey is asked the question in the text and encouraged to give up to three responses. Then, if more than one problem is raised, the respondent is asked which one is the single most important. The responses in Table 6-3 are from the latter question. Looking at the full array of responses, we find a broader range of alternatives suggested, yet the same outlines are apparent.

14. These measures were first used in the NES survey of the 1968 election. They were used extensively in presidential election surveys beginning in 1972. The issue measures used in Chapter 7 were also used extensively beginning in the 1970s. Therefore, in this and the next two chapters, we focus mainly on the last seven elections.

15. The median is based on the assumption that respondents can be ranked from most conservative to most liberal. The number of respondents who are more liberal than the median (or who see a candidate as more liberal than the median) is equal to the number who are more conservative (or see the candidate as more conservative) than the median. Because there are only 7 points on these scales, the median is computed using a procedure that derives a median for grouped data.

Note that in 1996, most placements of Perot were only made in interviews conducted early in the campaign. Those interviewed in late September or thereafter were not asked to place Perot on most of the issue scales. With so many not being asked their views of his stands, we have excluded the responses of those who were asked.

16. In the original government services and spending scale, "1" is the most conservative response, but it is the most liberal response on the other scales. To increase comparability, we have "reversed" the government services and spending scale, so that "1" in the text, tables, and figures corresponds to the response, "The government should provide many more services," while "7" corresponds to the other endpoint.

17. Angus Campbell et al., *The American Voter* (New York: Wiley, 1960), 168–187.

18. Until 1996, the NES interviewers did not ask those who failed to place themselves on an issue scale where they thought the candidates stood. Therefore, those who failed to meet the first criterion were not able to meet any of the remaining ones. Although some people who express no preference on an issue might know the position of one or both candidates (as is indeed the case in 1996), it is difficult to see how they could vote based on those perceptions if they had no opinion of their own. Therefore, we eliminate those with no personal opinion about the issue from further consideration in these calculations, just as we have to do in using earlier election surveys.

19. For details, see Abramson, Aldrich, and Rohde, *Change and Continuity in the 1980 Elections,* rev. ed., Table 6-3; *Change and Continuity in the 1984 Elections,* rev. ed., Table 6-2; *Change and Continuity in the 1988 Elections,* rev. ed., Table 6-2; and *Change and Continuity in the 1992 Elections,* rev. ed., Table 6-4.

20. The arguments made by Campbell and his colleagues in *The American Voter* about issue voting criteria are critiqued by Morris P. Fiorina, *Retrospective Voting in American National Elections* (New Haven, Conn.: Yale University Press, 1981), 9–11. Although many scholars have interpreted failure to meet these criteria as akin to failing a test, he argues that the criteria imply no such thing. We agree. Failure to satisfy these criteria in no way impugns the citizen. As we shall see, "failure" to satisfy these criteria is related to the strategies followed by the candidates in the campaign.

21. We use the term *apparent issue voting* to emphasize several points. First, voting involves too many factors to infer that closeness to a candidate on any one issue was the cause of the voter's choice. The issue similarity may have been purely coincidental, or it may have been only one of many reasons the voter supported that candidate. Second, we use the median perception of the candi-

dates' positions rather than the voter's own perception. Third, the relationship between issues and the vote may be caused by rationalization. Voters may have decided to support a candidate for other reasons and may also have altered their own issue preferences or misperceived the positions of the candidates to align themselves more closely with the candidate they already favored. See Richard A. Brody and Benjamin I. Page, "Comment: The Assessment of Policy Voting," *American Political Science Review* 66 (June 1972): 450–458.

22. Many individuals, of course, placed the candidates at positions different from those of the public on average. Using the average perceptions, however, reduces the effect of individuals' rationalizing their perceptions of candidates to be consistent with their own vote, rather than voting for the candidate whose views are actually closer to their own. See ibid.

23. This procedure counts every issue as equal in importance. It also assumes that what matters is that the voter is closer to the candidate on an issue; it does not consider how much closer the voter is to one candidate or the other. Because the balance of issues measure in 1992 was based on only three issue scales, it would be inappropriate to compare this measure to those created in 1996 and in earlier studies, which are based on a larger number of issue scales. For analysis and comparisons for the elections from 1972 through 1988, see Abramson, Aldrich, and Rohde, *Change and Continuity in the 1980 Elections,* rev. ed., 135–138; Abramson, Aldrich, and Rohde, *Change and Continuity in the 1984 Elections,* rev. ed., 179–183; and Abramson, Aldrich, and Rohde, *Change and Continuity in the 1988 Elections,* rev. ed., 169–173.

24. Scores of +6, +7, +8, and +9 were called strongly Republican, while similarly negative scores were called strongly Democratic. Scores of +4 and +5 were called moderately Republican; those of –4 and –5 were called moderately Democratic. Scores of +2 and +3 were called slightly Republican, those of –2 and – 3 being called slightly Democratic. Scores of –1, 0, and +1 were called neutral.

25. For the results from 1972 through 1988, see Abramson, Aldrich, and Rohde, *Change and Continuity in the 1988 Elections,* rev. ed., 172. For the results for 1992, see Abramson, Aldrich, and Rohde, *Change and Continuity in the 1992 Elections,* rev. ed., 188.

7. PRESIDENTIAL PERFORMANCE AND CANDIDATE CHOICE

1. See Paul R. Abramson, John H. Aldrich, and David W. Rohde, *Change and Continuity in the 1992 Elections,* rev. ed. (Washington, D.C.: CQ Press, 1995).

2. V. O. Key, Jr., *Politics, Parties, and Pressure Groups,* 5th ed. (New York: Crowell, 1964), 568. Key's theory of retrospective voting is most fully developed

in *The Responsible Electorate: Rationality in Presidential Voting, 1936–1960* (Cambridge, Mass.: Harvard University Press, 1966).

3. Anthony Downs, *An Economic Theory of Democracy* (New York: Harper and Row, 1957).

4. Morris P. Fiorina, *Retrospective Voting in American National Elections* (New Haven, Conn.: Yale University Press, 1981), 83.

5. See Benjamin I. Page, *Choices and Echoes in Presidential Elections: Rational Man and Electoral Democracy* (Chicago: University of Chicago Press, 1978). He argues that "party cleavages" distinguish the party at the candidate and mass levels.

6. Arthur H. Miller and Martin P. Wattenberg, "Throwing the Rascals Out: Policy and Performance Evaluations of Presidential Candidates, 1952–1980," *American Political Science Review* 79 (June 1985): 359–372. In this chapter we do not examine retrospective evaluations of foreign policy, both because of the low concern over it in the public and because (as a consequence) of the relative paucity of data about them. See the section in Chapter 2 titled "The Strategic Context and Candidates' Choices" for some available indications of approval of Clinton on "peace" as well as "prosperity."

7. Each respondent assesses governmental performance on the problem he or she considers the most important. In the six most recent surveys, respondents were asked, "How good a job is the government doing in dealing with this problem—a good job, only fair, or a poor job?"

8. Negative evaluations are not surprising. After all, if you thought the government had been doing a good job with the problem, then it probably would not be your major concern. This reasoning seems to underlie the very low proportions in every survey who thought the government was doing a good job with their most important concern.

9. Since 1976, this question has been worded as follows: "Which party do you think would be the most likely to get the government to do a better job in dealing with this problem—the Republicans, the Democrats, or wouldn't there be much difference between them?"

10. See Gerald H. Kramer, "Short-Term Fluctuations in U.S. Voting Behavior, 1896–1964," *American Political Science Review* 65 (March 1971): 131–143; Fiorina, *Retrospective Voting;* M. Stephen Weatherford, "Economic Conditions and Electoral Outcomes: Class Differences in the Political Response to Recession," *American Journal of Political Science* 22 (November 1978): 917–938; D. Roderick Kiewiet and Douglas Rivers, "A Retrospective on Retrospective Voting," *Political Behavior* 6, no. 4 (1984): 369–393; Kiewiet, *Macroeconomics and Micropolitics: The Electoral Effects of Economic Issues* (Chicago: University of Chicago Press, 1983); Michael S. Lewis-Beck, *Economics and Elections: The Major Western Democra-*

cies (Ann Arbor: University of Michigan Press, 1988); and Michael B. MacKuen, Robert S. Erikson, and James A. Stimson, "Peasants or Bankers? The American Electorate and the U.S. Economy," *American Political Science Review* 86 (September 1992): 597–611.

11. John E. Mueller, *War, Presidents, and Public Opinion* (New York: Wiley, 1973); Edward R. Tufte, *Political Control of the Economy* (Princeton, N.J.: Princeton University Press, 1978). For a perceptive critique of the business cycle formulation, see James E. Alt and K. Alec Chrystal, *Political Economics* (Berkeley: University of California Press, 1983).

12. Fiorina, *Retrospective Voting.*

13. This question was asked in both the preelection and the postelection waves of the 1984 and 1988 NES surveys. Since attitudes held by the public before the election are what count in influencing their choice, we use the first question. In both surveys, approval of Reagan's performance was more positive in the postelection interview: 66 percent approved of his performance in 1984, and 68 percent approved in 1988.

14. Gallup surveys, however, show lower approval rates for Ford. In Gallup's last major survey before the 1976 election (conducted in June), only 45 percent approved of Ford's performance as president. See George C. Edwards III with Alec M. Gallup, *Presidential Approval: A Sourcebook* (Baltimore: Johns Hopkins University Press, 1990), 74.

15. To construct this measure, we awarded respondents 2 points if they approved of the president's performance, 1 if they had no opinion, and 0 if they disapproved. Second, respondents received 2 points if they thought the government was doing a good job in handling the most important problem facing the country, 1 if they thought the government was doing only a fair job, and 0 if they thought it was doing a poor job. Finally, respondents received 2 points if they thought the incumbent president's party would do a better job at handling the most important problem, 1 point if they thought there was no difference between the parties, and 0 if they thought the challenger's party would do a better job. For all three questions, "don't know" and "not ascertained" responses were scored as 1, but respondents with more than one such response were excluded from the analysis. Scores on our measure were the sum of the individual values for the three questions, and thus ranged from a low of 0 (strongly against the incumbent's party) to 6 (strongly for the incumbent's party). Thus, the measure has seven possible values, corresponding to the seven categories in Figure 7-1.

16. For data from the 1976 and 1980 elections, see Paul R. Abramson, John H. Aldrich, and David W. Rohde, *Change and Continuity in the 1980 Elections,* rev. ed. (Washington, D.C.: CQ Press, 1983), 155–157, Table 7-8; for data from the 1984 elections, see Abramson, Aldrich, and Rohde, *Change and Continuity in the*

1984 Elections, rev. ed. (Washington, D.C.: CQ Press, 1987), 203–204, Table 7-8; and for data from the 1988 elections, see Abramson, Aldrich, and Rohde, *Change and Continuity in the 1988 Elections,* rev. ed. (Washington, D.C.: CQ Press, 1991), 195–198, Table 7-7. The small number of 7–point issue scales included in the NES survey precluded performing this analysis with 1992 data.

17. For comparable results for 1992, see Abramson, Aldrich, and Rohde, *Change and Continuity in the 1992 Elections,* rev. ed., 217.

8. PARTY LOYALTIES, POLICY PREFERENCES, AND THE VOTE

1. Angus Campbell et al., *The American Voter* (New York: Wiley, 1960). For the most recent statement of the "standard" view of party identification, see Warren E. Miller, "Party Identification, Realignment, and Party Voting: Back to the Basics," *American Political Science Review* 85 (June 1991): 557–568, and Warren E. Miller and J. Merrill Shanks, *The New American Voter* (Cambridge, Mass.: Harvard University Press, 1996), 117–183.

2. Campbell et al., *The American Voter,* 121. See also Morris P. Fiorina, *Retrospective Voting in American National Elections* (New Haven, Conn.: Yale University Press, 1981), 85–86.

3. For the full wording of the party identification questions, see Chapter 4, note 52.

4. Most "apoliticals" in this period were African-Americans living in the South. Because they were disenfranchised, questions about their party loyalties were essentially meaningless to them. For the most detailed discussion of how the NES creates its summary measure of party identification, see Arthur H. Miller and Martin P. Wattenberg, "Measuring Party Identification: Independent or No Partisan Preference?" *American Journal of Political Science* 27 (February 1983): 106–121.

5. For evidence of the relatively high level of partisan stability among individuals over time, see M. Kent Jennings and Gregory B. Markus, "Partisan Orientations over the Long Haul: Results from the Three-Wave Political Socialization Panel Study," *American Political Science Review* 78 (December 1984): 1000–1018.

6. V. O. Key, Jr., *The Responsible Electorate: Rationality in Presidential Voting 1936–1960* (Cambridge, Mass.: Harvard University Press, 1966).

7. Morris P. Fiorina, "An Outline for a Model of Party Choice," *American Journal of Political Science* 21 (August 1977): 601–625; Fiorina, *Retrospective Voting.*

8. Benjamin I. Page provides evidence of this. See his *Choices and Echoes in Presidential Elections: Rational Man and Electoral Democracy* (Chicago: University of Chicago Press, 1978). Anthony Downs, in *An Economic Theory of Democ-*

racy (New York: Harper and Row, 1957), develops a theoretical logic for such consistency in party stances on issues and ideology over time. For more recent theoretical and empirical development, see John H. Aldrich, *Why Parties? The Origin and Transformation of Political Parties in America* (Chicago: University of Chicago Press, 1995).

9. There is some controversy over how to classify these independent leaners. Some argue that they are mainly "hidden" partisans who should be considered identifiers. For the strongest statement of this position, see Bruce E. Keith et al., *The Myth of the Independent Voter* (Berkeley: University of California Press, 1992). In our view, however, the evidence on the proper classification of independent leaners is mixed. On balance, the evidence suggests that they are more partisan than independents with no partisan leanings, but less partisan than weak partisans. See Paul R. Abramson, *Political Attitudes in America: Formation and Change* (San Francisco: Freeman, 1983), 80–81, 95–96. For an excellent discussion of this question, see Herbert B. Asher, "Voting Behavior Research in the 1980s: An Examination of Some Old and New Problem Areas," in *Political Science: The State of the Discipline,* ed. Ada W. Finifter (Washington, D.C.: American Political Science Association, 1983), 357–360.

10. See, for example, Martin P. Wattenberg, *The Decline of American Political Parties, 1952–1992* (Cambridge, Mass.: Harvard University Press, 1994).

11. The surveys were conducted annually except for 1979, 1981, 1992, 1995, and 1997.

12. As we saw in Chapter 5, blacks have voted overwhelmingly Democratic since 1964. For that reason there is no meaningful relationship between partisanship and the vote among the black electorate. We therefore analyze the relationship between party identification and the vote among whites only.

13. Bernard R. Berelson, Paul F. Lazarsfeld, and William N. McPhee, *Voting: A Study of Opinion Formation in a Presidential Campaign* (Chicago: University of Chicago Press, 1954).

14. See Richard A. Brody and Benjamin I. Page, "Comment: The Assessment of Policy Voting," *American Political Science Review* 66 (June 1972): 450–458; Page and Brody, "Policy Voting and the Electoral Process: The Vietnam War Issue," *American Political Science Review* 66 (September 1972): 979–995; and Fiorina, "An Outline for a Model of Party Choice."

15. The question measuring approval of the president's handling of economic policy was not asked in NES surveys before 1984. In our study of these earlier elections, an alternative measure of economic retrospective evaluations was created and shown to be nearly as strongly related to party identification. See Paul R. Abramson, John H. Aldrich, and David W. Rohde, *Change and Continuity in the 1984 Elections,* rev. ed. (Washington, D.C.: CQ Press, 1987), Table 8-6. We

also found nearly as strong a relationship between partisanship and perceptions of which party would better handle the economy in the data from 1972, 1976, and 1980 as from later surveys reported here. See Paul R. Abramson, John H. Aldrich, and David W. Rohde, *Change and Continuity in the 1980 Elections,* rev. ed. (Washington, D.C.: CQ Press, 1983), 170, Table 8-6.

16. For a description of this measure, see Chapter 6. Since this measure uses the median placement of the candidates on the issue scales in the full sample, much of the projection effect is eliminated. For the relationship between party identification and the balance of issues measure in 1972, see Abramson, Aldrich, and Rohde, *Change and Continuity in the 1980 Elections,* rev. ed., Table 8-5.

17. Recall that the summary measure of retrospective evaluations includes the presidential approval measure, the job the government is doing in handling the most important problem the respondent sees facing the country, and which party would do better at handling that problem. This measure could not be created from the 1972 election data. In that survey the presidential approval measure was asked of a half of the sample different from the half of the sample that was asked the questions about the most important problems.

18. See, for example, Aldrich, *Why Parties?*

19. For the 1992 results, see Paul R. Abramson, John H. Aldrich, and David W. Rohde, *Change and Continuity in the 1992 Elections,* rev. ed. (Washington, D.C.: CQ Press, 1995), Table 8-10.

20. Ibid., 246.

21. The remaining 3 percent voted for other candidates or refused to say how they voted. According to the Voter News Service 1996 exit poll, among approximately 2,000 respondents who said they voted for Perot in 1992, 22 percent voted for Clinton, 33 percent for Perot, and 44 percent for Dole.

22. Two important articles assess some of these relationships: Gregory B. Markus and Philip E. Converse, "A Dynamic Simultaneous Equation Model of Electoral Choice," *American Political Science Review* 73 (December 1979): 1055–1070, and Benjamin I. Page and Calvin C. Jones, "Reciprocal Effects of Policy Preferences, Party Loyalties, and the Vote," *American Political Science Review* 73 (December 1979): 1071–1089. For a brief discussion of these articles, see Richard G. Niemi and Herbert F. Weisberg, *Controversies in Voting Behavior,* 2d ed. (Washington, D.C.: CQ Press, 1984), 89–95. For an excellent discussion of complex models of voting behavior and the role of party identification in these models, see Asher, "Voting Behavior Research in the 1980s," 341–354. For another excellent introduction to some of these issues, see Richard G. Niemi and Herbert F. Weisberg, "Is Party Identification Stable?" in *Controversies in Voting Behavior,* 3d ed., ed. Niemi and Weisberg (Washington, D.C.: CQ Press, 1993): 268–283.

INTRODUCTION TO PART 3

1. Elizabeth Drew, *Whatever It Takes: The Real Struggle for Political Power in America* (New York: Viking, 1997), 2.

2. As Steven J. Rosenstone and John Mark Hansen point out, between 1952 and 1988, seventeen states rescheduled their gubernatorial elections from presidential years to nonpresidential years. They estimate that in 1952, nearly half of the electorate could vote in a presidential election in which a governor was also being selected. In the 1988 presidential election, according to their estimates, only 12 percent of the electorate lived in states with competitive gubernatorial elections. See Rosenstone and Hansen, *Mobilization, Participation, and Democracy in America* (New York: Macmillan, 1993). According to our estimates, 12 percent of the U.S. population of voting age lived in the states that held gubernatorial elections in 1996. Rosenstone and Hansen argue that this change in the scheduling of gubernatorial elections is a major factor accounting for the decline of electoral participation during the postwar years.

Kansas held two Senate races in 1996, and both were won by Republicans. Pat Roberts was elected to a six-year term, filling the seat held by Republican Nancy Landon Kassebaum, who retired from the Senate, and Sam Brownback was elected to the two-year term created by Bob Dole's resignation.

3. Gary C. Jacobson, "The 105th Congress: Unprecedented and Unsurprising," in *The Elections of 1996*, ed. Michael Nelson (Washington, D.C.: CQ Press, 1997), 143.

4. The one exception was in 1934, when the Democrats increased their share of the House seats during Franklin D. Roosevelt's first term.

9. CANDIDATES AND OUTCOMES IN 1996

1. The independent was Bernard Sanders of Vermont, who was first elected to the House in 1990. He had previously been elected mayor of Burlington, Vermont, running as a Socialist. For convenience in presenting results, we shall treat Sanders as a Democrat throughout this chapter. This seems reasonable because he received committee assignments from the Democratic party, and the Democrats did not field a candidate against him in 1994. In 1996 a maverick Democrat ran without party support, receiving less than 10 percent of the vote, while Sanders won reelection with 55 percent of the vote to 33 percent for his Republican opponent.

2. The word *incumbents* here is used only for elected incumbents. This includes all members of the House because the only way to become a representa-

tive is by election. In the case of the Senate, however, vacancies may be filled by appointment. We do not count appointed senators as incumbents. In the 1996 cycle, the only appointed senator who had not subsequently won election was Sheila Frahm of Kansas, who was appointed to succeed Bob Dole when he resigned to pursue his presidential campaign. Senator Frahm was defeated for nomination in the Republican primary.

Special mention also needs to be made of the Louisiana and Texas House races. Louisiana has an unusual open primary system in which candidates from all parties run against one another in a single primary. If no candidate receives a majority, the top two vote getters, regardless of party, face each other in a runoff in November. In 1996 part of the Texas districting plan was declared unconstitutional, for reasons we discuss below. For the thirteen districts that were affected, the court ordered that an analogous procedure be used in the new districts for nominations in the November election, with similar runoffs to be held in December, if necessary. In both sets of races, we count the last round in each district as the controlling race. If that round only involved candidates of a single party, the race is counted as a primary and the winner as unopposed in the general election. If candidates of both parties were involved in the final round, it is treated as a general election.

3. The Republicans had won control of the House in eight consecutive elections from 1894 through 1908, far short of the Democratic series of successes.

4. In 1994 the Democrats won 19 percent of Republican House seats and no GOP Senate seats. In their own open seats, they retained only 31 percent in the House and none in the Senate. See Paul R. Abramson, John H. Aldrich, and David W. Rohde, *Change and Continuity in the 1992 Elections,* rev. ed. (Washington, D.C.: CQ Press, 1995), 319.

5. This is the idea behind the "exposure" thesis, which argues that a party that holds more seats than expected based on some historical average is more likely to lose ground than one that is at or below such an average. See Bruce I. Oppenheimer, James A. Stimson, and Richard W. Waterman, "Interpreting U.S. Congressional Elections: The Exposure Thesis," *Legislative Studies Quarterly* 11 (May 1986): 227–248.

6. The regional breakdowns used in this chapter are as follows: *East:* Connecticut, Delaware, Maine, Massachusetts, New Hampshire, New Jersey, New York, Pennsylvania, Rhode Island, and Vermont; *Midwest:* Illinois, Indiana, Iowa, Kansas, Michigan, Minnesota, Nebraska, North Dakota, Ohio, South Dakota, Wisconsin; *West:* Alaska, Arizona, California, Colorado, Hawaii, Idaho, Montana, Nevada, New Mexico, Oregon, Utah, Washington, and Wyoming; *South:* Alabama, Arkansas, Florida, Georgia, Louisiana, Mississippi, North Carolina, South Carolina, Tennessee, Texas, and Virginia; *Border:* Kentucky, Maryland, Missouri,

Oklahoma, and West Virginia. This classification differs somewhat from the one used in earlier chapters (and in Chapter 10), but it is commonly used for congressional analysis.

7. Over the years, changes in the southern electorate have made southern Democratic constituencies more like northern Democratic constituencies and less like Republican constituencies, North or South. These changes also appear to have enhanced the homogeneity of preferences within the partisan delegations in Congress. See David W. Rohde, "Electoral Forces, Political Agendas, and Partisanship in the House and Senate," in *The Postreform Congress,* ed. Roger H. Davidson (New York: St. Martin's, 1992), 27–47.

8. See, for example, the articles in the special issue (April 1995) of *American Politics Quarterly* on "Legislative Redistricting in the 1980s and 1990s," and the many other studies referenced therein.

9. See Abramson, Aldrich, and Rohde, *Change and Continuity in the 1992 Elections,* rev. ed., 226–269, 331–332.

10. See *Congressional Quarterly Weekly Report,* July 1, 1995, 1944–1946.

11. See Benjamin Sheffner, "High Court Rebuffs Census Challenge but Debate Rages about 2000 Count," *Roll Call,* March 21, 1996, 3.

12. See Holly Idelson, "States' Right Loses in Close Vote," *Congressional Quarterly Weekly Report,* May 27, 1995, 1480.

13. For an account of the Contract with America and its consideration by the House, see James G. Gimpel, *Fulfilling the Contract: The First 100 Days* (Needham Heights, Mass.: Allyn and Bacon, 1996).

14. The budget reconciliation bill is the vehicle for bringing tax and appropriations bills into conformity with the budget resolution adopted by Congress. Committees are instructed to adopt adjustments in revenues and expenditures of a certain amount, then the measures are combined into a single omnibus bill which has special procedural protections. As was especially true in the 104th Congress, this bill can also contain large-scale changes in government policy.

15. In all of 1995 Clinton vetoed eleven bills, and he was only overridden once, on a comparatively minor measure.

16. *Hotline,* November 20, 1995. *Hotline* is a commercial on-line service that covers politics and government.

17. *Congressional Quarterly Weekly Report,* January 27, 1996, 258.

18. NBC News/ *Wall Street Journal* poll, reported in the *National Journal,* March 23, 1996, 660.

19. *National Journal,* April 12, 1997, 714.

20. *Washington Post,* January 21, 1996, C7.

21. *Hill,* September 27, 1995, 14.

22. *Washington Post*, April 30, 1996, A5.

23. *Hotline*, January 4, 1996.

24. *Hill*, October 18, 1996, 17.

25. *Roll Call*, October 16, 1995, 1, 26.

26. Ibid., July 29, 1996, 1.

27. See Abramson, Aldrich, and Rohde, *Change and Continuity in the 1992 Elections*, rev. ed., 324–325.

28. *New York Times*, November 11, 1996, B3. For additional evidence of the public's improved view of the economy, based on NES surveys, see Chapter 7, Table 7-4.

29. Richard L. Berke, "A Coattails Reversal from '94 Races," *New York Times*, September 27, 1996, A11.

30. *Hill*, October 16, 1996, 1; *New York Times*, October 21, 1996, A1.

31. *New York Times*, October 27, 1996, A1.

32. Regina Dougherty, Everett C. Ladd, David Wilber, and Lynn Zayachkiwsky, eds., *America at the Polls, 1996* (Storrs, Conn.: Roper Center, 1997), 41.

33. *New York Times*, October 23, 1996, A12.

34. Richard F. Fenno, Jr., *Home Style: House Members in Their Districts* (Boston: Little, Brown, 1978).

35. For example, analysis of Senate races in 1988 indicated that both the political quality of the previous office held and the challenger's political skills had an independent effect on the outcome of the race. See Peverill Squire, "Challenger Quality and Voting Behavior in U.S. Senate Elections," *Legislative Studies Quarterly* 27 (May 1992): 247–263. For systematic evidence on the effect of candidate quality in House races, see Gary C. Jacobson, *The Electoral Origins of Divided Government: Competition in U.S. House Elections, 1946–1988* (Boulder, Colo.: Westview Press, 1990), chap. 4.

36. Data on office backgrounds were taken from *Congressional Quarterly Weekly Report*, October 26, 1996, 3089–3104.

37. Data on earlier years were taken from our studies of previous national elections.

38. Note that the figures in this paragraph include races in which only one of the parties fielded a candidate, as well as contests in which both did.

39. See Jacobson, *The Electoral Origins of Divided Government*; Jon R. Bond, Cary Covington, and Richard Fleischer, "Explaining Challenger Quality in Congressional Elections," *Journal of Politics* 47 (May 1985): 510–529; and David W. Rohde, "Risk-Bearing and Progressive Ambition: The Case of Members of the U.S. House of Representatives," *American Journal of Political Science* 23 (February 1979): 1–26.

40. L. Sandy Maisel and Walter J. Stone, "Determinants of Candidate Emergence in U.S. House Elections: An Exploratory Study," *Legislative Studies Quarterly* 22 (February 1997): 70–96.

41. See Peverill Squire, "Preemptive Fund-raising and Challenger Profile in Senate Elections," *Journal of Politics* 53 (November 1991): 1150–1164.

42. Jeffrey S. Banks and D. Roderick Kiewiet, "Explaining Patterns of Candidate Competition in Congressional Elections," *American Journal of Political Science* 33 (November 1989): 997–1015.

43. David Canon, *Actors, Athletes, and Astronauts: Political Amateurism in the United States Congress* (Chicago: University of Chicago Press, 1990).

44. See Kenneth J. Cooper, "Riding High Name Recognition to Hill," *Washington Post*, December 24, 1992, A4.

45. See Thomas E. Mann and Raymond E. Wolfinger, "Candidates and Parties in Congressional Elections," *American Political Science Review* 74 (September 1980): 617–632.

46. See David R. Mayhew, "Congressional Elections: The Case of the Vanishing Marginals," *Polity* 6 (Spring 1974): 295–317; Robert S. Erikson, "Malapportionment, Gerrymandering, and Party Fortunes in Congressional Elections," *American Political Science Review* 66 (December 1972): 1234–1245; Warren Lee Kostroski, "Party and Incumbency in Postwar Senate Elections: Trends, Patterns, and Models," *American Political Science Review* 67 (December 1973): 1213–1234.

47. Edward R. Tufte, "Communication," *American Political Science Review* 68 (March 1974): 211–213. The communication involved a discussion of Tufte's earlier article: "The Relationship between Seats and Votes in Two-Party Systems," *American Political Science Review* 67 (June 1973): 540–554.

48. See John A. Ferejohn, "On the Decline in Competition in Congressional Elections," *American Political Science Review* 71 (March 1977): 166–176; Albert D. Cover, "One Good Term Deserves Another: The Advantage of Incumbency in Congressional Elections," *American Journal of Political Science* 21 (August 1977): 523–541; and Albert D. Cover and David R. Mayhew, "Congressional Dynamics and the Decline of Competition in Congressional Elections," in *Congress Reconsidered*, 2d ed., ed. Lawrence C. Dodd and Bruce I. Oppenheimer (Washington, D.C.: CQ Press, 1981), 62–82.

49. Morris P. Fiorina, *Congress: Keystone of the Washington Establishment*, 2d ed. (New Haven, Conn.: Yale University Press, 1989), esp. chaps. 4–6.

50. See several conflicting arguments and conclusions in the following articles published in the *American Journal of Political Science* 25 (August 1981): John R. Johannes and John C. McAdams, "The Congressional Incumbency Effect: Is It Casework, Policy Compatibility, or Something Else? An Examination of the 1978

Election" (512–542); Morris P. Fiorina, "Some Problems in Studying the Effects of Resource Allocation in Congressional Elections" (543–567); Diana Evans Yiannakis, "The Grateful Electorate: Casework and Congressional Elections" (568–580); and McAdams and Johannes, "Does Casework Matter? A Reply to Professor Fiorina" (581–604). See also Johannes, *To Serve the People: Congress and Constituency Service* (Lincoln: University of Nebraska Press, 1984), esp. chap. 8; and Albert D. Cover and Bruce S. Brumberg, "Baby Books and Ballots: The Impact of Congressional Mail on Constituent Opinion," *American Political Science Review* 76 (June 1982): 347–359. The evidence in Cover and Brumberg, "Baby Books," for a positive electoral effect is quite strong, but the result may be applicable only to limited circumstances.

51. Ferejohn, "On the Decline of Competition," 174.

52. Cover, "One Good Term," 535.

53. The data for 1974–1990 were taken from "House Incumbents' Average Vote Percentage," *Congressional Quarterly Weekly Report,* November 10, 1990, 3800. The 1994 figures are from the *New York Times,* November 10, 1994. The data for 1992 and 1996 are from *USA Today,* November 8, 1996, 4A.

54. For an excellent analysis of the growth of, and reasons for, anti-Congress sentiment, see John R. Hibbing and Elizabeth Theiss-Morse, *Congress as Public Enemy* (Cambridge: Cambridge University Press, 1995).

55. Fenno, *Home Style,* 163–169.

56. The body of literature on this subject has grown to be quite large. Some salient examples, in addition to those cited later, are Gary C. Jacobson, *Money in Congressional Elections* (New Haven, Conn.: Yale University Press, 1980); Jacobson, "Parties and PACs in Congressional Elections," in *Congress Reconsidered,* 4th ed., ed. Lawrence C. Dodd and Bruce I. Oppenheimer (Washington, D.C.: CQ Press, 1989), 117–152; Jacobson and Samuel Kernell, *Strategy and Choice in Congressional Elections,* 2d ed. (New Haven, Conn.: Yale University Press, 1983); John A. Ferejohn and Morris P. Fiorina, "Incumbency and Realignment in Congressional Elections," in *The New Direction in American Politics,* ed. John E. Chubb and Paul E. Peterson (Washington, D.C.: Brookings Institution, 1985), 91–115.

57. See Jacobson, *The Electoral Origins of Divided Government,* 63–65.

58. The 1990 data were taken from *Politics in America, 1992: The 102nd Congress,* ed. Phil Duncan (Washington, D.C.: Congressional Quarterly Inc.); the 1992 data are from the *Washington Post,* May 26, 1993, A17. For both elections the data include all incumbents, not just those who had major-party opposition.

59. The 1996 spending data were obtained in March 1997 from the Web site of the Federal Election Commission (http://www.fec.gov).

60. Thirteen of the thirty-two targeted representatives (41 percent) lost. *Hotline,* November 6, 1997.

61. See Abramson, Aldrich, and Rohde, *Change and Continuity in the 1992 Elections,* rev. ed., 278–282, and the earlier work cited there.

62. See Jacobson, *The Electoral Origins of Divided Government,* 54–55, and the work cited in note 56 above.

63. Donald Philip Green and Jonathan S. Krasno, "Salvation for the Spendthrift Incumbent: Reestimating the Effects of Campaign Spending in House Elections," *American Journal of Political Science* 32 (November 1988): 884–907.

64. Gary C. Jacobson, "The Effects of Campaign Spending in House Elections: New Evidence for Old Arguments," *American Journal of Political Science* 34 (May 1990): 334–362.

65. Alan I. Abramowitz, "Explaining Senate Election Outcomes," *American Political Science Review* 82 (June 1988): 385–403.

66. Gary C. Jacobson, "Campaign Spending and Voter Awareness of Congressional Candidates" (paper presented at the Annual Meeting of the Public Choice Society, New Orleans, May 11–13, 1977), 16.

67. Challengers were categorized as having strong experience if they had been elected to Congress, to statewide office, to the state legislature, or to countywide or citywide office (for example, mayor, prosecutor, and so on).

68. Paul R. Abramson, John H. Aldrich, and David W. Rohde, *Change and Continuity in the 1980 Elections,* rev. ed. (Washington, D.C.: CQ Press, 1983), 202–203.

69. Quoted in Angela Herrin, "Big Outside Money Backfired in GOP Loss of Senate to Dems," *Washington Post,* November 6, 1986, A46.

70. See David W. Rohde, *Parties and Leaders in the Postreform House* (Chicago: University of Chicago Press, 1991), especially chap. 3; and Rohde, "Electoral Forces, Political Agendas, and Partisanship in the House and Senate," in *The Postreform Congress,* ed. Roger H. Davidson (New York: St. Martin's Press, 1992), 27–47.

71. See Abramson, Aldrich, and Rohde, *Change and Continuity in the 1992 Elections,* rev. ed., 339–342.

72. See Juliet Eilperin, "Committee Reform Fervor Fades as New Dreier Report Highlights Obstacles to Eliminating More House Panels," *Roll Call,* November 14, 1996, 5.

73. *Roll Call,* August 4, 1997, 8.

74. Cindy Skrzycki, "In Top Federal Jobs, Vacancies Mushroom," *Washington Post,* August 2, 1997, A1.

75. Albert Eisele, "Senate Stalls Judges over Activism," *Hill,* March 12, 1997, 1.

76. *Washington Post,* May 21, 1997, A1.

77. Ibid., June 16, 1997, A4.

78. Ibid., June 18, 1997, A1.

79. Earlier research indicated that for these purposes voters may tend to regard a president whose predecessor either died or resigned from office as a continuation of the first president's administration. Therefore, these data are organized by term of administration, rather than term of president. See Abramson, Aldrich, and Rohde, *Change and Continuity in the 1980 Elections,* rev. ed., 252–253.

80. Edward R. Tufte, "Determinants of the Outcomes of Midterm Congressional Elections," *American Political Science Review* 69 (September 1975): 812–826; and Tufte, *Political Control of the Economy* (Princeton, N.J.: Princeton University Press, 1978); Gary C. Jacobson and Samuel Kernell, *Strategy and Choice in Congressional Elections,* 2d ed. (New Haven, Conn.: Yale University Press, 1983).

81. The Jacobson-Kernell hypothesis was challenged by Richard Born in "Strategic Politicians and Unresponsive Voters," *American Political Science Review* 80 (June 1986): 599–612. Born argued that economic and approval data at the time of the election were more closely related to outcomes than were parallel data from earlier in the year. Jacobson, however, offered renewed support for the hypothesis in an analysis of both district-level and aggregate data. See Gary C. Jacobson, "Strategic Politicians and the Dynamics of House Elections, 1946–86," *American Political Science Review* 83 (September 1989): 773–793.

82. Alan I. Abramowitz, Albert D. Cover, and Helmut Norpoth, "The President's Party in Midterm Elections: Going from Bad to Worse," *American Journal of Political Science* 30 (August 1986): 562–576.

83. Bruce I. Oppenheimer, James A. Stimson, and Richard W. Waterman, "Interpreting U.S. Congressional Elections: The Exposure Thesis," *Legislative Studies Quarterly* 11 (May 1986): 228.

84. Robin F. Marra and Charles W. Ostrom, Jr., "Explaining Seat Change in the U.S. House of Representatives 1950–86," *American Journal of Political Science* 33 (August 1989): 541–569.

85. *National Journal,* July 19, 1997, 1484.

86. Ibid. The corresponding responses with regard to congressional Democrats were 49 percent yes and 45 percent no.

87. Stuart Rothenberg, "Coup's Bottom Line: If GOP War Continues, Dems Will Benefit in '98," *Roll Call,* July 24, 1997, 18.

88. *Hill,* June 4, 1997, 1.

89. *Roll Call,* August 7, 1997, 8.

90. Ibid., 11.

91. For a list, see *Hotline,* April 2, 1997.

92. See *Roll Call,* June 9, 1997, 1.

93. Ibid., August 4, 1997.

94. *Congressional Quarterly Weekly Report,* June 21, 1997, 1436. The projected

losers are New York and Pennsylvania (two seats each), and Connecticut, Illinois, Michigan, Mississippi, Ohio, Oklahoma, and Wisconsin, one each. The probable gainers are Arizona, Georgia, and Texas, two seats each; Colorado, Florida, Montana, Nevada, and Utah, one each.

95. *Roll Call,* February 27, 1997, 1, 29.

96. *Congressional Quarterly Weekly Report,* February 15, 1997, 403.

10. THE CONGRESSIONAL ELECTORATE IN 1996

1. As we saw in Chapter 5, the 1996 NES survey results overreported the Democratic share of the presidential vote. There is a small reverse (pro-Republican) bias in the House vote. According to the 1996 NES survey, the Republicans received 53 percent of the major-party vote; official results show they actually received only 50.2 percent. See "Counting the Vote: 1996 Totals," *Congressional Quarterly Weekly Report,* February 15, 1997, 444. To simplify the presentation, we have eliminated from consideration votes for minor-party candidates in all the tables in this chapter. Furthermore, to ensure that our study of choice is meaningful, in all tables except Tables 10-1 and 10-2 we include only voters who lived in congressional districts in which both major parties ran candidates.

2. We confine our attention in this section to voting for the House because this group of voters is more directly comparable to the presidential electorate. We employ the same definitions for social and demographic categories as used in Chapters 4 and 5.

3. Paul R. Abramson, John H. Aldrich, and David W. Rohde, *Change and Continuity in the 1980 Elections,* rev. ed. (Washington, D.C.: CQ Press, 1983), 213–216.

4. Alan I. Abramowitz, "Choices and Echoes in the 1978 U.S. Senate Elections: A Research Note," *American Journal of Political Science* 25 (February 1981): 112–118; and Abramowitz, "National Issues, Strategic Politicians, and Voting Behavior in the 1980 and 1982 Congressional Elections," *American Journal of Political Science* 28 (November 1984): 710–721.

5. Robert S. Erikson and Gerald C. Wright, "Voters, Candidates, and Issues in Congressional Elections," in *Congress Reconsidered,* 3d ed., ed. Lawrence C. Dodd and Bruce I. Oppenheimer (Washington, D.C.: CQ Press, 1985), 91–116.

6. Robert S. Erikson and Gerald C. Wright, "Voters, Candidates and Issues in Congressional Elections," in *Congress Reconsidered,* 6th ed., ed. Lawrence C. Dodd and Bruce I. Oppenheimer (Washington, D.C.: CQ Press, 1997), 148–150.

7. Albert D. Cover, "One Good Term Deserves Another: The Advantage of

Incumbency in Congressional Elections," *American Journal of Political Science* 21 (August 1977): 523–541. Cover includes in his analysis not only strong and weak partisans but also independents with partisan leanings.

8. It should be noted that the 1996 NES survey may contain biases that inflate the percentage who report voting for House incumbents. For a discussion of this problem in earlier years, see Robert B. Eubank and David John Gow, "The Pro-Incumbent Bias in the 1978 and 1980 National Election Studies," *American Journal of Political Science* 27 (February 1983): 122–139; and David John Gow and Robert B. Eubank, "The Pro-Incumbent Bias in the 1982 National Election Study," *American Journal of Political Science* 28 (February 1984): 224–230.

9. Richard F. Fenno, Jr., "If, As Ralph Nader Says, Congress Is 'The Broken Branch,' How Come We Love Our Congressmen So Much?" in *Congress in Change: Evolution and Reform,* ed. Norman J. Ornstein (New York: Praeger, 1975), 277–287. This theme is expanded and analyzed in Richard F. Fenno, Jr., *Home Style: House Members in Their Districts* (Boston: Little, Brown, 1978).

10. Abramson, Aldrich, and Rohde, *Change and Continuity in the 1980 Elections,* rev. ed., 220–221. For the 1984 results, see Abramson, Aldrich, and Rohde, *Change and Continuity in the 1984 Elections,* rev. ed. (Washington, D.C.: CQ Press, 1987), 272. For the 1988 results, see Abramson, Aldrich, and Rohde, *Change and Continuity in the 1988 Elections,* rev. ed. (Washington, D.C.: CQ Press, 1991), 273. And for the data on 1992, see Abramson, Aldrich, and Rohde, *Change and Continuity in the 1992 Elections,* rev. ed. (Washington, D.C.: CQ Press, 1995), 311.

11. Opinion on this last point is not unanimous, however. See Richard Born, "Reassessing the Decline of Presidential Coattails: U.S. House Elections from 1952–80," *Journal of Politics* 46 (February 1984): 60–79.

12. John A. Ferejohn and Randall L. Calvert, "Presidential Coattails in Historical Perspective," *American Journal of Political Science* 28 (February 1984): 127–146.

13. Randall L. Calvert and John A. Ferejohn, "Coattail Voting in Recent Presidential Elections," *American Political Science Review* 77 (June 1983): 407–419.

14. James E. Campbell and Joe A. Sumners, "Presidential Coattails in Senate Elections," *American Political Science Review* 84 (June 1990): 513–524.

15. See Abramson, Aldrich, and Rohde, *Change and Continuity in the 1980 Elections,* rev. ed., 222–223, for the corresponding data on 1980; Abramson, Aldrich, and Rohde, *Change and Continuity in the 1984 Elections,* rev. ed., 273–275, for the data on 1984; Abramson, Aldrich, and Rohde, *Change and Continuity in the 1988 Elections,* rev. ed., 272–275, for 1988 data; and Abramson, Aldrich, and Rohde, *Change and Continuity in the 1992 Elections,* rev. ed., 310–313, for the 1992 data.

11. THE 1998 CONGRESSIONAL ELECTIONS

1. The independent was Bernard Sanders of Vermont. As we indicated in Chapter 9 (note 1), we treat Sanders as a Democrat in our analyses.

2. The regional breakdowns can be found in footnote 6 of Chapter 9. The Democrats won 62 percent of the seats in the East, 48 percent in the Midwest, 47 percent in the West, 43 percent in the South, and 41 percent in the Border states.

3. In the Senate the Democrats held 55 percent of the seats in the East, 55 percent in the Midwest, 39 percent in the West, 36 percent in the South, and 40 percent in the Border states.

4. These data are drawn from *Vital Statistics on Congress 1995–1996*, ed. Norman J. Ornstein, Thomas E. Mann, and Michael J. Malbin (Washington, D.C.: Congressional Quarterly, 1996), 53.

5. See *Roll Call*, October 2, 1997, 14.

6. *The Hill*, October 1, 1997, 1.

7. *Roll Call*, July 30, 1998, 15.

8. *Roll Call*, July 16, 1998, 32.

9. *The Hill*, September 9, 1998, 4.

10. *Roll Call*, September 17, 1998, 15.

11. *Washington Post*, November 1, 1998, A1.

12. In July and August of 1998, the president's approval ratings ranged between 61 and 66 percent. (These figures were taken from the Gallup Poll's web site (www.gallup.com), December 28, 1998.) Comparable figures for other postwar presidents were: Truman, 39 percent; Eisenhower, 58 percent; Nixon, 28 percent; and Reagan, 64 percent. See Lynn Ragsdale, *Vital Statistics on the Presidency: Washington to Clinton* (Washington D.C.: CQ Press, 1996), 192.

13. *New York Times*, November 7, 1996, B3. The 1998 poll was based on a questionnaire completed by 10,017 voters as they were leaving 250 polling places around the country.

14. *National Journal*, November 8, 1998, 2667.

15. These figures were taken from the Gallup Poll's web site (www.gallup.com), December 28, 1998.

16. *The Hill*, April 1, 1998, 6.

17. Richard A. Brody, "The Lewinsky Affair and Popular Support for President Clinton," manuscript, Stanford University, November 3, 1998. The data are from the *Washington Post*/ABC polls.

18. *New York Times*, October 28, 1998, A1.

19. *Washington Post*, October 12, 1998, A1.

20. *New York Times*, November 5, 1998, B4.

21. *Washington Post*, October 29, 1998, A1.

22. *Washington Post*, October 30, 1998, A1.

23. *Roll Call,* October 29, 1998, 20.

24. *Washington Post,* October 25, 1998, A16.

25. Iver Peterson, "An Upset Is Traced, in Part, to a Partisan Song," *New York Times,* November 5, 1998, B16.

26. *Washington Post,* September 7, 1998, A14.

27. *Washington Post,* September 7, 1998, A14.

28. *Roll Call,* October 15, 1998, 11.

29. *USA Today,* November 2, 1998, 9A; *New York Times,* November 3, 1998, A22.

30. *New York Times,* November 3, 1998, A22.

31. The estimates are from analyst Curtis Gans of the Committee for the Study of the American Electorate and were taken from the web site at www.allpolitics. com, November 5, 1998.

32. See Robert Orme and David W. Rohde, "Presidential Surge and Differential Decline: The Effects of Changing Turnout on the Fortunes of Democratic House Incumbents in 1994," a paper presented at the 1995 Annual Meeting of the American Political Science Association, Chicago, August 30–September 3, 1995.

33. Norah M. O'Donnell, "Study Shows Black Vote Up in Eight States Last Month," *Roll Call,* December 7, 1998, 17. The declines in turnout were in California, Texas, New York, Florida, and Pennsylvania. Substantial increases occurred in Georgia, Illinois, Maryland, Michigan, North Carolina, and South Carolina, while there were smaller increases in Alabama and Ohio.

34. *New York Times,* November 6, 1998, A22.

35. *New York Times,* November 6, 1998, A22.

36. The data on vote choice for all elections and on the proportion of the electorate in 1998 are from the *New York Times,* November 9, 1998, A20. Data on the proportions of the electorate for 1996 and 1994 are from the *New York Times,* November 7, 1996, B3; data for 1992 are from the *New York Times,* November 5, 1992, B9.

37. See Richard Morin, "Citing Survey Change, Pollsters Retreat on Estimates of the Union Vote," *Washington Post,* November 6, 1998, A5.

38. *New York Times,* November 6, 1998, A22.

39. See Karlyn Bowman, "Tracking November's Exit Poll Results From A to Z," *Roll Call,* November 19, 1998, 14.

40. For a discussion of the increased role of national party organizations in congressional elections over the last two decades, see Paul S. Herrnson, *Congressional Elections,* 2d ed. (Washington, D.C.: CQ Press, 1998), Chapter 4.

41. For a discussion of the 1994 congressional elections, see Paul R. Abramson, John H. Aldrich, and David W. Rohde, *Change and Continuity in the 1992 Elections,* rev. ed. (Washington, D.C.: CQ Press, 1995), 317–336.

42. See ibid., 257–282.

43. *USA Today,* April 21, 1998, 4A.

44. These figures on the 1998 vote, and those used later in this chapter, are taken from the preliminary unofficial returns published in the November 7, 1998, issue of *Congressional Quarterly Weekly Report,* 3027–3035. At the time of writing the official results were not yet available.

45. For House races, the information regarding candidate experience was taken from the candidate descriptions in the summary tables of the state-by-state primary election coverage from *Congressional Quarterly Weekly Reports.* It was supplemented by state-by-state coverage from the web site http://www.washingtonpost.com/wp-srv/results98/national/statebystate.htm. Almost all of the Senate data were obtained from the *Washington Post* web site, supplemented in two instances by *Congressional Quarterly Weekly Reports.*

46. *The Hill,* February 4, 1998, 1.

47. See Charles E. Cook, "Recruiting Improves For Both Parties After Below-Average Start," *Roll Call,* February 23, 1998, 8.

48. *Hotline* (an on-line political news service), October 20, 1997. The report was quoting from a story in the *Atlanta Constitution.*

49. These numbers, and those cited below, are derived from Paul R. Abramson, John H. Aldrich, and David W. Rohde, *Change and Continuity in the 1988 Elections,* rev. ed. (Washington, D.C.: CQ Press, 1991), 240, 322; and Abramson, Aldrich, and Rohde, *Change and Continuity in the 1992 Elections,* rev. ed., 274, 334.

50. Herrnson, *Congressional Elections,* 40.

51. *Roll Call,* January 15, 1998, 1.

52. These figures, and all of those discussed below, were obtained from summary tables and descriptions posted on the Federal Elections Commission (FEC) web site (www.fec.gov) on December 30, 1998. Note that unlike the FEC data employed in Chapter 9 (which was stated in terms of average spending), these data were reported by the commission in terms of median spending.

53. *National Journal,* November 7, 1998, 2680.

54. *Roll Call,* September 24, 1998, 1.

55. *Roll Call,* October 8, 1998, 10.

56. *National Journal,* November 7, 1998, 2680.

57. *Roll Call,* November 5, 1998, 31.

58. *Washington Post,* November 8, 1998, A22.

59. *Roll Call,* November 9, 1998, 22.

60. *Roll Call,* November 9, 1998, 21.

61. *New York Times,* November 8, 1998, 22.

62. *Roll Call,* November 19, 1998, 1.

63. *Congressional Quarterly Weekly Report,* November 21, 1998, 3167.

64. *Congressional Quarterly Weekly Report,* November 21, 1998, 3167.

65. *Roll Call,* November 23, 1998, 19.

66. *Washington Post,* November 24, 1998, A4.

67. *Roll Call,* November 23, 1998, 19.

68. For a discussion of, and evidence on, this matter see John H. Aldrich and David W. Rohde, "The Consequences of Party Organizations in the House: Theory and Evidence on Conditional Party Government," a paper presented at the 1998 Annual Meeting of the Southern Political Science Association.

69. *Roll Call,* November 23, 1998, 1, 20.

70. *Roll Call,* December 3, 1998, 16.

71. *Washington Post,* December 11, 1998, A22.

72. Eric Pianin and Kevin Merida, "How GOP's Enforcer Propelled the Process." *Washington Post,* December 16, 1998, A22.

73. *Washington Post,* December 19, 1998, A38.

74. *Washington Post,* December 21, 1998, A19.

75. *Washington Post,* December 21, 1998, A19.

76. *Congressional Quarterly Weekly Report,* December 22, 1998, 3340.

77. These results were reported on the Pew Center's web site (www.people-press.org), December 23, 1998.

78. *New York Times,* December 21, 1998, A21.

79. *USA Today,* December 17, 1998, 12A; and December 21, 1998, 6A.

80. *USA Today,* December 31, 1998, 4A.

81. *Roll Call,* November 9, 1998, 13.

82. *Roll Call,* November 12, 1998, 11.

83. *Congressional Quarterly Weekly Report,* December 5, 1998, 3259.

84. Arizona and Texas would gain two seats each, while California, Florida, Georgia, Montana, and Nevada would gain one. The losers would be Pennsylvania and New York (two each), and Connecticut, Mississippi, Ohio, Oklahoma, and Wisconsin (one each). See the *Washington Post,* January 1, 1999, A23.

85. The Democratic states are California, Georgia, Massachusetts, and North Carolina; the GOP states are Florida, Michigan, New Jersey, Ohio, and Pennsylvania; split states are Illinois, Indiana, New York, Texas, and Virginia.

INTRODUCTION TO PART 4

1. Niccolò Machiavelli, *The Prince,* trans. Luigi Ricci (New York: Modern Library, 1950), 91.

2. Arend Lijphart, *Democracies: Patterns of Majoritarian and Consensus Government in Twenty-One Countries* (New Haven, Conn.: Yale University Press, 1984). Finland and France could also be considered to have presidential elections, but in Finland the president and the prime minister have roughly equal powers. Since Lijphart's book was published, experience has shown that France

is not as much of a presidential system as Lijphart thought. Lijphart wrote, "The French president . . . is not only the head of state but also the real head of government; the prime minister is merely the president's principal adviser and assistant" (73). This appeared to be true in 1984, but after the 1986 legislative election it became clear that the president's power is diminished substantially if he does not have support in the National Assembly.

3. In France a new election is held to elect a president to a full seven-year term. This has occurred twice: in 1969, after Charles de Gaulle resigned, and in 1974, when Georges Pompidou died in office.

12. THE 1996 AND 1998 ELECTIONS AND THE FUTURE OF AMERICAN POLITICS

1. Maurice Duverger, *Political Parties: Their Organization and Activity in the Modern World*, trans. Barbara North and Robert North (New York: Wiley, 1963), 308–309. In this book, we use the term *majority* to mean winning more than half of the vote. Duverger uses the term *majorité* to mean what we would call a plurality of the vote, that is, more votes than any other party received.

2. Other democracies that might also be classified as having, or having had, a dominant party include Denmark, Norway, Iceland, Chile, India, Venezuela, and Columbia. The four countries we discuss here are those discussed extensively in a book edited by T. J. Pempel, *Uncommon Democracies: The One-Party Dominant Regimes* (Ithaca, N.Y.: Cornell University Press, 1990). See Alan Arian and Samuel H. Barnes, "The Dominant Party System: A Neglected Model of Democratic Stability," *Journal of Politics* 36 (August 1974), 592–614, which compares Israel and Italy. Mapai is the Hebrew acronym for Israel Workers' Party. In 1968 Mapai merged with two smaller parties to become the Israel Labor party, and between 1969 and 1984 joined an electoral coalition called the Alignment. That coalition fell apart after the 1984 election, and the party is now generally referred to as the Labor party. See also Gøsta Esping-Andersen, "Single-Party Dominance in Sweden: The Saga of Social Democracy," in *Uncommon Democracies*, 33–57, and Scott C. Flanagan et al., *The Japanese Voter* (New Haven, Conn.: Yale University Press, 1991).

3. Duverger, *Political Parties*, 312.

4. Admittedly, Duverger was vague about the reasons dominant parties tend to fail. He suggests that they lose dominance because they become too bureaucratic to govern effectively. Although dominant parties lost their dominance in Israel, Italy, Japan, and Sweden, a variety of factors led to their decline.

5. Asher Arian, *The Second Republic: Politics in Israel* (Chatham, N.J.: Chatham House, 1998), 111.

6. For an analysis of the gradual decline of the Christian Democrats, see Sidney

Tarrow, "Maintaining Hegemony in Italy: 'The softer they rise, the slower they fall!' " in *Uncommon Democracies,* 306–332.

7. This conclusion was reached even before the LDP losses in the upper house in the summer of 1998. See Aiji Tanaka and Yoshitaka Nishizawa, "Critical Elections of Japan in the 1990s: Does the LDP's Comeback in 1996 Mean Voter Realignment or Dealignment?" (paper presented at the Seventeenth World Congress of the International Political Science Association, Seoul, Korea, August 17–21, 1997).

8. Duverger, *Les Partis Politiques,* 3d ed. (Paris: Armand Colin, 1958), 342. The English-language translation appeared in 1963 (see note 1).

9. For a discussion of the logic of coalition structures, and why large coalitions are often at risk, see William H. Riker, *The Theory of Political Coalitions* (New Haven, Conn.: Yale University Press, 1962).

10. See, for example, Michael Nelson, "Constitutional Aspects of the Elections," in *The Elections of 1988,* ed. Michael Nelson (Washington, D.C.: CQ Press, 1989), 181–209; Byron E. Shafer, "The Election of 1988 and the Structure of American Politics: Notes on Interpreting an Electoral Order," *Electoral Studies* 8 (April 1989), 5–21.

11. Evan Thomas, "Introduction," in *Back from the Dead: How Clinton Survived the Republican Revolution,* by Evan Thomas and others (New York: Atlantic Monthly Press, 1997), xiii.

12. James W. Ceaser and Andrew E. Busch, *Losing to Win: The 1996 Elections and American Politics* (Lanham, Md.: Rowman and Littlefield, 1997), 170, 171.

13. In the 1868 elections, three southern states, Mississippi, Texas, and Virginia, had not yet been readmitted into the Union, and Union troops helped Grant win in Alabama, Arkansas, Florida, North Carolina, South Carolina, and Tennessee.

14. In 1996 California voters enacted an open primary system in which voters could vote for any party, regardless of how they had registered. These open primary rules run counter to the procedures allowed for choosing delegates by the national Democratic party, and possibly violate Republican national rules as well. In 1998 leaders of both the Democratic and Republican parties in California supported a ballot measure that would have created a closed primary for the purpose of selecting delegates to the presidential nominating convention, but this proposal failed.

15. See Paul R. Abramson, John H. Aldrich, and David W. Rohde, *Change and Continuity in the 1984 Elections,* rev. ed. (Washington, D.C.: CQ Press, 1987), 25.

16. See Paul R. Abramson, John H. Aldrich, and David W. Rohde, *Change and Continuity in the 1988 Elections,* rev. ed. (Washington, D.C.: CQ Press, 1991), 13–15.

17. For an interesting account, see Larry J. Sabato, "Presidential Nominations: The Front-Loaded Frenzy of 1996," in *Toward the Millennium: The Elections of*

1996, ed. Larry J. Sabato (Needham Heights, Mass.: Allyn and Bacon, 1997), 48–49.

18. Kathy Kiely, "GOP Looks for Election Lessons," *USA Today,* November 5, 1998, 3A.

19. Ibid.

20. Laurie Goodstein, "Religious Conservatives, Stung by Vote Losses, Blame G.O.P. for Focusing on Clinton," *New York Times,* November 5, 1998, B3.

21. Ibid.

22. These states are Alabama, Alaska, Idaho, Indiana, Kansas, Mississippi, Nebraska, North Carolina, North Dakota, Oklahoma, South Carolina, South Dakota, Texas, Utah, Virginia, and Wyoming.

23. Arend Lijphart, *Electoral Systems and Party Systems: A Study of Twenty-Seven Democracies, 1945–1990* (New York: Oxford University Press, 1994), 160–162.

24. Based upon the Ballot Access News web site (www.ballot.access.org), November 8, 1998, and *Ballot Access News,* December 8, 1998, 5.

25. As Steven J. Rosenstone and his colleagues point out, most successful third parties in the twentieth century have been formed mainly to attempt to elect presidential candidates. See Steven J. Rosenstone, Roy L. Behr, and Edward H. Lazarus, *Citizen Response to Major Party Failure,* 2d ed. (Princeton, N.J.: Princeton University Press, 1996).

26. Joseph A. Schlesinger, *Political Parties and the Winning of Office* (Ann Arbor: University of Michigan Press, 1991).

27. For a discussion of the political importance of the difference between selective incentives and collective goods, see Mancur Olson, Jr., *The Logic of Collective Action: Public Goods and the Theory of Groups* (Cambridge, Mass.: Harvard University Press, 1965). For an application of this difference to political parties, see John H. Aldrich, *Why Parties? The Origin and Transformation of Political Parties in America* (Chicago: University of Chicago Press, 1995).

28. Based upon the Reform Party Official web site (www.reformparty.org/candidates).

29. We are grateful to Joseph A. Schlesinger for reminding us of this point.

30. See Philip E. Converse, *The Dynamics of Party Support: Cohort-Analyzing Party Identification* (Beverly Hills, Calif.: Sage, 1976).

31. The thesis of "hidden partisans" is advanced most forcefully by Bruce E. Keith et al., *The Myth of the Independent Voter* (Berkeley: University of California Press, 1992). For the strongest evidence supporting the position that independence indicates a lack of strong commitment to a party, see Martin P. Wattenberg, *The Decline of American Political Parties, 1952–1996* (Cambridge, Mass.: Harvard University Press, 1998), 31–46. See also Wattenberg, *The Rise of Candidate-Centered Politics: Presidential Elections of the 1980s* (Cambridge, Mass.: Harvard University Press, 1991), 31–46.

Suggested Readings

(Readings preceded by an asterisk include discussion of the 1996 elections.)

Chapter 1: The Nomination Struggle

Abramson, Paul R., John H. Aldrich, Phil Paolino, and David W. Rohde. "'Sophisticated' Voting in the 1988 Presidential Primaries." *American Political Science Review* 86 (March 1992): 55–69.

Abramson, Paul R., John H. Aldrich, and David W. Rohde. "Progressive Ambition among United States Senators: 1972–1988." *Journal of Politics* 49 (February 1987): 3–35.

Aldrich, John H. *Before the Convention: Strategies and Choices in Presidential Nomination Campaigns.* Chicago: University of Chicago Press, 1980.

Bartels, Larry M. *Presidential Primaries and the Dynamics of Public Choice.* Princeton, N.J.: Princeton University Press, 1988.

Brams, Steven J. *The Presidential Election Game.* New Haven, Conn.: Yale University Press, 1978, 1–79.

*Ceaser, James W., and Andrew E. Busch, *Losing to Win: The 1996 Elections and American Politics.* Lanham, Md.: Rowman and Littlefield, 1997, 57–87.

*Mayer, William G. "The Presidential Nominations." In *The Election of 1996: Reports and Interpretations,* by Gerald M. Pomper with colleagues. Chatham, N.J.: Chatham House, 1997, 21–76.

Polsby, Nelson W., and Aaron Wildavsky. *Presidential Elections: Strategies and Structures of American Politics,* 9th ed. Chatham, N.J.: Chatham House, 1996, 119–180.

*Sabato, Larry J. "Presidential Nominations: The Front-loaded Frenzy of '96." In *Toward the Millennium: The Elections of 1996,* edited by Larry J. Sabato. Needham Heights, Mass.: Allyn and Bacon, 1997, 37–91.

*Stanley, Harold W. "The Nominations: Republican Doldrums, Democratic Revival." In *The Elections of 1996,* edited by Michael Nelson. Washington, D.C.: CQ Press: 1997, 14–43.

*Thomas, Evan, with others. *Back from the Dead: How Clinton Survived the Republican Revolution.* New York: Atlantic Monthly Press, 1997, 45–134.

*Wayne, Stephen J. *The Road to the White House, 1996: The Politics of Presidential Elections,* postelection ed. New York: St. Martin's Press, 1997, 97–199.

Chapter 2: The General Election Campaign

Asher, Herbert B. *Presidential Elections and American Politics: Voters, Candidates, and Campaigns since 1952,* 5th ed. Pacific Grove, Calif.: Brooks/Cole, 1992, 239–314.

Brams, Steven J. *The Presidential Election Game.* New Haven, Conn.: Yale University Press, 1978, 80–133.

*Ceaser, James W., and Andrew E. Busch. *Losing to Win: The 1996 Elections and American Politics.* Lanham, Md.: Rowman and Littlefield, 1997, 89–118, 149–154.

*Herrnson, Paul S., and Clyde Wilcox. "The 1996 Presidential Election: A Tale of a Campaign That Didn't Seem to Matter." In *Toward the Millennium: The Elections of 1996,* edited by Larry J. Sabato. Needham Heights, Mass.: Allyn and Bacon, 1997, 121–142.

Hershey, Marjorie Randon. "The Constructed Explanation: Interpreting Election Results in the 1984 Presidential Race." *Journal of Politics* 54 (November 1992): 943–976.

*Just, Marion R. "Candidate Strategies and the Media Campaign." In *The Election of 1996: Reports and Interpretations,* by Gerald M. Pomper with colleagues. Chatham, N.J.: Chatham House, 1997, 77–106.

Kessel, John H. *Presidential Campaign Politics,* 4th ed. Pacific Grove, Calif.: Brooks/Cole, 1992.

*Nelson, Michael. "The Election: Turbulence and Tranquility in Contemporary American Politics." In *The Elections of 1996,* edited by Michael Nelson. Washington, D.C.: CQ Press, 1997, 44–80.

Polsby, Nelson W., and Aaron Wildavsky. *Presidential Elections: Strategies and Structures in American Politics,* 9th ed. Chatham, N.J.: Chatham House, 1996, 181–257.

Thomas, Dan B., and Larry R. Baas. "The Postelection Campaign: Competing Constructions of the Clinton Victory in 1992." *Journal of Politics* 58 (May 1996): 309–331.

*Thomas, Evan, with others. *Back from the Dead: How Clinton Survived the Republican Revolution.* New York: Atlantic Monthly Press, 1997, 135–201.

*Wayne, Stephen J. *The Road to the White House, 1996: The Politics of Presidential Elections,* postelection ed. New York: St. Martin's Press, 1997, 201–283.

Chapter 3: The Election Results

Abramson, Paul R., John H. Aldrich, Phil Paolino, and David W. Rohde. "Third-Party and Independent Candidates in American Politics: Wallace, Anderson, and Perot." *Political Science Quarterly* 110 (Fall 1995): 349–367.

Black, Earl, and Merle Black. *The Vital South: How Presidential Elections Are Won.* Cambridge, Mass.: Harvard University Press, 1992.

Burnham, Walter Dean. *Critical Elections and the Mainsprings of American Politics.* New York: Norton, 1970.

Clubb, Jerome M., William H. Flanigan, and Nancy H. Zingale. *Partisan Realignment: Voters, Parties, and Government in American History.* Beverly Hills, Calif.: Sage, 1980.

Kelley, Stanley, Jr. *Interpreting Elections.* Princeton, N.J.: Princeton University Press, 1983.

Lamis, Alexander P. *The Two-Party South,* 2d expanded ed. New York: Oxford University Press, 1990.

Nardulli, Peter F. "The Concept of a Critical Realignment, Electoral Behavior, and Political Change." *American Political Science Review* 89 (March 1995): 10–22.

Presidential Elections 1789–1992. Washington, D.C.: Congressional Quarterly Inc., 1995.

Schlesinger, Joseph A. *Political Parties and the Winning of Office*. Ann Arbor: University of Michigan Press, 1991.

Sundquist, James L. *Dynamics of the Party System: Alignment and Realignment of Political Parties in the United States*, rev. ed. Washington, D.C.: Brookings Institution, 1983.

Chapter 4: Who Voted?

Aldrich, John H. "Rational Choice and Turnout." *American Journal of Political Science* 37 (February 1993): 246–278.

Ansolabehere, Stephen, and Shanto Iyengar. *Going Negative: How Attack Ads Shrink and Polarize the Electorate*. New York: Free Press, 1996.

Burnham, Walter Dean. "The Turnout Problem." In *Elections American Style*, edited by James A. Reichley. Washington, D.C.: Brookings Institution, 1987, 97–133.

Hill, Kim Quaile, and Jan E. Leighley. "Political Parties and Class Mobilization in Contemporary United States Elections." *American Journal of Political Science* 40 (August 1996): 787–804.

Kleppner, Paul. *Who Voted? The Dynamics of Electoral Turnout, 1870–1980*. New York: Praeger, 1982.

Leighley, Jan E., and Jonathan Nagler. "Socioeconomic Class Bias in Turnout, 1964–1988: The Voters Remain the Same." *American Political Science Review* 86 (September 1992): 725–736.

Miller, Warren E., and J. Merrill Shanks. *The New American Voter*. Cambridge, Mass.: Harvard University Press, 1996, 95–114.

Rosenstone, Steven J., and John Mark Hansen. *Mobilization, Participation, and Democracy in America*. New York: Macmillan, 1993.

Teixeira, Ruy A. *The Disappearing American Voter*. Washington, D.C.: Brookings Institution, 1992.

Wolfinger, Raymond, and Steven J. Rosenstone. *Who Votes?* New Haven, Conn.: Yale University Press, 1980.

Chapter 5: Social Forces and the Vote

Alford, Robert R. *Party and Society: The Anglo-American Democracies.* Chicago: Rand McNally, 1963.

Axelrod, Robert. "Where the Votes Come From: An Analysis of Electoral Coalitions, 1952–1968." *American Political Science Review* 66 (March 1972): 11–20.

Dawson, Michael C. *Behind the Mule: Race and Class in American Politics.* Princeton, N.J.: Princeton University Press, 1994.

Hamilton, Richard F. *Class and Politics in the United States.* New York: Wiley, 1972.

Huckfeldt, Robert, and Carol Weitzel Kohfeld. *Race and the Decline of Class in American Politics.* Urbana: University of Illinois Press, 1989.

Lipset, Seymour Martin. *Political Man: The Social Bases of Politics,* expanded ed. Baltimore, Md.: Johns Hopkins University Press, 1981.

Miller, Warren E., and J. Merrill Shanks. *The New American Voter.* Cambridge, Mass.: Harvard University Press, 1996, 212–282.

Stanley, Harold W., and Richard G. Niemi. "The Demise of the New Deal Coalition: Partisanship and Group Support, 1952–92." In *Democracy's Feast: Elections in America,* edited by Herbert F. Weisberg. Chatham, N.J.: Chatham House, 1995, 220–240.

Tate, Katherine. *From Politics to Protest: The New Black Voters in American Elections,* enlarged ed. Cambridge, Mass.: Harvard University Press, 1994.

Wald, Kenneth D. *Religion and Politics in the United States,* 3d ed. Washington, D.C.: CQ Press, 1997.

Chapter 6: Candidates, Issues, and the Vote

Abramowitz, Alan I. "It's Abortion, Stupid: Policy Voting in the 1992 Presidential Election." *Journal of Politics* 57 (February 1995): 176–186.

Asher, Herbert B. *Presidential Elections and American Politics: Voters, Candidates, and Campaigns since 1952,* 5th ed. Pacific Grove, Calif.: Brooks/Cole, 1992, 122–195.

Campbell, Angus, Philip E. Converse, Warren E. Miller, and Donald E. Stokes. *The American Voter.* New York: Wiley, 1960, 168–265.

Carmines, Edward G., and James A. Stimson. *Issue Evolution: Race and the Transformation of American Politics.* Princeton, N.J.: Princeton University Press, 1989.

*Elshtain, Jean Bethke, and Christopher Beem. "Issues and Themes: Economics, Culture, and 'Small-Party' Politics." In *The Elections of 1996,* edited by Michael Nelson. Washington, D.C.: CQ Press, 106–120.

Gerber, Elisabeth R., and John E. Jackson. "Endogenous Preferences and the Study of Institutions." *American Political Science Review* 87 (September 1993): 639–656.

*Keeter, Scott. "Public Opinion and the Election." In *The Election of 1996: Reports and Interpretations,* by Gerald M. Pomper and colleagues. Chatham, N.J.: Chatham House, 1997, 107–133,

Popkin, Samuel L. *The Reasoning Voter: Communication and Persuasion in Presidential Campaigns.* Chicago: University of Chicago Press, 1991.

Shafer, Byron E., and William J. M. Claggett. *The Two Majorities: The Issue Context of Modern American Politics.* Baltimore, Md.: Johns Hopkins University Press, 1995.

Stimson, James A., Michael B. MacKuen, and Robert S. Erikson, "Dynamic Representation." *American Political Science Review* 89 (September 1995): 543–565.

Chapter 7: Presidential Performance and Candidate Choice

Alvarez, R. Michael, and Jonathan Nagler. "Economics, Issues and the Perot Candidacy: Voter Choice in the 1992 Presidential Election." *American Journal of Political Science* 39 (August 1995): 714–744.

Downs, Anthony. *An Economic Theory of Democracy.* New York: Harper and Row, 1957.

Fiorina, Morris P. *Retrospective Voting in American National Elections.* New Haven, Conn.: Yale University Press, 1981.

Hetherington, Marc J. "The Media's Role in Forming Voters' National Economic Evaluations in 1992." *American Journal of Political Science* 40 (May 1996): 372–395.

Key, V. O., Jr. *The Responsible Electorate: Rationality in Presidential Voting, 1936–1960.* Cambridge, Mass.: Harvard University Press, 1966.

Kiewiet, D. Roderick. *Macroeconomics and Micropolitics: The Electoral Effects of Economic Issues.* Chicago: University of Chicago Press, 1983.

Lewis-Beck, Michael S. *Economics and Elections: The Major Western Democracies.* Ann Arbor: University of Michigan Press, 1988.

MacKuen, Michael B., Robert S. Erikson, and James A. Stimson. "Peasants or Bankers? The American Electorate and the U.S. Economy." *American Political Science Review* 86 (September 1992): 597–611.

Riker, William H. *Liberalism Against Populism: A Confrontation Between the Theory of Democracy and the Theory of Social Choice.* San Francisco: Freeman, 1982.

Tufte, Edward R. *Political Control of the Economy.* Princeton, N.J.: Princeton University Press,1978.

Chapter 8: Party Loyalties, Policy Preferences, and the Vote

Abramson, Paul R. *Political Attitudes in America: Formation and Change.* San Francisco: Freeman, 1983.

Aldrich, John H. *Why Parties? The Origin and Transformation of Political Parties in America.* Chicago: University of Chicago Press, 1995.

Beck, Paul Allen. "The Dealignment Era in America." In *Electoral Change in Advanced Industrial Democracies: Realignment or Dealignment?* edited by Russell J. Dalton, Scott C. Flanagan, and Paul Allen Beck. Princeton, N.J.: Princeton University Press, 1984, 240–266.

Campbell, Angus, Philip E. Converse, Warren E. Miller, and Donald E. Stokes. *The American Voter.* New York: Wiley, 1960, 120–167.

Collet, Christian. "The Polls-Trends: Third Parties and the Two-Party System." *Public Opinion Quarterly* 60 (Fall 1996): 431–449.

DeSart, Jay A. "Information Processing and Partisan Neutrality: A Reexamination of the Party Decline Thesis." *Journal of Politics* 57 (August 1995): 776–795.

Keith, Bruce E., David B. Magleby, Candice J. Nelson, Elizabeth Orr, Mark C. Westlye, and Raymond E. Wolfinger. *The Myth of the Independent Voter.* Berkeley: University of California Press, 1992.

Miller, Warren E., and J. Merrill Shanks. *The New American Voter.* Cambridge, Mass.: Harvard University Press, 1996, 117–185.

Rapaport, Ronald B. "Partisanship Change in a Candidate-Centered Era." *Journal of Politics* 59 (February 1997): 185–199.

Wattenberg, Martin P. *The Decline of American Political Parties: 1952–1992.* Cambridge, Mass.: Harvard University Press, 1994.

Chapter 9: Candidates and Outcomes in 1996

*Ceaser, James W., and Andrew E. Busch. *Losing to Win: The 1996 Elections and American Politics.* Lanham, Md.: Rowman and Littlefield, 1997, 119–148.

*Cohen, Richard E. "Campaigning for Congress: The Echo of '94." In *Toward the Millennium: The Elections of 1996,* edited by Larry J. Sabato. Needham Heights, Mass.: Allyn and Bacon, 1997, 163–188.

Cox, Gary W., and Jonathan N. Katz. "Why Did the Incumbency Advantage in U.S. House Elections Grow?" *American Journal of Political Science* 40 (May 1996): 478–497.

*Drew, Elizabeth. *Whatever It Takes: The Real Struggle for Political Power in America.* New York: Viking, 1997.

Fenno, Richard F., Jr. *Home Style: House Members in Their Districts.* Boston: Little, Brown, 1978.

Fiorina, Morris P. *Congress: Keystone of the Washington Establishment,* 2d ed. New Haven, Conn.: Yale University Press, 1989.

*Hershey, Marjorie Randon. "The Congressional Elections." In *The Election of 1996: Reports and Interpretations,* by Gerald M. Pomper with colleagues. Chatham, N.J.: Chatham House, 1997, 205–239.

Hill, Kevin A. "Does the Creation of Majority Black Districts Aid Republicans? An Analysis of the 1992 Congressional Elections in Eight Southern States." *Journal of Politics* 57 (May 1995): 384–401.

*Jacobson, Gary C. "The 105th Congress: Unprecedented and Unsurprising." In

The Elections of 1996, edited by Michael Nelson. Washington, D.C.: CQ Press, 1997, 143–166.

Kiewiet, D. Roderick, and Langche Zeng. "An Analysis of Congressional Career Decisions, 1947–1986." *American Political Science Review* 87 (December 1993): 928–941.

Rohde, David W. *Parties and Leaders in the Postreform House.* Chicago: University of Chicago Press, 1991.

Schlesinger, Joseph A. *Ambition and Politics: Political Careers in the United States.* Chicago: Rand McNally, 1966.

Chapter 10: The Congressional Electorate in 1996

Abramowitz, Alan I., and Jeffrey A. Segal. *Senate Elections.* Ann Arbor: University of Michigan Press, 1992.

Beck, Paul Allen, Lawrence Baum, Aage R. Clausen, and Charles E. Smith, Jr. "Patterns and Sources of Ticket Splitting in Subpresidential Voting." *American Political Science Review* 86 (December 1992): 916–928.

Dalager, Jon K. "Voters, Issues, and Elections: Are the Candidates' Messages Getting Through?" *Journal of Politics* 58 (May 1996): 486–515.

Dimock, Michael A., and Gary C. Jacobson. "Checks and Choices: The House Bank Scandal's Impact on Voters in 1992." *Journal of Politics* 57 (November 1995): 1143–1159.

Fenno, Richard F., Jr. "If, as Ralph Nader Says, Congress Is 'The Broken Branch,' Why Do We Love Our Congressmen So Much?" In *Congress in Change: Elections and Reform,* edited by Norman J. Ornstein. New York: Praeger, 1975, 277–287.

Jacobson, Gary C. *The Electoral Origins of Divided Government: Competition in U.S. House Elections, 1946–1988.* Boulder, Colo.: Westview Press, 1990.

———. The Politics of Congressional Elections, 4th ed. Boston: Addison-Wesley, 1997.

Sigelman, Lee, Paul J. Wahlbeck, and Emmett H. Buell, Jr. "Vote Choice and the Preference for Divided Government: Lessons of 1992." *American Journal of Political Science* 41 (July 1997): 879–894.

Chapter 12: The 1996 and 1998 Elections and the Future of American Politics

*Burnham, Walter Dean. "Bill Clinton: Riding the Tiger." In *The Election of 1996: Reports and Interpretations,* by Gerald M. Pomper with colleagues. Chatham, N.J.: Chatham House, 1997, 1–20.

*Ceaser, James W., and Andrew E. Busch. *Losing to Win: The 1996 Elections and American Politics.* Lanham, Md.: Rowman and Littlefield, 1997, 156–173.

*Ladd, Everett Carll. "1996 Vote: The 'No Majority' Realignment Continues." *Political Science Quarterly* 112 (Spring 1997): 1–28.

*McWilliams, Wilson Carey. "The Meaning of the Election." In *The Election of 1996: Reports and Interpretations,* by Gerald M. Pomper with colleagues. Chatham, N.J.: Chatham House, 1997, 241–272.

*Nelson, Michael. "1997 and Beyond: The Perils of Second-Term Presidents." In *The Elections of 1996,* edited by Michael Nelson. Washington, D.C.: CQ Press, 1997, 1–13.

*Pomper, Gerald M. "The Presidential Election." In *The Election of 1996: Reports and Interpretations,* by Gerald M. Pomper with colleagues. Chatham, N.J.: Chatham House, 1997, 173–204.

*Sabato, Larry J. "The November Vote—A Status Quo Election." In *Toward the Millennium: The Elections of 1996,* edited by Larry J. Sabato. Needham Heights, Mass.: Allyn and Bacon, 1997, 143–161.

Additional Readings

(The following readings on the 1996 elections have appeared since *Change and Continuity in the 1996 Elections* was published.)

Abrams, Herbert L., and Richard Brody. "Bob Dole's Age and Health in the 1996 Election: Did the Media Let Us Down?" *Political Science Quarterly* 113 (Fall 1998): 471–491.

Alvarez, R. Michael, and Jonathan Nagler. "Elections, Entitlements, and Social Issues: Voter Choice in the 1996 Presidential Election." *American Journal of Political Science* 42 (October 1998): 1349–1363.

Asher, Herbert B., and Andrew R. Tomilson. "The Media and the 1996 Presidential Campaign." In *Reelection 1996: How Americans Voted,* edited by Herbert F. Weisberg and Janet M. Box-Steffensmeier. Chatham, N.J.: Chatham House, 1999, 125–142.

Bass, Harold F., Jr. "Partisan Rules, 1946–1996." In *Partisan Approaches to Post-war American Politics,* by Byron E. Shafer et al. Chatham, N.J.: Chatham House, 1998, 220–270.

Bibby, John F. "Party Organizations, 1946–1996." In *Partisan Approaches to Post-war American Politics,* by Byron E. Shafer et al. Chatham, N.J.: Chatham House, 1998, 142–185.

Bibby, John F. "State Party Organizations: Coping and Adapting to Candidate-Centered Parties and Nationalization." In *The Parties Respond: Changes in American Parties and Campaigns,* 3d ed., edited by L. Sandy Maisel. Boulder, Colo.: Westview Press, 1998, 23–49.

Crotty, William. "Political Parties in the 1996 Election: The Party as Team or the Candidates as Superstars." In *The Parties Respond: Changes in American Parties and Campaigns,* 3d ed., edited by L. Sandy Maisel. Boulder, Colo.: Westview Press, 1998, 202–224.

Dodenhoff, David, and Ken Goldstein. "Resources, Racehorses, and Rules: Nominations in the 1990s." In *The Parties Respond: Changes in American Parties and Campaigns,* 3d ed., edited by L. Sandy Maisel. Boulder, Colo.: Westview Press, 1998, 170–201.

Herrnson, Paul S. "National Party Organizations at the Century's End." In *The Parties Respond: Changes in American Parties and Campaigns,* 3d ed., edited by L. Sandy Maisel. Boulder, Colo.: Westview Press, 1998, 50–82.

Kerbel, Matthew Robert. "Parties in the Media: Elephants, Donkeys, Boars, Pigs, and Jackals." In *The Parties Respond: Changes in American Parties and Campaigns,* 3d ed., edited by L. Sandy Maisel. Boulder, Colo.: Westview Press, 1998, 243–259.

Lacy, Dean, and J. Tobin Grant. "The Impact of the Economy on the 1996 Election: The Invisible Foot." In *Reelection 1996: How Americans Voted,* edited by Herbert F. Weisberg and Janet M. Box-Steffensmeier. Chatham, N.J.: Chatham House, 1999, 99–110.

Maisel, L. Sandy. "Political Parties on the Eve of the Millennium." In *The Parties Respond: Changes in American Parties and Campaigns,* edited by L. Sandy Maisel. Boulder, Colo.: Westview Press, 1998, 356–371.

Mayer, William G. "Mass Partisanship, 1946–1996." In *Partisan Approaches to Postwar American Politics,* by Byron E. Shafer et al. Chatham, N.J.: Chatham House, 1998, 186–219.

Mitofsky, Warren J. "Was 1998 a Worse Year for Polls than 1948?" *Public Opinion Quarterly* 62 (Summer 1998): 230–249.

Mondak, Jeffrey J., Carl McCurley, and Steven R. L. Millman. "The Impact of Incumbents' Levels of Competence and Integrity in the 1994 and 1996 U.S. House Elections." In *Reelection 1996: How Americans Voted*, edited by Herbert F. Weisberg and Janet M. Box-Steffensmeier. Chatham, N.J.: Chatham House, 1999, 213–235.

Nichols, Stephen M., David C. Kimball, and Paul Allen Beck. "Voter Turnout in the 1996 Election: Resuming the Downward Spiral?" In *Reelection 1996: How Americans Voted*, edited by Herbert F. Weisberg and Janet M. Box-Steffensmeier. Chatham, N.J.: Chatham House, 1999, 23–44.

Norrander, Barbara. "Is the Gender Gap Growing?" In *Reelection 1996: How Americans Voted*, edited by Herbert F. Weisberg and Janet M. Box-Steffensmeier. Chatham, N.J.: Chatham House, 1999, 145–161.

Patterson, Samuel C., and Joseph Quin Monson. "Reelecting the Republican Congress: Two More Years." In *Reelection 1996: How Americans Voted*, edited by Herbert F. Weisberg and Janet M. Box-Steffensmeier. Chatham, N.J.: Chatham House, 1999, 183–212.

Shribman, David M. "End of Pretty Good Feelings: The Middle Way of Bill Clinton and America's Voters." In *The Parties Respond: Changes in American Parties and Campaigns,* 3d ed., edited by L. Sandy Maisel. Boulder, Colo.: Westview Press, 1998, 341–355.

Sinclair, Barbara. "Evolution or Revolution? Policy-Oriented Congressional Parties in the 1990s." In *The Parties Respond: Changes in American Parties and Campaigns,* 3d ed., edited by L. Sandy Maisel. Boulder, Colo.: Westview Press, 1998, 263–285.

Smith, Charles E., Jr., Peter M. Radcliffe, and John H. Kessel. "The Partisan Choice: Bill Clinton or Bob Dole?" In *Reelection 1996: How Americans Voted*, edited by Herbert F. Weisberg and Janet M. Box-Steffensmeier. Chatham, N.J.: Chatham House, 1999, 70–87.

Sorauf, Frank J. "Political Parties and the New World of Campaign Finance." In *The Parties Respond: Changes in American Parties and Campaigns,* 3d ed., edited by L. Sandy Maisel. Boulder, Colo.: Westview Press, 1998, 225–242.

Stanley, Harold M., and Richard G. Niemi. "Party Coalitions in Transition: Partisanship and Group Support, 1952–96." In *Reelection 1996: How Americans Voted*, edited by Herbert F. Weisberg and Janet M. Box-Steffensmeier. Chatham, N.J.: Chatham House, 1999, 162–180.

Stone, Walter J., and Ronald B. Rapoport. "A Candidate-Centered Perspective on Party Responsiveness: Nomination Activists and the Process of Party Change." In *The Parties Respond*, 3d ed., edited by L. Sandy Maisel. Boulder, Colo.: Westview Press, 1998, 83–105.

Wattenberg, Martin P. *The Decline of American Political Parties: 1952–1996*. Cambridge, Mass.: Harvard University Press, 1998.

Weisberg, Herbert F., and Stephen T. Mockabee. "Attitudinal Correlates of the 1996 Presidential Vote: The People Reelect a President." In *Reelection 1996: How Americans Voted*, edited by Herbert F. Weisberg and Janet M. Box-Steffensmeier. Chatham, N.J.: Chatham House, 1999, 45–69.

Index

358

Stimson, James A., 114, 229, 319*n*32, 324*n*10, 329*n*5, 335*n*83
Stockdale, James, 120
Stokes, Donald E., 61, 319*n*1
Stone, Alan, 293*n*2
Stone, Walter J., 332*n*40
Strategic voting. *See* Sophisticated voting
Sumners, Joe A., 246, 337*n*14
Sundquist, James L., 4, 294*n*9
"Superdelegates," 284, 286
Supreme Court appointments, 2, 137, 281, 282
Survey Research Center–Center for Political Studies (SRC-CPS) election studies. *See* Black National Election Study; National Election Studies; Vote validation studies
Sweden, 279, 280, 342*n*4
Switzerland, 62, 65

Taagepera, Rein, 301*n*8
Taft, William Howard, 68, 120
Tanaka, Aiji, 343*n*7
Tarrow, Sidney, 342*n*6
Tate, Katherine, 309*n*21, 316*n*3
Tate, Randy, 287
Tax policies, 2, 31, 35, 122, 123, 125, 226, 251
Taylor, Morry, 13
Taylor, Zachary, 4, 281
Teixeira, Ruy, 80, 81, 84, 311*nn*38, 42, 44, 47, 312*n*49
Tennessee, 47, 52, 56, 58, 343*n*13
Term limits, 207, 223, 231, 234
Tetlock, Philip E., 304*n*6
Texas, 14, 51, 56, 57, 205, 274, 285, 288, 329*n*2, 336*n*94, 339*n*33, 341*nn*82, 83, 343*n*13, 344*n*22
Theiss-Morse, Elizabeth, 333*n*54
"Thermometer" ratings, 116–121
Third parties, 118, 120, 185, 187, 288–291
Thomas, Clarence, 115
Thomas, Evan, 282, 343*n*11
Thompson, Fred, 288
Thompson, Mike, 231
Thompson, Tommy, 14
"Threshold" rules, 284
Thurmond, J. Strom, 300*n*7
Tilden, Samuel J., 48, 66, 300*n*2
Toner, Robert, 307*nn*11, 13
Trilling, Richard J., 4, 294*n*9
Truman, Harry S., 32, 38, 55, 56, 111, 174, 300*n*3, 338*n*12
Tsongas, Paul, 19, 20
Tufte, Edward R., 150, 216, 324*n*11, 332*n*47, 335*n*80

Turnout
 among African-Americans, 51, 52, 66, 71, 72, 79, 102, 104, 106, 107, 109, 111, 258, 259, 262
 and age, 72, 76, 81
 attempts to increase, 37, 70, 71, 85, 86, 194, 253, 256–260
 among Catholics, 5, 77, 78, 111
 decline of, 62, 65–71, 79–86, 104, 258, 328*n*2
 and education, 71, 72, 78–81, 84, 310*n*35
 among Hispanics, 72, 75
 implications for realignment, 5, 90, 291, 292
 and income, 76, 77, 80
 increase in, 62, 66, 68–71, 102
 and issue preferences, 88
 among Jews, 77
 measurement of, 65, 66, 72, 305*n*3, 306*n*8, 307*nn*15–17, 308*nn*19, 20
 among the middle class, 76, 78, 80, 109
 and party identification, 82–84, 86–88, 168, 172
 and perceived closeness of election, 85
 among Protestants, 77, 78, 111
 and retrospective evaluations, 88, 89
 and sense of political efficacy, 81–84
 in the South, 51, 52, 72, 75–78, 105
 among union members, 77, 107, 259
 among women, 65, 66, 70–72, 75
 and women's suffrage, 65, 66, 70, 71, 306*n*4
 among the working class, 5, 70, 76, 78, 109
Twenty-second Amendment, 41, 284

Unemployment
 concern with, 125
 rates of, 125, 143
Unions
 contribution of members to Democratic presidential coalition, 107
 and Democratic party, 71, 166, 219, 232, 333*n*60
 support for Clinton, 98
 turnout of members, 77, 107, 259
 and the vote of members, 92, 97–99, 106, 107, 113–115, 238, 259
U.S. Bureau of the Census for 2000, 273, 274
U.S. Bureau of the Census Surveys, 8, 71, 72, 75, 76, 79, 80, 306*n*8, 307*n*14
Utah, 42, 46, 306*n*4, 336*n*94